Wireless Technologies for Ambient Assisted Living and Healthcare:

Systems and Applications

Athina Lazakidou
University of Peloponnese, Greece

Konstantinos Siassiakos
University of Piraeus, Greece

Konstantinos Ioannou
University of Patras, Greece

T0320516

Medical Information Science
REFERENCE

MEDICAL INFORMATION SCIENCE REFERENCE

Hershey · New York

Director of Editorial Content: Kristin Klinger
Director of Book Publications: Julia Mosemann
Acquisitions Editor: Lindsay Johnston
Development Editor: Christine Bufton
Publishing Assistant: Deanna Jo Zombro
Typesetter: Deanna Jo Zombro
Production Editor: Jamie Snavely
Cover Design: Lisa Tosheff

Published in the United States of America by
Medical Information Science Reference (an imprint of IGI Global)
701 E. Chocolate Avenue
Hershey PA 17033
Tel: 717-533-8845
Fax: 717-533-8661
E-mail: cust@igi-global.com
Web site: http://www.igi-global.com

Library of Congress Cataloging-in-Publication Data

Wireless technologies for ambient assisted living and healthcare : systems and applications / Athina Lazakidou, Konstantinos Siassiakos and Konstantinos Ioannou, editors.
    p. ; cm.
 Includes bibliographical references and index.
 Summary: "This book provides explanations of concepts, processes and acronyms related to different areas, issues and trends in various areas of wireless technologies for ambient assisted living and healthcare, focusing on emerging wireless technologies and innovative wireless solutions for smart home environments"--Provided by publisher.
 ISBN 978-1-61520-805-0 (hardcover)
 1. Telecommunication in medicine. 2. Medical care--Data processing. 3. Medical telematics. 4. Wireless communication systems. 5. Older people--Long term care--Information services. 6. Life care communities--Information services. 7. Congregate housing--Information services. I. Lazakidou, Athina A., 1975- II. Siassiakos, Konstantinos M. III. Ioannou, Konstantinos G., 1975-
 [DNLM: 1. Assisted Living Facilities--trends. 2. Information Systems. 3. Aged. 4. Computer Communication Networks. 5. Delivery of Health Care. 6. Electronic Health Records. WT 26.5 W798 2011]
 R119.9.W56 2011
 610.285--dc22
               2009052765

British Cataloguing in Publication Data
A Cataloguing in Publication record for this book is available from the British Library.

All work contributed to this book is new, previously-unpublished material. The views expressed in this book are those of the authors, but not necessarily of the publisher.

Table of Contents

Chapter 12

Detailed Table of Contents

Chapter 1

Fotis Kitsios, University of Macedonia, Greece
Thanos Papadopoulos, University of Southampton, UK
Spyros Angelopoulos, The University of Warwick, UK

Pervasive healthcare is an emerging research discipline, which focuses on the development of pervasive and ubiquitous computing technology for healthcare environments. Information and Communication Technologies have dramatically evolved during the last decade, laying a solid foundation for the future generation of Ubiquitous Internet access. As a result, current efforts in research and development in the areas of pervasive healthcare, promote the formation of inter-disciplinary international teams of experts, scientists, researchers and engineers to create a new generation of applications and technologies that will facilitate the fully automated information cyberspace systems. The authors discuss the current state-of-the-art in the world of Telecommunications and Internet Technologies as well as new technological trends in the Internet and Automation Industries, while promoting research and development in the interdisciplinary projects conducted by multinational teams worldwide.

Chapter 2

Ibrahiem Mahmoud Mohamed El Emary, King Abdulaziz University, Saudi Arabia

This chapter is interested in discussing how to use data mining techniques to assist in achieving an acceptable level of quality of service of telecommunication systems. The quality of service is defined as the metrics which is are predicated by using the data mining techniques, decision tree, association rules and neural networks. Routing algorithms can use this metric for optimal path selection which in turn will affect positively on the system performance. Also , in this chapter management axis using data mining techniques was were handled, i.e., check the status of the telecommunication networks , role of data mining in obtaining optimal configuration , how to use data mining technique to assure high level of security for the telecommunication. The popularity of data mining in the telecommunications industry can be viewed as an extension of the use of expert systems in the telecommunications industry. These systems were developed to address the complexity associated with maintaining a huge network infrastructure and the need to maximize network reliability while minimizing labor costs (Liebowitz, J. 1988). The problem with these expert systems is that they are expensive to develop because it is both difficult and time consuming to elicit the requisite domain knowledge from experts.

Chapter 3

Konstantinos Siassiakos, University of Piraeus, Greece
Konstantinos Ioannou, University of Patras, Greece
Athina Lazakidou, University of Peloponnese, Greece

Rapid advances in information technology and wireless communications are leading to the emergence of a new type of information infrastructure that has the potential of supporting an array of advanced services for healthcare. Today's healthcare professionals need to be connected to the network always. Continuous connectivity is the watchword of these demanding users, who need to communicate over the network seamlessly and stay connected everywhere in emergency cases. TETRA technology provides several ways of protecting the privacy and security of communication, such as authentication, air interface encryption and end-to-end encryption. Using a TETRA network can benefit not only ambulance crews, but also medical personnel at remote locations. Even though doctors are rarely present in ambulances, they can use the transmitted medical data to make a formal diagnosis, enabling treatment to be started and saving several critical minutes before arrival at the hospital. The objective of this chapter is to study how simply can a healthcare professional collect physiological data from mobile and/or remote patients and how securely and reliably health information can be transferred from emergency places to hospitals through a TETRA network.

Chapter 4

Ibrahiem Mahmoud Mohamed El Emary, King Abdulaziz University, Saudi Arabia

This chapter gives a brief background on network management and how it is integrated into sensor network as well as the application of computational intelligence techniques in managing wireless sensor networks. Also discussed how Genetic Algorithms work in common and how they can be applied to sensor networks. Among the major management tasks rely on consumption power management, so there are many challenges associated with sensor networks but the primary challenge is energy consumption. Sensor networks are typically have little human interaction and are installed with limited battery supplies. This makes energy conservation a critical issue in deployed WSNs. All types of networks require monitoring and maintenance. A service that supplies a set of tools and applications that assist a network manager with these tasks is network management. It includes the administration of networks and all associated components. While all networks require some form of network management, different types of networks may stress certain aspects of network management. Some networks may also impose new tasks on network management. There are different types of network management architectures: centralized, hierarchical and distributed. In a centralized approach, one central server performs the role of the network management application. A hierarchical architecture will include multiple platforms, typically one server and several clients, performing network management functions.

Chapter 5

E. Patiniotakis, Hellenic Telecommunications Organization S.A. (OTE), Greece

St. Perdikouris, Hellenic Telecommunications Organization S.A. (OTE), Greece

G. Agapiou, Hellenic Telecommunications Organization S.A. (OTE), Greece

I. Chochliouros, Hellenic Telecommunications Organization S.A. (OTE), Greece

K. Voudouris, Technological Educational Institute of Athens, TEI-A, Greece

E. Dimitriadou, Hellenic Telecommunications Organization S.A. (OTE), Greece

I. Fraimis, Wireless Telecommunications Laboratory, University of Patras, Greece

A. Ioannou, Hellenic Telecommunications Organization S.A. (OTE), Greece

Wi-Fi mesh is a fast growing and mature technology which is widely used and has been proven very useful for healthcare including applications for ambient people. In this chapter, we attempt a quick introduction of the principles of 802.11s protocol that refers to mesh topology Wi-Fi networks. Specifically, we describe the main operations and functions performed in a Wi-Fi mesh network such as routing procedures, synchronization as well as QoS capabilities and security mechanisms that are crucial for carrying sensitive information like medical data. Finally, in the second part of this chapter, actual measurements are presented from an experimental network that consisted of four dual radio (2.4 GHz and 5 GHz) mesh access points. Key parameters are evaluated, such as maximum throughput for different distances, jitter, delay and data loss which affect the transmission of sensitive data. Moreover, the handover capability of the system is presented in terms of data throughput and voice quality degradation during the transition.

Chapter 6

A. Rigas, Hellenic Telecommunications Organization S.A. (OTE), Greece

E. Patiniotakis, Hellenic Telecommunications Organization S.A. (OTE), Greece

G. Agapiou, Hellenic Telecommunications Organization S.A. (OTE), Greece

I. Chochliouros, Hellenic Telecommunications Organization S.A. (OTE), Greece

K. Voudouris, Technological Educational Institute of Athens, Greece

E. Dimitriadou, Hellenic Telecommunications Organization S.A. (OTE), Greece

K. Ioannou, University of Patras, Greece

A. Ioannou, Hellenic Telecommunications Organization S.A. (OTE), Greece

The term WiMAX is an abbreviation of Worldwide Interoperability for Microwave Access and it is defined in IEEE, as the 802.16 family of standards. Unlike other legacy Point-to-Multipoint wireless technologies, WiMAX is able to offer higher transmission rates, quality of service assurance and hence it can be compared to other wireline technologies. Additionally, WiMAX is proven to be useful for telemedicine purposes (live surgeries and medical examinations, medical conferences etc.), especially in distant areas. WiMAX is based on two major standards; one is the IEEE802.16d that was developed specifically for fixed wireless communications and is dedicated mainly in LOS environments and can be used in many cases, where fixed infrastructure is not available. On the other hand, 802.16e can be used in cases of both fixed and moving subscribers, while providing better coverage, performance and even higher transmission rates. This paper describes the major capabilities of the WiMAX standard and presents the performance of WiMAX networks based on measurements taken during laboratory and field tests.

Chapter 7
    Alessia D'Andrea, IRPPS-CNR, Italy
    Arianna D'Ulizia, IRPPS-CNR, Italy
    Fernando Ferri, IRPPS-CNR, Italy
    Patrizia Grifoni, IRPPS-CNR, Italy

Wireless technologies are increasingly acquiring a considerable relevance in the field of Ambient Assisted Living. This contributes to independent living and quality of life for many elderly people by reducing the need of caretakers and personal nursing. In this paper we provide a classification of existing wireless technologies for Ambient Assisted Living based on the role they can have in the assistance to elderly people. Then, we provide an overview of several intelligent wireless systems applied in the Ambient Assisted Living on considering the different wireless technologies used in each of them.

Chapter 8
    Nicholas S. Samaras, TEI of Larissa, Greece
    Costas Chaikalis, TEI of Larissa, Greece
    Giorgios Siafakas, TEI of Larissa, Greece

Smart houses represent a modern technology which can secure and facilitate our life. The objective of this chapter is to adapt medical sensors to home automated systems, which collect medical data such as blood pressure, heart rate and electrical heart activity for elderly and/or disabled persons. Firstly, the collected data is transferred to a home server and to an external manager for further analysis. Subsequently, data is stored at a database and monitoring is available only for authorized users via a simple web interface. IEEE 802.15.4 wireless standard has been chosen as the optimal solution for communication in the smart house. Finally, two implementation scenarios of the smart house for an elderly and/or disabled person are simulated using Custodian software tool.

Chapter 9
    Ibrahiem Mahmoud Mohamed El Emary, King Abdulaziz University, Saudi Arabia

This chapter focuses on the management process of the wireless sensor networks in telemedicine applications. The main management tasks that are reported and addressed covers: topology management, privacy and security issues in WSN management, topology management algorithms, and route management schemes. Also, failure detection in WSN and fault management application using MANNA was presented and discussed. The major challenges and design issues facing WSN management was touched in a separate section. Typical telemedicine interactions involve both store-and-forward and live interaction. Both the traditional live and store-and-forward telemedicine systems provide an extension of healthcare services using fixed telecommunications networks (i.e. non-mobile). Various telemedicine solutions have been proposed and implemented since its initial use some 30 years ago in the fixed network environment using wired telecommunications networks (e.g. digital subscriber line). Technological advancements in wireless communications systems, namely wireless personal area networks (WPANs), wireless local area networks (WLANs), WiMAX broadband access, and cellular systems (2.5G, 3G and beyond 3G) now have the potential to significantly enhance telemedicine services by creating a flexible and heterogeneous network within an end-to-end telemedicine framework. In the future, integrating wireless solutions into healthcare delivery may well come to be a requirement, not just a differentiator, for accurate and efficient healthcare delivery. However, this raises some very significant challenges in terms of interoperability, performance and the security of such systems.

    Georgios Mantas, University of Patras, Greece
    Dimitrios Lymberopoulos, University of Patras, Greece
    Nikos Komninos, Athens Information Technology, Greece

This chapter presents the concept of Smart Home, describes the Smart Home networking technologies and discusses the main issues for ensuring security in a Smart Home environment. Nowadays, the integration of current communication and information technologies within the dwelling has led to the emergence of Smart Homes. These technologies facilitate the building of Smart Home environments in which devices and systems can communicate with each other and can be controlled automatically in order to interact with the household members and improve the quality of their life. However, the nature of Smart Home environment as well as the fact that it is always connected to the outside world via Internet and the open security back doors derived from the household members raise many security concerns. Finally, by reviewing the existing literature regarding Smart Homes and security issues that exist in Smart Home environments, the authors envisage to provide a base to broaden the research in Smart Home security.

    Lamprini T. Kolovou, University of Patras, Greece
    Dimitrios Lymberopoulos, University of Patras, Greece

E-Health considers the healthcare environment as an electronic workspace where different Medical Information Systems (MIS) supports the automation of information processing, the exchange of medical and administrative data and the automation of medical workflow. AAL systems are MISs of special purposes that use wireless technology to provide healthcare to citizens. By their nature AAL systems are totally distributed, they include various medical and other users' devices and the mobility of people increases their complexity and creates advanced requirements for the communication of data. Effectiveness and functionality of AAL premise interoperability at all levels of communication. In this chapter the definitions of interoperability are examined and how these are specialized for the healthcare area as well. In addition, the applied technologies and some significant issues that regard interoperability are analyzed.

E-government projects have a breadth of impact that extends far beyond their respective context. However, current e-government methodologies and models used are only tailored to specific requirements. Despite the use of interoperability in e-government, there has been a paucity of literature on adapting e-government frameworks in the healthcare context and in e-health in particular. Aiming to fill this gap, this chapter justifies why interoperability frameworks currently used in e-government may be useful in e-health. Therefore, this study attempts to address the issues faced by surveying the models consisting of effective practices in e-government IT integration management, as well as IT support. The overall aim of this chapter is to conduct a critical analysis of well-established e-government models and frameworks. Understanding e-government integration project management will ultimately help in the development of an effective practice model, which will improve e-government implementation.

Preface

Improving the quality of life for the disabled and the increasing fraction of elderly people is becoming more and more of an essential task for today's European societies, as Europe and industrialized countries worldwide are confronted with a demographic shift. The consequence of increasing life expectancy and decreasing birth rates is an EU population that is becoming increasingly older. On the social side of this issue, it is important for all these people having the need to be supported in their daily-life-activities to remain integrated in social life - despite their age and existing disabilities. On the economical side, ageing has enormous implications, since not only the income side of social schemes is affected, but also expenditures: health care systems for instance, are concerned. Facing these challenges of ageing societies there exist areas of opportunity, where technological and social-economic innovation can enhance the quality of life of older and impaired people, mitigate the economic problems of an ageing population, and create new economic and business opportunities.

Ambient Assisted Living (AAL) includes assistance to carry out daily activities, health and activity monitoring, enhancing safety and security, getting access to social, medical and emergency systems, and facilitating social contacts. Receiving social and/or medical support in various new intelligent ways consequently contributes to independent living and quality of life for many elderly and disabled people. Overall, AAL can improve the quality of life of elderly people at home and reduces the need of caretakers, personal nursing.

The book entitled "Wireless Technologies for Ambient Assisted Living and Health Care: Systems and Applications" provides a compendium of terms, definitions and explanations of concepts, processes and acronyms. Additionally, this volume features short chapters authored by leading experts offering an in-depth description of key terms and concepts related to different areas, issues and trends in various areas of Wireless Technologies for Ambient Assisted Living and Health Care. The book focuses on emerging wireless technologies and innovative wireless solutions for smart home environments.

The topics of this book covers useful areas of general knowledge including Information and Communication Technologies related to Health, New Developments in Distributed Applications and Interoperable Systems, Applications and Services, Wireless Technologies and Architectures for Health Monitoring Systems, Wireless Communication and Sensor Networks in Smart Living Space.

This book will be an excellent source of comprehensive knowledge and literature on the topic of Wireless Computing in the area of Health Care and Assisted Living.

All of us who worked on the book hope that readers will find it useful.

Athina A. Lazakidou, Konstantinos Siassiakos, Konstantinos Ioannou
Editors

Chapter 1
A Roadmap to the Introduction of Pervasive Information Systems in Healthcare

Fotis Kitsios
University of Macedonia, Greece

Thanos Papadopoulos
University of Southampton, UK

Spyros Angelopoulos
The University of Warwick, UK

ABSTRACT

Pervasive healthcare is an emerging research discipline, which focuses on the development of pervasive and ubiquitous computing technology for healthcare environments. Information and Communication Technologies have dramatically evolved during the last decade, laying a solid foundation for the future generation of Ubiquitous Internet access. As a result, current efforts in research and development in the areas of pervasive healthcare, promote the formation of inter-disciplinary international teams of experts, scientists, researchers and engineers to create a new generation of applications and technologies that will facilitate the fully automated information cyberspace systems. The authors discuss the current state-of-the-art in the world of Telecommunications and Internet Technologies as well as new technological trends in the Internet and Automation Industries, while promoting research and development in the interdisciplinary projects conducted by multinational teams worldwide.

INTRODUCTION

Over the last years, Information Technology (IT) has been implemented as a means to achieve competitive advantage for private firms, and provide better quality services to customers. The IT

artefacts have started to embrace all activities of human beings. They are embedded in more places than a desktop computer and provide innovative services in ways that have not been imagined in the past.

The paradigm shift (Kuhn, 1967) in the use of IT and Information Systems (IS) is usually referred to as ubiquitous or pervasive computing (Weiser,

DOI: 10.4018/978-1-61520-805-0.ch001

2002). Ubiquitous Internet and pervasive IS are active research areas that have recently started to mature. Literature suggests many applications and systems on futuristic and pervasive computing for the 21st century, and discusses possible scenarios of adoption and implementation (Angelopoulos *et al.*, 2008).

In the healthcare context pervasive computing is used widely, for instance through blood pressure cuffs and glucose meters that can upload data to a personal computer for collection and dissemination to professional caregivers (Borriello *et al.*, 2007). However, there is still research to be done in terms of its implementation and the role of stakeholders in the construction of such tools. Literature has not explored thoroughly the necessity of adopting and implementing pervasive IT/IS.

Aiming to address this gap, the chapter aims to shed light upon the complex configurations of stakeholders that construct Pervasive Information Systems (PIS). The structure of the chapter is as follows: after a brief introduction to pervasive computing, the introduction of PIS to the healthcare is examined and in particular literature regarding the implementation of PIS to the specific context. Additionally, issues regarding the role of stakeholders during the implementation process are highlighted. The chapter concludes by an overview of the PIS and their application in healthcare and suggests further research avenues.

PERVASIVE COMPUTING

Omnipresence is the ability to be everywhere at a certain point in time. Ubiquity postulates the omnipresence of networking; an unbounded and universal network (Angelopoulos *et al.*, 2008). The widely used definition of ubiquitous computing is the method of enhancing computer use by making many computers available throughout the physical environment, but making them effectively invisible to the user (Wang et al, 2007). Pervasive computing integrates computation into

the environment, rather than having computers, which are distinct objects. Ubiquitous activities are not so task-centric while the majority of usability techniques are. It is not at all clear how to apply task-centric techniques to informal everyday computing situations (Abowd & Mynat 2000).

There is no clear definition of pervasive computing in the current literature (Orwat et al., 2008). Pervasive computing is considered roughly as the opposite of virtual reality. Where virtual reality puts people inside a computer-generated world, pervasive computing forces the computer to live out there in the world with people. Visualisation and interaction of pervasive services can be implemented using context-aware augmented reality (Van de Kar, 2005). Thus, pervasive computing is considered a very difficult integration of human factors, computer science, engineering, and social sciences (Weiser, 1991). On the other hand, augmented reality (AR), another type of virtual reality, is considered as an excellent user interface for pervasive computing applications, because it allows intuitive information browsing of location-referenced information (Lee et al., 2006; Schmalstieg and Reitmayr, 2005). Moreover, pervasive computing is also different from traditional general purpose computers. This is because IT is not in the foreground, triggered and manipulated by humans; instead, IS resides in the background, monitoring the activities of humans and processing this information to other sources (Kourouthanassis et al., 2008).

The vision of pervasive computing consists of unobtrusively integrating computers with peoples everyday lives at home and at work (Chen et al., 2007) and has inspired many researchers to work on new hardware, networking protocols, human-computer interactions, security and privacy, applications, and social implications (Weiser, 1991; Satyanarayanan, 2001). In the last decade, a number of researcher articles presented the vision and illustrated the scenarios of futuristic computing systems in the year 2005 (Babulak, 2005). Much of the research on Ubiquitous Computing has been dominated by a focus upon the office environment since when Mark Weiser articulated the notion of Ubiquitous Computing back in 1994 the office has been the default domain. However, today, much of the foreseen technology is already implemented and fully integrated in industry, military, businesses, education and home. Mark Weiser in his article which was written back in 1996 wrote about futuristic computer technologies applied in "Smart House in the year 2005" (Weiser, 1996). Mark Weisers vision did indeed materialise and some of his concepts are currently part of ongoing research and implementation projects (Babulak, 2005).

Pervasive computing as well as the ubiquitous Internet technologies, include the potentials to make our everyday life more comfortable. As a distinguished Professor of Computer Science quite aptly once said: "Computer technology today has influenced almost every aspect of our lives, industry, business, and education. However, most unfortunately computer technology have mechanised the relationship between people due to e-mail and Internet technologies. It is important that the research, academic and industrial community work together to reverse that equation, whereby computer technology will be a tool that will improve human lives and mutual interaction." (Babulak, 2005b). The authors encourage reader to reflect on that statement.

Literature has focused on the differences of PIS with the old paradigm of Desktop Information Systems (DIS) (Kourouthanassis et al., 2008; Lyytinen & Yoo, 2002; Saha & Mukherjee, 2003; Satyanarayanan, 2001). PIS steps back from the original interaction of humans with the IS and views computing devices as seamlessly merging into the physical environment; the DIS is viewed as another access device. PIS also incorporate the interaction of devices with each other in a natural and unobtrusive manner (Maes, 2005; Quek et al., 2002). Therefore, PIS "enable the provision of more human-like communication capabilities, while at the same time effectively treating implicit actions as meaningful system inputs" (Abowd, Mynatt, & Rodden, 2002; cited in Kourouthanassis et al., 2008). The PIS extend the paradigm of DIS under six examination dimensions depicted in Table 1.

The most important benefit deriving from the deployment of the ubiquitous computing systems is the creation of new experiences for the end user. This is particularly important in the regional development, where the provision of complimentary consuming schemes and the urbanization of todays society have created the model of the new consumer who is more knowledgeable about comparable product costs, more changeable in retail and brand preferences, showing little loyalty to brands, self-sufficient, yet demanding more

Table 1. PIS and DIS differentiating elements (adopted from Kourouthanassis et al., 2008)

	Desktop Information Systems	**Pervasive Information Systems**
User	• Committed • Known • Trained Role Model: Office Clerk	• Opportunistic • Unknown • Untrained Role Model: Citizen
Task	• Specific • Focused on utility and productivity	• Generic • Focused on service delivery and experience
Medium	• Localised • Homogeneous • "Point and Click" paradigm	• Constant Presence • Heterogeneous • Natural interaction and multimodal paradigm
Space	• Cybernetic	• Physical
Product	• Virtual	• Tangible and Virtual
Time	• Reactive	• Proactive

information, who holds high expectations of service and personal attention and is driven by three new currencies: time, value, and information (Kourouthanassis *et al.*, 2007).

Let us imagine a scenario where a person lives in the "Smart House 2015" (Tolmie et al., 2002). It is already 8:00 am and the alarm clock wakes Alice up while half opening the blinds to let the morning light enter her bedroom. The soundtrack of her favourite music station plays on the home cinema set while she takes her bath and a cup of fresh coffee waits for her at the kitchen. She dresses up and leaves home on time while pressing the button "exit" on the touch panel. The door closes behind her and immediately, all unnecessary lights as well as the toaster that she forgot switched on, turn off. The security alarm sets on and waits for Alice to get back. As soon as Alice arrives from work, she gets in her house using the fingerprint reader at the front door. At the very same time, the in-house lighting is set in the "welcome mode" and the air-conditioning system is set to suit her preferences. While she is entering the living room, TV switches on her favourite news station in order to inform her about the current affairs. She takes a look at the remote control, in order to check that everything is perfect and she initializes the multi-zone entertainment system. Her favourite music plays on the home cinema set and she is now ready to enjoy her bath, since the water is ready at the desired temperature. The ventilation works silently in order not to disturb the music listening, and it maximizes its power only when Alice gets out of the bathroom. She has not had the time to cook and the delivery boy rings the bell to deliver her favourite Chinese food. Immediately, the monitor that can be found closer to her location, shows the view of the man smiling at the front door and with the touch of a button, she opens the door and the front lighting to facilitate his entrance into the house. This example explicates in detail the pervasiveness of IT in a home environment, and the subsequent benefits that stem out of the implementation of PIS.

Therefore, ubiquity represents the concept of having a network connection everywhere (Watson, 2004) with all consumer devices, with the intelligence and information widely dispersed and always accessible, as well as smart entities including appliances, buildings, signs, street smart communities, etc. The main focus is to enable one global network that would be available 24 hours a day, seven days a week, whole year round, and will provide best quality of services to anyone, anywhere and anytime (Babulak, 2005a).

PIS projects are yet to be implemented. The aforementioned challenges reveal that there is more work to be done in respect to the way the PIS is implemented and evaluated. In the implementation of such a system implementation, issues regarding the disclosure of information, as well as in the relationships between different actors entailed in the process, and their views and agendas. There is a burgeoning population of effectively invisible computers around us, embedded in the fabric of our homes, shops, vehicles, farms and some even in our bodies. They are invisible in that they are part of the environment and we can interact with them as we go about our normal activities. However, they can range in size from large plasma displays on the walls of buildings to microchips implanted in the human body. They help us command, control, communicate, do business, travel and entertain ourselves, and these "invisible" computers are far more numerous than their desktop counterparts.

However, pervasive computing brings to the foreground new security threats, ranging from loss of privacy and financial damages, to bodily injuries. For instance, PIS are vulnerable to security threats, known from conventional IT systems, but new threats may come to existence due to the unique nature of the pervasiveness of the devices. At the same time, strong security in pervasive applications, for example, fee-based feature activation in products, offers new opportunities for businesses as well as for users. Therefore, security in pervasive computing and PIS stems out as an emerging research theme, since there is an active academic and industrial community working on strong security solutions (Paar & Weimerskirch 2007). Several approaches are developed to protect information for pervasive environments against malicious users. Nonetheless, ad hoc mechanisms or protocols are typically added in the approaches by compromising disorganized policies or additional components to protect from unauthorized access (Wang et al., 2007).

PERVASIVE INFORMATION SYSTEMS IN THE HEALTHCARE CONTEXT

A system is context-aware if it can extract, interpret, and use context information and adapt its functionality to the current context of use (Korkea-aho, 2000). In particular, context-awareness is also considered as one of the most important issues in pervasive computing, which is used to provide relevant services and information to users by exploiting contexts. By contexts, we mean information about locations, software agents, users, devices, and their relationships (Daftari et al, 2003; Gu et al, 2004). Recently, several researches have been in progress for developing flexible middlewares, which can supply context-aware service infrastructure such as Context Toolkit (Dey et al, 2001), Reconfigurable Context-Sensitive Middleware for Pervasive Computing (Yau et al, 2003), SOCAM (Service-oriented Context-aware Middleware) (Gu et al, 2004), and GAIA (Biegel & Cahill, 2004).

There are three main reasons why context is important (Hong et al, 2005). First, context reduces the input cost. Second, context may provide an exciting user experience without much effort on the users part. Third, users benefit through context sharing. User preferences and security may vary depending on the device capabilities and other context conditions. Therefore, the context adaptability should provide for means to

express conditions and reason them applicable to adaptable ubiquitous services (Gandon and Sadeh, 2004; Held *et al.*, 2002). One particular important issue is to combine context awareness with more natural and intuitive interfaces like AR for providing more human-oriented visualization, interaction and collaboration of various pervasive services (Lee *et al.*, 2006). Further, in a dynamic heterogeneous environment, context adaptation for user-oriented services is a key concept to meet the varying requirements of different clients. In order to enable context-aware adaptation, context information must be gathered and eventually presented to the application performing the adaptation (Held *et al.*, 2002).

Pervasive healthcare seeks to respond to a variety of pressures on healthcare systems, including the increased incidence of life-style related and chronic diseases, emerging consumerism in healthcare, need for empowering patients and relatives for self-care and management of their health, and need to provide seamless access for health care services, independent of time and place. PIS and ubiquitous Internet increasingly influences health care and medicine (Orwat *et al.*, 2008). According to Kohn and Corrigan (2000), thousands of patients die each year in hospitals due to medical errors caused by inefficient patient pathways and care procedures. In the U.S., such errors are estimated to account for 7000 deaths annually and are often due to bad handwriting and similar problems (Menezes *et al.*, 1997). This indicates that there exists high potential in applying PIS to process improvement. For example, medication errors could be largely eliminated through better auditing capabilities, introduced by pervasive computing technology, such as RFID. Therefore, PIS can contribute to the elimination of errors since it improves the improvement or procedures through which care is provided.

PIS assists in the improvement of other hospital processes (Bohn *et al.*, 2003). Decisions are based upon information about the physical location of a person or object. For instance, if the health condition of a patient deteriorates and needs to be taken to the Emergency Unit, the system could locate the nearest doctor and call him/her to the scene so that (s)he can take further actions. Moreover, PIS can facilitate the exchange of information to authorised users at any time and any place and secure the confidentiality of medical data. This means that doctors do not need to be accompanied with a large folder of diagnostic files, since all written information as well as X-ray images and other data are accessible on touchpads in the patients rooms, the offices, on handheld devices, through headsets and wherever else they are needed. Consequently, healthcare personnel focus on their work and do not need to be worried about access to information.

Pervasive computing is mentioned in the context of improving healthcare (Borriello *et al.*, 2007). In the specific context, applications include psychotherapy (Sa *et al.*, 2007); autism and children with special needs (Kientz et al., 2007); simultaneous assessment of multiple individuals (Hayes et al., 2007); continuous measurement of physiological signals such as limb motion, respiration, and skin temperature (Wade and Asada, 2007). Arguably, then, PIS are actually starting to be deployed. For instance, telesurgery is becoming a practical reality, with remote surgeons taking part in a surgical procedure, or are able to consult on the condition of a patient (Borriello *et al.*, 2007). These researchers advocate towards the use of PIS, as it benefits healthcare organisations in three ways: firstly, PIS lower costs since they enable faster and more appropriate care to patients; secondly, care is made accessible to more people and the scale at which healthcare can be applied is increased; and thirdly, healthcare is becoming more personalised, enabling thereby individuals to be more responsible for maintaining their health.

In a not-so-imaginary example, Black *et al.* (2004) describe the use of PIS in healthcare environments: "Patients are instrumented with vital-sign monitors and with a means of determining their location. Physicians and nurses have wireless PDAs, also instrumented with a means of determining their location. Context-aware applications help optimize physician rounds, support nurse triage, simplify the user interface to pervasive devices, provide additional data for billing reconciliation, and provide clinical communications." Fully automated environments will require sophisticated MIMO antenna systems and small smart devices that will be able to communicate within themselves all the time. These devices will have self healing capabilities to make sure that they are recharged regularly and will be operational without any interruption. In contrast to humans who have breakfast, lunch, dinner and snack on accession to make sure that they are able to do their job, and yet they sleep anywhere from 6 to 14 hours each day, the devices creating the fully automated space cannot sleep, perhaps they may wait or be on pause mode, but as soldiers they must be in full operational readiness at anytime and anywhere.

PIS may improve productivity, but it also introduces costs, for instance in deployment, administration, and maintenance. Healthcare may be an area on which people are willing to spend a significant part of their income, but, however, the amount of money that can be actually invested by governments on new treatment methods, the benefit of which is mostly marginal, is certainly limited. Considering though the prospective proliferation of pervasive computing technology, we can conclude that the cost might as well drop below the level where its application in the healthcare domain becomes economically attractive (Bohn *et al.*, 2003).

Research is yet to be conducted to shift from design to actual implementation (Tolmie *et al.*, 2002). Apart from benefits related to the implementation of PIS in healthcare, there are also challenges to researchers in several ways. For instance, clinical staff needs to deal with large volumes of shared data, such as patient records and x-rays. Additionally, the work of clinical staff is team-oriented and requires collaboration in

Figure 1. PIS roadmap

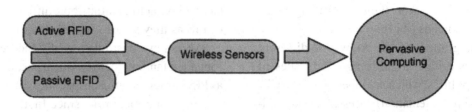

order to solve complex problems; it is also no-madic, as it requires them to attend conferences and exchange views with colleagues. The working environment is filled with disruptions, and hence they should be able to memorise parallel pending activities during the treatment process. They also need quick access to relevant data, while at the same time, keeping sensitive medical data private (Borriello *et al.*, 2007). To assist with these issues, PIS suggests an integration platform between different artefacts, which come together to suggest improvements in the way health is provided to citizens.

Taking into account the aforementioned challenges in the implementation of PIS in healthcare, we suggest that two issues should be addressed in order to successfully implement PIS, namely technical factors, such as interoperability, battery capacity, (data) security and connectivity, and social and organisational factors and in particular the focus on stakeholders and their acceptance of the new technology (Newell, 2007). This is because the healthcare context is peculiar in terms of the multiplicity of stakeholders and users of PIS –e.g. doctors, nurses, managers, administrative staff– and the diverse settings, that is, accident settings, intensive care and adapted domestic environments; there is also the patient factor, people who are suffering and need to be treated as soon as possible.

The aforementioned stakeholders should accept the new PIS; acceptance is defined as the adoption and use of objects by persons (Scheermesser *et al.*, 2008) and can be studied using the Technology Acceptance Model (TAM) (Davis *et al.*, 1989; Davis, 1989), and the Theory of Planned

Behaviour (TPB) (Ajzen and Fishbein, 1980; Ajzen, 1991). TAM refers to a model that aims to reveal the user acceptance of IS. It postulates that perceived ease of use and perceived usefulness should be considered for the acceptance of IS. The former factor can be translated as the degree to which a person believes that using the system will enhance his/her job performance, whereas the latter medical or therapeutical use (Davis *et al.*, 1989; Scheermesser *et al.*, 2008). The TPB model, stemming from social psychology, is concerned with intended behaviour and the factors that determine it, that is, intended attitudes, subjective norms and perceived behaviour control (Scheermesser *et al.*, 2008). These factors are concerned mainly with the fit of the PIS to the social norms and "the persons perception that most people who are important to him think he should or should not perform the behaviour in question" (Fishbein and Ajzen, 1975; Scheermesser *et al.*, 2008).

Using TAM and TPB models, Scheermesser *et al.* (2008) explore the implementation of pervasive computing in healthcare, using two case studies in pre- and post-clinical healthcare, namely the treatment of acute cardiovascular diseases, and the potential for the treatment of multiple sclerosis. Using a qualitative user acceptance analysis of the two studies, the researchers suggest that the main factor of user acceptance is the perceived medical usefulness; usability is a decisive factor of acceptance if the perceived usefulness is reduced by problems with usability. Moreover, acceptance is inhibited if data privacy or if subjective norms are violated. Finally, the successful implementation of PIS depends on the active integration of different stakeholders, physicians, medical staff and patients, each with their specific agendas, priorities and needs (ibid).

The integration of the views of different stakeholders brings to the foreground issues of power and politics, which are inherent in every IT innovation implementation process. As stakeholders have different views regarding the PIS and its implementation due to their different agendas, they many associate in order to influence the outcome of the process. Stakeholders, their associations, and their dynamics are the starting point for implementation, shaping the process depending on their vested interests and agendas (Harrisson and Laberge, 2002; Swan and Scarbrough, 2005).

To address the politics and dynamics inherent in the implementation of IT innovation –and in our case PIS– Harrisson and Laberge (2002), in their study of diffusion amongst workers of a large microelectronics firm, use Actor-Network Theory (ANT) and its uniqueness in treating artefacts and technologies as well as people and organisations as members of a network (Callon, 1986; Latour, 1987/2005; Latour and Woolgar, 1986). In particular, they regard innovation as a network, constructed through the associations of actors, shaped by pre-existing ideologies and workers perceptions regarding collective relationships, and based on the translation of identities of actors who participate in the implementation.

In the case of PIS implementation, ANT focuses on the chains of actions and events which have to do with the implementation and more specifically to the actors involved in the spread of ideas, objects or artefacts that may modify it, deflect it, betray it, add to it, or appropriate it (Sarker *et al.*, 2006). The emphasis lies in how actors not only react towards PIS, but how their actions create and appropriated PIS. Secondly, ANT considers the different identities and meanings constructed by different actors during the implementation process. Latour (1987) suggests that the identity of innovation and technological change depend

on how actors enact and enrol them. Therefore, it studies how actors can attribute different meanings of PIS as they seek to achieve their own goals.

ANT may constitute a useful theoretical lens for understanding socio-political phenomena such as PIS implementation, especially where technology plays a critical role, since firstly it does not exclude non-human actors (e.g. technologies) from the analysis, allowing thereby for a more explicit examination of the enabling or restricting role of IT in the implementation process; and secondly, it acknowledges the inherently unstable nature of actors, as they can change their associations with others, depending on their different agendas and views of the PIS in question; and thirdly, it suggests that IT –PIS in this case– when it is introduced into an organization, it has to be translated, that is, adjusted to local conditions (localised) (Czarniawska and Sevon, 2006). Therefore, ANT brings to the fore a political analysis which is important in the implementation of IT innovations, and in this case the PIS.

CONCLUSION

In this research we aimed to provide an overview pervasive concerning from a healthcare point of view. IT/IS did inspire a number of outstanding scientists and engineers in the past centuries to find new solutions to make life easier for all mankind. The emergence and accessibility of advanced data and telecommunications technologies combined with the convergence of industry standards, as well as the convergence of data and telecommunications industries contribute towards the ubiquitous access to information resources via the Internet.

The automated environment and cyberspace systems for the 21st century entered a new era of innovation and technological advancements. The worlds industry and commerce are becoming increasingly dependent on web-based solutions, with regards to a global vision for the future.

With increased benefits and improvements in overall information technology, the benefit-to-cost ratio has never been higher. It is essential to continue the development of industry standards and the application of information technologies in order to increase the automation and ultimate success of modern logistics, the E-Commerce and E-manufacturing industries (Kropft, 2002; Shade, 2001).

The advancement of current technologies in the fields of data and telecommunications, ubiquitous Internet access and sensor technologies combined with the new revolutionary explorations and concepts in biotechnology and nanotechnology, computer human interface-interaction, etc., present a great challenge for the research community not only as a result of mathematical complexity, but most of all as a result of the users perception (Babulak, 2005).

Future efforts should be focused on designing a communication language and transmission media that will allow for instantaneous communication transfer and control between smart devices and humans. Additionally, despite the benefits of PIS, it is important to shed light upon the evaluation of such technologies and the cost-benefit ratio of PIS in healthcare. Finally, since their implementation is challenging and the user acceptance is a crucial factor in the process, research should shed more light upon the role of actors and their emerging associations during the implementation, focusing on the way in which PIS is introduced, interpreted, defined, and modified in healthcare context.

REFERENCES

Abel, D. J., Taylor, K., Ackland, R., & Hungerford, S. (1998). An exploration of GIS architectures for Internet environments. *Computers, Environment and Urban Systems*, 22(1), 7–23. doi:10.1016/S0198-9715(98)00016-7

Abowd, D., & Mynat, D. (2000). Charting past, present and future research in Ubiquitous computing. *AC Transactions on Computer-Human Interaction*, 7(1), 29–58. doi:10.1145/344949.344988

Ajzen, I. (1991). The theory of planned behaviour. *Organizational Behavior and Human Decision Processes*, 50, 179–211. doi:10.1016/0749-5978(91)90020-T

Ajzen, I., & Fishbein, M. (1980). *Understanding attitudes and predicting social behaviour*. Englewood Cliffs, NJ: Prentice-Hall.

Angelopoulos, S., Kitsios, F., & Babulac, E. (2008). From e to u: Towards an innovative digital era. In Prof. Stavros Kotsopoulos and Dr. Konstantinos Ioannou (eds.), *Heterogeneous Next Generation Networking: Innovations and Platform*, (pp 427-444), Hershey, PA: Idea Group Publishing.

Babulak, E. (2005a). Automated Environment via Cyberspace. In *Proceedings of the International Conference on Applied Computing* (IADIS), Algarve, Portugal.

Babulak, E. (2005b). Quality of Service Provision Assessment in the Healthcare Information and Telecommunications Infrastructures. Accepted for publication in the *International Journal of Medical Informatics*.

Biegel, G., & Cahill, V. (2004). A Framework for Developing Mobile, Context-aware Applications. In *Proceedings of the Second IEEE International Conference on Pervasive Computing and Communications* (PerCom04), IEEE Computer Society.

Black, J. P., Segmuller, W., Cohen, N., Leiba, B., Misra, A., Ebling, M. R., & Stern, E. (2004). Pervasive Computing in Health Care: Smart Spaces and Enterprise Information Systems. In MobiSys Workshop on Context, Boston Massachusetts, USA.

Bohn, J., Gaertner, F., & Vogt, H. (2003). Dependability Issues of Pervasive Computing in a Healthcare Environment. Proceedings of the First International Conference on Security in Pervasive Computing.

Borriello, G., Stanford, V., Naranayaswami, C., & Menning, W. (2007). Pervasive Computing in Healthcare. [Editorial]. *IEEE Pervasive Computing / IEEE Computer Society [and] IEEE Communications Society, 6*(1), 17–19. doi:10.1109/MPRV.2007.11

Callon, M. (1986). Some elements in sociology of translation: domestication of the scallops and fishermen of St. Brieuc Bay. In Law, J. (Ed.), *Power, action and belief* (pp. 196–233). London: Routledge.

Chen, G., & Kotz, D. (2000). A survey of context-aware mobile computing research, Technical Report TR2000-381, Department of Computer Science, Dartmouth College.

Czarniawska, B., & Sévon, G. (Eds.). (2005). *Global Ideas: How Ideas, Objects and Practices Travel in the Global Economy*. Malmö: Liber & Copenhagen Business School Press.

Daftari, A., Mehta, N., Bakre, S., & Sun, X. H. (2003). *On design framework of context aware embedded systems*. Chicago: Monterey Workshop.

Davis, F. (1989). Perceived Usefulness, Perceived Ease of Use, and User Acceptance of Information Technology. *Management Information Systems Quarterly, 13*, 319–340. doi:10.2307/249008

Davis, F., Bagozzi, R. P., & Warshaw, P. R. (1989). User Acceptance of computer technology – A comparison of two theoretical models. *Management Science, 35*, 982–1003. doi:10.1287/mnsc.35.8.982

De Sa, M., Carrico, L., & Antunes, P. (2007). Ubiquitous Psychotherapy. *IEEE Pervasive Computing / IEEE Computer Society [and] IEEE Communications Society, 6*(1), 20–27. doi:10.1109/MPRV.2007.23

Dey, A. K., Abowd, G. D., & Salber, D. (2001). A conceptual framework and a toolkit for supporting the rapid prototyping of context-aware applications. *Human-Computer Interaction, 16*, 97–166. doi:10.1207/S15327051HCI16234_02

Dickson, K. Chiu, W. & Leung, H. (2005). Towards ubiquitous tourist service coordination and integration: a multi-agent and semantic web approach. In *Proceedings of the 7th international conference on Electronic commerce ICEC 05*. ACM Press

Dix, A., Finlay, J., Abowd, G. D., & Beale, R. (2004). *Human-Computer Interaction*. Upper Saddle River, NJ: Prentice Hall.

Fishbein, M., & Ajzen, I. (1975). *Belief, Attitude, Intention and Behavior: An Introduction to Theory and Research*. Reading, MA: Addison-Wesley.

Funk, J. L. (1998). Competition between regional standards and the success and failure of firms in the world-wide mobile communication market. *Telecommunications Policy, 22*(4/5), 419–441. doi:10.1016/S0308-5961(98)00024-X

Gandon, F., & Sadeh, N. (2004). Semantic Web Technologies to Reconcile Privacy and Context Awareness, *Web Semantics Journal, 1*(3).

Garlan, D., Siewiorek, D., Smailagic, A., & Steenkiste, P. (2002). Project Aura: Towards Distraction-Free Pervasive Computing. *IEEE Pervasive Computing / IEEE Computer Society [and] IEEE Communications Society, 1*(2), 22–31. doi:10.1109/MPRV.2002.1012334

Gu, T., Wang, X. H., Pung, H. K., & Zhang, D. Q. (2004). An Ontology-based Context Model in Intelligent Environments. In *Proceedings of Communication Networks and Distributed Systems Modeling and Simulation Conference*. San Diego.

Harrisson, D., & Laberge, M. (2002). Innovation, identities and resistence: The social construction of innovation. *Journal of Management Studies, 39*(4), 497–521. doi:10.1111/1467-6486.00301

Hayes, T. L., Pavel, M., Larimer, N., Tsay, I. A., & Nutt, J. (2007). Simultaneous assessment of multiple individuals. *IEEE Pervasive Computing / IEEE Computer Society [and] IEEE Communications Society, 6*(1), 36–43. doi:10.1109/MPRV.2007.9

Held, A., Buchholz, S., & Schill, A. (2002). Modelling of Context Information for Pervasive Computing Applications. In *Proceedings of the 6th World Multiconference on Systemics, Cybernetics and Informatics*. Orlando, FL.

Hong, D., Chiu, D. K. W., & Shen, V. Y. (2005). Requirements elicitation for the design of context-aware applications in a ubiquitous environment. In *Proceedings of the 7th international conference on Electronic commerce ICEC 05*. ACM Press. Jackson, J., & Murphy, P. (2006). Clusters in regional tourism: An Australian case. *Annals of Tourism Research, 33*(4), 1018–1035.

Jennings, N. R., Faratin, P., Lomuscio, A. R., Parsons, S., Sierra, C., & Wooldridge, M. (2002). Automated negotiation: prospects, methods and challenges. *International Journal of Group Decision and Negotiation, 10*(2), 199–215. doi:10.1023/A:1008746126376

Kientz, J. A., Hayes, G. R., Westeyn, T. L., Starner, T., & Abowd, G. D. (2007). Pervasive computing and autism: assisting caregivers of children with special needs. *IEEE Pervasive Computing / IEEE Computer Society [and] IEEE Communications Society, 6*(1), 28–35. doi:10.1109/MPRV.2007.18

Kitsios, F., Angelopoulos, S., & Zannetopoulos, I. (2008). *Innovation and e- government: an in depth overview on e-services*, Heterogeneous Next Generation Networking: Innovations and Platform, Handbook edited by Prof. Stavros Kotsopoulos and Dr. Konstantinos Ioannou, pp 415-426, Idea Group Publishing.

Kohn, L. T., & Corrigan, J. (2000). (eds). *To Err Is Human: Building a Safer Health System*. National Academy Press, 2000. Available at: http://books.nap.edu/books/0309068371/html/index.html

Korkea-aho, M. (2000). Context-aware application surveys, available at: http://users.tkk.fi/~mkorkeaa/doc/context-aware.html

Kourouthanassis, E., P., Giaglis, M., G., & Vrechopoulos, A. P. (2007). Enhancing user experience through pervasive information systems: The case of pervasive retailing. *International Journal of Information Management, 27*, 319–335. doi:10.1016/j.ijinfomgt.2007.04.005

Kraus, S. (2001). *Strategic Negotiation in Multiagent Environments*. Cambridge, MA: The MIT Press.

Kropft, P. (2002). What is Pervasive Computing. Series of Lecture notes.

Latour, B. (1987). *Science in Action: How to Follow Scientists and Engineers through Society*. Milton Keynes: Open University Press.

Latour, B. (2005). *Reassembling the Social: An Introduction to Actor-Network-Theory*. Oxford: Oxford University Press.

Latour, B., & Woolgar, S. (1986). *Laboratory Life: The Construction of Scientific Facts*. Chichester: Princeton University Press.

Lee, K. J., Ju, J., & Jeong, J. M. (2006). Mobile and pervasive commerce track: A payment & receipt business model in U-commerce environment, Proceedings of the 8th international conference on Electronic commerce: The new e-commerce: innovations for conquering current barriers, obstacles and limitations to conducting successful business on the internet ICEC 06. ACM Press.

Lee, K. J., & Seo, Y. H. (2006). A pervasive comparison shopping business model for integrating offline and online marketplace, Proceedings of the 8th international conference on Electronic commerce: The new e-commerce: innovations for conquering current barriers, obstacles and limitations to conducting successful business on the internet ICEC 06. ACM Press.

Lukkari, J., Korhonen, J., & Ojala, T. (2004). SmartRestaurant: mobile payments in context-aware environment, Proceedings of the 6th international conference on Electronic commerce ICEC 04. ACM Press. Mark Weisers Vision, retrieved February 3, 2005, from Ubiq Website: http://www.ubiq.com/hypertext/weiser/SciAmDraft3.html

Menezes, A. J., van Oorschot, P. C., & Vanstone, S. A. (1997). *Handbook of Applied Cryptography*. Boca Raton: CRC Press.

Noble, B., Satyanarayanan, M., Narayanan, D., Tilton, T., Flinn, J., & Walker, K. (1997). Agile application-aware adaptation for mobility, in: Proceedings of the 16th ACM SOSP.

Norman, D. A. (1999). *The Invisible Computer: Why Good Products Can Fail, the Personal Computer Is So Complex, and Information Appliances Are the Solution*. The MIT Press.

Orwat, C., Graefe, A., & Faulwasser, T. (2008). Towards pervasive computing in health care – A literature review. *BMC Medical Informatics and Decision Making, 8*(26).

Pike, R., Presotto, D., Dorward, S., Flandrena, B., Thompson, K., Trickey, H., & Winterbottom, P. (1995). Plan 9 from Bell Labs. *Computing Systems, 8*(3), 221–254.

Roussos, G. (2003). Appliance design for pervasive computing. *IEEE Pervasive Computing / IEEE Computer Society [and] IEEE Communications Society, 2*(4), 75–77.

Ruta, M., Noia, T. D., Sciascio, E. D., Piscitelli, G., & Scioscia, F. (2007). Session M5: e-business systems and applications: RFID meets bluetooth in a semantic based u-commerce environment, Proceedings of the ninth international conference on Electronic commerce ICEC 07. ACM Press.

Salvi, A. B., & Sahai, S. (2002). Dial m for money, Proceedings of the 2nd international workshop on Mobile commerce WMC 02. ACM Press.

Sarker, S., Sarker, S., & Sidirova, A. (2006). Understanding business process change failure: an actor-network perspective. *Journal of Management Information Systems, 23*(1), 51–86. doi:10.2753/MIS0742-1222230102

Scheermesser, M., Kosow, H., Rashid, A., & Holtmann, C. (2008). User acceptance of pervasive computing in healthcare: Main findings of two case studies. Second International Conference on Pervasive Computing.

Schilit, B. N., Adams, N., & Want, R. (1994). Context-aware computing applications, In IEEE Workshop on Mobile Computing Systems and Applications, pp. 85-90, Santa Cruz, CA, US.

Schmalstieg, D., & Reitmayr, G. (2005). The World as a User Interface: Augmented Reality for Ubiquitous Computing. Central European Multimedia and Virtual Reality Conference 2005 (CEMVRC 2005), Prague, Czech Republic.

Shade, B. (2001). Increased Productivity Through E-Manufacturing, by Cahners Business Information.

Shafer, S., Krumm, J., Brumitt, B., Meyers, B., Czerwinski, M., & Robbins, D. (1998). *The new easyliving project at microsoft research*. Gaithersburg, Maryland: In DARPA / NIST Smart Spaces Workshop.

Stajano, F. (2002). *Security for Ubiquitous Computing*. Wiley press. doi:10.1002/0470848693

Sun, S., Su, C., & Ju, T. (2005). A study of consumer value-added services in mobile commerce: focusing on domestic cellular phone companies in Taiwan, China, Proceedings of the 7th international conference on Electronic commerce ICEC 05. ACM Press.

Swan, J., & Scarbrough, H. (2005). The politics of networked innovation. *Human Relations, 58*, 913–943. doi:10.1177/0018726705057811

Tolmie, P., Pycock, J., Diggins, T., MacLean, A., & Karsenty, A. (2002). *Unremarkable Computing*. Xerox Research Centre Europe.

van de Kar, E. (2005). The design of a mobile information and entertainment service on a UMTS testbed, Proceedings of the 7th international conference on Electronic commerce ICEC 05. New York: ACM Press.

Wade, E., & Asada, H. (2007). Conductive-Fabric Garment for a Cable-Free Body Area Network. *IEEE Pervasive Computing / IEEE Computer Society [and] IEEE Communications Society*, *6*(1), 52–58. doi:10.1109/MPRV.2007.8

Wang, H., Cao, J., & Zhang, Y. (2006). Ubiquitous computing environments and its usage access control. In *Proceedings of the First International Conference on Scalable Information Systems, INFOSCALE*. Hong Kong: ACM Press.

Wang, H., Cao, J. and Zhang, Y. (2007). *Access control management for ubiquitous computing. Future Generation Computer Systems*, accepted for publication in Future Generation Computer Systems journal.

Wang, Y., van de Kar, E., & Meijer, G. (2005). Designing mobile solutions for mobile workers: lessons learned from a case study. In *Proceedings of the 7th international conference on Electronic commerce ICEC 05*. New York: ACM Press.

Watson, R. T. (2000). U-commerce: the ultimate. *Ubiquity, 1*(33). ACM Press.

Watson, R. T. (2004). *Data management: Databases and Organizations 4th edition*. New York: Willey press.

Weiser, M. (1991). The computer for the 21st century. *Scientific American*, *265*(3), 66–75. doi:10.1038/scientificamerican0991-94

Weiser, M. (1996). *Open House, Web magazine of the Interactive Telecommunications Program of New York University*. Appeared in March, 1996 ITP, Review 2.0. http://www.itp.tsoa.nyu.edu/~review/

Wohlwend, H. (2001). *An E-Factory Vision*. 2nd European Advanced Equipment Control/Advance Process Control Conf., April 18-20.

Yau, S. S., Gupta, S. K. S., Karim, F., Ahamed, S. I., Wang, Y., & Wang, B. (2003). Smart Classroom: Enhancing Collaborative Learning Using Pervasive Computing Technology. In *Proceedings of the 6th WFEO World Congress on Engineering Education and the 2nd ASEE International Colloquium on Engineering Education* (ASEE 2003).

Chapter 2
Role of Data Mining and Knowledge Discovery in Managing Telecommunication Systems

Ibrahiem Mahmoud Mohamed El Emary
King Abdulaziz University, Saudi Arabia

ABSTRACT

This chapter is interested in discussing how to use data mining techniques to assist in achieving an acceptable level of quality of service of telecommunication systems. The quality of service is defined as the metrics which are predicated by using the data mining techniques, decision tree, association rules and neural networks. Routing algorithms can use this metric for optimal path selection which in turn will affect positively on the system performance. Also, in this chapter management axis using data mining techniques were handled, i.e., check the status of the telecommunication networks, role of data mining in obtaining optimal configuration, how to use data mining technique to assure high level of security for the telecommunication. The popularity of data mining in the telecommunications industry can be viewed as an extension of the use of expert systems in the telecommunications industry. These systems were developed to address the complexity associated with maintaining a huge network infrastructure and the need to maximize network reliability while minimizing labor costs (Liebowitz, J. 1988). The problem with these expert systems is that they are expensive to develop because it is both difficult and time consuming to elicit the requisite domain knowledge from experts.

INTRODUCTION

Normally collecting and storing data is outpaced the ability to analyze, summarize and extract knowledge from the continuous stream of input data. In database, knowledge discovery represents the complex process of identifying valid, novel, potentially useful and ultimately understandable patterns of data. Data mining which is a particular step in the KDD process consists of particular algorithms that under acceptable computational efficiency limitations produce a particular enumeration of patterns (models) over the data. Data mining technology has emerged as a means of

DOI: 10.4018/978-1-61520-805-0.ch002

identifying patterns and trends from large quantities of data. The Data Mining technology normally adopts data integration method to generate data warehouse, on which to gather all data into a central site, and then run an algorithm against that data to extract the useful module prediction and knowledge evaluation.

The major Data Mining (DM) tasks are: classification which means assigning each record of a database to one of a predefined set of classes, clustering that deals with finding groups of records that are close according to some user defined metrics or association rules that determines implication rules for a subset of record attributes. In research community, Data Mining have many challenges covering the following:

- In various application domains, the mined data is produced with high rate or come in stream, so in those cases, knowledge has to be mined fast and efficiently in order to be updated and useful. Accordingly, the input data is changed rapidly.
- In a lot of organizations, security is of major concern. Here, there may be willing to release data mining results but not the source data itself.
- It is urgently to partition and distribute the data for parallel processing to achieve an acceptable space and time performance. Based on this fact, data mining is very computationally intensive process involving very large data sets.
- Data mining deal with huge amounts of data located at different sites where the amount of data can easily exceed the terabyte limit;

According to the above challenges, a basic approach for data mining which is to move all of the data to a central data repository and then to analyze them with a single data mining system, even though it guarantees accurate results of data analysis, it might be infeasible in many cases.

A an alternative approach to the above is to use high level learning with in-place strategies in which all the data can be locally analyzed, and the local results at their local sites are combined at the central site to get the final result which mean building a global data model. This approach is less expensive but may produce incorrect and ambiguous global results.

Telecommunication sector represents one of the tremendous growths among the technology during the last century. With the debut of intelligent networks (INs), service providers and specialized ISVs gained a hand in developing new services. The basic function of a service management system is to manage a service network for contracted customers. This system can efficiently support proactive troubleshooting in case of a network error, analyzing errors on the service level and correlating the network level error messages with the service topology purchased by the specific client. If any matching result is found, the operators receive an error message on the service involved. A service is defined as a network with a P2P or VPN topology running on any network technology based on customer needs and technical conditions.

In order to perform the tasks above, the service management system must be in contact with the network management systems managing the network technologies. The service management system receives the network-level alarms from these network management systems. The provider receives the network topology needed to interpret the specific alarms from the technical inventory management system using a special interface as well, although they often took a long time to deliver to customers. One of the major requirements for IT systems in telecommunications environments is achieving an acceptable level of reliability and scalability. In addition, there is a strong need for integration due to the above-average number and significance of heterogeneous IT support systems in modern day telecommunications companies. Accordingly, the IT industry attempts to meet those requirements by deploying innovative software technologies like distributed and database technologies, application server based systems.

In the current time, the telecommunication industry has quickly evolved from offering local and long distance telephone services to provide many other comprehensive communication services including voice, fax, pager, cellular phone, images, e-mail, computer and web data transmission and other data traffic. There is another phase of challenges comes as a result of the integration between telecommunication, computer network, internet and numerous other means of communication and computing are too interest to telecommunication networks management which covers: configuration, performance monitoring, accounting, fault detection and security.

As mentioned above, performance monitoring represents one of the major management processes. The main performance job that should be managed well is related to the routing in the communication networks. Routing involves two basic activities which are determining optimal routing paths to achieve high performance measure represented by system throughput (quality of service) and delay (quantity of service) and transporting information groups. The telecommunications industry was one of the first to adopt data mining technology. This is most likely because telecommunication companies routinely generate and store enormous amounts of high-quality data, have a very large customer base, and operate in a rapidly changing and highly competitive environment. So, telecommunication companies try to utilize data mining to improve the following: marketing efforts, identify fraud, and better manage their telecommunication networks. However, these companies also face a number of data mining challenges due to: enormous size of their data sets, the sequential and temporal aspects of their data, and the need to predict very rare events such as customer fraud and network failures in real-time.

The telecommunications industry generates and stores a tremendous amount of data. These data include:

- Network data, which describes the state of the hardware and software components in the network
- Customer data, which describes the telecommunication customers
- Call detail data, which describes the calls that traverse the telecommunication networks

The amount of data is so great that manual analysis of the data is difficult, if not impossible. The need to handle such large volumes of data led to the development of knowledge-based expert systems. These automated systems performed important functions such as identifying fraudulent phone calls and identifying network faults. The problem with this approach is that it is time consuming to obtain the knowledge from human experts and, in many cases; the experts do not have the requisite knowledge. The advent of data mining technology promised solutions to these problems and for this reason, the telecommunications industry was an early adopter of data mining technology. Telecommunication data pose several interesting issues for data mining. The first concerns scale, since telecommunication databases may contain billions of records and are amongst the largest in the world. A second issue is that the raw data is often not suitable for data mining (Liebowitz, J. 1988). For example, both call detail and network data are time-series data that represent individual events. Before this data can be effectively mined, useful "summary" features must be identified and then the data must be summarized using these features. Because many data mining applications in the telecommunications industry involve predicting very rare events, such as the failure of a network element or an instance of telephone fraud, rarity is another issue that must be dealt with. The fourth and final data mining issue concerns real-time performance: many data mining applications, such as fraud detection, require that any learned model/rules be applied in real-time. Each of these four issues is discussed throughout this chapter, within the context of real data mining applications.

The data mining applications for any industry depend on two factors: the data that are available and the business problems facing the industry. This section provides background information about the data maintained by telecommunications companies. The challenges associated with mining telecommunication data are also described in this section. Telecommunication companies maintain data about the phone calls that traverse their networks in the form of call detail records, which contain descriptive information for each phone call. In 2001, AT&T long distance customers generated over 300 million call detail records per day (Cortes, C., 2001) and, because call detail records are kept online for several months, this meant that billions of call detail records were readily available for data mining. Call detail data is useful for marketing and fraud detection applications.

Telecommunication companies also maintain extensive customer information, such as billing information, as well as information obtained from outside parties, such as credit score information. This information can be quite useful and often is combined with telecommunication- specific data to improve the results of data mining. For example, while call detail data can be used to identify suspicious calling patterns, a customer's credit score is often incorporated into the analysis before determining the likelihood that fraud is actually taking place. Telecommunications companies also generate and store an extensive amount of data related to the operation of their networks. This is because the network elements in these large telecommunication networks have some self-diagnostic capabilities that permit them to generate both status and alarm messages. These streams of messages can be mined in order to support network management functions, namely fault isolation and prediction (Rosset, S., 2003).

The telecommunication industry faces a number of data mining challenges. According to (Rosset, S., 2003), the three largest databases all belong to telecommunication companies, with France Telecom, AT&T, and SBC having databases with 29, 26, and 25 Terabytes, respectively. Thus, the scalability of data mining methods is a key concern. A second issue is that telecommunication data is often in the form of transactions/events and is not at the proper semantic level for data mining. For example, one typically wants to mine call detail data at the customer (i.e., phone line) level but the raw data represents individual phone calls. Thus it is often necessary to aggregate data to the appropriate semantic level (Sasisekharan, R., 1996) before mining the data. An alternative is to utilize a data mining method that can operate on the transactional data directly and extract sequential or temporal patterns (Klemettinen, M., 1999).

Another issue arises because much of the telecommunications data is generated in real-time and many telecommunication applications, such as fraud identification and network fault detection, need to operate in real-time. Because of its efforts to address this issue, the telecommunications industry has been a leader in the research area of mining data streams (Fawcett, T., 1997). One way to handle data streams is to maintain a signature of the data, which is a summary description of the data that can be updated quickly and incrementally (Cortes, C., 1998) developed signature-based methods and applied them to data streams of call detail records. A final issue with telecommunication data and the associated applications involves rarity. For example, both telecommunication fraud and network equipment failures are relatively rare. Predicting and identifying rare events has been shown to be quite difficult for many data mining algorithms (Weiss, G., 2003) and therefore this issue must be handled carefully in order to ensure reasonably good results.

MAJOR DATA MINING APPLICATIONS IN TELECOMMUNICATION

The telecommunications industry was an early adopter of data mining technology and therefore many data mining applications exist. Numerous data mining applications have been deployed in the telecommunications industry. However, most applications fall into one of the following three categories: marketing, fraud detection, and network fault isolation and prediction.

Telecommunication Marketing

Telecommunication companies maintain an enormous amount of information about their customers and, due to an extremely competitive environment, have great motivation for exploiting this information. For these reasons the telecommunications industry has been a leader in the use of data mining to identify customers, retain customers, and maximize the profit obtained from each customer. Perhaps the most famous use of data mining to acquire new telecommunications customers was MCI's Friends and Family program. This program, long since retired, began after marketing researchers identified many small but well connected subgraphs in the graphs of calling activity (Han, J., 2002). By offering reduced rates to customers in one's calling circle, this marketing strategy enabled the company to use their own customers as salesmen. This work can be considered an early use of social-network analysis and link mining (Getoor, L., 2005). A more recent example uses the interactions between consumers to identify those customers likely to adopt new telecommunication services (Hill, S., 2006). A more traditional approach involves generating customer profiles (i.e., signatures) from call detail records and then mining these profiles for marketing purposes. This approach has been used to identify whether a phone line is being used for voice or fax (Kaplan, H., 1999) and to classify a phone line as belonging to a either business or residential customer (Cortes, C., 1998).

Over the past few years, the emphasis of marketing applications in the telecommunications industry has shifted from identifying new customers to measuring customer value and then taking steps to retain the most profitable customers. This shift has occurred because it is much more expensive to acquire new telecommunication customers than retain existing ones. Thus it is useful to know the total lifetime value of a customer, which is the total net income a company can expect from that customer over time. There are 45 data mining methods used to model customer lifetime value for telecommunication customers (Rosset, S., 1999).

A key component of modeling a telecommunication customer's value is estimating how long they will remain with their current carrier. This problem is of interest in its own right since if a company can predict when a customer is likely to leave, it can take proactive steps to retain the customer. The process of a customer leaving a company is referred to as churn, and churn analysis involves building a model of customer attrition. Customer churn is a huge issue in the telecommunication industry where, until recently, telecommunication companies routinely offered large cash incentives for customers to switch carriers. Numerous systems and methods have been developed to predict customer churn (Wei, C., 2002). These systems almost always utilize call detail and contract data, but also often use other data about the customer (credit score, complaint history, etc.) in order to improve performance. Churn prediction is fundamentally a very difficult problem and, consequently, systems for predicting churn have been only moderately effective—only demonstrating the ability to identify some of the customers most likely to churn (Masand, B., 1999).

Telecommunication companies maintain a great deal of data about their customers. In addition to the general customer data that most businesses collect, telecommunication companies also store call detail records, which precisely describe the calling behavior of each customer. This information can be used to profile the customers and these profiles can then be used for marketing and/or forecasting purposes.

This chapter begins with one of the most well-known and successful marketing campaigns in the telecommunications industry: MCI's Friends and Family promotion. This promotion was initially launched in the United States in 1991 and, although now retired, was responsible for significant growth in MCI's customer base. The promotion offered reduced calling fees when calls are placed to others in one's calling circle. This promotion purportedly originated when market researchers noticed small sub graphs in the call graph of network activity—which suggested the possibility of adding entire calling circles rather than the costly approach of adding individual subscribers (Han, J., 2002). It is worth noting that MCI relied primarily on its customers to bring in members of their calling circle, even though MCI could have utilized its call detail data to generate a list of the people in each calling circle. The most likely reason for this is that MCI did not want to anger its customers by using highly personal information (calling history). This demonstrates that privacy concerns are an issue for data mining in the telecommunications industry, especially when call detail data is involved.

The MCI Friends and Family promotion relied on data mining to identify associations within data. Another marketing application that relies on this technique is a data mining application for finding the set of non-U.S. countries most often called together by U.S. telecommunication customers (Cortes, C., 1998). One set of countries identified by this data mining application is: {Jamaica, Antigua, Grenada, Dominica}. This information is useful for establishing and marketing international calling plans. A serious issue with telecommunication companies is customer churn. Customer churn involves a customer leaving one telecommunication company for another. Customer churn is a significant problem because

of the associated loss of revenue and the high cost of attracting new customers. Some of the worst cases of customer churn occurred several years ago when competing long distance companies offered special incentives, typically $50 or $100, for signing up with their company a practice which led to customers repeatedly switching carriers in order to earn the incentives.

Data mining techniques now permit companies the ability to mine historical data in order to predict when a customer is likely to leave. These techniques typically utilize billing data, call detail data, subscription information (calling plan, features, contract expiration data) and customer information (e.g., age). Based on the induced model, the company can then take action, if desired. For example, a wireless company might offer a customer a free phone for extending their contract. One such effort utilized a neural network to estimate the probability h(t) of cancellation at a given time t in the future (Mani, D., 1999).

In the telecommunications industry, it is often useful to profile customers based on their patterns of phone usage, which can be extracted from the call detail data. These customer profiles can then be used for marketing purposes, or to better understand the customer, which in turn may lead to better forecasting models. In order to effectively mine the call detail data, it must be summarized to the customer level. Then, a classifier induction program can be applied to a set of labeled training examples in order to build a classifier. This approach has been used to identify fax lines (Kaplan, H., 1999) and to classify a phone line as belonging to a business or residence (Cortes, C., 1998). Other applications have used this approach to identify phone lines belonging to telemarketers and to classify a phone line as being used for voice, data, or fax.

There are two sample rules for classifying a customer as being a business or residential customer shown below (using pseudo-code). These rules were generated using SAS Enterprise Miner, a sophisticated data mining package that supports multiple data mining techniques. The rules shown below were generated using a decision tree learner. However, a neural network was also used to predict the probability of a customer being a business or residential customer, based solely on the distribution of calls by time of day (i.e., the neural network had 24 inputs, one per hour of the day). The probability estimate generated by the neural network was then used as an input (i.e., feature) to the decision tree learner. Evaluation on a separate test set indicates that rule 1 is 88% accurate and rule 2 is 70% accurate (Kaplan, H., 1999).

Rule 1: if < 43% of calls last 0-10 seconds and < 13.5% of calls occur during the weekend and neural network says that P (business) > 0.58 based on time of day call distribution then business customer

Rule 2: if calls received over two-month period from at most 3 unique area codes and <56.6% of calls last 0-10 seconds' then residential customer

It is worth noting that because a telecommunications company generates a call detail record if the calling (paying) party is its customer, the company will also have a sample of (received) calls for non-customers. If a company has high overall market penetration, this sample may be large enough for data mining. Thus, telecommunication companies have the technical ability to profile non-customers as well as customers.

Telecommunication Fraud Detection

Telecommunications Fraud Detection is very serious problem for telecommunication companies, resulting in billions of dollars of lost revenue each year. Fraud can be divided into two categories: subscription fraud and superimposition fraud (Fawcett, T., 2002). Subscription fraud occurs when a customer opens an account with the intention of never paying the account and superimposi-

tion fraud occurs when a perpetrator gains illicit access to the account of a legitimate customer. In this latter case, the fraudulent behavior will often occur in parallel with legitimate customer behavior (i.e., is superimposed on it). Superimposition fraud has been a much more significant problem for telecommunication companies than subscription fraud. Ideally, both subscription fraud and superimposition fraud should be detected immediately and the associated customer account deactivated or suspended. However, because it is often difficult to distinguish between legitimate and illicit use with limited data, it is not always feasible to detect fraud as soon as it begins. This problem is compounded by the fact that there are substantial costs associated with investigating fraud, as well as costs if usage is mistakenly classified as fraudulent.

The most common technique for identifying superimposition fraud is to compare the customer's current calling behavior with a profile of his past usage, using deviation detection and anomaly detection techniques. The profile must be able to be quickly updated because of the volume of call detail records and the need to identify fraud in a timely manner (Cortes, C., 1998) generated a signature from a data stream of call-detail records to concisely describe the calling behavior of customers and then they used anomaly detection to "measure the unusualness of a new call relative to a particular account." Because new behavior does not necessarily imply fraud, this basic approach was augmented by comparing the new calling behavior to profiles of generic fraud—and fraud is only signaled if the behavior matches one of these profiles. Customer level data can also aid in identifying fraud. For example, price plan and credit rating information can be incorporated into the fraud analysis (Roset, S., 1999). More recent work using signatures has employed dynamic clustering as well as deviation detection to detect fraud (Aggarwal, C., 2007). In this work, each signature was placed within a cluster and a change in cluster membership was viewed as a potential indicator of fraud.

There are some methods for identifying fraud that do not involve comparing new behavior against a profile of old behavior. Perpetrators of fraud rarely work alone. For example, perpetrators of fraud often act as brokers and sell illicit service to others and the illegal buyers will often use different accounts to call the same phone number again and again. (Cortes, C., 1998) exploited this behavior by recognizing that certain phone numbers are repeatedly called from compromised accounts and that calls to these numbers are a strong indicator that the current account may be compromised. A final method for detecting fraud exploits human pattern recognition skills. (Cortes, C., 1998) built a suite of tools for visualizing data that was tailored to show calling activity in such a way that unusual patterns are easily detected by users. These tools were then used to identify international calling fraud. Telecommunication Network Fault Isolation and Prediction Monitoring and maintaining telecommunication networks is an important task. As these networks became increasingly complex, expert systems were developed to handle the alarms generated by the network elements (Weiss, G., 1998). However, because these systems are expensive to develop and keep current, data mining applications have been developed to identify and predict network faults. Fault identification can be quite difficult because a single fault may result in a cascade of alarms—many of which are not associated with the root cause of the problem. Thus an important part of fault identification is alarm correlation, which enables multiple alarms to be recognized as being related to a single fault.

Fraud is a serious problem for telecommunication companies, leading to billions of dollars in lost revenue each year. Fraud can be divided into two categories: subscription fraud and superimposition fraud. Subscription fraud occurs when a customer opens an account with the intention of never paying for the account charges. Superimposition fraud involves a legitimate account with some legitimate activity, but also includes some "superimposed" illegitimate activity by a person other than the account holder. Superimposition fraud poses a bigger problem for the telecommunications industry and for this reason we focus on applications for identifying this type of fraud. These applications should ideally operate in realtime using the call detail records and, once fraud is detected or suspected, should trigger some action. This action may be to immediately block the call and/or deactivate the account, or may involve opening an investigation, which will result in a call to the customer to verify the legitimacy of the account activity.

The most common method for identifying fraud is to build a profile of customer's calling behavior and compare recent activity against this behavior. Thus, this data mining application relies on deviation detection. The calling behavior is captured by summarizing the call detail records for a customer, as described earlier in this chapter. If the call detail summaries are updated in realtime, fraud can be identified soon after it occurs. Because new behavior does not necessarily imply fraud, one fraud-detection system augments this basic approach by comparing the new calling behavior to profiles of generic fraud—and only signals fraud if the behavior matches one of these profiles (Mani, D., 1999).

Customer level data can also aid in identifying fraud. For example, one sample rule that combines call detail and customer level data for detecting cellular fraud is: "People who have a price plan that makes international calls expensive and who display a sharp rise in international calls are likely the victim of cloning fraud." This same basic approach has been used to identify cellular cloning fraud, which occurs when the identification information associated with one cell phone is monitored and then programmed into a second phone (cloning fraud was a very serious problem in the 1990's, until authentication methods were developed to eliminate this type of fraud). This data mining application analyzed large amounts of cellular call data in order to identify patterns of fraud (Fawcett, T., 2002). These patterns were then used to generate monitors, each of which watches a customer's behavior with respect to one pattern of fraud. These monitors were then fed into a neural network, which determined when there is sufficiently evidence of fraud to raise an alert. Data mining can also help detect fraud by identifying and storing those phone numbers called when a phone is known to be used fraudulently. If many calls originate from another phone to numbers on this list of "suspect" phone numbers, one may infer that the account is being use fraudulently (Mani, D., 1999).

Fraud applications have some characteristics that require modifications to standard data mining techniques. For example, the performance of a fraud detection system should be computed at the customer level, not at the individual call level. So, if a customer account generates 20 fraud alerts, this should count, when computing the accuracy of this system, as only one alert; otherwise the system may appear to perform better than it actually does (Rosset, S., 1999). More sophisticated cost based metrics can also be used to evaluate the system. This is important because misclassification costs for fraud are generally unequal and often highly skewed (Weiss, G., 1998). For this reason, when building a classifier to identify fraud, one should ideally know the relative cost of letting a fraudulent call go through versus the cost of blocking a call from a legitimate customer.

Another issue is that since fraud is relatively rare—and the number of verified fraudulent calls is relatively low—the fraud application involves predicting a relatively rare event where the underlying class distribution is highly skewed. Data mining algorithms often have great difficulty dealing with highly skewed class distributions and predicting rare events. For example, if fraud makes up only .2% of all calls, many data mining systems will not generate any rules for finding fraud, since a default rule, which never predicts

fraud, would be 98.8% accurate. To deal with this issue, the training data is often selected to increase the proportion of fraudulent cases. For example, (Ezawa, K., 1995) increase the percentage of fraudulent calls from 1-2% to 9-12%. However, the use of a non-representative training set can be problematic because it does not provide the data mining method with accurate information about the true class distribution (Weiss, G. 2003).

Network Fault Isolation

The Telecommunication Alarm Sequence Analyzer (TASA) is a data mining tool that aids with fault identification by looking for frequently occurring temporal patterns of alarms (Klemettinen, M., 1999). Patterns detected by this tool were then used to help construct a rule-based alarm correlation system. Another effort, used to predict telecommunication switch failures, employed a genetic algorithm to mine historical alarm logs looking for predictive sequential and temporal patterns (Weiss, G., 1998). One limitation with the approaches just described is that they ignore the structural information about the underlying network. The quality of the mined sequences can be improved if topological proximity constraints are considered in the data mining process (Devitt, A., 2005) or if substructures in the telecommunication data can be identified and exploited to allow simpler, more useful, patterns to be learned (Baritchi, A., 2000). Another approach is to use Bayesian Belief Networks to identify faults, since they can reason about causes and effects (Fawcett, T, 1999).

Telecommunication networks are extremely complex configurations of hardware and software. Most of the network elements are capable of at least limited self-diagnosis, and these elements may collectively generate millions of status and alarm messages each month. In order to effectively manage the network, alarms must be analyzed automatically in order to identify network faults in a timely manner—or before they occur and degrade network performance. A proactive response is essential to maintaining the reliability of the network. Because of the volume of the data, and because a single fault may cause many different, seemingly unrelated, alarms to be generated, the task of network fault isolation is quite difficult. Data mining has a role to play in generating rules for identifying faults.

The Telecommunication Alarm Sequence Analyzer (TASA) is one tool that helps with the knowledge acquisition task for alarm correlation (Klemettinen, M., 1999). This tool automatically discovers recurrent patterns of alarms within the network data along with their statistical properties, using a specialized data mining algorithm. Network specialists then use this information to construct a rule-based alarm correlation system, which can then be used in real-time to identify faults. TASA is capable of finding episodic rules that depend on temporal relationships between the alarms. For example, it may discover the following rule: "if alarms of type link alarm and link failure occur within 5 seconds, then an alarm of type high fault rate occurs within 60 seconds with probability 0.7."

Before standard classification tasks can be applied to the problem of network fault isolation, the underlying time-series data must be rerepresented as a set of classified examples. This summarization, or aggregation, process typically involves using a fixed time window and characterizing the behavior over this window. For example, if n unique alarms are possible, one could describe the behavior of a device over this time window using a scalar of length n. In this case each field in the scalar would contain a count of the number of times a specific alarm occurs. One may then label the constructed example based on whether a fault occurs within some other time frame, for example, within the following 5 minutes. Thus, two time windows are required. Once this encoding is complete, standard classification tools can be used to generate "rules" to predict future failures.

Such an encoding scheme was used to identify chronic circuit problems (Klemettinen, M., 1999). The problem of reformulating time-series network events so that conventional classification based data mining tools can be used to identify network faults has been studied. (Weiss, G. M., 1998) View this task as an event prediction problem while (Fawcett, T, 1999) view it as an activity monitoring problem. Transforming the time-series data so that standard classification tools can be used has several drawbacks. The most significant one is that some information will be lost in the reformulation process. For example, using the scalar-based representation just mentioned, all sequence information is lost.

Time weaver (Weiss, G. M., 1998) is a genetic-algorithm based data mining system that is capable of operating directly on the raw network-level time series data (as well as other time-series data), thereby making it unnecessary to re-represent the network level data. Given a sequence of time stamped events and a target event T, Time weaver will identify patterns that successfully predict T. Time weaver essentially searches through the space of possible patterns, which includes sequence and temporal relationships, to find predictive patterns. The system is especially designed to perform well when the target event is rare, which is critical since most network failures are rare. In the case studied, the target event is the failure of components in the 4ESS switching system.

TYPES OF TELECOMMUNICATION DATA

The first step in the data mining process is to understand the data. Without such an understanding, useful applications cannot be developed. In this section we describe the three main types of telecommunication data. If the raw data is not suitable for data mining, then the transformation steps necessary to generate data that can be mined are also described.

Call Detail Data

Every time a call is placed on a telecommunications network, descriptive information about the call is saved as a call detail record. The number of call detail records that are generated and stored is huge. For example, AT&T long distance customers alone generate over 300 million call detail records per day (Cortes, C., 2001). Given that several months of call detail data is typically kept online, this means that tens of billions of call detail records will need to be stored at any time. Call detail records include sufficient information to describe the important characteristics of each call. At a minimum, each call detail record will include the originating and terminating phone numbers, the date and time of the call and the duration of the call. Call detail records are generated in real time and therefore will be available almost immediately for data mining. This can be contrasted with billing data, which is typically made available only once per month. Call detail records are not used directly for data mining, since the goal of data mining applications is to extract knowledge at the customer level, not at the level of individual phone calls. Thus, the call detail records associated with a customer must be summarized into a single record that describes the customer's calling behavior. The choice of summary variables (i.e., features) is critical in order to obtain a useful description of the customer. Below is a list of features that one might use when generating a summary description of a customer based on the calls they originate and receive over some time period P:

1. Average call duration
2. % no-answer calls
3. % calls to/from a different area code
4. % of weekday calls (Monday – Friday)
5. % of daytime calls (9am – 5pm)

6. Average # calls received per day
7. Average # calls originated per day
8. # unique area codes called during P

These eight features can be used to build a customer profile. Such a profile has many potential applications. For example, it could be used to distinguish between business and residential customers based on the percentage of weekday and daytime calls. Most of the eight features listed above were generated in a straightforward manner from the underlying data, but some features, such as the eighth feature, required a little more thought and creativity. Because most people call only a few area codes over a reasonably short period of time (e.g., a month), this feature can help identify telemarketers, or telemarketing behavior, since telemarketers will call many different area codes.

The above example demonstrates that generating useful features, including summary features, is a critical step within the data mining process. Should poor features be generated, data mining will not be successful. Although the construction of these features may be guided by common sense and expert knowledge, it should include exploratory data analysis. For example, the use of the time period 9am-5pm in the fifth feature is based on the commonsense knowledge that the typical workday is 9 to 5 (and hence this feature may be useful in distinguishing between business and residential calling patterns). However, more detailed exploratory data analysis, shown in Figure 1, indicates that the period from 9am to 4pm is actually more appropriate for this purpose.

Figure 1 plot, for each weekday hour, h, the business to residential call ratio, which is computed as: % weekday business calls during h / % weekday residential calls during h. Thus, this figure shows that during the period of 9am to 4pm, businesses place roughly 1.5 times as many of their total weekday calls as does a residence. Note that at 5pm the ratio is close to 1, indicating that the calls during this timeframe are not very useful for distinguishing between a business and

Figure 1. Comparison of business and residential hourly calling patterns

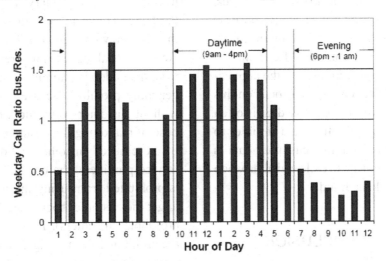

a residence. However, calls in the evening time-frame (6pm – 1am) are also useful in distinguishing between the two types of customers. For some applications, such as fraud detection, the summary descriptions, sometimes called signatures (Kaplan, H., 1999), must be updated in real-time for millions of phone lines. This requires the use of fairly short and simple summary features that can be updated quickly and efficiently.

Network Data

Telecommunication networks are extremely complex configurations of equipment, comprised of thousands of interconnected components. Each network element is capable of generating error and status messages, which leads to a tremendous amount of network data. This data must be stored and analyzed in order to support network management functions, such as fault isolation. This data will minimally include a timestamp, a string that uniquely identifies the hardware or software component generating the message and a code that explains why the message is being generated. For example, such a message might indicate that "controller 7 experienced a loss of power for 30 seconds starting at 10:03 pm on Monday, May 12. Due to the enormous number of network messages

generated, technicians cannot possibly handle every message. For this reason expert systems have been developed to automatically analyze these messages and take appropriate action, only involving a technician when a problem cannot be automatically resolved (Cox, K., 1997).

Data mining technology is now helping identify network faults by automatically extracting knowledge from the network data. As was the case with the call detail data, network data is also generated in real-time as a data stream and must often be summarized in order to be useful for data mining. This is sometimes accomplished by applying a time window to the data. For example, such a summary might indicate that a hardware component experienced twelve instances of a power fluctuation in a 10-minute period.

Customer Data

Telecommunication companies, like other large businesses, may have millions of customers. By necessity this means maintaining a database of information on these customers. This information will include name and address information and may include other information such as service plan and contract information, credit score, family income and payment history. This information may be supplemented with data from external sources, such as from credit reporting agencies. Because the customer data maintained by telecommunication companies does not substantially differ from that maintained in most other industries, the applications described in Section 3 do not focus on this source of data. However, customer data is often used in conjunction with other data in order to improve results. For example, customer data is typically used to supplement call detail data when trying to identify phone fraud.

SUMMERY AND CONCLUSION

This chapter describes how data mining is used in the telecommunications industry. Three main sources of telecommunication data (call detail, network and customer data) were described, as were common data mining applications (fraud, marketing and network fault isolation). This chapter also highlighted several key issues that affect the ability to mine data, and commented on how they impact the data mining process. One central issue is that telecommunication data is often not in a form—or at a level—suitable for data mining. Other data mining issues that were discussed include the large scale of telecommunication data sets, the need to identify very rare events (e.g., fraud and equipment failures) and the need to operate in real time (e.g., fraud detection).

Data mining applications must always consider privacy issues. This is especially true in the telecommunications industry, since telecommunication companies maintain highly private information, such as whom each customer calls. Most telecommunication companies utilize this information conscientiously and consequently privacy concerns have thus far been minimized. A more significant issue in the telecommunications industry relates to specific legal restrictions on how data may be used. In the United States, the information that a telecommunications company acquires about their subscribers is referred

to as Customer Proprietary Network Information (CPNI) and there are specific restrictions on how this data may be used. The Telecommunications Act of 1996, along with more recent clarifications from the Federal Communications Commission, generally prohibits the use of that information without customer permission, even for the purpose of marketing the customers other services. In the case of customers who switch to other service providers, the original service provider is prohibited from using the information to try to get the customer back (e.g., by only targeting profitable customers). Furthermore, companies are prohibited from using data from one type of service (e.g., wireless) in order to sell another service (e.g. landline services). Thus, the use of data mining is restricted in that there are many instances in which useful knowledge extracted by the data mining process cannot be legally exploited. Much of the rationale for these prohibitions relates to competition. For example, if a large company can leverage the data associated with one service to sell another service, then companies that provide fewer services would be at a competitive disadvantage.

The telecommunications industry has been one of the earliest adopters of data mining technology, largely because of the amount and quality of the data that it collects. This has resulted in many successful data mining applications. Given the fierce competition in the telecommunications industry, one can only expect the use of data mining to accelerate, as companies strive to operate more efficiently and gain a competitive advantage. The telecommunications industry has been one of the early adopters of data mining and has deployed numerous data mining applications. The primary applications relate to marketing, fraud detection, and network monitoring. Data mining in the telecommunications industry faces several challenges, due to the size of the data sets, the sequential and temporal nature of the data, and the real-time requirements of many of the applications. New methods have been developed and existing methods have been enhanced to respond to these challenges. The competitive and changing nature of the industry, combined with the fact that the industry generates enormous amounts of data, ensures that data mining will play an important role in the future of the telecommunications industry.

Data mining should play an important and increasing role in the telecommunications industry due to the large amounts of high quality data available, the competitive nature of the industry and the advances being made in data mining. In particular, advances in mining data streams, mining sequential and temporal data, and predicting/classifying rare events should benefit the telecommunications industry. As these and other advances are made, more reliance will be placed on the knowledge acquired through data mining and less on the knowledge acquired through the time-intensive process of eliciting domain knowledge from experts—although we expect human experts will continue to play an important role for some time to come. Changes in the nature of the telecommunications industry will also lead to the development of new applications and the demise of some current applications.

As an example, the main application of fraud detection in the telecommunications industry used to be in cellular cloning fraud, but this is no longer the case because the problem has been largely eliminated due to technological advances in the cell phone authentication process. It is difficult to predict what future changes will face the telecommunications industry, but as telecommunication companies start providing television service to the home and more sophisticated cell phone services become available (e.g., music, video, etc.), it is clear that new data mining applications, such as recommender systems, will be developed and deployed. Unfortunately, there is also one troubling trend that has developed in recent years. This concerns the increasing belief that U.S. telecommunication companies are too readily sharing customer records with governmental agencies. This concern arose in 2006 due to

revelations—made public in numerous newspaper and magazine articles—that telecommunications companies were turning over information on calling patterns to the National Security Agency (NSA) for purposes of data mining (Klemettinen, M., 1999). If this concern continues to grow unchecked, it could lead to restrictions that limit the use of data mining for legitimate purposes.

REFERENCES

Aggarwal, C. (Ed.). (2007). *Data Streams: Models and Algorithms*. New York: Springer.

Baritchi, A., Cook, D., & Holder, L. *(2000), Discovering structural patterns in telecommunications data. In* Proceedings of the Thirteenth Annual Florida AI Research Symposium *(pp. 82-85).*

Cortes, C., Pregibon. (2001). D. Signature-based methods for data streams. *Data Mining and Knowledge Discovery*, 5(3), 167–182. doi:10.1023/A:1011464915332

Cortes, C., & Pregibon, D. *(1998), Giga-mining. In* Proceedings of the Fourth International Conference on Knowledge Discovery and Data Mining *(pp. 174-178). New York: AAAI Press.*

Cortes, C., & Pregibon, D. *(1998), Giga-mining. In* Proceedings of the Fourth International Conference on Knowledge Discovery and Data Mining, *(pp.174-178), New York: AAAI Press*

Cox, K., Eick, S., & Wills, G. (1997). Visual data mining: Recognizing telephone calling fraud. *Data Mining and Knowledge Discovery*, 1(2), 225–231. doi:10.1023/A:1009740009307

Devitt, A., Duffin, J., & Moloney, R. *(2005), Topographical proximity for mining network alarm data.* In Proceedings of the 2005 ACM SIGCOMM Workshop on Mining Network Data *(pp. 179-184). New York: ACM Press.*

Ezawa, K. *Norton (1995), S. Knowledge discovery in telecommunication services data using Bayesian network models. In* Proceedings of the First International Conference on Knowledge Discovery and Data Mining; *Montreal Canada. Menlo Park, CA: AAAI Press.*

Fawcett, T., & Provost, F. (1997). Adaptive fraud detection. *Data Mining and Knowledge Discovery, 1*(3), 291–316. doi:10.1023/A:1009700419189

Fawcett, T., & Provost, F. *(1999), Activity monitoring: Noticing interesting changes in behavior. In* Proceedings of the Fifth ACM SIGKDD International Conference on Knowledge Discovery and Data Mining, *53-62. New York: ACM Press.*

Fawcett, T., & Provost, F. (2002). Fraud Detection. In Klosgen, W., & Zytkow, J. (Eds.), *Handbook of Data Mining and Knowledge Discovery* (pp. 726–731). New York: Oxford University Press.

Getoor, L., & Diehl, C. P. (2005). Link mining: A survey. *SIGKDD Explorations, 7*(2), 3–12. doi:10.1145/1117454.1117456

Han, J., Altman, R. B., Kumar, V., Mannila, H., & Pregibon, D. (2002). Emerging scientific applications in data mining. *Communications of the ACM, 45*(8), 54–58. doi:10.1145/545151.545179

Hill, S., Provost, F., & Volinsky, C. (2006). Network based marketing: Identifying likely adopters via consumer networks. *Statistical Science, 21*(2), 256–276. doi:10.1214/088342306000000222

Kaplan, H., Strauss, M., & Szegedy, M. *(1999), Just the fax—differentiating voice and fax phone lines using call billing data. In* Proceedings of the Tenth Annual ACM-SIAM Symposium on Discrete Algorithms *(pp. 935-936). Philadelphia, PA: Society for Industrial and Applied Mathematics.*

Klemettinen, M., Mannila, H., & Toivonen, H. (1999). Rule discovery in telecommunication alarm data. *Journal of Network and Systems Management, 7*(4), 395–423. doi:10.1023/A:1018787815779

Klemettinen, M., Mannila, H., & Toivonen, H. (1999). Rule discovery in telecommunication alarm data. *Journal of Network and Systems Management, 7*(4), 395–423. doi:10.1023/A:1018787815779

Liebowitz, J. (1988). *Expert System Applications to Telecommunications*. New York: John Wiley & Sons.

Mani, D., Drew, J., Betz, A., & Datta, P. *(1999), Statistics and data mining techniques for lifetime value modelin. In* Proceedings of the Fifth ACM SIGKDD International Conference on Knowledge Discovery and Data Mining *(pp. 94-103). New York, NY: ACM Press.*

Masand, B., Datta, P., Mani, D., & Li, B. (1999). CHAMP: A prototype for automated cellular churn prediction. [Apologize]. *Data Mining and Knowledge Discovery, 3*(2), 219–225. doi:10.1023/A:1009873905876

Roset, S., Murad, U., Neumann, E., Idan, Y., & Pinkas, G. *(1999), Discovery of fraud rules for telecommunications—challenges and solutions. In* Proceedings of the Fifth ACM SIGKDD International Conference on Knowledge Discovery and Data Mining; *pp. 409-413. New York: ACM Press.*

Rosset, S., Murad, U., Neumann, E., Idan, Y., & Gadi, P. (1999), Discovery of fraud rules for telecommunications—challenges and solutions. Proceedings of the Fifth ACM SIGKDD International Conference on Knowledge Discovery and Data Mining (pp. 409-413). New York: ACM Press.

Rosset, S., Neumann, E., & Eick, U., & Vatnik. (2003). Customer lifetime value models for decision support. *Data Mining and Knowledge Discovery, 7*(3), 321–339. doi:10.1023/A:1024036305874

Sasisekharan, R., Seshadri, V., & Weiss, S. (1996). Data mining and forecasting in large-scale telecommunication networks. *IEEE Expert, 11*(1), 37–43. doi:10.1109/64.482956

Wei, C., & Chiu, I. (2002). Turning telecommunications call details to churn prediction: A data mining approach. *Expert Systems with Applications*, *23*(2), 103–112. doi:10.1016/S0957-4174(02)00030-1

Weiss, G., & Hirsh, H. *(1998), Learning to predict rare events in event sequences. In R. Agrawal & P. Stolorz (Eds.),* Proceedings of the Fourth International Conference on Knowledge Discovery and Data Mining *(pp.359-363). Menlo Park, CA: AAAI Press.*

Weiss, G. M., & Hirsh, H. *(1998), learning to predict rare events in event sequences. In* Proceedings of the Fourth International Conference on Knowledge Discovery and Data Mining. *359-363. AAAI Press*

Weiss, G. M., & Provost, F. (2003). Learning when training data are costly: The effect of class distribution on tree induction. *Journal of Artificial Intelligence Research*, *19*, 315–354.

KEY TERMS AND DEFINITIONS

Call Detail Data: It is the data that describes the calls traverse the telecommunication components in the network.

Customer Data: It is the data that describes the telecommunication customers.

Data Mining Applications: Is to extract knowledge at the customer level, not at the level of individual phone calls. Thus, the call detail records associated with a customer must be summarized into a single record that describes the customer's calling behavior.

Data Mining: Is a particular step in the Knowledge Discovery (KDD) process which consists of particular algorithms that under acceptable computational efficiency limitations produce a particular enumeration of patterns (models) over the data.

Network Data: It is the data that describes the state of the hardware and software networks.

Telecommunication Alarm Sequence Analyzer (TASA): Is a data mining tool that aids with fault identification by looking for frequently occurring temporal patterns of alarms.

Telecommunication Network: It is extremely complex configurations of equipment, comprised of thousands of interconnected components.

Chapter 3
Utilization of TETRA Networks for Health Information Transfer

Konstantinos Siassiakos
University of Piraeus, Greece

Konstantinos Ioannou
University of Patras, Greece

Athina Lazakidou
University of Peloponnese, Greece

ABSTRACT

Rapid advances in information technology and wireless communications are leading to the emergence of a new type of information infrastructure that has the potential of supporting an array of advanced services for healthcare. Today's healthcare professionals need to be connected to the network always. Continuous connectivity is the watchword of these demanding users, who need to communicate over the network seamlessly and stay connected everywhere in emergency cases. TETRA technology provides several ways of protecting the privacy and security of communication, such as authentication, air interface encryption and end-to-end encryption. Using a TETRA network can benefit not only ambulance crews, but also medical personnel at remote locations. Even though doctors are rarely present in ambulances, they can use the transmitted medical data to make a formal diagnosis, enabling treatment to be started and saving several critical minutes before arrival at the hospital. The objective of this chapter is to study how simply can a healthcare professional collect physiological data from mobile and/or remote patients and how securely and reliably health information can be transferred from emergency places to hospitals through a TETRA network.

INTRODUCTION

Cost reduction pressures and the need for shortened in-patient stays are promoting the use of wireless patient monitoring systems in hospitals.

DOI: 10.4018/978-1-61520-805-0.ch003

Their contribution to better process management, superior flexibility and increased efficiency within hospitals is further underlining the appeal of wireless networking options for patient monitoring systems.

Wireless connectivity has encouraged an overall rise in productivity through improved workflow and data management. Wireless patient monitors have also supported enhanced flexibility within the hospital environment by enabling remote monitoring of patients.

Telemedicine applications, including those based on wireless technologies, span the areas of emergency health care: telecardiology, teleradiology, telepathology, teledermatology, teleophtlalmology, teleoncology, and telepsychiatry. In addition, health telematics applications, enabling the availability of prompt and expert medical care, have been exploited for the provision of healthcare services at understaffed areas, such as rural health centers, ambulance vehicles, ships, trains, and airplanes, as well as for home monitoring.

The primary problem with tiny, low power sensors is establishing and maintaining wireless links in the presence of so many high power devices radiating noise. This noise will change through out the day so that a continuously adapting routing technique is needed. Unfortunately, several challenges exist such as:

1. Deploying sensors to provide propser sensor converage.
2. Balancing resource usage to maximize sensor lifetime.
3. Communicating messages reliably among the nodes (healthcare provider, patient, emergency vehicles) using multihop paths.
4. Prioritizing routing messages, i.e., emergency call vs. outgoing patients.
5. Authenticating data links as well as securing the data to ensure patience confidentiality.

BACKGROUND

High quality health care requires individuals to share sensitive personal information with their doctors and other healthcare professionals. This information is necessary to make the most accurate diagnoses and provide the best treatment. It may be shared with others, such as insurance companies, pharmacies, researchers, and employers, for many reasons. If patients are not confident that this information will be kept confidential, they will not be forthright and reveal accurate and complete information. If healthcare providers are not confident that the organization that is responsible for the healthcare record will keep it confidential they will limit what patients add to the record. Either of these actions is likely to result in inferior healthcare. The privacy and security of personal health information has become a major public concern.

Most common security problem within the healthcare systems is the access of the employees (threat from inside). Specifically people who work in a hospital have the ability to view protected health information (PHI) of anybody. This raises the probability for a legal action, which cause major impacts. It is conceivable how important is to enforce security policies. It is important the introduction of security policies which the decisions made by people who have the authority and set boundaries under which the staff could operate. Exclusive of the inside threat, it is possible to occur damage in a healthcare system from outside threat such as hackers. In this case it is very important to develop mechanisms which minimize the risk. So we have not to allow an insecure Internet connection in the internal network of the healthcare system.

The *first security risk* is the failure to protect sensitive data beyond encryption.

The *second security risk* is the inability to accurately manage mobile computer assets. Under HIPAA, healthcare organizations must be able to audit how many computers they have in their inventory, where they are assigned, who is logging into them, what software is installed and where the computer is located.

The *third security risk* is sensitive information on public terminals. Nursing stations, public information terminals and help stations allow for greater risk of data breaches. Unattended stationary computers should always be monitored and protected with an authentication prompt.

The *fourth security risk* is difficulty implementing a comprehensive data security plan. Healthcare facilities must have a comprehensive data security plan including asset tracking and recovery software that has cable locks, encryption software and secure passwords. Plan updates and reviewing should be done to ensure maximum effectiveness.

The *fifth security risk* is reluctance to create a data breach policy. In the event of a data breach there should be a standard procedure in place for timely notification of supervisors, law enforcement, patients and the media.

TETRA NETWORKS

Terrestrial Trunked Radio (TETRA) comprises a suite of open digital trunked radio standards defined by the European Telecommunications Standards Institute (ETSI) to meet the needs of the most demanding of Professional Mobile Radio (PMR) users. TETRA is an Interoperability standard that allows equipment from multiple vendors to interoperate with each other. TETRA is used by PMR users such as Public Safety, Transportation, Utilities, Government, Commercial & Industrial, Oil & Gas and Military. TETRA is also used by Public Access Mobile Radio (PAMR) Operators.

The Professional Mobile Radio market, which includes Private and Public Access Mobile Radio (PMR and PAMR), has traditionally been scattered

in many dimensions in terms of technologies, frequency allocation etc.

The first clear change towards international standardization was the introduction of the analogue MPT1327 trunked radio standard, that lead to a market success in most parts of the world.

Terrestrial Trunked Radio (TETRA) is the first truly open digital private mobile radio standard. TETRA is opening an even more international Professional Mobile Radio market.

The high level of user involvement in the creation of the standard ensures that it will meet the needs of the demanding users.

To ensure an open multivendor market, TETRA specifies the following essential interfaces:

- **Air Interface** ensures the interoperability of terminal equipment from different manufacturers.
- **Terminal Equipment Interface (TEI)** facilitates the independent development of mobile data applications.
- **Inter-System Interface (ISI)** allows the interconnection of TETRA networks from different manufacturers.
- **Direct Mode Operation (DMO)** guarantees communication between terminals also beyond network coverage.

TETRA terminals can act as mobile phones (cell phones), with a direct connection to the PSTN. It is common also for them to operate in a group calling mode in which a single button push will connect the user to a dispatcher and all

Figure 1. Interfaces specified by TETRA

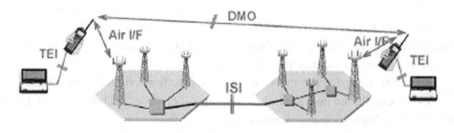

the other users in a group. It is also possible for the terminal to act as a one-to-one walkie talkie but without the normal range limitation since the call still uses the network. Emergency buttons, provided on the terminals, enable the users to transmit emergency signals, to the dispatcher, overriding any other activity taking place at the same time.

TETRA uses Time Division Multiple Access (TDMA) with four user channels on one radio carrier and 25 kHz spacing between carriers. Both point-to-point and point-to-multipoint transfer can be used. Digital data transmission is also included in the standard though at a low data rate.

TETRA Mobile Stations (MS) can communicate Direct Mode or using Trunked infrastructure (Switching and Management Infrastructure or SwMI) made of TETRA Base Stations (TBS). As well as allowing direct communications in situations where network coverage has been lost, Direct Mode or DMO also includes the possibility of using one (or a chain) of TETRA terminals as relays for a signal. This functionality is called DMO gateway (from DMO to TMO) or DMO Repeater (DMO to DMO). In rescue situations this feature could allow direct communications underground or in areas of bad coverage.

In addition to voice and dispatch services, the TETRA system supports several types of data communication. Status messages and short data services (SDS) are provided over the system's main control channel, while Packet Data or Circuit switched data communication uses specifically assigned traffic channels.

All traffic is normally encrypted. TETRA provides both over the air encryption and end-to-end encryption.

The main advantages of TETRA over other technologies (such as GSM) are:

- The much lower frequency used gives longer range, which in turn permits very high levels of *geographic* coverage with a smaller number of transmitters, thus cutting infrastructure costs.

- High spectral efficiency - 4 channels in 25 kHz and no guard bands, compared to GSM with 8 channels in 200 kHz and guard bands.

- Very fast call set-up - a one too many group call is generally set-up within 0.5 seconds (typical less than 250 msec for a single node call) compared with the many seconds (typically 7 to 10s) that are required for a GSM network.

- Works at high speeds >400 km/h. TETRA was used during the French TGV train speed record on 3 April 2007 at 574.8 km/h.

- The system contains several mechanisms, designed into the protocols and radio parameters, to ensure communication success even during overload situations (e.g. during major public events or disaster situations), thus calls will always get through unlike in cellular systems. The system also supports a range of emergency calling modes.

- TETRA infrastructure is usually separate from (but connected to) that of the public (mobile) phone networks, resulting in (normally) no call charges for the system owners, substantially more diverse and resilient communications and it is easy to customise and integrate with data applications (vehicle location, GIS databases, dispatch systems etc).

- Unlike most cellular technologies, TETRA networks typically provide a number of fall-back modes such as the ability for a base station to process local calls. So called Mission Critical networks can be built with TETRA where all aspects are fail-safe/multiple-redundant.

- In the absence of a network mobiles/portables can use 'direct mode' whereby they share channels directly (walkie-talkie mode).

- Gateway mode - where a single mobile with connection to the network can act as a relay for other nearby mobiles that are out of range of the infrastructure.
- TETRA also provides a point-to-point function that traditional analogue emergency services radio systems did not provide. This enables users to have a one-to-one trunked 'radio' link between sets without the need for the direct involvement of a control room operator/dispatcher.
- Unlike the cellular technologies, which connect one subscriber to one other subscriber (one-to-one) then TETRA is built to do one-to-one, one-to-many and many-to-many. These operational modes are directly relevant to the public safety and professional users.
- TETRA supports both air-interface encryption and End-to-end encryption
- Rapid deployment (transportable) network solutions are available for disaster relief and temporary capacity provision.
- Equipment is available from many suppliers around the world, thus providing the benefits of competition.
- Network solutions are available in both the older circuit-switched (telephone like) architectures and flat, IP architectures with soft (software) switches.

SECURITY FUNCTIONS

TETRA contains a wealth of security functions designed to protect users' information. This information can consist of the users' speech and data traffic and also other information that relates to the identities and operations of the users themselves. When describing these TETRA security functions it is important to make a distinction between the different categories of functions and their specific application.

In TETRA the following categories can be identified:

- **Security Mechanisms:** These are independent self-contained functions that aim to achieve a specific security objective such as confidentiality of information or authentication of mobile terminals. Security mechanisms are the main building blocks for a security system.
- **Security Management Features:** These are functions that are used to control, manage and operate the individual security mechanisms. They form the heart of the resulting security and should guarantee that the security features are integrated into a consistent security system. Furthermore they are used to realize interoperability of the security mechanisms over different networks. Key management is the most essential security management function.
- **Standard Cryptographic Algorithms:** These are standardized system specific mathematical functions that are used, normally in combination with parameters called "cryptographic keys", to provide an adequate security level for the security mechanisms and the security management features. Standardized cryptographic algorithms are offered in TETRA to support interoperability between different TETRA systems.
- **Lawful Interception Mechanisms:** These are functions that are used within some communication systems to provide the lawfully required access to information and communication, with the aim to fulfill national regulatory requirements. It is essential that such functions do not undermine the regular security of the system. Therefore these functions should be

controlled through security management features.

- **Evaluation of Security Mechanisms:** It is very important to be aware of the different roles and objectives of these classes. In certain proprietary systems the first two classes are often confused. This results in a "knot" of security features, which is difficult to analyze and even harder to correctly implement and control in an operational environment. But also mechanisms and algorithms get confused. Sometimes one tends to assess security provided by a certain mechanism only by the strength of the algorithm used, ignoring the environment in which it is used.

UTILIZATION OF TETRA NETWORK FOR HEALTH INFORMATION TRANSFER

The *TETRA* network has many advantages over traditional analog communication systems. Digital coding and transmission greatly enhances the sound quality and practically eliminates the problems with cracks and sound distortions. Contrary to analog networks, when using *TETRA*, one may address a voice connection to a single user or to a group of users.

Another important feature of the *TETRA* network is the possibility to associate the connections with certain priority numbers so that the low-priority connections can be terminated in case the network is overloaded.

The most important aspect is that the advanced communication solutions have the potential to save more lives; the lives of the public and those who work for the emergency services. The new generation of communications has been designed specifically for the emergency services, are generally being implemented to support multi-agency operation, and include unique features demanded by emergency service users.

In an emergency, every second counts. A life could be saved if a rescue crew can get an early, accurate diagnosis. Fast diagnosis could depend on being able to monitor and record the patient's vital signs and transmit the data wirelessly to a medical expert for consultation.

Using a TETRA network, such a solution can be used to monitor and transmit hospital quality diagnostics to remote specialists. Experts at the hospital can suggest proper treatment earlier, saving vital minutes. Knowing the history of the patient's condition during the trip to hospital will also cut delays when the patient arrives in the emergency room. The integration of data into the voice channel enhances the functionality of automated vehicle tracking systems and digitized mapping. Telemetry enables ambulance crews to transmit heart rhythms and other patient monitoring to hospital casualty units. Video enables also emergency units to view accident scenes remotely. Digitizing of the mobile network has the added benefit of improving the speed of traditional manual in-house processes such as: patient report forms, database management and vehicle management.

CONCLUSION

Cost and return on investment is always a consideration. The TETRA network can enable existing information and resources to be extended out to the point of care, helping medical professionals deliver top medical care in a more timely and efficient manner. In medicine, time savings equals hospital savings. Instant access to clinical and drug information or the ability to electronically prescribe drugs can save several minutes per situation and decrease errors. Improved care in less time enables more patients to be treated and better results for patient and hospital.

Using a TETRA network can benefit not only ambulance crews, but also medical personnel at remote locations. They can be sure that accurate patient diagnostic information is transmitted securely and reliably, allowing them to determine the correct treatment as soon as possible. Not every chest pain is a heart attack: more than 40% of patients admitted to hospital with chest pains are eventually diagnosed as having non-cardiac or non-life threatening symptoms. Transporting a patient for such an "unnecessary" hospital admission is not only expensive but can also delay an ambulance from more critical emergencies.

Provide discussion of the overall coverage of the chapter and concluding remarks.

REFERENCES

Berreti, D. (1998). Default set of BSS Parameters for Cosmote Network and set of BSS parameters for umbrella cells, Nokia Productivity Services. *Technical Report, Nokia Telecommunications, 7.8.1998,* (pp. 2-16).

Bhargava, A., & Zoltowski, M. (2003). Sensors and wireless communication for medical care. In *Proc. 14th International Workshop on Database and Expert Systems Applications*, (pp. 956–960).

Chakravorty, R. (2006). A programmable service architecture for mobile medical care. In *Proceedings of the 4th Annual IEEE International Conference on Pervasive Computing and Communications Workshops (PerCom '06)*, Pisa, Italy, (pp. 532–536).

Dimitriadou, E., Ioannou, K., Panoutsopoulos, I., Garmpis, A., & Kotsopoulos, S. (2005). Priority to Low Moving Terminals in TETRA Networks. *WSEAS Transactions on Communications, 11*(4), 1228–1236.

Dunlop, J. (1999). *Digital Mobile Communications and the TETRA System*. New York: John Wiley & Sons.

Hong, D., & Rappaport, S. (1986). Traffic model and performance analysis for cellular mobile radio telephone systems with prioritized and non prioritized handoff procedures. *IEEE Trans., VT-35*, 77–92.

Ioannou, K., Louvros, S., Panoutsopoulos, I., Kotsopoulos, S., & Karagiannidis, G. (2002). Optimizing the Handover Call Blocking Probability in Cellular Networks with High Speed Moving Terminals. *IEEE Communications Letters, 6*(10). doi:10.1109/LCOMM.2002.802048

Jafari, R., Dabiri, F., Brisk, P., & Sarrafzadeh, M. (2005). CustoMed: A power optimized customizable and mobile medical monitoring and analysis system. In *Proceedings of ACM HCI Challenges in Health Assessment Workshop in Conjunction with Proceedings of the Conference on Human Factors in Computing Systems (CHI '05)*, Portland, OR.

Jea, D., & Srivastava, M. B. (2006). A remote medical monitoring and interaction system, In *Proceedings of the 4th International Conference on Mobile Systems, Applications, and Services (MobiSys '06)*, Uppsala, Sweden, June 2006.

Kyriacou, E., Pavlopoulos, S., Koutsouris, D., Andreou, A., Pattichis, C., & Schizas, C. (2001). Multipurpose Health Care Telemedicine System. In *Proceedings of the 23rd Annual International Conference of the IEEE/EMBS*, Istanbul, Turkey.

Lin, Y., Jan, I., Ko, P., Chen, Y., Wong, J., & Jan, G. (2004). A wireless PDA-based physiological monitoring system for patient transport. *IEEE Transactions on IT in Biomedicine, 8*(4), 439–447. doi:10.1109/TITB.2004.837829

Mandellos, G., Lymperopoulos, D., Koukias, M., Tzes, A., Lazarou, N., & Vagianos, C. (2004). A Novel Mobile Telemedicine System for Ambulance Transport: Design and Evaluation. In *Proceedings of the 26th Annual International Conference of the IEEE EMBS*, San Francisco, pp. 3080-3083.

Pattichis, C., Kyriacou, E., Voskarides, S., Pattichis, M., Istepanian, R., & Schizas, C. (2002). Wireless Telemedicine Systems: An Overview. *IEEE Antennas and Propagation, 44*(2), 143–153. doi:10.1109/MAP.2002.1003651

Pavlopoulos, S., Kyriacou, E., Berler, A., Dembeyiotis, S., & Koutsouris, D. (1998). Novel emergency telemedicine system based on wireless communication technology—AMBULANCE. *IEEE Transactions on Information Technology in Biomedicine, 2*(4), 261–267. doi:10.1109/4233.737581

Rasid, M., & Woodward, B. (2005). Bluetooth Telemedicine Processor for Multichannel Biomedical Signal Transmission via Mobile Cellular Networks. *IEEE Transactions on Information Technology in Biomedicine, 9*(1). doi:10.1109/TITB.2004.840070

Stavroulakis, P. (2007). *TErrestrial Trunked RAdio - TETRA: A Global Security Tool (Signals and Communication Technology.* Berlin, Germany: Springer.

Varshney, U. (2005). Pervasive healthcare: applications, challenges and wireless solutions. *Communications of the AIS* 16.

Varshney, U. (2006). Patient monitoring using infrastructure oriented wireless LANs. *International Journal of Electronic Healthcare, 2*(2), 149–163.

Varshney, U. (2006). Using wireless technologies in healthcare. *Int. Journal on Mobile Communications, 4*(3), 354–368.

Zander, J. Kim, S.-L. (2001). *Radio Resource Management for Wireless Networks.* Norwood, MA: Artech House.

KEY TERMS AND DEFINITIONS

Confidentiality: Confidentiality has been defined by the International Organization for Standardization (ISO) in ISO-17799 as "ensuring that information is accessible only to those authorized to have access" and is one of the cornerstones of information security. Confidentiality is one of the design goals for many cryptosystems, made possible in practice by the techniques of modern cryptography. Confidentiality also refers to an ethical principle associated with several professions (e.g., medicine, law, religion, professional psychology, and journalism). In ethics, and (in some places) in law and alternative forms of legal dispute resolution such as mediation, some types of communication between a person and one of these professionals are "privileged" and may not be discussed or divulged to third parties. In those jurisdictions in which the law makes provision for such confidentiality, there are usually penalties for its violation.

Data Integrity: Data integrity is a term used in computer science and telecommunications that can mean ensuring data is "whole" or complete, the condition in which data is identically maintained during any operation (such as transfer, storage or retrieval), the preservation of data for their intended use, or, relative to specified operations, the a priori expectation of data quality. Put simply, data integrity is the assurance that data is consistent and correct.

Health Information: The recorded information in any format (e.g., oral, written, or electronic) regarding the physical or mental condition of an individual, health care provision, or health care payment.

Information Security: Information security means protecting information and information systems from unauthorized access, use, disclosure, disruption, modification or destruction. The terms information security, computer security and information assurance are frequently incorrectly used interchangeably. These fields are interrelated often and share the common goals of protecting the confidentiality, integrity and availability of information; however, there are some subtle differences between them.

TETRA: Terrestrial Trunked Radio (TETRA) is a set of standards developed by the European Telecommunications Standardization Institute (ETSI) that describes a common mobile radio communications infrastructure throughout Europe.

This infrastructure is targeted primarily at the mobile radio needs of public safety groups (such as police and fire departments), utility companies, and other enterprises that provide voice and data communications services.

Chapter 4

Application of Computational Intelligence Techniques in Managing Wireless Sensor Networks

Ibrahiem Mahmoud Mohamed El Emary
King Abdulaziz University, Saudi Arabia

ABSTRACT

This chapter gives a brief background on network management and how it is integrated into sensor network as well as the application of computational intelligence techniques in managing wireless sensor networks. Also discussed how Genetic Algorithms work in common and how they can be applied to sensor networks. Among the major management tasks rely on consumption power management, so there are many challenges associated with sensor networks but the primary challenge is energy consumption. Sensor networks are typically have little human interaction and are installed with limited battery supplies. This makes energy conservation a critical issue in deployed WSNs. All types of networks require monitoring and maintenance. A service that supplies a set of tools and applications that assist a network manager with these tasks is network management. It includes the administration of networks and all associated components. While all networks require some form of network management, different types of networks may stress certain aspects of network management. Some networks may also impose new tasks on network management. There are different types of network management architectures: centralized, hierarchical and distributed. In a centralized approach, one central server performs the role of the network management application. A hierarchical architecture will include multiple platforms, typically one server and several clients, performing network management functions.

INTRODUCTION

Network management means the process of controlling and monitoring the behavior of a network.

In traditional networks the major goal is to minimize the response time, but in sensor networks the primary goal is minimizing energy use and the main means for doing this is by reducing the amount of communication between nodes. WSNs are highly dynamic and prone to faults, mainly

DOI: 10.4018/978-1-61520-805-0.ch004

because of energy shortages, connectivity interruptions, and environmental obstacles. Network failures are common events rather than exceptional ones. Thus, in WSNs, we are mainly concerned with monitoring and controlling node communication in order to optimize the efficiency of the network, ensure the network operates properly, maintain the performance of the network, and control large numbers of nodes without human intervention. A network management system designed for WSNs should provide a set of management functions that integrate configuration, operation, administration, security, and maintenance of all elements and services of a sensor network. The ideal wireless sensor is networked and scaleable, consumes very little power, is smart and software programmable, capable of fast data acquisition, reliable and accurate over the long term, costs little to purchase and install, and requires no real maintenance. Selecting the optimum sensors and wireless communications link requires knowledge of the application and problem definition. Battery life, sensor update rates, and size are all major design considerations.

A wireless sensor network (WSN) generally consists of a base station or "gateway" that can communicate with a number of wireless sensors via a radio link. Data is collected at the wireless sensor node, compressed, and transmitted to the gateway directly or, if required, uses other wireless sensor nodes to forward data to the gateway. The transmitted data is then presented to the system by the gateway connection. A functional block

diagram of a versatile wireless sensing node is provided in Figure 1. A modular design approach provides a flexible and versatile platform to address the needs of a wide variety of applications. For example, depending on the sensors to be deployed, the signal conditioning block can be re-programmed or replaced. This allows for a wide variety of different sensors to be used with the wireless sensing node. Similarly, the radio link may be swapped out as required for a given applications' wireless range requirement and the need for bidirectional communications. The use of flash memory allows the remote nodes to acquire data on command from a base station or by an event sensed by one or more inputs to the node. Furthermore, the embedded firmware can be upgraded through the wireless network in the field. The microprocessor has a number of functions including:

1. Managing the data collection of the sensors;
2. Performing power management functions;
3. Interfacing the sensor data to the physical radio layer; and
4. Managing the radio network protocol

A key feature of any wireless sensing node is to minimize the power consumed by the system. Generally, the radio subsystem requires the largest amount of power. Therefore, it is advantageous to send data over the radio network only when required. This sensor event-driven data collection

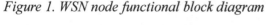

Figure 1. WSN node functional block diagram

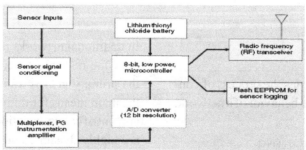

model requires an algorithm to be loaded into the node to determine when to send data based on the sensed event. Additionally, it is important to minimize the power consumed by the sensor itself. Therefore, the hardware should be designed to allow the microprocessor to judiciously control power to the radio, sensor, and sensor signal conditioner.

The main task of WSN monitoring is to collect information about the following parameters: node states (e.g., battery level and communication power), network topology, wireless bandwidth, link state, and the coverage and exposure bounds of WSNs. A sensor network management system can perform a variety of management control tasks based on the collected network states such as controlling sampling frequency, switching node on/off (power management), controlling wireless bandwidth usage (traffic management), and performing network reconfiguration in order to recover from node and communication faults (fault management).

Monitoring individual nodes in a large sensor network may be impractical. It is sufficient to control the network by ensuring specific network coverage. Furthermore, sensor nodes are typically deployed in remote or harsh conditions and the configuration of nodes in WSNs changes dynamically. Thus, a sensor network management system should allow the network to self-forming, self-organize, and ideally to self-configure in the event of failures without prior knowledge of the network topology. Despite the importance of sensor network management, there is no existing generalized solution for WSN management. However, most sensor network applications are designed with network management in mind and thus no extra network management layer is required.

Wireless sensor networks are emerging applications of pervasive computing, consisting of many small, low power and intelligent sensor nodes (or motes) and one or more base stations. Sensor nodes gather information in diverse settings

including natural ecosystems, battlefields, and manmade environments and send the information to one or more base stations. Sensor nodes work under severe resource constraints such as limited battery power, computing power, memory, wireless bandwidth, and communication capability, while the base station has more computational, energy and communication resources. The base station acts as a gateway between sensor nodes and the end user. Sensor network applications use a data-centric approach that views a network as a distributed system consisting of many autonomously cooperating sensor nodes, any of which may have a role in routing, data gathering, or data processing. Every node will communicate through other nodes in a sensor network to produce information-rich results. Furthermore, intermediate nodes can perform data aggregation and caching that is useful to reduce communication overheads. Sensor network applications can be categorized according to its operational paradigm: data gathering and event-driven. The data gathering application requires sensor nodes to periodically report their data to the base station. In the event-driven application, nodes only send data when an event of interest occurs.

Due to the fact that WSNs are composed of a large number of low-cost but energy-constrained sensor nodes, along with the notorious timer-varying and error-prone natures of wireless links, scalable, robust, and energy-efficient data disseminating techniques are requisite for the emerging WSN applications such as environment monitoring and surveillance. There are various techniques for managing the power requirements of WSN, one of them is called view of supply chain in which we conceptually partition a whole sensor field into several functional regions based on the supply chain management methodology, and apply different routing schemes to different regions in order to provide better performance in terms of reliability and energy usage. For this purpose, a novel zone flooding scheme, essentially a combination of geometric routing and flooding techniques was proposed. The hybrid data dissemination framework features low overhead, high reliability, good scalability and flexibility, and preferable energy efficiency.

Recent advances in MEMS technology and wireless communications have resulted in small, low-cost sensors with more and more powerful processing and networking capabilities. This makes wireless sensor networks (WSNs) be identified as one of the most important technologies that will change the world. WSNs can furnish us with fine-granular observations about the physical world where we are living. Recent advances in MEMS technology and wireless communications have resulted in small, low-cost sensors with more and more powerful processing and networking capabilities. Potential applications include disaster rescue, energy management, medical monitoring, logistics and inventory management, and military reconnaissance, etc. While much research has focused on making sensor networks feasible and useful, some important problems resulting from the error-prone and resource constrained natures of WSNs are not well addressed yet. Of note are the issues associated with scalability, reliability, and network lifetime. For instance, a data dissemination technique should work well not only in small-scale sensor networks but also in large-scale sensor networks. In addition, it should be robust against harsh environmental effects and temporal or permanent failures of sensors and wireless links in between them. Moreover, it should have good energy-efficiency in terms of both low average energy consumption per observation report and balanced energy usage instead of overusing a small set of the network.

Wireless sensor networks are networks consisting of very small sensors that are limited in power, both battery and processing. These sensor networks are often used in monitoring applications, for monitoring such things as the environment, structures and animal habitats. Network management is a critical function of any

network, including wireless sensor networks. The nature of wireless sensor networks makes network management a more difficult task than that of traditional networks. One key aspect of network management of wireless sensor networks is topology management. The primary goal of topology management is developing algorithms to maintain a connected network while conserving energy. It consists of knowing the physical connection and logical relationships of the sensors. This type of architecture helps to distribute the functions thus eliminating the bottleneck at the one central server. In order to distribute network management functions even more would be to move to a distributed architecture. This type of network management architecture utilizes multiple peer-to-peer platforms sharing all management tasks. This provides better scalability, availability, reliability and modularity.

Recent advances in MEMS technology and wireless communications have resulted in small, low-cost sensors with more and more powerful processing and networking capabilities. This makes wireless sensor networks (WSNs) be identified as one of the most important technologies that will change the world [B. Warneke, 2002]. Wireless sensor networks are emerging applications of pervasive computing, consisting of many small, low power, and intelligent sensor nodes and one or more base stations. Sensor nodes gather information in diverse settings and send the information to one or more base stations. Sensor nodes work under severe resource constraints such as limited battery power, computing power, memory, wireless bandwidth, and communication capability, while the base station has more computational, energy and communication resources. The base station acts as a gateway between sensor nodes and the end user.

Sensor network applications use a data-centric approach that views a network as a distributed system consisting of many autonomously cooperating sensor nodes [K. Holger, 2003], any of which may have a role in routing, data gathering, or data processing. Every node will communicate with other nodes in a sensor network to produce information-rich results (e.g., temperature and soil moisture in a certain region of the network). Furthermore, intermediate nodes can perform data aggregation and caching that is useful to reduce communication overheads [A.A. Ahmed, 2003], [C. Shen, 2001]. Sensor network applications can be categorized according to its operational paradigm: data gathering and event-driven. The data gathering application requires sensor nodes to periodically report their data to the base station. In the event-driven application, nodes only send data when an event of interest occurs.

WSNs can furnish us with fine-granular observations about the physical world where we are living. Potential applications of WSN include disaster rescue, energy management, medical monitoring, logistics and inventory management, and military reconnaissance, etc. While much research has focused on making sensor networks feasible and useful [R. Min, 2001], [I. Akyildiz, 2002], some important problems resulting from the error-prone and resource constrained natures of WSNs are not well addressed yet. Of note are the issues associated with scalability, reliability, and network lifetime. For instance, a data dissemination technique should work well not only in small-scale sensor networks but also in large-scale sensor networks. In addition, it should be robust against harsh environmental effects and temporal or permanent failures of sensors and wireless links in between them. Moreover, it should have good energy-efficiency in terms of both low average energy consumption per observation report and balanced energy usage instead of overusing a small set of the network.

The ideal wireless sensor is networked and scaleable, consumes very little power, is smart and software programmable, capable of fast data acquisition, reliable and accurate over the long term, costs little to purchase and install, and requires no real maintenance. Selecting the optimum

sensors and wireless communications link requires knowledge of the application and problem definition. Battery life, sensor update rates, and size are all major design considerations. Examples of low data rate sensors include temperature, humidity, and peak strain captured passively. Examples of high data rate sensors include strain, acceleration, and vibration. Recent advances have resulted in the ability to integrate sensors, radio communications, and digital electronics into a single integrated circuit (IC) package. This capability is enabling networks of very low cost sensors that are able to communicate with each other using low power wireless data routing protocols.

A wireless sensor network (WSN) generally consists of a base station (or "gateway") that can communicate with a number of wireless sensors via a radio link. Data is collected at the wireless sensor node, compressed, and transmitted to the gateway directly or, if required, uses other wireless sensor nodes to forward data to the gateway. The transmitted data is then presented to the system by the gateway connection. The main purpose of this chapter is to highlight and discuss as well as analyze the management process of WSN through using computational intelligence techniques. We are interested in this track because WSN management represents one of the main functions that should be executed to guaranty the safety operation of WSN, to be more specific; network management is defined as the process of managing, monitoring, and controlling the behavior of a network. Wireless sensor networks (WSNs) pose unique challenges for network management that make traditional network management techniques impractical. In traditional networks the primary goals are minimizing response time and providing comprehensive information, but in sensor networks the primary goal is minimizing energy use [B. Warneke, 2002] and the main means for doing this is by reducing the amount of communication between nodes. Optimizing the operational and functional properties of WSNs may require a unique solution for each application problem [R.

Min, 2001]. WSNs are highly dynamic and prone to faults, mainly because of energy shortages, connectivity interruptions, and environmental obstacles. Network failures are common events rather than exceptional ones [I. Akyildiz, 2002]. Thus, in WSNs, we are mainly concerned with monitoring and controlling node communication in order to optimize the efficiency of the network, ensure the network operates properly, maintain the performance of the network, and control large numbers of nodes without human intervention.

This chapter is organized from ten sections. Section two describes the architecture of wireless sensor networks as well as the power consumption of WSN. In section three, we review Communications Architecture for Wireless Sensor Networks. Section five deals with design factors that affect WSN and major requirements from WSN. Architecture of the Protocol Stack for Wireless Sensor Networks was described in section five. Section six covers the various application of WSN. WSN routing protocols was discussed in details in section seven. In section eight, we describe and analyze WSN management techniques. Application of Genetic Programming and Sensor Networks was explained in section nine. Section ten explains briefly how to use Intelligent Agents in controlling and managing the Wireless Sensor Networks. Finally, this chapter was terminated in section eleven with summary and conclusion.

WIRELESS SENSOR NETWORKS ARCHITECTURE & POWER CONSUMPTION

WSN Various Topologies

There are of different topologies for radio communications networks to represent the architecture of WSN. A brief discussion of the network topologies that apply to wireless sensor networks are outlined below.

Star Network (Single Point-to-Multipoint)

A star network represents one of the communications topology in which there exists a single base station send and/or receives a message to a number of remote nodes. The remote nodes can only send or receive a message from the single base station; they are not permitted to send messages to each other. The advantage of this type of network topology to use it for wireless sensor networks is in its simplicity and the ability to keep the remote node's power consumption a minimum value. It also allows for low latency communications between the remote node and the base station. The disadvantage of such a network is that the base station must be within radio transmission range of all the individual nodes and is not as robust as other networks due to its dependency on a single node to manage the network.

Mesh Network

A mesh network allows any node in the network to transmit to any other node in the network that is within its radio transmission range. This allows for what is known as multihop communications; that is, if a node wants to send a message to another node that is out of radio communications range, it can use an intermediate node to forward the message to the desired node. This network topology has the advantage of redundancy and scalability. If an individual node fails, a remote node still can communicate with any other node in its range, which in turn, can forward the message to the desired location. In addition, the range of the network is not necessarily limited by the range in between single nodes; it can simply be extended by adding more nodes to the system. The disadvantage of this type of network is in power consumption of the nodes that implement the multihop communications are generally higher than for the nodes that don't have this capability, often limiting the battery life. Additionally, as the number of communication hops to a destination increases, the time to deliver the message also increases, especially if low power operation of the nodes is a requirement.

Hybrid Star: Mesh Network

A hybrid between the star and mesh network provides for a robust and versatile communications network, while maintaining the ability to keep the wireless sensor nodes power consumption to a minimum. In this network topology, the lowest power sensor nodes are not enabled with the ability to forward messages. This allows for minimal power consumption to be maintained. However, other nodes on the network are enabled with multi-hop capability, allowing them to forward messages from the low power nodes to other nodes on the network. Generally, the nodes with the multihop capability are higher power, and if possible, are often plugged into the electrical mains line [Chris Townsend Steven Arms 2004].

Power Consideration in Wireless Sensor Networks

The single most important consideration for a wireless sensor network is power consumption. While the concept of wireless sensor networks looks practical and exciting on paper, if batteries are going to have to be changed constantly, widespread adoption will not occur. Therefore, when the sensor node is designed, power consumption must be minimized. There are various strategies used to reduce the average supply current of the radio, including the following:-

- Reduce the amount of data transmitted through data compression and reduction.
- Lower the transceiver duty cycle and frequency of data transmissions.
- Reduce the frame overhead.
- Implement strict power management mechanisms (power-down and sleep modes).

- Implement an event-driven transmission strategy; only transmit data when a sensor event occurs.

Power reduction strategies for the sensor itself include:

- Turn power on to sensor only when sampling.
- Turn power on to signal conditioning only when sampling sensor.
- Only sample sensor when an event occurs.
- Lower sensor sample rate to the minimum required by the application

COMMUNICATIONS ARCHITECTURE FOR WIRELESS SENSOR NETWORKS

Wireless sensor network (WSN) is a network made of a numerous number of sensor nodes with sensing, wireless communications and computation capabilities. These sensor nodes are scattered in an unattended environment (i.e., sensor field) situated far from the user as shown in Figure 2. The upper side of the architecture represents the communication architecture for (WSNs). The main entities that build up the architecture are [S. Tilak, 2002]:

- The Sensor nodes; form the sensor network. Their main objectives are making discrete, local measurement about phenomenon surrounding these sensors, forming a wireless network by communicating over a wireless medium, and collect date and rout data back to the user via sink (Base Station).
- The sink (Base Station); communicates with the user via Internet or satellite communication. It is located near the sensor field or well-equipped nodes of the sensor network. Collected data from the sensor

Figure 2. Sensor nodes scattered in a sensor field and the components of a single sensor node

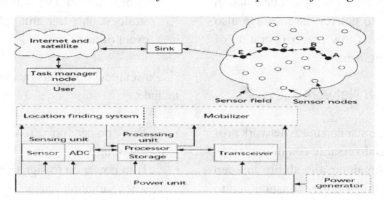

field routed back to the sink by a multi-hop infra structureless architecture through the sink.

- Phenomenon; which is an entity of interest to the user to collect measurements about. This phenomenon sensed and analyzed by the sensor nodes. The user; who is interested in obtaining information about specific phenomenon to measure/monitor its behavior.

DESIGN FACTORS OF WSN AND THE MAJOR REQUIREMENTS SATISFYING WSN STANDARDS

In this sub-section, we intend to describe the design factors of overall wireless sensor networks communications architecture as well as the design factors of protocols and algorithms for wireless sensor networks (WSNs). Many design factors have been addressed by many researchers in this field. These design factors are surveyed below. These factors serve as hints or guidelines to design a protocol or algorithm for WSNs.

- Reliability: reliability or fault tolerance of a sensor node is the ability to maintain the sensor network functionalities without any interruption due to sensor node failure [C. Shen, 2001], [K. G. Hoblos, 2000]. Sensor

node may fail due to lack of energy, physical damage, communications problem, inactivity (a node becomes suspended), or environmental interference. Reliability is modeled in [K. G. Hoblos, 2000] using the Poisson distribution to capture the probability of not having a failure within the time interval (0,t):

$$R_k(t) = e^{-k^t} \qquad (1)$$

where k is the failure rate of sensor node k and t is the time period.

- Density and Network Size/Scalability: hundreds, thousands or millions of sensor nodes may be deployed to study a phenomenon of interest to users. The density of these nodes affects the degree of coverage area of interest. The networks size affects reliability, accuracy, and data processing algorithms [Eiko Yoneki, 2005]. The density can range from a fewer sensor nodes to a hundred in a region that can be less than 10m in diameter. The density [1] is calculated as in [K. G. Hoblos, 2000]:

$$\mu(R) = (N \pi R^2)/A \qquad (2)$$

where N is the scattered sensor nodes in region A, and R is the radio transmission range. Basically, (R) gives the number of nodes within the transmission radius of each node in region A.

- Sensor Network Topology: the topology of a network affects many of its characteristics like; latency, capacity, and robustness. Also, the complexity of data routing and processing depends on the network topology. Densely deploying thousands of sensor nodes in sensor field (Figure 1) requires careful handling of network topology maintenance [I. Akyildiz, 2002], [Eiko Yoneki, 2005]. Paper [I. Akyildiz, 2002] defined three phases related to topology maintenance and changes (e.g., malfunctioning of some sensor nodes); Predeployment and deployment phase, Postdeployment phase, and Redeployment of additional nodes phase.

- Energy Consumption: one of the components of sensor nodes is the power source which is limited enough. A sensor node is battery-operated. Hence; life time of a sensor node depends strongly on the battery life time, especially where no power source replenishment is possible in some applications scenarios. Since the main objectives of sensor nodes are sensing/ collecting events, data processing, and data transmission through routing; then the power resource can be divided among these three operations (sensing, computation, and communications). On the other hand; life time of a sensor node plays a key role on energy efficiency and robustness of sensor node [I. Akyildiz, 2002], [R. C. Shah, 2002], [Eiko Yoneki, 2005].

- Hardware Constraints: sensor node consists of four main components (the lower side of Figure 1): a sensing units, processing unit, transmission unit, and power unit. They may also have application-dependent additional components such as position/ location finding systems, power genera-

tor, and mobilizer. Sensing units are usually composed of two subunits: Sensors and ADC (Analog to Digital Converter). The Analog signals produced by sensors based on the observed phenomenon are converted by ADC to digital signal and fed into the processing unit to be processed. Processing unit, generally associated with storage unit, manages the procedures that make the sensor node collaborate with other nodes to perform the assigned sensing tasks. Transmission unit that connects the sensor node to the network. Power unit may be supported by a power scavenging such as solar cells. Since most of the sensor network routing techniques and sensing tasks require knowledge of location with high accuracy, thus it is common that a sensor node has a position/ location finding system. Sometimes, a mobilizer is needed to move sensor node to carry out the assigned tasks. Hence, the size of sensor node is of a great design issue [I. Akyildiz, 2002].

- Data Aggregation/Data Fusion: it is the task of reducing data size by summarizing the data into a set of meaningful information via computation while data are propagating through the wireless sensor network (in this context). As sensor networks made of large number of sensor nodes; this can easily congest the network and flooding it with information [H. Cam, 2003]. Hence; a solution to data congestion in sensor networks is to use computation to aggregate or fuse data within WSN, then transmit only the aggregated data to the controller. Many approaches within the context of WSNs are proposed to facilitate data aggregation, also known as data fusion, such as; (1) diffusion algorithms which assume that homogeneous data propagate to destination throughout the network by transmitting data from one node to another, then these data may be aggregated using diffusion algorithms, (2) Streaming queries are based on SQL extension for continuous querying, And (3) Event Algebra which assists in composing simple events into composite ones with the help of event graph [Eiko Yoneki, 2005].

- Transmission Media: in a multi-hop sensor network, a wireless medium is used to link nodes for communications goal. These links can be formed by radio (e.g., Bluetooth compatible 2.4 GHz transceiver), Infrared which is license free and robust to interference from electrical devices, and Optical media.

- Security: security aspects in WSNs have been focused on the centralized communications approaches. Some of the threats to a WSN are described in [Perrig, A.,2004], [Avancha, S. 2003], [E. Shi, 2004] and categorized as follows: Passive Information Gathering, False Node, Node Outage, Supervision of a Node, Node Malfunction, Message Corruption, Denial of Service, and Traffic Analysis [Perrig, A., 2004], [E. Shi, 2004]. There is a need to develop distributed security approaches for wireless sensor network.

- Self-Configuration: it is essential for wireless sensor network to be self-organize; since the densely deployed sensor nodes in a sensor field may fail due to many reasons (e.g., lack of energy, physical destruction, environment interference, communications problem, inactivity, etc) and new nodes may join the network. On the other hand; sensor nodes work unattended in a dynamic environment; so they need to be self-configuration to establish a topology that supports communications under severe energy constraints. It is worthy mention that self-configuration in WSN is an essential factor to maintain a WSN functions properly and serve its purpose [N. Bulusu, 2001], [B. Krishnamachari, 2003].

- Network dynamics: in many applications, the movement of sensor nodes or the base station (sink) is essential. This means that sensor nodes are moving nodes (i.e., not stationary as assumed by many of network architectures). This has arisen the routing stability issues as well as energy, bandwidth, etc. Moreover, the specific sensed phenomenon may be either dynamic (e.g., target detection/ tracking applications) or stationary (e.g., forest monitoring) depending on the applications.

- Quality of Service: for some applications, data delivery within a bounded latency (i.e., time constrained applications) is of great importance; otherwise, the sensed data that delivered after certain latency will be useless. In other applications (e.g., not time-constrained applications), the conservation of power is more important than the quality of the sent data. Hence; there is a tradeoff between the quality of service/the quality of data sent and the energy conservations or consumption depending on the applications [Iyer, R., 2003], [J. Kay, 2004].

- Coverage: the sensor node's view of the environment that it is situated in is limited both in range and in accuracy. This means the ability of sensor nodes to cover physical area of the environment is limited [Eiko Yoneki, 2005], [Kay Romer, 2004].

- Connectivity: a permanent connection between any two individual sensor nodes that are densely deployed in a sensor network defines the network connectivity. The connectivity is of great importance, since it influences communications protocols' design and data dissemination techniques. Also, it is worth mentioning that connectivity of sensor network may not prevent the network topology from being variable and the network size from reduction as a result of the death or failure of some sensor nodes due to the reasons mentioned earlier in the paper [Eiko Yoneki, 2005], [Kay Romer, 2004].

PROTOCOL STACK ARCHITECTURE OF THE WIRELESS SENSOR NETWORKS

The architecture of protocol stack [I. Akyildiz, 2002] used by the sink and sensor nodes is shown in Figure 3. This protocol stack integrates power and routing awareness (i.e., energy-aware routing), integrates data with networking protocols (i.e., data aggregation), communicates power efficiently through the wireless medium, and promotes cooperative efforts of sensor nodes (i.e., task management plane). This protocol stack (Figure 3) is made up of physical layer, data link layer, network layer, transport layer, application layer, power management plane, mobility management plane, and task management plane. The physical layer addresses the needs of a robust modulation, transmission and receiving techniques.

In Figure 3, the network layer takes care of routing the data supplied by the transport layer. The transport layer helps to maintain the flow of data if the wireless sensor network application requires it. Depending on the sensing tasks, different types of application Software can be set up and used on the application layer. The power management plane manages how a sensor node uses its power and manages its power consumption among the three operations (sensing, computation, and wireless communications). For instance, to avoid getting duplicated messages, a

sensor node may turn off it receiver after receiving a message from one of its neighbors. Also, a sensor node broadcasts to its neighbors that it is low in power and can not take part in routing messages. The remaining power is reserved for sensing and detecting tasks. The mobility management plane detects and registers the movement/ mobility of sensor nodes as a network control primitive. Hence; a route back to the user is always kept, and sensor nodes can keep track of who their neighbors of other sensor nodes are. Therefore, the nodes can balance their power and task usage by knowing this situation. The task management plane (i.e., cooperative efforts of sensor nodes) balances and schedules the events' sensing and detecting tasks from a specific area. Hence; not all of the sensor nodes in that specific area are required to carry out the sensing tasks at the same time. Depending on their power level, some nodes perform the sensing task more than others.

WIRELESS SENSOR NETWORKS APPLICATIONS

Sensor networks are applied in a wide range of areas, such as military applications, public safety, medical, surveillances, environmental monitoring, commercial applications, habitat and tracking [i. Khemapech, 2005], [Ning Xu, 2005], [V. Rajaravivarma, 2003]. In general, sensor networks will be ubiquitous in the near future, since they support new opportunities for the interaction between humans and their physical world. In addition, sensor networks are expected to contribute significantly

Figure 3. The wireless sensor networks protocol stack

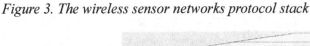
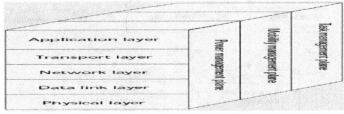

to pervasive computing and space exploration in the next decade. Deploying sensor nodes in an unattended environment will give much more possibilities for the exploration of new applications in the real world. In this context, we will look briefly at some of these applications. The idea behind these applications is that; densely deploying sensor nodes with capabilities of sensing, wireless communications, and computation in an unattended environment, will assist in measuring its ambient conditions, and obtaining the characteristics about phenomenon of interest surrounding these sensors; by transforming these sensed/gathered data into electrical signals that can be processed. Moreover, other applications for wireless sensor networks can be seen in environmental monitoring and control field (e.g., robot control), high-security smart homes, tracking, and identifications and personalization [R. Min, 2001]. Among these applications the following (Figure 4):

- Military applications; such as environment monitoring, tracking and surveillance applications. Sensor nodes that from sensor network are dropped to the field of interest (e.g., behind the hostile forces, spy, etc), and remotely controlled by user who is situated far from them. User may assign

new tasks to be performed by these sensor nodes.

- Environmental monitoring; such as animals tracking, forest detection and flood detection, and weather prediction and forecasting.
- Commercial applications; such as seismic activities monitoring and prediction, and smart environment applications.
- Health applications; such as tracking and monitoring of doctors and patients in or out the hospitals by providing them with sensors.
- Automation and control (e.g., robotics control).

SENSOR NETWORKS ROUTING PROTOCOLS

Design Challenges

Among the design factors and challenges for wireless sensor networks protocol are energy depletion, robustness to dynamic environment, and scalability to numerous number of sensor nodes. Some recommended solutions to these challenges are as follows: a reduction in the active duty cycle for each sensor node, a minimization of data communications over the wireless channel (i.e.,

Figure 4. Various sensor network applications

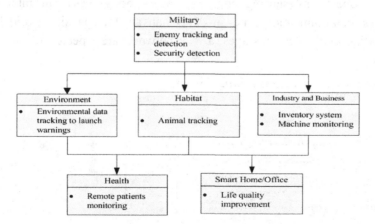

aggregation, communicate network state summaries instead of actual data), and maximization of network life time (i.e., minimum energy routing) will give hand to the energy depletion challenge. Scalability, on another hand; may be enhanced by organizing network in a hierarchical manner (e.g., clustering) and utilizing localized algorithms with localized interactions among sensor nodes, while robustness to environmental changes, may be improved through self-organizing, self-healing, self configuring, and self-adaptive networks.

Classification of Sensor Networks Routing Protocols

There are different ways by which we can classify the sensor networks' routing protocols. According to network structure, these routing protocols can be classified as: flat, hierarchical, and location-based protocols. Also, these protocols can be classified into: multipath-based, query-based, negotiation-based, Quality of Service (QoS)-based or coherent based depending on the protocol operation. Moreover, these protocols can be classified into three categories, namely, reactive, proactive, and hybrid protocols depending on route discovery. In flat-based routing, all nodes are assigned the same roles or functionalities. In hierarchical-based routing, nodes will play different roles or functionalities, aiming at routing techniques clustering the nodes with different roles so that the heads of the cluster can do some data aggregation or confusion in order to save power, while in location based routing; sensor nodes' positions are exploited to route the data to specific regions other than the whole network. On the other hand; in reactive protocols, routes are computed on demand. In proactive protocols, routes are computed before they are needed, while hybrid protocols utilize a combination of the ideas of both reactive and proactive protocols.

WSN vs. MANET

A realization of sensor networks' characteristics, design, and applications require wireless ad hoc networking mechanisms. Among the existing ad hoc networks models, the mobile ad hoc networks (MANETs) are the closest to sensor networks. Although MANETs and Wireless Sensor Networks (WSNs) share some similar characteristics, such as; network topology is ad hoc (i.e., not fixed), power and bandwidth are an expensive resources, wireless communication mediums (i.e., wireless communications links) are used to connect nodes, the protocols and algorithms developed for MANETs are not suitable for the unique features and application requirements of WSNs because these two types of networks have different differences [I. Akyildiz, 2002]. The main difference between WSN and MANETs are:-

- The number of sensor nodes in WSNs can be several orders of magnitude higher than that in MANETs.
- Unlike a node in MANETs, sensor node may not have a unique global IP address because of the large amount of overhead and the numerous numbers of sensors.
- Sensor nodes are extremely cheaper and more tiny devices, not like ad hoc network nodes (e.g., PDAs, Laptops, etc), and usually they deployed in thousands.
- The communication paradigm used in WSNs is broadcasting, whereas MANETs are based on point-to-point communications.
- The topology of a WSN changes very frequently.
- Energy and bandwidth conservation is the main concern in WSN protocol design since power resources of sensor noses are very limited as well as computation, communication capabilities than their MANETs counterparts because of their low cost.

- Sensor nodes are prone to failure much more than nodes in MANETs. Consequently, it is so important to study new routing protocols for wireless sensor networks that will fulfill the above requirements.

ROUTING PROTOCOLS IN WIRELESS SENSOR NETWORKS

The most well-known routing protocols for wireless sensor networks will be introduced in this subsection as follows:-

Flooding

Flooding [W. R. Heinzelman, 1999] is an old routing mechanism that may also be used in sensor networks. In flooding, a node sends out the received data or the management packets to its neighbors by broadcasting, unless a maximum number of hops for that packet are reached or the destination of the packets is arrived. However; there are some deficiencies for this routing technique [[W. R. Heinzelman, 1999] like:-

- Implosion: is the case where a duplicated data or packets are sent to the same node. Flooding is a function of the network topology. For instance; node A has K neighbor nodes which are neighbors of the node B, then node B will receive K copies of the data or message sent from node A.
- Overlap: if two sensor nodes cover an overlapping measuring region, both of them will sense/detect the same data. As a result, their neighbor nodes will receive duplicated data or messages. Overlapping is a function of both the network topology and the mapping of sensed data to sensor nodes.
- Resource blindness: In flooding, nodes do not take into account the amount of energy resource available to them at a given time.

A WSN protocol must be energy resource-aware and adapts its sensing, communication and computation to the state of its energy.

Gossiping

Gossiping protocol is an alternative to flooding mechanism. In Gossiping [S. M. Hedetniemi, 1988], nodes can forward the incoming data/packets to randomly selected neighbor node. Once a gossiping node receives the messages, it can forward the data back to that neighbor or to another one randomly selected neighbor node. This technique assists in energy conservation by randomization. Although, gossiping can solve the implosion problem, it cannot avoid the overlapping problem. On the other hand; gossiping distribute information slowly, this means it consumes energy at a slow rate, but the cost is long-time propagation is needed to send messages to all sensor nodes.

SPIN

SPIN (Sensor Protocols for Information via Negotiation) [J. Kulik, 2002] is a family of adaptive protocols for WSNs. Their design goal is to avoid the drawbacks of flooding protocols mentioned above by utilizing data negotiation and resource adaptive algorithms. SPIN is designed based on two basic ideas; (1) to operate efficiently and to conserve energy by sending meta-data (i.e., sending data about sensor data instead of sending the whole data that sensor nodes already have or need to obtain), and (2) nodes in a network must be aware of changes in their own energy resources and adapt to these changes to extend the operating lifetime of the system. SPIN has three types of messages, namely, ADV, REQ, and DATA.

- ADV: when a node has data to send, it advertises via broadcasting this message containing meta-data (i.e., descriptor) to all nodes in the network.

- REQ: an interested node sends this message when it wishes to receive some data.
- DATA: Data message contains the actual sensor data along with meta-data header. SPIN is based on data-centric routing where the sensor nodes send ADV message via broadcasting for the data they have and wait for REQ messages from interested sinks or nodes.

The semantics of SPIN's meta-data format is application dependent and not supported by SPIN. In another words; SPIN uses application specific meta-data to name the sensed data. Although, SPIN has some advantages, such as (1) solving the problems associated with classic flooding protocols, and (2) topological changes are localized, it has its own drawbacks like; (1) scalability, SPIN is not scalable, (2) if the sink is interested in too many events, this could make the sensor nodes around it deplete their energy, and (3) SPIN's data advertisement technique can not guarantee the delivery of data if the interested nodes are far away from the source node and the nodes in between are not interested in that data. SPIN- 1 starts when a node has new data to share. This node sends out an ADV message containing a descriptor (i.e., meta-data) about the data it has to its neighbor nodes. An interested neighbor in that data sends out a REQ message to the broadcasting node, which then in turns sends out the actual data along with the meta-data. In SPIN-2, which is simply SPIN-1 with a low-energy threshold, if a node has new data to share or received an ADV message, it will not take part in the protocol if it does not have enough energy.

Directed Diffusion

Directed diffusion [C. Intanagonwiwat, 2003] is another data dissemination and aggregation protocol. It is a data-centric and application aware routing protocol for WSNs. It aims at naming all data generated by sensor nodes by attribute-value pairs.

Directed diffusion consists of several elements; first of all, naming; where task descriptors, sent out by the sink, are named by assigning attribute-value pairs. Secondly, interests and gradients; the named task description constitutes an interest that contains timestamp field and several gradient fields. Each node stores the interest in its interest cache. As the interests propagate throughout the network, the gradients from the source back to the sink are set up. Thirdly, data propagation, when the source has data for the interest, it sends out the data to the interest (i.e., sink) along the interest's gradient path. Fourthly, after the interest (sink) starts receiving low rate data events, it reinforce one particular neighbor to draw down higher quality (higher data rate) events. This feature of directed diffusion is achieved by data-driven local rules. Directed diffusion assists in saving sensors' energy by selecting good paths by caching and processing data in-network since each node has the ability for performing data aggregation and caching. On the other hand; Directed diffusion has its limitations such as; implementing data aggregation requires deployment of synchronization techniques which is not realizable in WSNs. Also, the overhead in data aggregation involves recording information. These two drawbacks may contribute to the cost of sensor node, which is not desired.

LEACH

LEACH (Low Energy Adaptive Clustering Hierarchy) [W. Heinzelman, 2000] is a self-organizing, adaptive clustering-based protocol that uses randomized rotation of cluster-heads to evenly distribute the energy load among the sensor nodes in the network. LEACH based on two basic assumptions: (a) base station is fixed and located far away from the sensors, and (b) all nodes in the network are homogeneous and energy constrained. The idea behind LEACH is to form clusters of the sensor nodes depending on the received signal strength and use local cluster heads as routers to route data to the base station. The key features of LEACH are:-

- Localized coordination and control for cluster set-up and operation.
- Randomized rotation of the cluster"base stations" or"cluster-heads" and the corresponding clusters.
- Local compression to reduce global communication.

In LEACH, the operation is separated into fixed-length rounds, where each round starts with a setup phase followed by a steady-state phase. The duration of a round is determined priori.

PEGASIS

PEGASIS (Power-Efficient GAthering in Sensor Information Systems) is a greedy chain-based power efficient algorithm [S. Lindsey, 2002]. Also, PEGASIS is based on LEACH (the scenario and the radio model in PEGASIS are the same as in LEACH). The key features of PEGASIS are:

- The BS is fixed at a far distance from the sensor nodes.
- The sensor nodes are homogeneous and energy constrained with uniform energy.
- No mobility of sensor nodes.

PEGASIS is based on two ideas; Chaining, and Data Fusion. In PEGASIS, each node can take turn of being a leader of the chain, where the chain can be constructed using greedy algorithms that are deployed by the sensor nodes. PEGASIS assumes that sensor nodes have a global knowledge of the network, nodes are stationary (no movement of sensor nodes), and nodes have location information about all other nodes. PEGASIS performs data fusion except the end nodes in the chain. PEGASIS outperforms LEACH by eliminating the overhead of dynamic cluster formation, minimizing the sum of distances that non leader-nodes must

transmit, limiting the number of transmissions and receives among all nodes, and using only one transmission to the BS per round. PEGASIS has the same problems that LEACH suffers from. Also, PEGASIS does not scale, can not be applied to sensor network where global knowledge of the network is not easy to get.

GEAR

GEAR (Geographical and Energy Aware Routing) [Y. Yu, 2001] is a recursive data dissemination protocol WSNs. It uses energy aware and geographically informed neighbor selection heuristics to rout a packet to the targeted region. Within that region, it uses a recursive a geographic informed mechanism to disseminate the packet. GEAR, like other sensor networks protocols, developed according to some assumptions given by:

- Sensor nodes are static (i.e., immobile).
- There is an existence of a localization system that enables each node to know its current position.
- Sensor nodes are energy-constrained accompanied with location information about all other nodes (i.e., each node knows its location and its energy level, and its neighbor's location and remaining energy level.
- The link that connects nodes is bi-directional, i.e., if node N can hear from a neighbor node Mi, then its transmission range can reach node Mi. GEAR has two phases: (1) forwarding the packets toward the targeted region, and (2) forwarding the packets within the targeted region. During the first phase; packets/queries are routed to the region R using energy-aware and geographically informed neighbor selection heuristics. In the second phase, and within that region R, it uses a recursive a geographic informed forwarding mechanism or restricted flooding to disseminate the packets inside R.

- Data Aggregation; we believe that reducing the data size quickly using computation will play a key role in supporting efficient query processing, and reducing the overall network overhead. Hence saving power.

- Dynamic clustering architecture is required since such architecture will preclude cluster heads from depleting their energy quickly. Hence, long network's lifetime.

- Threshold for sensor nodes on data transmission and dissemination: this will help in saving energy by reducing unnecessary transmissions (i.e., redundancy) and giving the network long lifetime.

- Randomized path selection; multi-path selection to destination could improve fault tolerance and handle the overhead of network load.

- Mobility; most of the current protocols assume that sensor nodes are static (i.e., immobile). However, for some applications or in some situations, nodes need to be mobile. Hence, new routing algorithms are needed to handle the mobility and network topology changes.

- Self-configuration; since sensor nodes are prone to failure due to some factors or new sensor nodes may join the network, an update, self-configuration, self-healing, and adaptation to changes in network topology or environmental changes should be considered.

- Security; there is a desperate need to develop distributed security approaches for wireless sensor network. Hence, achieving secure routing.

- Quality-of-Service; dependability, and localization need to be considered and given more attention. Time synchronization: time synchronization techniques are required since time plays a key role in WSNs.

WIRELESS SENSOR NETWORKS MANAGEMENT

In this section, our aim is to provide a discussion of the management issues for WSNs, their design impact on WSNs, and to highlight some guidelines and directions to be considered when designing a management system for WSNs. Throughout this work, we identified that wireless sensor networks are large networks made of densely deployed (hundreds, thousands or magnitude of order of ten thousands in some situations) sensor nodes in an unattended environment. In essence, nodes are of magnitude of order more than those in traditional computer networks. These nodes are characterized by constraints, namely, energy and bandwidth constraints, and nodes-as a common fact-are prone to faults. Sensor networks have different architecture than traditional wired data networks. Sensor networks are set up in a random manner. On the other hand, the WSNs are applications-dependent which implies that the management requirements also change among sensor networks, and a configuration error of a WSN in unpredictable situations may cause the fail/loss of the whole entire network even before it starts to operate [L.B. Ruiz, 2005], [L.B. Ruiz, 2003], [L. B. Ruiz, 2004]. Also, the behavior of WSN is highly unpredictable and dynamic [S. B. B. Deb, 2002]. All these factors have to be incorporated by various sensor network models that describe the current network's states.

WSN Models

- Network Topology Model; it describes the actual topology map and the connectivity and/or reachability of the network. It also may assist routing operations and obtaining information about future deployment of nodes [S.B. B. Deb, 2002], since the topology of a network affects many of its characteristics, such as latency, capacity, and robustness, as well as the complexity of data routing and processing. This requires careful handling of network topology maintenance [A.A. Ahmed, 2003], [Perrig, 2004]. Paper [A.A. Ahmed, 2003] defined three phases related to topology maintenance and changes (e.g., malfunctioning of some sensor nodes); Predeployment and deployment phase, Post-deployment phase, and Re-deployment of additional nodes phase.

- Residual Energy Model; describes the remaining energy level of the nodes or the network. Using this information as well as the data from network topology, coupled together; would make it possible to identify the weak areas (i.e., areas that have short lifetime) of the network [S.B.B. Deb, 2002].

- Cost Model; describes the cost of equipment, energy, and human cost to maintain the desired performance levels of the network.

- Usage Patterns Model; represents the activity of the network in terms of period of time for nodes' activity, quantity of data transmitted per sensor unit or the movements made by the target, and tracking of hot spots in the network to avoid hot spot problem [S. B. B. Deb, 2002].

- Behavioral Model; describes the behavior of the network. Since sensor networks are highly unpredictable, dynamic, and unreliable, statistical and probabilistic models may be much more efficient in estimating the network behavior than estimating the network behavior than deterministic models.

- Coverage Area Model; a sensing coverage area map that represents the actual sensor's view of the environment and communications coverage map that describes the communication coverage area from the range of the RF transceiver [S.B.B. Deb, 2002].

The above models would build up the MIB (management Information base). Also, these models could be used for different network management functions such as: deployment of sensors, network operating parameters, coverage area supervision function, topology map discovery function, network connectivity discovery function, node localization discovery function, prediction function for future network states, monitored area definition function, design of sensor networks, energy level function, self-test function, etc [L. B. Ruiz, 2003], [S.B.B. Deb, 2002].

Since sensor nodes are unattended as well as the environment these sensors are situated in; human intervention to perform some network maintenance tasks, such as configuration, protection, healing, and energy replenishment is becoming impractical. So, it is our belief that self-management solutions (self-configuration, self-healing, self-optimization, self protection, self-service, self awareness, and self knowledge) [IBM, 2003], [IBM, 2004], are a promising functional key management solution that can cope with the various unique requirements and constraints, imposed on the wireless sensor networks due to resource restrictions introduced by some factors (e.g., small size, memory, low-power consumption, fault-tolerance, low latency, scalability, adaptively, and robustness). Attempts to build up management system that can combine all of these features are proposed by some interested researchers in this field. L. B. Ruiz, et al. [L. B. Ruiz, 2004], [S.B.B. Deb, 2002], [IBM, 2003], have proposed an architecture for WSN management called"MANNA". The MANNA management architecture took into account three management dimensions: (1) the management functional areas (i.e., Fault, Configuration, Accounting, Performance, and Security), (2) the management levels (i.e., Business management, Service management, Network management, Network element management, and Network element), and (3) WSN functionalities, such as

Configuration, Maintenance, Sensing, Processing, and Communication.

In the work [L.B. Ruiz, 2004], [S.B.B. Deb, 2002], [IBM, 2003], the authors argue that; "in WSNs, all operational, administrative and maintenance characteristics of the network elements, the network, the services, and business, as well as the adequate execution in the activities of configuration, maintenance, sensing, processing and communication are dependent on the configuration of the WSN". Also, other attempts have been carried out on the power management for WSNs [M. A. M. Viera, 2003], [R.M. Passos, 2005], [A. Sinha, 2001], [R.Tynan, 2005]. Also, it is our belief that sensor network management could borrow from artificial intelligence approach, in general, swarm intelligence [E. Bonabeau, 1999], in particular, to achieve scalable, robust, and adaptable management system for WSNs. Different algorithms, optimization techniques, and collective intelligence could be adapted and brought to the field of wireless sensor network.

Management Functionality

The function of network management systems is to monitor and control a network. These activities are wide ranging, and in this section we classify existing sensor network management systems in terms of the functionality they provide. Systems for sensor networks that are based on traditional network management systems include BOSS [H. Song, 2005] and MANNA [L.B. Ruiz, 2003]. BOSS serves as a mediator between UpnP networks and sensor nodes. MANNA provides a general framework for policy-based management of sensor networks. sNMP [B. Deb, 2005] provides network topology extraction algorithms for retrieving network state. Other researchers have designed novel routing Protocols for network management. For example, TopDisc [B. Deb, 2001] and STREAM [B. Deb, 2004] are used in sNMP for extracting network topology, RRP [W. Liu, 2004] uses a zone-flooding protocol, SNMS

[G. Tolle, 2005] introduces the Drip protocol, and WinMS [W. Louis, 2006] is based on the Flexi-MAC protocol. Fault detection is an important focus of the systems TP [C. Hsin, 2006], Sympathy [N. Ramanathan, 2005], MANNA [L. B. Ruiz, 2004], and WinMS [W. Louis, 2006].

In TP, each node monitors its own health and its neighbors' health, so providing local fault detection. Sympathy goes one step further by providing a debugging technique to detect and localize faults that may occur from interactions between multiple nodes. MANNA performs centralized fault detection based on analysis of gathered WSN data. In WinMS, there is a scheduled period where nodes listen to their environment activities and can self-configure themselves in the event of failure without prior knowledge of the full network topology. In addition, WinMS provides a centralized fault management scheme that analyses network states to detect and to predict potential failures and takes corrective and preventive actions accordingly. TP, Sympathy, and MANNA focus solely on fault detection and debugging, they provide no automatic network reconfiguration to allow the network to recover from faults and failures. WinMS differs from the rest as it adaptively adjusts the network by providing local and central recovery mechanisms.

TinyDB [S. Madden, 2005] and MOTE-VIEW [M. Turon, 2005] are visualization tools that provide graphical representations of network states to the end user. TinyDB is a query-based interface that allows the end user to retrieve information from sensor nodes in a network. MOTE-VIEW also allows the end user to control sensor node settings such as transmission power, radio frequency, and sampling frequency. In these systems the central server analyses data collected from the network. The main disadvantage of such passive monitoring schemes is that they are not adaptive to current network conditions, and provides no self configuration in the event of faults. The end user must manually manage the network and interpret the graphical representation of collected data. Several network management systems focus on managing power resources in the network: Agent-Based Power Management [R. Tynan, 2005], SenOS [T. H. Kim, 2003], AppSleep [N. Ramanathan, 2005], and Node-Energy Level Management [A. Boulis, 2003]. Agent-Based Power Management utilizes intelligent mobile agents to manage sub-networks and perform local power management processing. It can reduce the sampling rate of nodes with critical battery and reduce node transmission power. Other systems such as SenOS, AppSleep, and Node-Energy Level Management [A. Boulis, 2003] use common sensor nodes to perform power management. SenOS and AppSleep put nodes to sleep when they are not needed Node-Energy Level Management [A. Boulis, 2003] allows nodes to reject a management task based on the importance of that task. Traffic management functions are provided in Siphon [C. Y. Wan, 2005], DSN RM [J. Zhang, 2001] and WinMS [W. Louis, 2006].

Siphon [C. Y. Wan, 2005] uses multi-radio nodes to redirect traffic from common nodes in a network in order to prevent congestion at the central server and in the primary radio network. In contrast, DSN RM [J. Zhang, 2001] uses single-radio common-nodes to evaluate each of their incoming and outgoing links and apply delay schemes to these links when necessary in order to reduce the amount of traffic in the network. Congestion can also be avoided by modifying sensor nodes' reporting rate based on the reliability level of sensor node data [M. Perillo, 2003]. By reducing a node's reporting rate, the number of packets transmitted in the network is reduced, so avoiding potential congestion. WinMS [W. Louis, 2006] can reconfigure nodes to report their data more rapidly or slowly depending on the significance and importance of their data to the end-user. The WinMS scheme supports nonuniform and reactive sensing in different parts of a network.

Several network management protocols reviewed are application specific rather than general purpose schemes. RRP [W. Liu, 2004] is tailored for real-time data gathering applications with bursty and bulky traffic. App-Sleep is designed for latency-tolerant applications. TP is a fault detection system best suited for monitoring and surveillance applications. SenOS power management is designed for SenOS operating system-based sensor networks. Network management systems such as RRP and Siphon [C.Y. Wan, 2004] require special hardware: RRP uses GPS nodes for implementing the proposed zone flooding protocol, while Siphon requires multi-radio nodes to act as virtual sinks. There are two main choices for the system organization of sensor network management protocols: central vs distributed control, and reactive vs proactive monitoring. Table I summarizes state of the art sensor network management systems according to these system choices.

Table 1. Network management system organization

Network Management System	Reactivity	Architecture
WinMS	Proactive	Hierarchical
DSN RM	Proactive	Hierarchical
Mobile agent-based policy management	Proactive	Hierarchical
Intelligent agent-based power management	Proactive	Distributed
Siphon	Proactive	Distributed
BOSS	Proactive	Centralized
Sympathy	Proactive	Centralized
SenOS	Reactive	Hierarchical
Agilla	Reactive	Distributed
Node-energy level management	Reactive	Distributed
Two-phase monitoring system	Fault-detection	Distributed
TopDisc	Passive	Hierarchical
AppSleep	Passive	Hierarchical
RRP	Passive	Hierarchical
STREAM	Passive	Hierarchical
Sectoral Sweeper	Passive	Distributed
TinyDB	Passive	Centralized
MOTE-VIEW	Passive	Centralized
SNMS	Passive	Centralized
MANNA	N/A	N/A

Management Reactivity

Sensor network management systems can be classified according to the approach taken to monitor and control of WSN:-

- Passive monitoring; the system collects information about network states. It may perform postmortem analysis of data.
- Fault detection monitoring; the system collects information about network states in order to identify whether faults have occurred.
- Reactive monitoring; the system collects information about network states to detect whether events of interest have occurred and then adaptively reconfigure the network.
- Proactive monitoring; the system actively collects and analyses network states to detect past events and to predict future events in order to maintain the performance of the network.

Management Architecture

Sensor network management systems can also be classified according to their network architecture [C. Fok, 2005]: centralized, distributed, or hierarchical. In centralized management systems, such as BOSS [H. Song, 2005], MOTE-VIEW [M. Turon, 2005], SNMS [G. Tolle, 2005], and Sympathy [N. Ramanathan, 2005], the base station acts as the manager station that collects information from all nodes and controls the entire network. The central manager with unlimited resources can perform complex management tasks, reducing the processing burden on resource-constrained nodes in the sensor network. Since the central manager also has the global knowledge of the network, it can provide accurate management decisions. But, this approach has some problems. First, it incurs a high message overhead (bandwidth and energy) from data polling, and this limits its scalability.

Second, the central server is a single point of data traffic concentration and potential failure. Lastly, if a network is partitioned, then nodes that are unable to reach the central server are left without any management functionality.

Distributed management systems employ multiple manager stations. Each manager controls a subnetwork and may communicate directly with other manager stations in a cooperative fashion in order to perform management functions. Distributed management has lower communication costs than centralized management, and so provides better reliability and energy efficiency. But it is complex and difficult to manage. Distributed management algorithms may be computationally too expensive for resource-constrained sensor network nodes. Distributed management systems include DSN RM [60], Node-energy level management [A. Boulis, 2003], App- Sleep [N. Ramanathan, 2005], and sensor management optimization [M. Perillo, 2003]. Another disadvantage of distributed systems is memory costs. For example, neighborhood state transition diagram maintenance in TP [C. Hsin, 2006], task usage profile maintenance in Node-Energy Level Management [A. Boulis, 2003], and tuple space maintenance in Agilla [C. Fok, 2005] all require significant memory resources.

A mobile agent-based framework is an example of distributed management system implementation. Network management systems that use this approach are Agilla, Sectoral Sweeper [A. Erdogan, 2003], Mobile Agent-Based Policy Management [Z. Ying, 2005], Agent-Based Power Management [R. Tynan, 2005], and MANNA [L. B. Ruiz, 2003]. The main advantages of these approaches are that local processing reduces network bandwidth requirements and prevents network bottlenecks by reducing processing at the central server [Z. Ying, 2005]. Furthermore, agents can be designed to distribute tasks in the network. For example, agents can relay some tasks from overloaded nodes to other nodes with lower workloads.

In addition, agents can be moved flexibly to cover an area of interest [L.B. Ruiz, 2003] and agents can shift debugging and transmission operation from low-power sensor nodes to extend network lifetime. There are several drawbacks of agent-based approaches. First, there is a need for special nodes to perform management tasks. Second, the human manager needs to locate these agents 'intelligently' in order to cover all nodes in the network. Thus, this approach requires a network to be configured manually and the human manager needs to have expertise about the optimal number of agents as well as agent location for a particular sensor network application. Third, the agent based approach introduces delays when a manager wants to retrieve network states of a node because the manager needs to wait for an agent to visit the node [B. Deb, 2004]. Fourth, the agent-based approach does not scale for large WSNs because as the number of sensor nodes increases, the number of agents deployed must be increased. Alternatively, reducing the number of agents increases the time required for an agent to visit nodes in a network.

Finally, since the agent typically sends aggregated management information from a set of managed nodes in a network, fine-grained information from individual nodes is compromised. Hierarchical network management is a hybrid between the centralized and distributed approach. Intermediate managers are used to distribute management functions, but do not communicate with each other directly. Each manager is responsible for managing the nodes in its sub-network. It passes information from its sub-network to its higher-level manager, and also disseminates management functions received from the higher-level manager to its sub-network. For example, in AppSleep [N. Ramanathan, 2005], TopDisc [B. Deb, 2001], STREAM [B. Deb, 2004], and SenOS [T. H. Kim, 2003], some common-nodes are selectively elected as cluster heads to act as distributed managers. There is a non-trivial energy overhead for selecting cluster heads. Agent-based

policy management [Z. Ying, 2005] uses mobile agents as distributed managers. In RRP [W. Liu, 2004], individual nodes have distinct roles: acquiring raw sensor data, transporting data, or filtering data. Unlike other systems, DSN RM [J, Zhang, 2001] and WinMS [W. Louis, 2006] allow individual nodes to act as agents and perform management functions autonomously based on their neighborhood states.

TRAFFIC MANAGEMENT SYSTEMS

Siphon

Siphon is an on-demand overload traffic management system [C. Y. Wan, 2005]. It uses a small number of wireless multi radio virtual sinks to prevent congestion at or near base stations. Siphon proposes distributed algorithms that provide virtual sink discovery and selection, congestion detection, traffic redirection, and congestion avoidance in the secondary radio network. Virtual sinks (VSs) are intermediaries between sensor nodes and base stations in the network and are responsible for redirecting data from regions of the sensor network that have increasing traffic loads. Siphon uses an in-band signaling approach to allow nodes with data overload to discover local VSs that could be multiple hops away. Siphon does this by piggybacking a signature byte into a control packet that is periodically advertised by the base station. The signature byte contains the scope (hop-count) of a VS and this information is used to control the visibility of the VS to nodes in its neighborhood. Siphon uses two techniques to detect congestion: node-initiated congestion detection and physical sink initiated post-facto congestion control. Siphon uses a CSMA-based congestion detection technique [C. V. Wan, 2003] to detect local congestion, whereby VS redirects the traffic of nodes within its visibility when their data generation rates exceed a predefined threshold.

Siphon also performs post-mortem analysis of event data at the base station. Siphon activates VS signaling originating at the base station if the reliability of the network degrades below a predefined threshold. This scheme is useful for preventing congestion close to the base station. Siphon uses a secondary radio network to propagate VS signaling in a timely manner without interfering with the operation of the primary-radio network. In addition, VS constantly monitors its congestion level on both primary and secondary radio channels to avoid congestion at any channel. When a channel is overloaded, VS may not advertise its existence or may reduce its service scope. If both channels are overloaded, Siphon uses a traditional fallback mechanism such as controlling data rates at the source node and at forwarding nodes to ease congestion.

Advantages of Siphon are that it prevents the funneling effect at a base station from the many-to-one traffic pattern and it is able to accommodate various traffic load demands in a network. Furthermore, the VS second radio infrastructure allows traffic redirection in a timely manner without degrading the performance of forwarding operations in the primary-radio network. Lastly, VS can detect congestion locally and globally. Global congestion detection performed by the base station is beneficial for avoiding premature funneling problems. Disadvantages of Siphon are that it requires pre-deployment expertise in determining the optimal VS scope (value of hop-count) under different conditions, distributing or selectively placing virtual sinks across the sensor field, and determining the minimum number of virtual sinks required to achieve optimum traffic management performance. In addition, the monetary cost for deploying a multi-radio sensor platform is much higher than a single radio platform. VS with a large number of hop counts may create a funneling problem at the VS. In contrast, a VS with smaller hop counts provides shorter redirection paths from congested nodes to its primary and secondary radio channels to avoid congestion at

any channel. When a channel is overloaded, VS may not advertise its existence or may reduce its service scope. If both channels are overloaded, Siphon uses a traditional fallback mechanism such as controlling data rates at the source node and at forwarding nodes to ease congestion.

Advantages of Siphon are that it prevents the funneling effect at a base station from the many-to-one traffic pattern and it is able to accommodate various traffic load demands in a network. Furthermore, the VS second radio infrastructure allows traffic redirection in a timely manner without degrading the performance of forwarding operations in the primary-radio network. Lastly, VS can detect congestion locally and globally. Global congestion detection performed by the base station is beneficial for avoiding premature funneling problems. Disadvantages of Siphon are that it requires pre-deployment expertise in determining the optimal VS scope (value of hop-count) under different conditions, distributing or selectively placing virtual sinks across the sensor field, and determining the minimum number of virtual sinks required to achieve optimum traffic management performance. In addition, the monetary cost for deploying a multi-radio sensor platform is much higher than a single radio platform. VS with a large number of hop counts may create a funneling problem at the VS. In contrast, VS with smaller hop counts provides shorter redirection paths from congested nodes to it and hence improves delivery latency and energy consumption. However, it requires the application to deploy more VSs to cover the network and this increases the cost of deploying the network, defeating the benefit of using fewer VSs. Furthermore, some nodes may not be covered by any VS as a result of random distribution or limited availability of VSs in a sensor network.

DSN Resource Management

Zhang et al. [J. Zhang, 2001] propose a resource management technique for task oriented distributed sensor networks (DSN) that avoids network congestion while meeting the overall objectives of the network. They propose a 'perflow' method to analyze data streams among nodes at different hierarchical levels of the DSN. In DSNs, the decision stations act as managers for each hierarchical level. Each manager gathers data from nodes in its level, processes their data, and sends the resulting information to the next level manager for further processing. Thus, the information produced at lower levels affects the management decision making process at higher levels, and low level information can be used to meet global objectives set by the highest level.

The per-flow method provides a set of measures for evaluating the importance (degradation and relevance) of incoming data associated with each link at a node. It uses fuzzy logic techniques to determine suitable degradation and relevance values. Basically, each node in the network assigns three weight measures to each of its network links: 1) data quality measured at the node's parent, 2) data timeliness: latency incurred for data to arrive at the node, and 3) data significance in achieving the overall DSN objectives, measured at the node's child. These measurements are used to allocate resources among nodes in a network in which higher weight links get priority over lower weight links. This scheme can reduce data flows in the network and hence prevent network congestion. An advantage of per-flow priority-based resource management is that it integrates and propagates relevant information from the network for achieving the overall objectives of a DSN, hence providing intelligent resource management and congestion avoidance. A limitation of the proposed technique is that its effectiveness depends on finding reliable data weight values, which are prone to WSN uncertainties.

Applications of Network Management Functions

In addition to applications dedicated to network management, many WSN applications incorporate network management functions. For example, TinyDB [S. Madden, 2005] is a query-based processing system for extracting information from sensors in a network. It maintains meta-data describing the types of sensor readings available in the network. It also provides a network topology map to manage the network by monitoring connectivity among nodes, maintaining routing tables, and ensuring that every sensor node in the network delivers its data to the end user efficiently [S. Madden, 2005]. A limitation of TinyDB from a management perspective is that it requires the human manager to control network management operations manually and to interpret the collected management information. Hence, it is necessarily a reactive system in which nodes cannot manage their own behavior based on their sensor readings and topology changes are difficult to capture [M. Welsh, 2004]. Zhao et al. [W. Liu, 2004] utilize in-network aggregation of network states to provide an abstraction of sensor network health, such as a residual energy scan that represents the remaining energy level of sensor nodes [G. Tolle, 2005].

In WSNs, sensor nodes may have overlapping coverage areas and so these nodes produce redundant data. It is beneficial for energy conservation to shut down redundant nodes temporarily or reduce their reporting rates. Tilak et al. [S. Tilak, 2002] propose a congestion avoidance scheme that modifies sensor node reporting rates when the data collected has met a desired reliability. This scheme can reduce the number of transmissions in the sensor network and so prevent network congestion. Perillo and Heinzelman [M. Perillo, 2003] propose a sensor management optimization method to maximize the lifetime of a sensor network while meeting a desired level of reliability. The balance is achieved by selecting and scheduling a set of nodes to be active in monitoring the environment and determining how long and how the data from these nodes should be routed in the network. Redundant nodes are turned off during this time. The management scheme is designed for event-driven applications in which event triggers occur infrequently and only for a short period of time. A set of active nodes is valid if the total bandwidth requirement of the set is within the network's bandwidth capacity and the set meets the desired reliability level. Furthermore, the management scheme models the scheduling and routing requirement as a generalized maximum flow graph problem in order to ensure that active nodes are routed as often as possible. A drawback of the proposed scheme is that the optimization algorithm for solving the graph problem is computationally too complex and expensive for resource-constrained sensor nodes.

Genetic Programming and Sensor Networks

For a long time, Genetic Algorithms have been used in science to derive solutions for any type of problems, from construction of wind turbines to pattern-recognition systems. The application of Genetic Algorithms with the goal to evolve computer programs is called Genetic Programming. This section will give a brief overview on how Genetic Algorithms work in common and how they can be applied to sensor networks. As explained in [Holger Karl, 2003], such devices are restricted in resources like memory size, processing speed, and battery power. The communication among them is costly in terms of energy and not reliable either. Furthermore, the topology of sensor networks is volatile and usually cannot be determined a priori, enforcing self organization. Algorithms and protocols normally applied to distributed systems are therefore often insufficient and need to be replaced with specialized counterparts.

These requirements make programming sensor nodes a demanding task for software developers because the design of sensor network applications must pay attention to aspects that are not directly related to the application functionality itself. We claim that Genetic Programming techniques are an effective means to automatically discover powerful programming solutions for sensor networks.

Clearly, Genetic Programming is not suited to produce very large programs for general application tasks. However, we view sensor nodes as ideal targets for Genetic Programming since these nodes can only perform a limited functionality due to their resource constraints. The Distributed Genetic Programming Framework [DGPF] [Thomas Weise, 2006] allows us to automatically discover distributed algorithms for given problems. Additionally, such algorithms can be optimized in various ways, taking energy consumption into account as well as memory usage or code size. In the next section we describe how Genetic Programming can be applied to sensor networks followed by an example in the third section.

Genetic Algorithms

Genetic Algorithms start with an initial population of random solution candidates called individuals. In our case, the individuals are small programs that can be executed on sensor nodes. As in nature, the population will be refined step by step in a cycle of computing the fitness of its individuals, selecting the best individuals and creating a new generation derived from these. If a reasonable good solution has evolved, the algorithm will terminate. Randomized optimization algorithms are called "multiobjective" if they permit the specification of more than one optimization objective.

Using DGPF, several fitness functions can be defined, allowing optimizing programs not only for functionality but also for nonfunctional requirements like energy consumption and communication frequency. Furthermore, different search algorithms like randomized Hill Climbing and Genetic Algorithms can be combined to speed up the optimization process. In our case the individuals that are being evolved are algorithms in the form of small programs. The functionality and effectiveness of such an algorithm can be determined by simulating it on a virtual hardware representing a single sensor node. In terms of distributed algorithms, it is not sufficient to simulate only one sensor node. Thus multiple instances of the program will be executed in a network simulator in parallel. The following two subsections describe the virtual hardware and the network model used in simulations.

Virtual Hardware

A sensor node is modeled as an automaton that consists of a virtual hardware holding its execution state and a program running on that hardware. Unlike most other approaches in Genetic Programming which grow stateless functions, architecture with a fixed-sized memory have been developed. The instruction set can be reduced to the one introduced by Teller, granting the Turing completeness needed to model real distributed algorithms or network protocols. Like real microprocessors, direct and indirect memory access and a collection of arithmetic expressions are included in the instruction set as well as conditional jumps. Communication is also modeled with primitive directives which allow storing memory words in an output buffer and transmitting the buffered data. A single message can be received into the input buffer and will be processed by reading the received words sequentially. Newly incoming messages get lost if the input buffer is already occupied. The example in the next section displays some of the available instructions.

Network Simulation

The network simulation provides additional statistical data for each automaton, holding information on the number of messages sent, lost, and successfully processed. As in real networks, many automata run asynchronously at approximately the same speed which, however, might differ from node to node and cannot be regarded as constant either. To grant realistic simulations, the network model has the following properties:

- The links between the nodes are randomly created, yet it will be ensured that there are no network partitions.
- Messages are simple word sequences with no predefined structure.
- Messages cannot be sent directly. Like radio broadcasts they will be received by any node in transmission distance. Finding out which message is of concern will be in the responsibility of each node.
- Messages can get lost without special cause.
- Transmissions may take a random time until they reach their target.
- The collision of two transmissions underway leads to the loss of both messages.

Example Algorithms

One example problem that has been solved with the DGPF is the so-called election problem. This problem is well known in the area of distributed computing and therefore we have used it to validate our approach. Election means to select one node out of a group of nodes, for instance to act as a communication relay. Each node owns a unique identifier and all nodes must know the ID of the elected node after the election algorithm has terminated. One method to perform such an election would be to select the node with the maximum ID. Therefore, a functional fitness function that evaluates how many nodes know the maximum ID after a given amount of time should be introduced. Additionally, we enter three non-functional fitness functions into the evolution appear: parsimony pressures for minimum code size, minimum memory size and a minimum transmission count. Each automaton is initialized with its own ID in its memory cell. It took several hours to obtain the solution depicted in the following algorithm using an older version of our framework on a 3 GHz Pentium 4 PC. Most time was spent on the network simulation.

The genetically evolved election algorithm

```
@0:
Send mem[0]
@1:
mem[1]=Receive
If(mem[1]<=mem[0]) Goto @1
@2:
mem[0]=mem[1]
Goto @0
```

Due to many optimizations, the current version of the DGPF runs significantly faster and also incorporates various new distribution schemes [Thomas Weise, 2006] for Genetic Algorithms resulting in further speedup, depending on the number of available computers. The discovered algorithm seems to be simple and quite efficient for the problem definition: The nodes initially send the contents of their first memory cell (their ID) to all neighbors. If and only if a node then receives a greater ID, it stores it in the first memory cell and starts the cycle again. Otherwise, no message is sent which pays respect to the parsimony pressure for minimum transmission count. The node waits instead for incoming transmissions.

APPLICATION OF INTELLIGENT AGENTS IN MANAGING WIRELESS SENSOR NETWORKS

Intelligent agents can be used as a valuable asset when deployed within a wireless sensor network. Wireless sensor networks have a number of limitations, which need to be addressed before creating successful agents. These limitations include issues with energy conservation, mitigating resource limitations and wireless link availability to name a few. Middleware software can be used to overcome these shortcomings and provide a feature-rich environment for intelligent agents to operate in. This section looks at the feasibility of deploying intelligent agents in a wireless sensor network, the requirements for using a middleware solution effectively and evaluates a variety of different commercial and academic middleware currently available for implementing agents in distributed sensor networks.

As we mentioned previously, Wireless sensor networks consist of spatially distributed autonomous devices that take advantage of sensors. Sensor networks typically have a peer-to-peer ad-hoc topology that is common to most other distributed networks. Sensors arrogate data from the environment in which they are deployed. Sensor networks measure a variety of conditions such as temperature, location, sound, motion or other physical activities. When the individual nodes that make up the sensor network are connected wirelessly in an ad-hoc way, the data discovered can have a more profound impact than any one sensor or device. When deployed in situations such as fire detection, pollution detection, traffic monitoring, military reconnaissance, object tracking or various other application domains, the overall ability of wireless sensor networks is impressive. Sensor networks are typically deployed in hostile, unfriendly, and unforgiving environments where fixing, recharging, or replacing individual sensors may be difficult or impossible. Therefore, sensors must be constructed to be robust, redundant and autonomous in order to reduce the dependencies any one sensor has on another.

To reduce dependencies a variety of techniques such as adding redundant sensors, increasing the ability of the sensors to route communications using multi-hop techniques, and adding intelligent agents which analyze data to determine whether or not to transmit results. One focus of this section is on the ability and utility of deploying intelligent agents on a sensor network. Computational power along with the ability to communicate is often diminished significantly due to the severe power constraints put on a node when in a rugged environment. A wireless radio transmitter is almost always the biggest power consumer for a node. Thus reducing communications often provides a significant boost in the lifespan of a node. This requires an intelligent node to effectively balance the need to send data with the amount of power available to transmit and receive data. Sensor networks are designed to have the ability to scale up or down dynamically. Because of the distributed peer-to-peer nature of sensor networks, it is (or should be) trivial for new nodes to be deployed on the fly and seamlessly integrate into the already existing network and instantly contribute to its success. It is possible for nodes to lose contact due to environmental changes, loss of power, or destruction. The robustness of each node can make a real difference in the efficacy of the entire network.

Intelligent Agents

Intelligent agents offer many interesting advantages to sensor networks which cannot be received otherwise. An example is using an agent to preserve battery power by queuing data and limiting the need to transmit data whenever possible, which requires intelligent decisions to be made. Frequently, the biggest consumer of battery power in nodes is the wireless radio device. Reducing its output causes a measurable effect on battery life even if it means consuming a bit more computational resources. People who argue against the use of intelligent agents in a sensor network state that an agent will consume more CPU power than normal, making intelligent agents less desirable. While intelligent agents may consume more resources, they can be used to save more power by making decisions to disable some or all functionality of a node's sensors or effectors (such as GPS or a wireless transmitter). Based on different factors perceived, an agent can choose to hibernate for a given amount of time, suspend other activities, or even turn off the radio entirely to conserve battery life. This simple intelligent decision-making can dramatically increase the lifetime of the network by reducing the need to replace or repair nodes with drained batteries. Assuming there is enough

processing power available on the node, an agent can perform some data analysis at the node level. It is possible the agent will be able to draw conclusions and act independently using any effectors on the node. Aggregating of data will mean sending less unimportant information through the wireless transmitter and therefore contribute to better power consumption. A node can have enough intelligence to communicate with other nodes in the network to gather additional information and make more global decisions, even though the node itself is much localized.

It is possible for intelligent agents to be in some way mobile. There are two types of mobility, physical and logical. Physical mobility involves the agent moving the node physically to a different location in space in order to gather new data. This is often times very costly and hard to do. Instead, an agent can be logically mobile and mode it's code and execution state from one node to another in order to perform data collection or analysis on an entirely new dataset. It's also possible for an agent to clone itself within a network. This would allow the sensor network to use distributed processing available in a peer-to-peer system to its advantage. If middleware does support this logical mobility, it's also important to have a way to remotely monitor and control the agents in case a rogue agent causes a disruption in the network. This alone may be a very difficult solution to solve due to a sensor network's distributed nature. There are some fundamental issues with creating and deploying intelligent agents on a wireless sensor network. Because wireless sensor networks are deployed in rugged and sometimes hostile environments, they are designed to be self sufficient for very long periods of time. Often, the nodes are battery powered, so the hardware needs to be slow to consume minimal energy. Smaller, more robust AI techniques such as goal or utility driven models or expert systems shells are often better formatted to run in a computationally limited embedded environment. Some of the fuzzy systems can work in a sensor network; however they usually require more power than expert systems and may not be feasible in most cases.

Middleware Requirements

Middleware is defined as software that connects software components to applications in order to overcome complex issues in distributed computing. Middleware solutions usually interface with the OS and sometimes hardware devices directly and provide a feature-rich environment for applications to build from. This homogeneous environment allows agents to run on any node with the middleware, leaving all portability issues to the middleware itself. Because middleware solutions have an extensive Application Programming Interface (API), applications need to have less specific code and therefore tend to have a smaller footprint. This is especially advantageous in a wireless sensor network. The smaller the agent application, the easier it fits onto the node or move to other nodes. Middleware for sensor networks needs to accomplish a variety of different tasks in order to be useful. First, the middleware must provide a way for agents to communicate with other agents on different nodes within the network. This includes interfacing with the wireless transmitter/receiver, routing packets to other parts of the network, providing discovery techniques, and solving other peer-to-peer communication problems. Second, the middleware should try to assist agents to correctly and efficiently use the sensors on the node. This will simplify agent development and allow more time and space for

implementing intelligence within the agent itself. A good middleware (Figure 5) solution could have support for an artificial intelligence technique built within the software itself. This could include an expert system or support for fuzzy logic assuming the node is powerful and stable enough to handle the processing requirements (which may or may not be the case). If all of these conditions are met, then the successful intelligent agent or agents can be used to their fullest extent within a wireless sensor network.

SUMMARY AND CONCLUSION

The sensor network management systems reviewed in this chapter have been designed from many different management perspectives. The systems are characterized by their power consumption, memory consumption, bandwidth consumption, fault tolerance, adaptability, and scalability. The development of general purpose network management layer protocols is a challenging problem and remains a largely unexplored area for wireless sensor networks. Wireless sensor networks have continually proven their usefulness in many different fields ranging from temperature regulation to traffic monitoring. Intelligent agents are allowing such sensor networks to be more usable, productive, and available and they will continue to do so as the technology continues to develop.

Because of hardware constraints, using intelligent agents on wireless sensor networks can be

Figure 5. Middleware structure

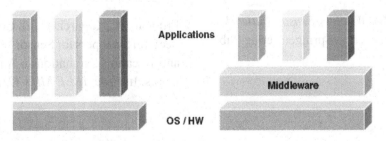

a very difficult task, which is why middleware technologies are needed. Middleware software can reduce the memory footprint, provide mobility to agents, help maintain agents in the network and significantly reduce development time. There are different middleware software solutions for wireless sensor networks available today, each with their own advantages and disadvantages. The final solution depends upon the existing requirements of the implemented wireless sensor network coupled with the best possible middleware to create the desired outcomes. A significant open problem is the development of management policies and expressive languages or metadata for representing management policies and for representing the information exchanged between sensor nodes, managers, and end users.

REFERENCES

Ahmed, A. A., Shi, H., & Shang, Y. (2003). A Survey on Network Protocols for Wireless Sensor Networks. In *Proc. of International Conference on Information Technology: Research and Education* (ITRE'03), (pp. 301 – 305).

Akyildiz, I., Su, W., Sankarasubramaniam, Y., & Cayirci, E. (2002). A survey on Sensor Networks. *IEEE Communications Magazine, 40*(8), 102–114. doi:10.1109/MCOM.2002.1024422

Astro Teller. (1994). Turing completeness in the language of genetic programming with indexed memory. In *Proceedings of the 1994 {IEEE} World Congress on Computational Intelligence, 1,* IEEE Press. Retrieved from http://dgpf.sourceforge.net/documents/006-2006-07-17-kuvs_paper.pdf

Avancha, S. (2003). *Wireless Sensor Networks.* Boston: Kluwer Academic/Springer Verlag Publishers.

Bonabeau, E., Dorigo, M., & Theraulaz, G. (1999). *Swarm Intelligence: From Natural to Artificial Systems, Santa Fe Institute Studies in the Sciences of Complexity.* New York: Oxford University Press.

Boulis, A., & Srivastava, M. B. (2003), "Node-level Energy Management for Sensor Networks in the Presence of Multiple Applications," in Proc. IEEE PerCom Conf.

Bulusu, N., et al. (2001). Scalable coordination for wireless sensor networks: Self-configuring localization systems. In *Proc. of the 6th International Symposium on Communication Theory and Applications* (ISCTA'01), Ambleside, UK

Cam, H., Ozdemir, S., Nair, P., & Muthuavinashippan, D. (2003). (in press). ESPDA [IEEE Sensor, Toronto, Canada]. *Energy-Efficient and Secure Pattern Based Data Aggregation for Wireless Sensor Networks.*

Deb, B., Bhatnagar, S., & Nath, B. (2001). A Topology Discovery Algorithm for Sensor Networks with Applications to Network Management. (Tech. Rep. DCS-TR-441), East Rutherford, NJ: Rutgers University

Deb, B., Bhatnagar, S., & Nath, B. (2004). STREAM: Sensor Topology Retrieval at Multiple Resolutions. *Kluwer Journal of Telecommunications Systems, 26*(2), 285–320. doi:10.1023/B:TELS.0000029043.27689.3f

Deb, S. B. B., & Nath, B. (2002). *A Topology Discovery Algorithm for Sensor Networks with Applications to Network Management.* (Tech. rep. DCSTR-441), Dept. of Computer Science, Rutgers Univ.

Erdogan, A., Cayirci, E., & Coskun, V. (2003). Sectoral Sweepers for Sensor Node Management and Location Estimation in Adhoc Sensor Networks. In *Proc. IEEE MILCOM Conf.*

Fok, C., Roman, G., & Lu, C. (2005). Mobile Agent Middleware for Sensor Networks: An Application Case Study. In *Proc. IEEE ICDCS Conf.*

Hedetniemi, S. M., Hedetniemi, S. H., & Liestman, A. (1988). A Survey of Gossiping and Broadcasting in Communication Networks. *Networks, 18.*

Heinzelman, W., Chandrakasan, A., & Balakrishnan (2000). Energy-Efficient Communication Protocol for Wireless Micro-Sensor Networks. In *Proc. of the 33rd Annual Hawaii International Conf. on System Sciences*, (pp. 3005- 3014).

Heinzelman, W. R., Kulik, J., & Balakrishnan, H. (1999). Adaptive Protocols for Information Dissemination in Wireless Sensor Networks. In *Proc. ACM MobiCom '99*, Seattle, WA.

Hoblos, K. G. Staroswiecki, M., & Aitouche, A. (2000). *Optimal Design of Fault Tolerant Sensor Networks.* IEEE Int'l. Conf. Cont. Apps., Anchorage, AK, (pp. 467-72)

Holger, K., & Andreas, W. (2003). *A short Survey of Wireless Sensor Networks.* (TKN Technical Report) TKN-03-018, Berlin.

Hsin, C., M. Liu (2006), "A Two-Phase Self-Monitoring Mechanism for Wireless Sensor Networks. *Journal of Computer Communications special issue on Sensor Networks, 29*(4), 462–476.

IBM. (2003). *An Architectural Blueprint for Autonomic Computing.* IBM and Autonomic Computing. Retrieved from http://www.redbooks.ibm.com/redbooks/pdfs/sg246635.pdf

Intanagonwiwat, C. Estrin, D., & Gonvindan, R. (2001). *Impact of Network Density on Data Aggregation in Wireless Sensor Networks.* In Proc. IEEE ICDCS Conf.

Intanagonwiwat, C., Govindan, R., & Estrin, D. Heidemann, J., & Silva, F. (2003), "Directed Diffusion for Wireless Sensor Networking," IEEE/ACM Transactions on Networking, vol. 11, pp. 2-16

Iyer, R., & Kleinrock, L. (2003). *QoS Control for Sensor Networks.* Presented at the IEEE International Communications Conference (ICC' 03), Anchorage, AK, May 11-15.

Karl, H., & Willig, A. (2003). *A Short Survey of Wireless Sensor Networks. (Technical Report).* Telecommunication Networks Group, Technische Universität Berlin.

Kay, J., & Frolik, J. (2004). Quality of Service Analysis and Control for Wireless Sensor Networks. In *Proc. of the 21st International Conf. on Mobile Ad-Hoc and Sensor Systems* (MASS'04), pp. 359-368, Fort Lauderdale, FL.

Kim, T. H., & Hong, S. (2003). Sensor Network Management Protocol for State-Driven Execution Environment. In *Proc. ICUC Conf.*

Krishnamachari, B. (2003). On the Complexity of Distributed Self-Configuration in Wireless Networks. Kluwer Academic Springer Publishers. *Telecommunication Systems, 22*(1-4), 33–59. doi:10.1023/A:1023426501170

Kulik, J., Heinzelman, W. R., & Balakrishnan, H. (2002). Negotiation-base protocols for Disseminating Information in Wireless Sensor Networks. *Wireless Networks, 8,* 169–185. doi:10.1023/A:1013715909417

Lindsey, S., & Raghavendra, C. S. (2002). PEGASIS: Power-Efficient Gathering in Sensor Information Systems. In *Proc. of IEEE Aerospace Conference*, Montana.

Liu, W., Zhang, Y., Lou, W., & Fang, Y. (2004). Managing Wireless Sensor Network with Supply Chain Strategy. In *Proc. IEEE QSHINE Conf.*

Louis Lee, W., Datta, A., & Cardell-Oliver, R. (2006). *WinMS: Wireless Sensor network-Management system, An Adaptive Policy-based Management for Wireless Sensor Networks* (Tech. Rep. UWA-CSSE-06-001), The University of Western Australia.

Min, R., et al. (2001). Low Power Wireless Sensor Networks. In *Proceedings of International Conference on VLSI Design*, Bangalore, India

Passos, R. M., Coelho, C. J. N., Loureiro, A. A. F., & Mini, R. A. F. (2005). Dynamic Power Management in Wireless Sensor Networks: An Application-Driven Approach. In *Proc. of the 2nd Annu. Conference on Wireless On-demand Network Systems and Services* (WONS '05), (pp. 109 – 118)

Perillo, M., & Heinzelman, W. B. (2003). Providing Application QoS through Intelligent Sensor Management. In *Proc. IEEE SNPA Conf.*

Perrig, A., et al. (2004). Security in wireless sensor networks," Communications of the ACM (CACM), *Wireless sensor networks, Special Issue: Wireless sensor networks, 47*(6), 53-57.

Rajaravivarma, V., Yang, Y., & Yang, T. (2003). An Overview of Wireless Sensor Network and Applications. In *Proc. of the 35th Southeastern Symposium on System Theory*, (pp. 432-436).

Ramanathan, N., Kohler, E., & Estrin, D. (2005). Towards a Debugging System for Sensor Networks. *International Journal of Network Management, 15*(4), 223–234. doi:10.1002/nem.570

Ramanathan, N., & Yarvis, M. (2005). A Stream-oriented Power Management Protocol for Low Duty Cycle Sensor Network Applications. In Proc. IEEE EmNetS-II Workshop

Romer, K., & Mattern, F. (2004). *The Design Space of Wireless Sensor Networks* (pp. 54–61). IEEE Wireless Communications.

Ruiz, L. B., Braga, T. R. M., Silva, A., Assuncao, H. P., Nogueira, J. M. S., & Loureiro, A. A. F. (2005). On the Design of a Self- Managed Wireless Sensor Network. *Communications Magazine, IEEE, 43*(8), 95–102. doi:10.1109/MCOM.2005.1497559

Ruiz, L. B., Nogueira, J. M., & Loureiro, A. A. F. (2003). MANNA: A Management Architecture for Wireless Sensor Networks. *IEEE Communications Magazine, 41*(2), 116–125. doi:10.1109/MCOM.2003.1179560

Ruiz, L. B., Nogueira, J. M. S., & Loureiro, A. A. F. (2003). MANNA: A Management Architecture for Wireless Sensor Networks. *IEEE Communications Magazine, 41*(2), 116–125. doi:10.1109/MCOM.2003.1179560

Ruiz, L. B., Silva, F. A., Braga, T. R. M., Nogueira, J. M. S., & Loureiro, A. A. F. (2004). On Impact of Management in Wireless Sensors Networks. In *Proc. of the 9th IEEE/IFIP Network Operations and Management Symposium* (NOMS' 04) vol. 1, pp. 657 - 670, Seoul, Korea

Ruiz, L. B., Siqueira, I. G., Oliveira, L. B., Wong, H. C., Nogueira, J. M. S., & Loureiro, A. A. F. (2004). Fault Management in Event-Driven Wireless Sensor Networks. In *Proc. ACM MSWiM Conf.* Retrieved from http://telegraph.cs.berkeley.edu/tinydb/tinydb.pdf, 2005.

Shah, R. C., & Rabaey, J. M. (2002). Energy Aware Routing for Low Energy Ad Hoc Senso Networks. In *Proceedings of IEEE Wireless Communications and Networking Conference* (WCNC), Orland, FL

Shen, C. Srisathapornphat, C., & Jaikaeo, C. (2001). *Sensor Information Networking Architecture and Applications*. IEEE Personal Communication. (pp. 52-59).

Shi, E., & Perrig, A. (2004). *Designing Secure Sensor Networks* (pp. 38–43). IEEE Wireless Communications.

Sinha, A., & Chandrakasan, A. (2001). Dynamic power management in wireless sensor networks. *Design and Test of Computers, IEEE, 18*(2), 62–74. doi:10.1109/54.914626

Song, H. Kim, D. Lee, K., & Sung, J. (2005). Upnp-Based Sensor Network Management Architecture. In *Proc. ICMU Conf.*

Tilak, S. Abu-Ghazaleh, N. B., & Heinzelman, W. (2002). Infrastructure tradeoffs for sensor networks. In Proc. *ACM WSNA Conf.*

Tilak, S., Abu-Ghazaleh, N., & Heinzelman, W. (2002). A taxonomy of Wireless Micro-senor Network Models. *ACM SIGMOBILE. Mobile Computing and Communications Review, 6*(2), 28–36. doi:10.1145/565702.565708

Tolle, G., & Culler, D. (2005). Design of an Application- Cooperative Management System for Wireless Sensor Networks. In *Proc. EWSN*

Townsend, C., & Arms, S. (2004). *Wireless Sensor Networks: Principles and Applications*. Williston, VT: Micro Strain Inc.

Turon, M. (2005). Mote-View: A Sensor Network Monitoring and Management Tool," in Proc. IEEE EmNetS-II Workshop

Tynan, R., & Marsh, D. OKane, D., & OHare, G. M. P. (2005). Agents for Wireless Sensor Network Power Management. In *Proc. IEEE ICPPW Conf.*

Tynan, R., Marsh, D., O'Kane, D., & O'Hare, G. M. P. (2005). Agents for wireless sensor network power management. In *Proc of International Conference workshops on Parallel Processing* (ICPP '05) Workshops, (pp. 413-418).

Viera, M. A. M. Viera, L. F. M. Ruiz, L. B. Loureiro, A. A. F. Fernandes, A. O. Nogueira, J. M. S. (2003). Scheduling Nodes in Wireless Sensor Networks: A Voronoi Approach. In *Proc. of the 28th Annual IEEE International Conference on Local Computer Networks* (LCN '03), (pp.423 – 429), 20-24.

Wan, C.-Y., Eisenman, S. B., & Campbell, A. T. (2003). CODA: COngestion Detection and Avoidance in Sensor Networks. In *Proc. ACM SenSys Conf.*

Wan, C.-Y., Eisenman, S. B., Campbell, A. T., & Crowcrof, J. (2005). Siphon: Overload Traffic Management using Multi-radio Virtual Sinks in Sensor Networks. In *Proc. ACM SenSys Conf.*

Warneke, B., & Pister, K. S. J. (2002, September). MEMS for Distributed Wireless Sensor Networks. In *Proc. of 9th International Conf. on Electronics, Circuits and Systems*. Dubrovnik, Croatia.

Weise, T., & Geihs, K. (2006). *DGPF - An Adaptable Framework for Distributed Multi-Objective Search Algorithms Applied to the Genetic Programming of Sensor Networks*. The 2nd International Conference on Bioinspired Optimization Methods and their Applications, Ljubljana, Slovenia

Welsh, M., & Mainland, G. (2004). Programming Sensor Networks Using Abstract Regions. In *Proc. USENIX NSDI Conf.*

Ying, Z., & Debao, X. (2005). Mobile Agent-based Policy Management for Wireless Sensor Networks. *In Proc. IEEE WCNM Conf.*

Yoneki, E., & Bacon, J. (n.d.). *A survey of Wireless Sensor Network technologies: research trends and middleware's role*. (Technical Report, no: 646), UCAM ¡CL¡TR¡646,

Yu, Y., Govindan, R., & Estrin, D. (2001). *Geographical and Energy Aware Routing: A Recursive Data Dissemination Protocol for Wireless Sensor Networks*. UCLA Computer Science Department UCLA-CSD TR-01-0023

Zhang, J., Kulasekere, E. C., Premaratne, K., & Bauer, P. H. (2001). Resource Management of Task Oriented Distributed Sensor Networks. In *Proc. IEEE ICASSP Conf.*

Zhao, Y. J., Govindan, R., & Estrin, D. (2002). Residual Energy Scan for Monitoring Sensor Networks. In Proc. IEEE WCNC Conf.

KEY TERMS AND DEFINITIONS

Connectivity: A permanent connection between any two individual sensor nodes that are densely deployed in a sensor network defines the network connectivity.

Coverage: The sensor node's view of the environment that it is situated in is limited both in range and in accuracy. This means the ability of sensor nodes to cover physical area of the environment is limited

Data Aggregation/Data Fusion: It is the task of reducing data size by summarizing the data into a set of meaningful information via computation while data are propagating through the wireless sensor network (in this context)

Directed Diffusion: It is a data dissemination and aggregation protocol. It is a data-centric and application aware routing protocol for WSNs. It aims at naming all data generated by sensor nodes by attribute-value pairs.

Flooding: It is an old routing mechanism that is used in sensor networks. In flooding, a node sends out the received data or the management packets to its neighbors by broadcasting, unless a maximum number of hops for that packet are reached or the destination of the packets is arrived.

Geographical and Energy Aware Routing (GEAR): It is a recursive data dissemination protocol WSNs. It uses energy aware and geographically informed neighbor selection heuristics to rout a packet to the targeted region

Gossiping Protocol: It is a mechanism in which nodes can forward the incoming data/packets to randomly selected neighbor node. Once a gossiping node receives the messages, it can forward the data back to that neighbor or to another one randomly selected neighbor node.

Implosion: It is the case where a duplicated data or packets are sent to the same node.

Low Energy Adaptive Clustering Hierarchy (LEACH): It is a self-organizing, adaptive clustering-based protocol that uses randomized rotation of cluster-heads to evenly distribute the energy load among the sensor nodes in the network.

Mesh Network: It is a network which allows any node in the network to transmit to any other node in the network that is within its radio transmission range.

Power-Efficient GAthering in Sensor Information Systems (PEGASIS): A greedy chain-based power efficient algorithm]. PEGASIS is based on LEACH (the scenario and the radio model in PEGASIS are the same as in LEACH).

Reliability: reliability or fault tolerance of a sensor node is the ability to maintain the sensor network functionalities without any interruption due to sensor node failure

Siphon: It is an on-demand overload traffic management system which uses a small number of wireless multi radio virtual sinks to prevent congestion at or near base stations.

Star Network: It is a network which represents one of the communications topology in which there exists a single base station send and/or receives a message to a number of remote nodes.

Wireless Sensor Network (WSN): It is a network made of a numerous number of sensor nodes with sensing, wireless communications and computation capabilities.

Chapter 5
Mesh Wi–Fi Networks:
Architectures and Experimental Results

E. Patiniotakis
Hellenic Telecommunications Organization S.A. (OTE), Greece

St. Perdikouris
Hellenic Telecommunications Organization S.A. (OTE), Greece

G. Agapiou
Hellenic Telecommunications Organization S.A. (OTE), Greece

I. Chochliouros
Hellenic Telecommunications Organization S.A. (OTE), Greece

K. Voudouris
Technological Educational Institute of Athens, TEI-A, Greece

E. Dimitriadou
Hellenic Telecommunications Organization S.A. (OTE), Greece

I. Fraimis
Wireless Telecommunications Laboratory, University of Patras, Greece

A. Ioannou
Hellenic Telecommunications Organization S.A. (OTE), Greece

ABSTRACT

Wi-Fi mesh is a fast growing and mature technology which is widely used and has been proven very useful for healthcare including applications for ambient people. In this chapter, we attempt a quick introduction of the principles of 802.11s protocol that refers to mesh topology Wi-Fi networks. Specifically, we describe the main operations and functions performed in a Wi-Fi mesh network such as routing procedures, synchronization as well as QoS capabilities and security mechanisms that are crucial for carrying sensitive information like medical data. Finally, in the second part of this chapter, actual measurements

DOI: 10.4018/978-1-61520-805-0.ch005

are presented from an experimental network that consisted of four dual radio (2.4 GHz and 5 GHz) mesh access points. Key parameters are evaluated, such as maximum throughput for different distances, jitter, delay and data loss which affect the transmission of sensitive data. Moreover, the handover capability of the system is presented in terms of data throughput and voice quality degradation during the transition.

INTRODUCTION

The hot spot networks also called Wide Local Area Network (WLAN) was proved unable to offer high bit rate capacities in large geographical areas. WLAN mesh technologies declare that they can offer an economic way of deploying broadband, large scale wireless networks. As the mesh technology became very popular and many vendors started to adopt it, there was an extended need for standardization and interoperability, mainly due to market requirements. For this reason, IEEE 802.11s Task Group was formed (September 2004). At the time of this article, 802.11s draft version 2.02 has been approved while the final 802.11s was scheduled for completion in August 2009.

The aim of this Task is to work out all the essential operations and energies to extend the traditional WLAN networks in order to efficiently support further mesh networking. The existing standard needs to be amended so that it will include new operations or modifications of the already existing ones, like Quality of Service (QoS), power saving, routing and forwarding as much as the management and configuration of a mesh network is concerned. The ultimate goal is to address all the issues for the creation of a self-configuring, self-healing, and self-monitoring WLAN mesh network. The main effort of the Task is to make the necessary changes to the basic 802.11 MAC protocol so that the delivery of unicast, multicast and broadcast frames would be feasible, by using radio-aware metrics; on the contrary, the PHY layer is not expected to change at all.

TECHNOLOGY OVERVIEW

WLAN mesh networks are targeted primarily for home, commercial, neighborhood, community, municipality, rural broadband, emergency and first responder, and public safety. Also for small to medium business, large enterprise and military networks.

The 802.11 mesh network is created from a collection of access points (APs) interconnected via wireless transmission that enables automatic topology learning and dynamic path configuration to occur. The network is decentralized and simplified because each node needs to transmit only as far as the next node. The frequency used for the communication between access points is either 2.4 GHZ (802.11g) or 5 GHz (802.11a). The maximum throughput in all cases is 54 Mbps. At this point it is important to mention that the upcoming 802.11n standard which uses Multiple Input- Multiple Output (MIMO) techniques promises rates up to 300 Mbps. The mesh access points (MAPs) are typical 802.11 access points that have routing and/or forwarding capabilities so that they can connect to each other and identify all the possible hops from source to destination. If one mesh point has also the capability to serve client stations or non-mesh nodes, it is called mesh point (MP). In most mesh Wi-Fi networks; there exists an access point (often called as "root MP") that has two interfaces. The one is a wireless interface so that it establishes connections with all neighboring MPs, while it has also a contact to the wired network. This MP is referred as Mesh Portal (MPP).

WLAN mesh networks are defined as:

Figure 1. Typical mesh network

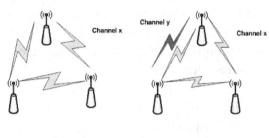

WLAN mesh is an IEEE 802.11-based wireless distribution system (WDS), which is a part of a distribution system (DS), consisting of a set of two or more MPs interconnected by IEEE 802.11 links and communicating through the WLAN mesh services. A WLAN mesh may support zero or more entry points (mesh portals [MPPs]), automatic topology learning, and dynamic path selection (including across multiple hops) [1].

A set of MP radio interfaces that are interconnected to each other using the same channel are referred to as a unified channel graph (UCG).

WLAN MEDIUM ACCESS CONTROL

Classical 802.11 MAC protocol is contention based, using distributed coordination function (DCG) or contention free, using point coordination function. The typical 802.11 MAC is adapted in WLAN mesh 802.11s with same amendments. A new service that needs to be added is the ability of multichannel mode. In this mode, it is assumed that each MP possesses multiple WLAN interfaces and that they use different channels in order to connect with peer MPs. Such an MP is able to dynamically allocate a frequency channel to each wireless link in accordance with network topology and traffic conditions. This can lead to increasing network capacity by load balancing and can solve the problem of a "hidden node". An example of multichannel mode is shown

in Figure 2. The advantage of using dual radio capable MPs is that the 802.11a band can be used for backhauling purposes (mesh connections between the APs) and the other (802.11g) is available for the end users (network access part). This essentially doubles the bandwidth offered by the system, because the access points do not need to switch, i.e. from reception to transmission mode, like they have to do when they use a single radio. In addition, when access points have a single radio, network capacity per node scales as $\Theta\left(\frac{1}{\sqrt{n}}\right)$ due to interference and half duplex radios.

Another addition to the 802.11 is the so called Mesh Deterministic Access (MDA) mechanism. This mechanism allows MPs that possibly interfere with each other, to access the channel with lower contention at certain times. Power saving (PS) mode is an optional feature of 802.11s. If an MP is a PS-capable MP, it advertises its PS state via the beacons. While in the PS mode, MPs periodically wake and listen for Delivery Traffic Indication Message (DTIM) beacons and remain awake for the time window specified within the Announcement Traffic Indication Message (ATIM). MPs that want to communicate with PS

Figure 2. Different channel modes

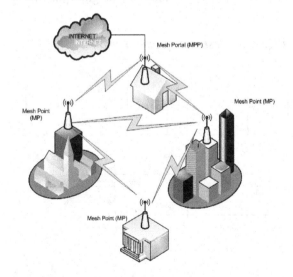

MPs, buffer data and deliver it in one of the following ways:

- By sending the traffic in the agreed upon schedule as part of the Automatic Power Save Delivery (APSD).
- By sending traffic during the ATIM window to request PS-enabled MP to stay awake past the ATIM window.
- By sending a single Null-Data packet during ATIM window to reactivate a suspended flow or change PS state [2].

The frame format of WLAN mesh frames is similar to the standard 802.11 MAC frame format but it has been enhanced so that it can be used for Extended Service Set (ESS) mesh services where mesh APs are connected in a distributed mode. In order to prevent infinite frame forwarding and loops, the mesh forwarding control field in MAC header (24 bits) contains an extra field which has the same functionality as the Time to Live (TTL) IP field. In addition, the MAC header incorporates a sequence number which is useful for controlling broadcast and other services. Mesh data frame format is illustrated in Figure 3.

The first draft of 802.11s has proposed two new control frames for backhauling channel selection: Request to Switch (RTX) and Clear to Switch (CTX). As it is obvious, all neighboring MPs

Figure 3. Mesh data frame format

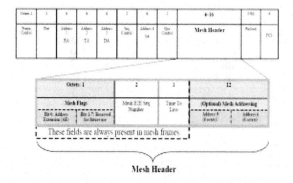

Mesh Header

should be capable of exchanging management frames which contain additional elements, related with the mesh operation beyond the already existed one in typical 802.11 frames. Some among the main elements are:

- Mesh ID
- Mesh capability
- Neighbor list
- MPP (root MP) reachability
- Peer request
- Peer response
- Active profile management

Functions such as neighbor discovery and synchronization use 802.11 management frames and encode the appropriate information elements by each mechanism.

As it was mentioned earlier, a wireless mesh network may include MPs with one or multiple radio interfaces. Furthermore, each MP may utilize more than one channel for its communication with other neighboring access points. The channel can be the same and unique at a specific time, if channel switching capability is absent. In this case, the entire wireless mesh cloud becomes one (giant) Ethernet switch. If such a multichanneling capability exists, then the MP can communicate simultaneously at multiple channels, even in different mesh networks. Dynamic frequency selection (DFS) is a crucial feature that all mesh access points have to adopt. The frequency range that 802.11g as much as 802.11a utilize, belongs to the unlicensed band. This means that a lot of other devices (rogue access points, radars, etc.) are possible interferers which may lead to significant degradation on the WLAN's mesh performance and in "extreme" situations, even to the disability of offering services. For that reason, all MPs should scan periodically all the available range for interference and change channel, according to criteria depending on the topology and the application requirements.

NETWORK DISCOVERY

When a mesh access point which belongs to a single UCG boots, it starts scanning all the available channels for neighbors. If it discovers other MPs, then it chooses a mesh ID from its profile, an operation channel, as well as an initial arbitrary channel precedence value. When it discovers other mesh access points that advertise various channels, it prefers the one with the highest precedence value. During the network discovery process, an MP executes two sub-operations: (a) Topology discovery, and; (b) Neighbor discovery. The first operation depends on the profile that each MP carries. [A profile consists of elements like mesh ID, path selection protocol identifier and path selection metric identifier].

Thus, in order to discover neighboring mesh access points, an MP starts scanning. The type of scanning is either "active" or "passive". In the latter case, an MP considers another one as a neighbor, if some specific attributes received on the beacon are the same with the ones stored in its profile (e.g. mesh ID). A neighbor MP needs to satisfy some further requirements in order to be considered as a "candidate peer". In the case when a newly discovered MP has a different path selection protocol and metric(s), it is ignored.

An MP tries to establish connections with all peer (same mesh ID) MPs. In the case where it is not capable of being associated with all its neighbors, it has to make a "choice", on the basis of signal quality criteria measured during the discovery phase or informed by other neighboring MPs. Such criteria are often the following:

- The current bit rate which can be achieved, depending on the highest possible modulation scheme.
- The packet error rate at the current bit rate.

CHANNEL ALLOCATION

During the lifetime of a mesh network, one or more MPs may choose to change their operation channel as a result of the Dynamic Frequency Selection (DFS) feature. When an MP determines the need to switch the channel of the UCG in which it belongs, it builds a Mesh Channel Switch Announcement (MCSA) element in order to advertise the transition to a new channel. This frame includes the Mesh ID, the new channel number and the corresponding precedence value. Then, the MP chooses a mesh channel switch timer until it actually switches to the new channel and sends the MCSA to all peer MPs that belong to the same UCG. After sending the advertisement, it updates its candidate channel (and its candidate channel precedence indicator), and sets the Channel Switch count (CSC) field value to the chosen wait time.

If an MP receives a MCSA with a channel precedence value larger than the current channel precedence value at the PHY on which the frame was received, the MP shall set an Mesh Channel Switch (MCS) timer equal to the channel switch count value of the frame; then it sends a mesh channel announcement to its peers, by copying the values from the received MCSA. It is possible that more than one MPs inside the unified channel graph may independently detect the need to switch channel, and so to be able to send separate MCSA. The main principle that an MP which receives multiple MCSAs follows is that it takes action only when the channel precedence value is larger than the channel precedence value of a previously received announcement frame. If it receives two announcements with the same precedence value, it makes a choice, on the basis of the source address (smaller is the prevailing one).

The channel switch should be scheduled so that all neighbor peer MPs (including MPs in power save mode) have the opportunity to receive at least one MCSA element before switching. The MP may send the MCSA frame after determining that the wireless medium is idle for one PIFS period and performing backoff. It is possible that a channel switch is successful in moving all neighbor peer MPs to the new channel selected. After changing to the new channel, the peer link should be re-established [3].

SYNCHRONIZATION

MPs can be either synchronized or not. In the first case, MPs use their own independent timer; in the other case, MPs update their timer, conformant to information received by the beacons and probe responses from other synchronized MPs. Any MP may choose to send beacon frames at specific intervals. Such an interval shall vary between unsynchronized and synchronized mesh access points. Unsynchronized MPs use the Mesh Beacon Collision Avoidance (MBCA) protocol in order to minimize the possibility of transmitting a beacon at the same time as a neighboring MP. MPs which are not capable of transmitting beacons designate other MPs to send beacons on their behalf.

ROUTING-FORWARDING

One of the most essential functions on Wi-Fi mesh architectures is the routing-forwarding. The terms "path selection" and "mesh forwarding" describe the selection of single hop or multihop paths and the forwarding of data through these paths. WLAN mesh routing framework is mainly based on layer-2 or MAC layer routing. Layer 2 routing offers faster access to more status information of layer 2 and physical layer, faster forwarding, and improvements of media access with respect to wireless multihop communication.

In mesh networks consisting of multiple hops it is likely to have out-of-order or duplicated frames. This possibility becomes considerable when the number of MPs increases or when the network is heavily loaded. The legacy 802.11 standard does not offer an end-to–end (E2E) protection mecha-

nism. For this reason, a new field is implemented in mesh networks, called as E2E sequence number, in order to identify data frames sent from a given source MP. Out-of-order frames are stored in a buffer for a specific time so that they can be served to LLC in right sequence while duplicated frames get discarded. 802.11s Task Group declares a desired maximum of 32 routing nodes participating as APs forwarders in a mesh network and larger configurations may also be contemplated by the standard. Thus, the ultimate maximum size of a mesh network is unclear at this time.

The format used in mesh networks is the same as the 802.11 standard [i.e. a four address link layer format] enriched with additional information that is relative to mesh operation (see Figure 3).

It is important to have a default routing protocol and radio metric that all devices from different vendors should be required to implement, to ensure interoperability and to have an extensible framework enabling the implementation of various routing protocols and radio metrics optimized for different usage environments. Only one protocol can be active on a particular link at a certain time, although an MP may have multiple routing protocols stored in its profile(s).

Certainly, 802.11s allows any path selection metric to be implemented on a selected path. All nodes have to employ radio aware path selection metric, so that to ensure a common routing metric. The cost function for the establishment of the radio-aware paths is based on airtime cost. The Airtime Link Metric is used to calculate each pairwise link within a mesh network and it is defined as the amount of channel recourses consumed by transmitting the frame over a particular link. This metric is easily implemented and can enforce interoperability. The airtime cost is calculated as:

$$C_a = (O_{ca} + O_p + \frac{B_t}{r}) \times \left(\frac{1}{1 - e_{pt}}\right),$$

O_{ca} is the channel access overhead (75μs for 802.11a and 335 μs for 902.11b),

O_p is the protocol overhead (110 μs 802.11a, 364 μs 802.11b),

B_t represents the number of bits of a test frame of 1000 bytes,

r equals to (the) bit rate in Mbps and

e_{pt} is the frame error rate.

HYBRID WIRELESS MESH PROTOCOL

The current IEEE mesh draft mandates the use of a specific frame routing protocol. A mesh point may support the default Hybrid Wireless Mesh Protocol (HWMP), another routing protocol called as Routing Aware Optimizes Link State Routing (RA-OLSR) as it will be later discussed in the scope of the present work, or a vendor specific protocol. HWMP offers the flexibility of on-demand routing with proactive topology tree extensions. This combination allows MPs to discover and sustain the best routes or to rely on the formation of a tree structure based on a root node (logically placed in a MPP). HWMP uses a single set of protocol primitives deriving from the Ad Hoc on Demand Distance Vector (AODV) protocol. It supports two modes of operation depending on the configuration. These are the following:

- On demand mode. This mode allows MPs to communicate using peer-to-peer routes. This mode is used when the mesh network has no root node configured and in certain circumstances even if a root node exists.
- Proactive tree building mode. In that case, other MPs proactively maintain routes to the root node and a proactive, distance vector routing tree is created and maintained.

These modes are not exclusive and therefore may be used concurrently.

At this point it is very important to distinguish reactive from proactive protocols. Reactive protocols compute a route only when it is needed. This reduces the control overhead but introduces latency for the first packet to be sent due to the time needed for building the route path. In proactive protocols, every node knows a route to every other node at all times. In this case there is no latency, but permanent maintenance of unused routes increases the control overhead especially if the network topology changes frequently. Hybrid protocols try to combine the best features of each one of the protocols mentioned before. This means that a hybrid routing protocol uses on-demand routes for peer-to-peer communication and establishes proactive routes for communications with gateway and other important nodes. Some of the advantages of HWMP hybrid routing are:

- It suits to a variety of usage scenarios.
- Low complexity.
- Reduced flooding of route discovery packets when a root node exists.
- If one on-demand route fails or becomes temporarily unavailable, tree topology routes can be used as a backup.

TREE BASED ROUTING

When a mesh portal (MPP) exists in a mesh network, then it can be used as a reference node for all routes. The MPP announces itself to all nodes using a broadcast route announcement message which includes the distance metric and a sequence number. Any MP receiving this message, creates or updates its forwarding information to the root MP (MPP), updates the metric and hops count of the route request message, records the metric and hops count to the root and retransmits the updated route request. Thus, information about the presence and the distance to an available root is disseminated to all MPs in the network. An MP which receives multiple route requests updates its current forwarding information if and only if one of the route requests (RREQ) messages contains a greater sequence number, or the sequence number is the same but the metric offered is better. When a node needs to send a frame to another node but does not have any routing information (specific path to this node) for it, it sends the frame to the root. Then the root checks its forwarding table and resends the frame either to its uplink (frame destination out of the mesh network) or to the next node which belongs to the path (beginning) from the root towards the destination. This MP which actually knows the address of the destination node sends a route request back to the source. As a result, an optimal on-demand route is created between the source and (the) destination. All the remainder frames will be forwarded across this new path. A key point about this tree topology mode is that when there are multiple MPPs, only one undertakes the role of the root node.

ON DEMAND ROUTING IN HWMP

On demand routing in HWMP uses route request and route reply messages in order to discover link metric information from a source to a destination. When an MP wants to send a frame to an unknown address it sends a broadcast RREQ with the destination MP specified in the destination list and metric field initialized to zero. When a MP receives a RREQ it behaves like in tree topology mode. When an intermediate MP forwards a RREQ, it changes the value of the metric field so that it represents the metric of the route to the RREQ's source. After creating or updating a route to the source, the destination MP sends a unicast RREP back to the source. Legacy STAs which do not have the ability to send and manage the frames used with on-demand routing, authorize the MAPs with which they are associated to do all the necessary operation(s) on behalf of them.

Except of the Hybrid Wireless Mesh Protocol which is a mandatory protocol of 802.11s draft,

there is an optional routing protocol called Radio-Aware Optimized Link-State Routing Protocol (RA-OLSR). RA-OLSR is a proactive, link state wireless mesh path selection protocol based on Optimized Link State Routing [IETF RFC 3626] with extensions from another routing protocol named Fisheye State Routing (FSR) protocol [4]. RA-OLSR enables the discovery and maintenance of optimal routes based on a predefined metric, given that each MP has a mechanism to determine the metric cost of a link to each of its neighbors. A metric field is used in information elements so that the metric link cost propagates between MPs. In disseminating topology information over the network, RA-OLSR adopts some specific approaches in order to reduce the related control overhead. It also includes an association discovery and maintenance protocol to support STAs that implement the legacy 802.11 standard. RA-OLSR offers the stability of a link-state protocol and at the same time it can immediately have routes available when needed because of its proactive nature.

SECURITY ON MESH WLAN NETWORKS

New security mechanisms must be defined for authenticating and securing MP-to-MP links. Multiple credential(s) types are supported for authentication such as pre-shared keys and digital

Figure 4. WLAN mesh security framework

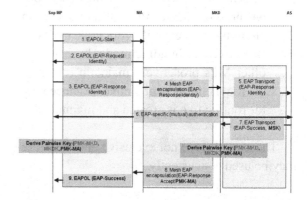

certificates. Before allowing a user or an MP to join the network, the device must be authenticated. 802.11s security proposals secure only links between MPs so it cannot offer an end-to-end solution. This can be achieved in upper layers (e.g. IPSec/VPN). The protocol requirements for secure mesh formation are dynamically generation of ephemeral keys, not susceptible to passive or active attacks and DoS resistance. For link by link security, 802.11s uses the main principles of 802.11i Robust Security Network Association (RSNA) with some necessary extensions. Figure 4 shows the proposed mesh authentication approach which extends the IEEE 802.11 EAP based authentication.

An MP operates as a supplicant, authenticator and in some cases it can play the role of the Authentication Server (AS). When a new node joins the mesh network (see Figure 5), it negotiates its role in the authentication process with its neighbor(s). If this new node cannot reach an AS and the other MP can (common case), then the MP which has a path to the AS becomes the Authenticator. If both of them have a connection to an AS then the one with the higher MAC address is assumed to be the Authenticator and the other becomes the supplicant. When the roles have been defined, the MPs perform a 4-way handshake. The result of this handshake is the creation of a pairwise key used for unicast transmissions and a separate group key for broadcasting/multicasting. These keys are renewed periodically by the AS. The pre-shared security mode, although it

can be used, it is not scalable for mesh networks that inherently include multiple hops.

QOS ON MESH NETWORKS

QoS provision over a wireless multihop mesh network is a real challenge. 802.11s includes mechanisms that allow voice, video and other QoS-demanding applications to be forwarded successfully over the mesh network. IEEE 802.11e and Enhanced Distribution channel access (EDCA) are used for accomplishing QoS. Each MP contends for the channel independently without caring about the status of other nodes. Local congestion occurs when an intermediate MP receives more packets than it can transmit which may lead to serious degradation on QoS handling of other nodes because a hop is not isolated from other hops.

Nodes blindly transmit as many packets as possible, regardless of how many reach their destination. This results in throughput degradation and performance inefficiency. Congestion control for real time applications is very important across multiple hops. Because all of these use UDP, a transport layer congestion control is meaningless. There is a single hop-by-hop Intra-Mesh Congestion Control which includes three basic steps:

- Local congestion monitoring: Each node actively monitors local channel utilization. If congestion is detected, it notifies previous-hop neighbors and/or the (whole) neighborhood.
- Congestion control signaling:
  ○ Congestion Control Request (unicast)
  ○ Congestion Control Response (unicast)
  ○ Neighborhood Congestion Announcement (broadcast)
- Local rate control: Each node that receives either a unicast or broadcast congestion notification message should adjust its traffic generation rate accordingly.

Figure 5. A new MP joins the network

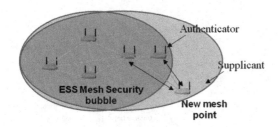

WLAN MESH MEASUREMENTS

Mesh networks are self healing and self-configuring. Mesh nodes discover each other and determine the optimum frequency scheme for communicating with their neighboring nodes and (with) local clients. Mesh nodes are constantly aware of the network conditions and promptly respond to any changes in the environment and to fault conditions by rerouting traffic or by reconfiguring the frequency channel scheme.

The measurements were performed using access points at 802.11a for backhauling purposes and 802.11b/g for the access part. At the 802.11a mode the AP operates in backhauling mode in a way that collects traffic from APs and transmits it to another AP. As it will be shown in the results, a combination of Wi-Fi and Mesh radio techniques provides a flexible, auto-forming and self healing backbone capable of supporting data, voice and video at high speeds, low latency and high reliability.

Key performance requirements for communications networks are throughput and quality of service (QoS). In a Wi-Fi mesh system, throughput degrades with increased number of hops as it will be shown by the presented data.

QoS for services such as voice and video is highly dependent on throughput, packet loss, delay and jitter, all of which degrade per hop. Therefore, it is very significant to measure throughput, packet loss, delay and jitter in relation to the number of hops in a test network. The topology of the test network is shown at Figure 6.

Specifically, the test network consists of four Mesh access points which/that interconnect with 5GHz band of frequency. All the MAPs were provided with dual radio so that they could offer access ability to 802.11b/g users. All the measurements were performed at the field emulating lots of scenarios. Before proceeding with the measurements' results, it is useful to give a brief explanation of the parameters that were measured.

MEASUREMENTS' PARAMETERS

Some of the key parameters that were used to evaluate the mesh network are the following:

- **Jitter:** It shows the mean statistical deviance of packet inter-arrival times over a period of time.
- **Latency:** It is the time elapsed between the transmission and the reception of a packet.
- **Packet Loss:** It is the number of packets that are lost during the transmission.
- **Mean Opinion Score:** It provides a numerical measure of the quality of human. The scheme uses parameters such as latency, jitter, and packet loss that are mathematically averaged to obtain a quantitative indicator of the system's performance.

Figure 6. Test network topology

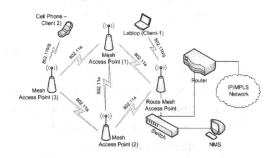

Figure 7. Throughput when distance changes

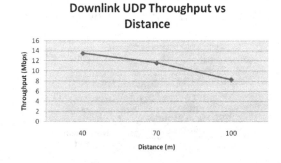

Figure 8. Throughput for different number of hops

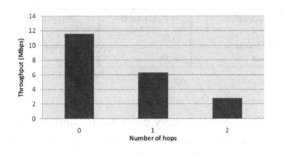

MOS is defined by one number, from 1 to 5.

TEST MEASUREMENTS

Throughput Tests

In this section, we will discover the dependency between the maximum throughput a user can achieve and the number of hops that data travels along the mesh network, as well as how throughput varies according to the distance from the MAP that the user is associated with. Figure 7 shows the results for various distances when there is no obstacle between the user and the MAP (LOS conditions) and user is associated with the Mesh portal (or root MP, 0 hops):

The throughput decreases while the user moves further from the MAP. This is expected because the modulation and the spectral efficiency are getting worse when the distance increases, so that the range of a MAPs signal covers larger areas even when SNR is quite low.

An interesting outcome derives from Figure **8** which shows how the throughput changes in case the user associates with diffent MAPs (multiple number of hops) while the distance from each associated MAP remains constant and equal to 70m.

It is obvious that for each additional hop data needs to travel across, thoughput almost remains the half of its previous value. This is happening due to the fact that the MPs that carry the data

have to switch from transmiting mode to receiving and vice versa which causes a degradation of their performance. At this point it is important to mention that the number of hops has a more severe impact in throughput than the distance.

Figure 9 illustrates the results of the scenario in which the users first associate with the MAP having clear line of sight conditions in a distance of 40m and then disassociate and move to another point that lies in the same distance but now the user has no optical view of the MAP.

The performance of the system differs when the protocol used (TCP/UDP) changes and the RF conditions are non line of sight. The reason for this is because TCP offers error correction. When the TCP protocol is used there is a "guaranteed delivery." This is mainly due to a method called "flow control". Flow control determines when data needs to be resent, and pauses the flow of data until the previous packets are successfully

Figure 9. Throughput in LOS-NLOS

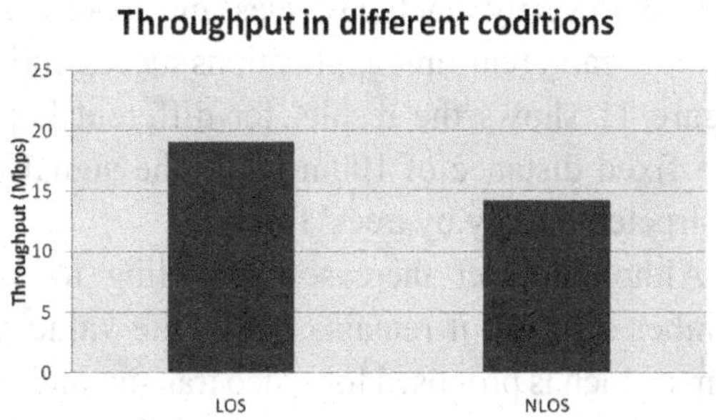

Throughput in different coditions

Figure 10. Performance with different transport protocols

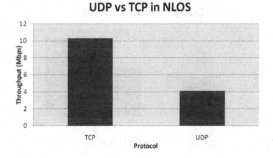

Figure 11. Jitter measurements

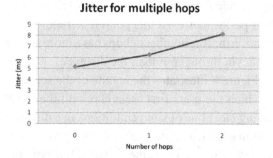

transferred. In NLOS conditions where there are many erroneous or lost packets, this retransmission mechanism helps achieving higher data rates than UDP transport where there is no way of recovering lost data.

Jitter Tests

Jitter plays a crucial role and affects the performance of real-time applications. The jitter measurements took place in LOS/NLOS environments and for different number of hops. This was done in order to verify that the wireless mesh network is able to carry real-time applications successfully. Figure 11 shows the results for different hops in a fixed distance of 100m while the signal is obstructed mainly by trees' foliage.

Although jitter increases according to the number of hops, it remains below the value of 10ms which is proposed for video transfer and 50 ms which is a tolerated value for VoIP. For 2 hops

Figure 12. Delay dependency by hop number

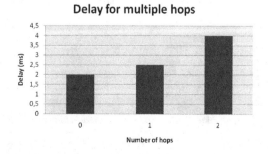

Table 1. Acceptable values for VoIP and video

Application	Delay (ms)	Jitter (ms)
VoIP	< 150	< 30
Video	< 250	< 10

the jitter value is very close to the limit, which may indicate that if we introduce another hop, a video may experience poor performance. The same tests were repeated for distances smaller than 100m and for better conditions. The results were acceptable as expected. Specifically, jitter values in LOS condition were 15% lower than those shown in Figure 11.

DELAY MEASUREMENTS

Real time applications such as VoIP or streaming video are more sensitive to fluctuations and large values of delay. A mesh network needs to add as little delay as possible to packets, especially to those that carry real time information. End-to-end delay of a flow is highly dependent on the number of hops that the flow traverses through.

Figure 12 illustrates how the delay changes for various distances from the MAP when the user communicates with a wired user and the number of hops to the MPP is equal to one.

Delay value seems to be independent from the distance between the user and the MAP. In all cases the delay value is ideal for real time applications. Recommended acceptable values of

Figure 13. Delay vs. distance

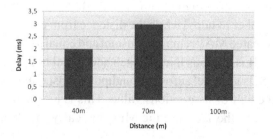

Figure 14. Packet loss for multiple hops and distances

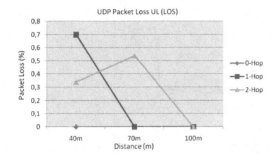

jitter and delay for VoIP and video streaming are summarized at Table 1.

PACKET LOSS MEASUREMENTS

Another parameter that has an important impact on real-time applications' performance is the number of lost packets. If this number becomes too big the receiver cannot decode the data properly and as a result we have corruptions in the video or voice. Tests for several hops and various distances for each hop show that the mesh network was very robust in losses. In all cases the lost data was a small fraction of the overall data sent. The results are shown in Figure 14.

HANDOVER EXPERIMENTS

A big advantage of mesh networks compared to classic Wi-Fi networks is that they offer the capability of handover which means that users can move all over the coverage area of the network without experiencing any disruption of their connection. Figures 16, 17 illustrate the impact of handover procession to user's performance.

As shown in Figure 15, the user moves from point A to point B. The speed of the user was roughly 2 km/h while executing at the same time a VoIP call and a FTP download. WMM choice was activated to both the wireless interface of the

user as well as to all access points of the mesh network.

As it is shown in Figure 13, the average MOS value during the execution of the experiment is higher than the acceptable limits (>3). At the moment of the user's transition from the field of coverage of one MAP to the field of another, MOS

Figure 15. Handover test conditions

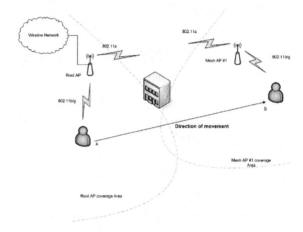

Figure 16. Handover impact on MOS value

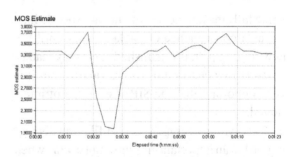

Figure 17. Throughput degradation during handover process

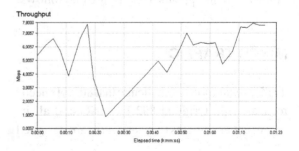

Figure 18. (a) Traffic separation in mixed traffic scenario (b) VoIP MOS value

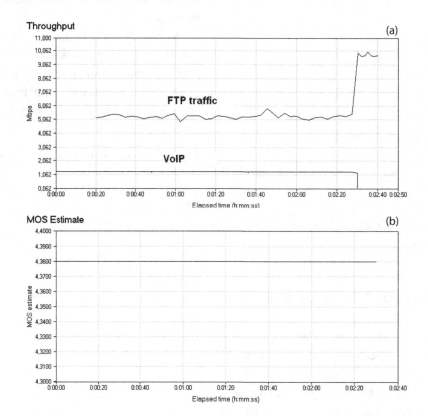

value falls instantaneously to not acceptable limits, as a consequence of packet losses until the new routing path is established. This may lead to a transitory deterioration of call quality, but it is very important that the SIP session is not interrupted.

Finally, the average speed of file transferring is high but an important turning-point occurs when the MAP at which the user is connected to changes. When the transfer to the new MAP is completed, the value of throughput increases gradually. This appears in the figure that follows:

MIXED TRAFFIC

Traffic separation is a challenge that 802.11s needs to deal with. Original 802.11 MAC and all its recent enhancements (e.g., 802.11e) are designed primarily for single hop wireless networks. Neither 802.11 DFC nor 802.11e EDCA can provide any QoS over a multihop wireless LAN. For this reason, QoS must be based on traffic separation with information of upper layers such as the IP header. In order to evaluate the ability of the test mesh network to carry mixed type of data, one user starts 20 VoIP sessions and after 20s the user begins downloading a file (FTP session). Traffic prioritization relies on the information of the IP header (value of Type Of Service -TOS- byte). According to this value, traffic is categorized to one of the available WMM classes. VoIP has the highest priority while other traffic is considered as 'best effort'. As shown below, the VoIP sessions are not affected by the file transfer and achieve a MOS of about 4.3 which is interpreted as excellent voice quality.

CONCLUSION

This chapter has outlined the main concepts of the WiFi Mesh technology including the main characteristics and properties, architectures and finally measurements taken in a test lab and outdoors.

REFERENCES

Camp, J. D., & Knightly, E. W. (2008). The IEEE 802.11s Extended Service Set Mesh Networking Standard. *IEEE Communications Magazine*, 46.

Conner, S. W., Kruys, J., Kyeongsoo, K., & Zuniga, J. C. (2006). *IEEE 802.11s Tutorial*. Retrieved February, 03, 2009, from http://www.ieee802.org/802_tutorials/06-November/802.11s_Tutorial_r5.pdf

Daniilidis, A. (2007). IEEE *802.11s Wireless Mesh Networks*. Retrieved March 23, 2009 from http://ece-classweb.ucsd.edu/winter10/ece287/homework/802.11s_tutorial.pdf

Ghumman, S. A. (2009). *Security in Wireless Mesh Networks* (*Master's Thesis in Computer Network Engineering, School of Information Science, Computer and Electrical Engineering, Halmstad University, 2009*). Retrieved August 13, 2009, from http://hh.diva-portal.org/smash/get/diva2:306340/fulltext01

Glass, S., Portmann, M., & Muthukkumarasamy, V. (2008). Securing Wireless Mesh Networks. *IEEE Internet Computing Magazine, 12*(4).

Hiertz, G., Max, S., Zhao, R., Denteneer, D., & Berlemann, L. (2007). *Principles of IEEE 802.11s*. Retrieved February 05, 2009 from http://user.cs.tu-berlin.de/~hornant/ieee_802_11s/ 04428715.pdf

Lassila, P. (2006). *Performance Challenges in Wireless Mesh Networks*. Retrieved January 15, 2009, from http://www.netlab.tkk.fi/tutkimus/abi/publ/ist2006-lassila.pdf

Zhang, Y., Luo, J., & Hu, H. (2006). *Wireless Mesh Networking: Architectures, Protocols and Standards*. Boca Raton, FL: Auerbach Publications.

Chapter 6
WiMAX Networks:
Performance and Measurements

A. Rigas
Hellenic Telecommunications Organization S.A. (OTE), Greece

E. Patiniotakis
Hellenic Telecommunications Organization S.A. (OTE), Greece

G. Agapiou
Hellenic Telecommunications Organization S.A. (OTE), Greece

I. Chochliouros
Hellenic Telecommunications Organization S.A. (OTE), Greece

K. Voudouris
Technological Educational Institute of Athens, Greece

E. Dimitriadou
Hellenic Telecommunications Organization S.A. (OTE), Greece

K. Ioannou
University of Patras, Greece

A. Ioannou
Hellenic Telecommunications Organization S.A. (OTE), Greece

ABSTRACT

The term WiMAX is an abbreviation of Worldwide Interoperability for Microwave Access and it is defined in IEEE, as the 802.16 family of standards. Unlike other legacy Point-to-Multipoint wireless technologies, WiMAX is able to offer higher transmission rates, quality of service assurance and hence it can be compared to other wireline technologies. Additionally, WiMAX is proven to be useful for telemedicine purposes (live surgeries and medical examinations, medical conferences etc.), especially in distant areas. WiMAX is based on two major standards; one is the IEEE802.16d that was developed specifically for fixed wireless communications and is dedicated mainly in LOS environments and can be used in many cases, where fixed infrastructure is not available. On the other hand, 802.16e can be used in cases

DOI: 10.4018/978-1-61520-805-0.ch006

of both fixed and moving subscribers, while providing better coverage, performance and even higher transmission rates. This chapter describes the major capabilities of the WiMAX standard and presents the performance of WiMAX networks based on measurements taken during laboratory and field tests.

INTRODUCTION

Broadband communications can be considered one of the most significant steps in modern communications systems. The requirement for new services like video conferencing, fast Internet and Voice over IP (VoIP), has set new standards for both fixed and wireless technologies. WiMAX is a wireless technology that aims at providing broadband services to wireless users similar to those of xDSL technologies. WiMAX is required to cover the needs of both broadband and wireless markets, both of which are the major markets in communications while high potentials for the future are also foreseen.

WiMAX is a point to multipoint wireless technology introduced by the Institute of Electrical and Electronics Engineers (IEEE) and it is described in the 802.16 framework of specifications. The first official meeting of the 802.16 group, took place in 1999 but the form of the technology was quite different than the one defined in latest standards. Since its first steps, WiMAX technology has gone through four development phases. The first phase was a narrowband version which was followed by the broadband edition for

line-of-sight (LOS) conditions only. The third phase enhanced WiMAX for operation in non line-of-sight link conditions (NLOS) while the latest stage is the one that is described in the current standards of 802.16 group.

The latest standard of WiMAX is the 802.16e-2005 with a major emphasis in introducing mobility of users for speeds up to 120 km/h with full handover support between base stations. The transmission characteristics and handover times are within the required limits in order to support real time applications such as VoIP, video streaming and online gaming. The support of the aforementioned applications is a real challenge for all wireless technologies especially in meeting the high requirements and the quality of service that is necessary for delivering the above services. Those transmission characteristics can be achieved by means of offering the required Quality of Service (QoS) mechanisms that will assure prioritization in services that are sensitive to delays (e.g. VoIP) over other types of services that are not delay sensitive or are not real-time (e.g. file transfer).

Figure 1. Global growth trend for mobile, internet and broadband markets (taken from ITU)

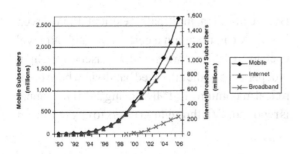

Figure 2. Communications market statistics for 2007 (taken from ITU)

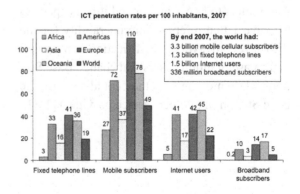

HISTORY OF WIMAX

The 802.16 standard was formed by IEEE in 1998 for defining and specifying the specs of a broadband wireless technology. The proposed technology would mostly fit LOS environments with frequencies ranging from 10-66GHz. The initial standard was to define the PHY and MAC layers including for single carries signals.

The next version of 802.16 was an amendment that allowed provision of services in NLOS environments by using frequencies from 2GHz up to 11GHz. This was the 802.16a standard that was published by IEEE in 2003. 802.16a was the first version of the standard that supported Orthogonal Frequency Division Multiplexing (OFDM) for the PHY layer as far as Orthogonal Frequency Division Multiple Access (OFDMA) for the MAC.

The revision that was published one year later (802.16d-2004), replaced all previous standards and came with the name of WiMAX. The 2004 version is also known as "Fixed WiMAX" since it did not support mobility functionality. This mobility functions were initiated with the version 2005.

802.16e-2005 is the latest version of WiMAX standards that is also known as "Mobile WiMAX". Its major differences compared to 802.16d include support for nomadic users (fixed users that can be attached to different Base Stations without handover support) and also support for mobile users. Another feature of mobile WiMAX is full interoperability between equipment of different vendors, a feature that was not mandatory in all previous versions. The latter is also known as Wave 2 and refers to MAC interoperability as opposed to Wave 1 that refers to interoperability for the PHY layer only. Wave 2 certification is important in the case of mobile users that change Base Stations while moving (e.g. they could also use the Base Station of another service provider) [1-3].

TECHNOLOGY OVERVIEW

WiMAX provides a range of functional options concerning both the PHY and MAC layer. The standard defines for example single-carrier, OFDM and OFDMA options for PHY and Time Division Multiplexing (TDM) or Frequency Division Multiplexing (FDM) schemes for the MAC layer. Additionally there are options applied to different channel bandwidths, central frequencies etc. In terms of central frequencies, WiMAX makes use of licensed frequencies but there is also an initiative to expand the technology in license exempt bands. This undertaking is still in progress at the time of writing and it will be defined in 802.16h standard. The expected date for the standard is around 2010.

Some of the competitive features of WiMAX are mentioned below.

High Performance in NLOS Environments

The PHY layer of WiMAX uses OFDM, which is a technique widely accepted for many broadband communication systems. Performance improvement in multipath environments due to the design of OFDM, allows operation in NLOS environments. This is important especially in mobile subscriber scenarios, where the end user's line of sight with the base station, could be obstructed by objects due to the low height of the receiver (e.g. pedestrian users).

High Throughput

By means of a multipath resilient PHY layer, WiMAX can maintain a certain throughput level even in NLOS scenarios. The end user throughput is dependent on the allocated bandwidth but a theoretical maximum of 74Mbps using 20MHz channel is reported. This throughput refers to physical layer and is the sum of uplink and downlink, while it assumes ideal transmission characteristics. In the following sections, real cases field measurements are described.

Bandwidth Flexibility

WiMAX provides a range of choices concerning the used bandwidth. The bandwidths used start from 1.25MHz up to 20MHz, allowing various implementations of WiMAX networks depending on the needs and available spectrum of the provider. It has to be mentioned that this set of bandwidths could pose some limits in terms of interoperability and this is the reason that WiMAX forum has defined specific profiles concerning used frequencies and bandwidths for its interoperability tests.

Adaptive Modulation & Coding

WiMAX is operating in various link conditions and ranges. This can be achieved by adapting the modulation and coding used for data transmission, allowing for smaller signal to noise ratios in case of non ideal link conditions. This has a negative effect on maximum throughput for the end user but it allows for better link availability.

Automatic Repeat Requests (ARQs)

This is a technique that is implemented in MAC layer and it improves the total link performance by performing error correction, instead of waiting for other mechanisms to improve transmission delay especially for services that use TCP protocols that request retransmission of data and may increase the transmission delay. In 802.16e-2005, many vendors implement Hybrid Automatic Repeat Requests (HARQ), which is a technique that is similar to ARQ but it occurs in the PHY layer and the final delays are even smaller than those of ARQ.

Multiple Duplexing Pptions

The WiMAX standard defines two options for multiplexing of uplink and downlink channels. This could be either Frequency Division Duplex (FDD) or Time Division Duplex. In general, TDD is preferred over FDD since it is more flexible in the provision of asymmetric services (e.g. Internet Services) or for services that require a relative small amount of bit rate for the uplink (such as VoIP).

Orthogonal Frequency Division Multiple Access (OFDMA)

In 802.16e-2005, OFDMA allows the set of carriers included in an OFDM symbol to be distributed to different users. This is important in frequency planning of the systems and can be used in an effective way, especially in cases of NLOS link conditions [4-5].

End to End IP Design

WiMAX was designed from the very beginning as an all IP technology. As a matter of fact, it can be used without any adaptations as an access technology of already established IP networks, while at the same time has the requirements towards the expected all IP convergence.

Quality of Service Support

WiMAX was designed as a technology to support differentiation of services. Quality of Service implemented in WiMAX, ensures that delay sensitive applications like VoIP and video streaming, will have the priority required against other kind of data like file transfer data. 802.16d standard defines four traffic classes (Best Effort, non-Real Time, Real Time and Unsolicited Grant Service) that correspond to specific kind of traffic. In

802.16e an additional Traffic Class "Extended Real Time Variable Rate" is defined that can be used in services with variable bit rate, like Voice over IP with silence suppression.

Mobility Support

The standard 802.16e-2005 introduces mobility functions that support mobile subscribers in terms of inter and intra base station handover. End users are able to roam without interruption of their services. This is important especially in real time applications where delay due to handover can result in poor service quality. Additionally, Mobile WiMAX supports high mobility end users with speeds up to 120 km/h.

Usage of Advanced Antenna Systems

In order to support mobile subscribers, advanced antenna techniques are being used. This applies also to fixed users but their advantages are beneficial when mobility and NLOS are involved. Advanced Antenna Techniques include Multiple Input - Multiple Output (MIMO) Antennas and Beamforming techniques that maximize performance in cases of multipath and fading.

Enhanced Security

WiMAX uses the Advanced Encryption Standard (AES) to encrypt user data as far as Extended Authentication Protocol in order to authenticate users by means of usernames and passwords, X.509 certificates etc.

WIMAX PHYSICAL LAYER

As mentioned above, PHY layer of WiMAX is using OFDM as its modulation scheme. OFDM offers more efficient performance in NLOS and multipath environments. It should be mentioned that OFDM was also adopted by 3GPP as a physical layer technique for most of the 4th generation broadband communication systems such as Long Term Evolution (LTE) and or mobile WiMAX, a fact that proves its efficiency.

OFDM is in general a frequency division multiplexing technique, which is using multiple carriers of orthogonal frequencies to transfer user data. By using adjacent orthogonal carriers, that is carriers with appropriate spacing and central frequency to eliminate interference between them, OFDM performs better than other schemes in NLOS environments where multipath effect can distort the received signal [6].

The concept behind OFDM is that transmitted data is split into channels of lower bit rate and those streams consist of a number of sub-carriers with orthogonal frequencies. This orthogonality is achieved by proper sub-carrier frequency selection so that the total OFDM symbol duration (allocated by all carriers) is at least 10 times greater than the maximum expected delay of data transmission. The condition that should be satisfied is thus:

$$\Delta f = \frac{k}{Tu}$$

where Δf is the sub-carrier spacing, k is a positive integer and Tu is the symbol duration. By using orthogonal carriers, inter symbol interference (ISI) is minimized and this is important in multipath environments. Another advantage of OFDM is the relatively high spectral efficiency, since almost all available bandwidth is used for data transmission. It can be proved that the achieved symbol rate under ideal link conditions is close to that given by Nyquist rate.

The OFDM symbol in 802.16d-2004 standard has a fixed number of 256 sub-carriers. Out of those, 192 are data sub-carriers, 8 are pilot sub-carriers for channel quality estimation, 1 is the Center Carrier that contains no data and the rest 55 are guard carriers with zero amplitude, which

Figure 3. OFDM sub-carrier structure for 802.16d-2004

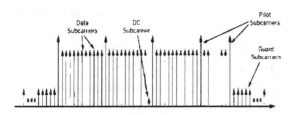

Figure 4. Sub-channels in 802.16e-2005

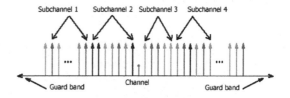

are used for achieving data sub-carrier separation. Figure 3 shows the allocation described above for an 802.16d-2004 OFDM symbol.

Mobile WiMAX introduces a new version of what was described, which is the Scalable-OFDM. For this implementation, the number of sub-carriers (FFT size) is not constant as it is in fixed WiMAX. By having a specific sub-carrier spacing of 10.94 kHz, the FFT size in 802.16e-2005 could vary from 128 to 2048 depending on the channel size that could range from a lower of 1.25 MHz up to 20 MHz.

By keeping the sub-carrier spacing constant, the OFDM symbol duration is always the same and this is important in high mobility environments, where Doppler Shifts can severely affect ISI. The sub-carrier separation was chosen to have this value so that a fair tradeoff between performance and robustness was obtained. Fixed applications, where link conditions are better in average, could afford a denser carrier allocation that would result in better total throughput. On the other hand this would not be appropriate for users with high mobility in which case multipath effects would introduce limitations in providing the required service quality.

Subchannelization is another major feature that was introduced by the 802.16d standard. By allocating a part of the available sub-carriers (either adjacent or not), a number of subchannels can be defined in the uplink and dedicated to each subscriber station (SS). The standard defines 16 sub-channels and according to the needs, one or more can be allocated to a subscriber station. Apart

from multiple subscribers, sub-channelization has significant performance improvement under suboptimal link conditions. For example, if a subscriber station is transmitting 1/16 of the available bandwidth, there is a gain of 12 dB in link budget or a significant improvement in SS power consumption.

Dividing the available spectrum into subchannels, reduces the available bandwidth for each subscriber but this does not have significant effects on system's performance since WiMAX services are asymmetric in most of the cases without significant uplink demands. Mobile WiMAX standard with its OFDMA PHY layer, defines sub-channelization in downlink too. By means of sub-channelization in both uplink and downlink, a multiple access mechanism using Orthogonal sub-carriers is defined and this is the reason for the Orthogonal Frequency Division Multiple Access name that was given to the PHY layer defined by 802.16e. In mobile WiMAX, specific sets of sub-channels are defined for uplink and downlink and their total number depends on the available bandwidth. There are certain sub-carrier allocation schemes described in the standard, including partial usage of sub-carriers (PUSC) that defines 15 uplink and 17 downlink sub-channels for 5MHz channel bandwidth. This number is doubled for 10MHz channel. PUSC theoretically allows network implementation with a single frequency being used (frequency reuse factor = 1). This is achieved by allocating different channels for subscribers at cell edge, reducing thus interference at cell edge. Even though this idea may seem ideal for network planning pur-

Figure 5. Frequency Reuse 1 Deployment in 802.16e using different sub-channels

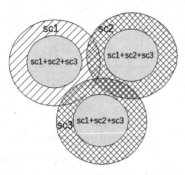

poses, it should be mentioned that it causes significant performance degradation and this should be carefully considered before implementation. The following diagram shows a typical implementation using a single frequency throughout the network.

Concerning modulation of carriers, WiMAX uses some already known digital modulation schemes such as BPSK (used only in 802.16d-2004), QPSK, 16QAM and 64QAM. It also uses adaptive modulation to ensure link availability under bad link conditions. Higher modulation schemes such as 64QAM achieve higher bit rates but require low noise compared to the received signal strength. In case this cannot be achieved

because for example of NLOS conditions or distance between user and base station, lower modulation is chosen and operation is achieved with lower bit rates.

For sakes of error control, WiMAX implements Forward Error Correction schemes, so that packet retransmissions are avoid and hence delay of data stays within the required thresholds for delay sensitive traffic. In FEC, redundant information is transmitted so that the receiver detects the error and corrects it locally, without propagating the error to upper layers that will be responsible to ask for retransmission and hence increase total delay. The amount of redundant information transmitted is noted as 1/2, 2/3 or 3/4 denoting the fraction of useful to total information sent. Similarly to the concept of adaptive modulation, FEC with higher percentage of redundant information are used in cases where Signal-to-Noise ratio is small, compensating thus the low bit rate due to increased redundancy with link availability.

WiMAX defines a certain structure of the PHY layer resources based on the concept of "slot" which is the smallest part of the spectrum that can be allocated to a subscriber for the smallest possible time interval. The size of the slot in not

Figure 6. Modulation vs. signal-to-noise (E/N) ratio

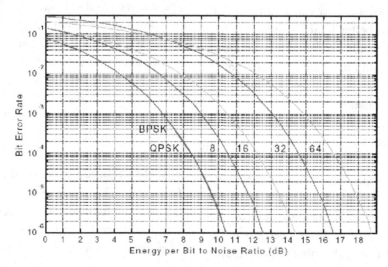

Figure 7. TDD frame structure

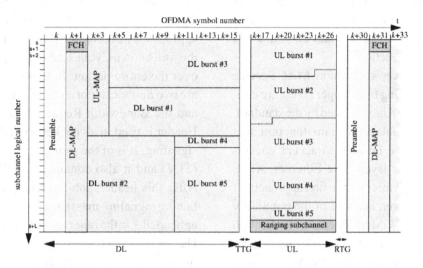

constant in all cases, but it depends on the usage of sub-carriers of each OFDM symbol. As an example, when PUSC is not used, 48 carriers in one symbol are allocated for each slot. In case of sub-channelization, 24 carriers are allocated in downlink for duration of two OFDM symbols. An integer number of slots is used to create a sub-frame that is expanded in both frequency (allocated carriers) and time (allocated OFDM symbols). WiMAX standard defines downlink and uplink sub-frame structures that depending on the duplexing scheme (FDD/TDD) are transmitted in parallel or one after the other. Sub-frames have predefined elements that are either mandatory or optional. The position of each element within the frame is included in the control frames that are transmitted at the beginning of downlink sub-frames. Other elements of the frame include preambles, downlink and uplink channel information etc. A typical TDD frame structure is shown in Figure 7.

WIMAX MAC LAYER

As mentioned above, WiMAX standards define the PHY and MAC layers. MAC layer is an interface between upper protocols of OSI stack and the PHY layer, while it also handles signaling required for WiMAX functionality. MAC layer comprises of three sublayers: the Convergence, the Common Part and the Security sublayers. The basic structure of MAC layer is presented in Figure 8.

One of the major characteristics of MAC layer is that it is connection oriented. All traffic is classified by means of various connection identifiers (CID) which are used to represent virtual connections between the base station and the subscriber. CIDs can be statically allocated from the beginning of the connection or upon demand. This is essential for the entire operation of MAC layer functionality like scheduling. It

Figure 8. WiMAX MAC layer

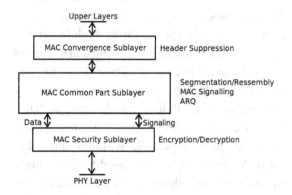

should be mentioned that CIDs represent flows of data and hence multiple CIDs can be allocated for a user, not only in uplink and downlink but also on the same direction.

During MAC layer's operation, MAC Service Data Units originating from upper layers are converted into MAC PDUs as defined by the standard.

Convergence sublayer's main function was initially designed to be able to accept packets from various upper layers like Ethernet, ATM, and IP. Even though this was the first approach for convergence sublayer, because of the popularity of IP architectures, WiMAX Forum's certification includes only Ethernet and IP. An additional function of the convergence sublayer is MAC header compression. In case that some packets have similar contents, like e.g. common IP headers, those are compressed, reducing thus the required bandwidth for data transmission. Convergence sublayer classifies received packets from upper layers to the appropriate CIDs and keeps track of the active connections. The CID for each packet could also differ in case of Quality of Service Rules applied by Service Flow IDs defined at WiMAX base station. As an example, voice traffic with same destination as data, will use a different CID because those two packet flows will belong to different Service Flows. Identification of different service flows and classification per CID is also a function of Convergence Sublayer.

Common Part Sublayer (CPS) is the major sublayer of MAC and that is where most of MAC layer functionality is implemented. Network initialization, packet scheduling, Automatic Repeat Request, bandwidth management, mobility management (for 802.16e) as far as modulation and coding selection are all implemented in Common Part Sublayer. It is a task of CPS to accept an SDU and convert them by means of segmentation or reassembling into PDU. CPS also groups PDUs that have for example common destination and transmits them, if possible within a single DL burst. A similar approach is used for ARQ functionality, where either packets are requested for retransmission or group acknowledgements are

sent, achieving thus better PHY layer utilization. A MAC SDU is converted into PDU by adding the appropriate headers and trailers to it. The trailer is the well known Cyclic Redundancy Check (CRC) over the entire packet. In terms of headers there are two major categories of headers: The Generic and the Bandwidth Request Header. A Generic Header is used in all packets containing data and signaling. It is of the format Type, Length, Value (TLV) and it also contains the CID it refers to. After this header, sub-headers may follow containing signaling messages while payload is also appended. On the other hand, Bandwidth Request Header does not contain any payload and it is sent by the subscriber to the Base Station, indicating how many bytes the user requires to complete the transmission. Those bandwidth requests are additions on the initial allocations made by the BS to the SS and they always refer to specific CIDs.

The packet scheduler of WiMAX is also implemented in Common Part Sublayer. Packet scheduling is essential to maintain fair bandwidth allocation between subscribers as far as to maintain a certain Quality of service between different types of traffic. The assurance of Quality of Service in WiMAX is achieved by defining specific traffic classes depending on the characteristics of each application. By considering the Traffic Class, each packet stream is prioritized against others, maintaining thus e.g. transmission delays within the required thresholds for real time applications. The Traffic classes defined by 802.16 standard are:

- **Best Effort (BE):** It has the lowest priority and bandwidth is allocated when no requests for other classes are pending. Appropriate for non critical types of data that require no QoS like web browsing.
- **non Real Time Polling Service (nrtPS):** Higher priority than best effort with bandwidth requests available to SS. It refers to traffic that is not delay sensitive but in cases where minimum bandwidth must be guaranteed.

- **Real Time Polling Service (rtPS):** Similar to nrtPS but supports real time traffic, such as voice and video by frequent polling for bandwidth requests.
- **extended Real Time Polling Service (ertPS):** Can be used for real time services with big variations bit rate like voice with silence suppression.
- **Unsolicited Grant Service (UGS):** This traffic class has the highest priority and it provides dedicated bandwidth to applications. It can be used with real time traffic of continuous bit rate.

Finally, Security Sublayer of MAC performs encryption of data and signaling before those reach the PHY layers and are transmitted over the air. Before encryption, authentication of users is performed by security sublayer as far as security key exchange between the base station and subscribers for the encryption process.

Apart from the functions described above, MAC layer provides power saving functions, which is essential for mobile terminals with limited power supply capacity. 802.16 standard defines sleep mode and idle mode. Sleep mode allows a subscriber to temporarily suspend its active connections for a predefined time interval. After this timer expires, the SS reactivates the connection

Figure 9. WiMAX reference model

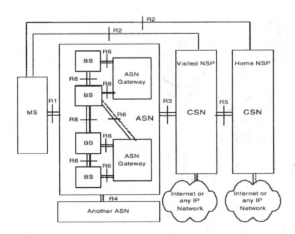

and receives data. Idle mode on the other hand allows a subscriber to receive broadcast downlink frames without being registered to a specific BS. This could be used for example in mobile users when there is no traffic towards/from a subscriber and change in BS occurs. If the idle mode is supported, then no handover processes need to be started and this is the suitable case in favor of the available network resources.

WIMAX REFERENCE ARCHITECTURE

For interoperability purposes, 802.16 standard defines a reference model, indicating the basic elements of a WiMAX network. The network reference model is shown in Figure 9.

The major elements of the Reference Model are:

- Mobile Subscriber (MS): Any 802.16 CPE
- Base Station (BS)
- Access Service Node (ASN-GW): Can be connected to many BSs. It is an access element responsible for keeping information about the MSs that are connected to the BSs. Mobility and radio resource management functions are also implemented in ASN.
- Connectivity Service Node (CSN-GW): Can be connected to many ASNs. CSN is the main core element of the model and provides IP connectivity and the main network functions like user authentication and authorization.

BASE STATION REGISTRATION SCENARIO

The process that is followed by a subscriber station when joining a network is the following:

- The SS scans for downlink channels to determine if it is in coverage of a Base Station and synchronizes with it.
- After synchronization, the required parameters are obtained from the downlink frames received. Those include channel conditions as far as MAC and PHY parameters.
- SS performs initial ranging procedure to achieve optimal power level of transmitted power and proper synchronization between uplink and downlink frames.
- Basic Capabilities of SS are negotiated and initial bandwidth allocation requests are sent. Basic Capabilities include Current Transmit Power, FEC support, FFT size etc.
- SS registers to BS and receives CIDs required for operation. IP connectivity is also established.
- Finally, service flows are established as soon as traffic reaches the SS or BS.

PERFORMANCE ANALYSIS

WiMAX performance has been tested from many telecom operators and various researchers, to understand better its capabilities and have a clear state of mind of its weaknesses, in order to accept or discard this new upcoming technology.

In order to qualify the benefits of using WiMAX systems, various measurements under different conditions, were done. Different scenarios were created by changing either channel size (3,5GHz, 7GHz) or by tranceiving TCP or UDP data packets. Also, WiMAX performance was tested by having ARQ functionality on or off and by using different antenna implementations (with or without diversity).

NETWORK TOPOLOGY

The network topology that was used comprised of the WiMAX Base Station (BS), 3 WiMAX CPEs, 3 Client PCs, an Ethernet switch, a DHCP Server and a Server PC. Figure 10 illustrates the above mentioned topology.

Before proceeding to the results of measurements, it is important to make some commends, concerning at the network topology. Every CPE supports IEEE802.3af standard, which means that a power injector is used for the power supply. The other port of the power injector is connected to the Client PC. The WiMAX BS is connected to

Figure 10. Network topology

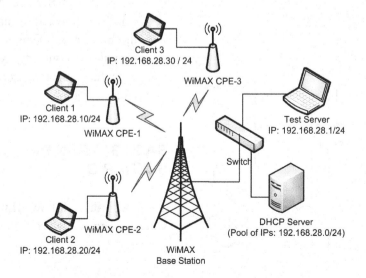

an Ethernet switch, which is also used as the connection point for both the DHCP Server and the PC Server. The DHCP Server is responsible for giving IP addresses, from a pool of IPs that are predefined to it. In our case, it a private LAN area of IP addresses was chosen, which is the 192.168.28.0/24 network. So, all Client PCs and Server, belong to the same LAN.

For every WiMAX CPE a specific Service Flow (SF) was defined for each BS. SFs have great importance, because an exact data rate can be defined for an end user to whom any service can be defined like (VoIP, Video etc.). The DL/UL ratio was 65/35, the channel size was 3,5GHz or 7GHz and all measurements accomplished at highest modulation rate of 64-QAM ¾.

MEASUREMENTS

To illustrate the WiMAX throughput behavior and its influence when changing some characteristics, such as channel size, cyclic prefix etc, different measurements were done.

In most countries, telecom operators are using 7MHz channel size and this means that the available throughput for both uplink and downlink directions, is fairly increased. With this channel size, more bandwidth-demanding services can be offered as well as specific service flows such as leased lines.

Figure 11 illustrates throughput levels, when channel size was changed. For the scopes of this measurement, UDP data packets were tranceived. Throughput includes both downlink and uplink traffic. So, for 3,5MHz channel size the total throughput is around 8 Mbps, while for 7MHz channel size, the total throughput is around 18Mbps.

UDP and TCP are both the major core protocols of the TCP/IP. Many applications are using one or the other protocol. So, it is crucial to know the behavior of both protocols when they are used in different channel sizes, in WiMAX.

Figure 12 illustrates TCP and UDP total throughput levels (uplink & downlink) for 7MHz channel size. So, TCP data rates reach up to 14Mbps, while UDP are little more than 18Mbps. This is happening because UDP does not guarantee reliability and specific ordering of data packets in data transmission, as TCP does. Also, UDP does not demand acknowledgement (ACK) packets as TCP, to ensure the proper delivery of each one. Thus, UDP achieves higher data rates, in comparison to TCP.

The IEEE 802.16 technology defines the ARQ mechanism that enables a connection to resend data at the MAC level if an erroneous packet is detected. Generaly, without the ARQ feature enabled, if any error is detected, data resending

Figure 12. TCP & UDP throughputs for 7MHz channel

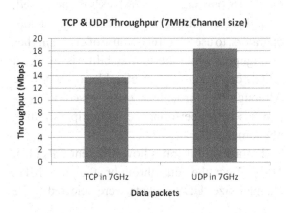

Figure 11. Throughput for different channel sizes

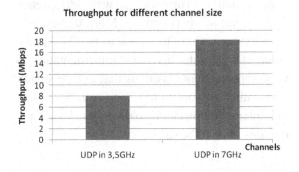

Figure 13. Throughput with ARQ on / off

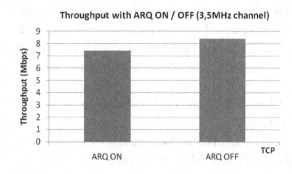

Figure 14. Throughput vs. cyclic prefix

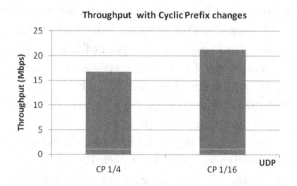

is done at the transport layer (Layer 4 TCP/IP). This causes throughput degredation.

Figure 13 illustrates throughput reaction when ARQ is enabled or disabled. This measurment was took under Line Of Sight (LOS) conditions. Throughput level with ARQ mechanism enabled is close to 7,5Mbps, while with ARQ disabled reaches close to 8,5Mbps. This measurment was as expected, because by enabling ARQ mechanism, additional overhead is added and thus throughput decresed. In Non Line Of Sight (NLOS) conditions, where retransmission of data packets are very common to happened, when ARQ mechanism is enabled, throughput values are increased.

Cyclic Prefix (CP) is another characteristic of WiMAX that can be changed, in order to achieve increased throughput or more robustness. CP is a quantity that carries an amount of data, but not payload. When it is used CP ¼, then 25% of the total amount of WiMAX frame is dedicated to carry CP data. At the same way, when CP is defined to be 1/16, only 6,25% of WiMAX's frame is used.

In LOS conditions it is preferable by telecom operators, to use CP 1/16, because of giving higher throughput, while the link stability is ideal. In NLOS conditions, it is preferable to use CP ¼. Although that throughput is decreased, the system has better performance in multipath-fading phenomena.

Figure 14 illustrates how different CPs (1/4, 1/16) affect the total throughput of a 7 MHz channel size. UDP packets were selected to be

send in both directions (uplink & downlink). So when having CP ¼ the total UDP throughput is up to 16,5Mbps, while with CP 1/16, throughput is aroung 21Mbps.

All the above mentioned measurements, belong to IEEE802.16-familly characteristics. Special antenna characteristics like 2nd and/or 4th order diversity, defined only for the IEEE802.16e standard for the first time. So, in terms of network planning, a telecom operator by using improved antenna techniques, is expected to have better coverage and thus more throughput and capacity, which leads in the offer of real time services, such as VoIP and Video.

Figure 15 illustrates throughput levels in LOS conditions, when a 2nd order diversity is used and/ or when no diversity systems at 3,5MHz channel size are used. Throughput measurements were taken for different distances, up to 0,9km. So, throughput level for the 2nd order diversity implementation was the same at all distances and its value was at 3,54 Mbps, while throughput in the implementation of no diversity, was a little higher. Throughput was between 3,52Mbps to 3,6Mbps. Those values where too close to the throughput value of a 2nd order diversity implementation. A very important conclusion is that in LOS conditions, either we work with systems with diversity or in implementations with no diversity, throughput remains almost the same.

Figure 15. Throughput vs. distance for line of sight (LOS)

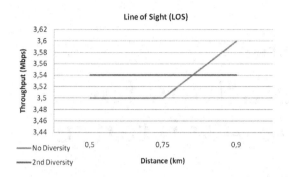

Figure 16. Throughput vs. distance for non line of sight (NLOS)

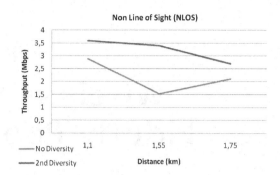

Figure 16 illustrates throughput levels in NLOS conditions, for different distances and for a chosen channel size of 3,5MHz. In this measurment 2nd order diversity and no diversity utilizations were used, for a channel size of 3,5MHz. Throughput levels with no diversity applied, varied between 1,5Mbps to 3Mbps, for distances up to 1,75km. Throughput levels while using a 2nd order diversity system, were significantly increased, as they ranged between 2,5Mbps and 3,6Mbps. So, using antennas in NLOS conditions with improved characteristics, offered improved throughput values and thus the ability to offer faster data rates and improved services.

REFERENCES

Andrews, J. G., Ghosh, A., & Muhamed, R. (2007). *Fundamentals of WiMAX: Understanding Broadband Wireless Networking*. Upper Saddle River, NJ: Prentice Hall.

IEEE. 802.16d-2004.(2004).*Standard for Local and metropolitan area networks*. IEEE

IEEE. 802.16e-2005. (2005).*Standard for Local and metropolitan area networks (Amendment 2)*. IEEE

Kwang-Cheng Chen, J., & de Marca, R. B. (2008). *Wiley Mobile WiMAX*. New York: Wiley-IEEE Press. doi:10.1002/9780470723937

Motorola White Paper on WiMAX. (2007). *D vs. E, Motorola*: The advantages of 802.16e over 802.16d. Motorola. Retrieved from http://www.motorola.com/staticfiles/Business/Solutions/Industry%20Solutions/Service%20Providers/Wireless%20Operators/Wireless%20Broadband/wi4%20WiMAX/_Document/StaticFile/WiMAX_E_vs._D__White_Paper.pdf

Sargeant, P. (2008). *White Paper on WiMAX*: The Promise of WiMAX. *Motorola*. Retrieved from http://www.motorola.com/staticfiles/Business/B2B_Internationalization_Patni/_Documents/White%20Papers/Static%20Files/The_Promise_of_WiMAX_WP.pdf?pLibItem=1&keywords=White%20papers&localeId=252.

Chapter 7
Wireless Solutions for Elderly People Assistance

Alessia D'Andrea
IRPPS-CNR, Italy

Arianna D'Ulizia
IRPPS-CNR, Italy

Fernando Ferri
IRPPS-CNR, Italy

Patrizia Grifoni
IRPPS-CNR, Italy

ABSTRACT

Wireless technologies are increasingly acquiring a considerable relevance in the field of Ambient Assisted Living. This contributes to independent living and quality of life for many elderly people by reducing the need of caretakers and personal nursing. In this chapter we provide a classification of existing wireless technologies for Ambient Assisted Living based on the role they can have in the assistance to elderly people. Then, we provide an overview of several intelligent wireless systems applied in the Ambient Assisted Living on considering the different wireless technologies used in each of them.

INTRODUCTION

During the last two decades, the life-time expectancy increased significantly in developed countries (Chande, 2001). This has given rise to a considerable increase on the elderly people percentage; we are living in the midst of an unprecedented transition, characterized on one hand by the rapid ageing of the industrialised world and on the other hand by the decreasing number of young people. As life expectancy increases, the need for assistance to elderly people also raises drastically. Hence a major challenge of health institutions is to allow elderly people to pursue an independent life in their preferred environment reducing the need of hospitalisation. In this direction, the scientific and technological innovations in wireless communications offer important means to address these challenges associated to the ageing population, such as, the rise in number of people with high disability rates, fewer family carers,

DOI: 10.4018/978-1-61520-805-0.ch007

and a smaller productive workforce. In particular, wireless technologies are increasingly acquiring a considerable relevance in the field of Ambient Assisted Living (AAL) (Fischer et al., 2003) that includes the monitoring of physical activities and health of elderly person at home in order to detect unusual events and give care support.

In this chapter we provide a classification of existing wireless technologies for AAL based on the role they can have in the assistance to elderly people. Then, we provide an overview of several intelligent wireless systems applied in the AAL.

The use of wireless technologies (such as Bluetooth, Wi-Fi, RFID, etc.) in the field of AAL has the potential to change healthcare services by enhancing the quality of elderly people care. In particular they allow to:

- collect and access of all records of the elderly person;
- track the movements of the elderly person at home;
- monitor the health of the elderly person.

Starting from this consideration we will classify wireless technologies in three different classes:

- *Acquisition wireless technologies*: they enable healthcare professionals to access and collect all records of the elderly person (such as problems, medications, past medical history, immunizations, laboratory data, and radiology reports) wherever they are in the country and potentially worldwide. This allows both to automate and streamline the clinician's workflow and generate a complete record of clinical encounters, as well as supporting other care-related activities directly or indirectly via interface, including evidence-based decision support, quality management, and outcomes reporting.
- *Location-tracking wireless technologies* that are used to track the movement of the

elderly person. Depending on the desired level of user monitoring, the indoor user position can be acquired on a sub-meter level accuracy, or tracking in room/apartment level accuracy. Both infrastructure and infrastructureless deployments can be considered for the provision of safety and emergency services to the elderly person. Infrastructureless position techniques are cheap to deploy, but less accurate. On the contrary, infrastructure based techniques give an exact position on the expense of high cost and installations.

- *Monitoring wireless technologies* that enable doctors and carers to continuously monitor the health status of the elderly person providing the transmission of information such as live vital signs. This allows the delivery of related information of the elderly person to one or more healthcare professionals in reasonable time. Any changes in medication can be updated immediately, and any contra-indications automatically cross-checked.

Moreover we provide an overview of several intelligent wireless systems applied in the AAL. The systems are analysed by considering the different wireless technologies used to monitor the health and daily activities of elderly people at home. The systems provide early warning to medical specialists, record information (in electronic format) that can help to set the cause of a health problem and assist elderly person as soon as possible.

The chapter is organised as follow. After a brief illustration of common daily activities and problems that elderly people face due to the health degradation as a consequence of aging, the chapter gives an overview of wireless technologies. Afterwards, a classification of wireless technologies, applied to the healthcare sector, is given, along with an overview of existing wireless systems applied in the AAL. Finally, the last section provides some conclusions and future works.

Elderly User Target Group and Problem to be Solved

Elderly people are typically experiencing reduced vision or hearing capabilities as well as reduced walking ability, leading to difficulties in pursuing their own life independently or performing their daily life activities. They fear of getting lost when out of their homes, getting injured or communicating with strangers. The next step of being afraid to pursue ordinary life outside the safety of home is loneliness, social exclusion, and, eventually, institutionalization. Furthermore, the reduced vision and/or hearing capabilities may also present a barrier for the use of ICT solutions. Specific wireless systems must be incorporated to ensure usability and acceptance issues of technological aids.

Generally, elderly people perform the following common activities in the daily life:

- Entertainment (e.g. movies, theatre, restaurants, bars, elderly communities)
- Shopping, paying bills
- Taking a walk
- Meeting relatives & friends

- Visiting a health specialist (e.g. Hospital or a General Practitioner)
- Transactions with public authorities

In Figure 1, we depict the most common daily activities of elderly people classified by their gender (Cis-IMSERSO, 2000).

Moreover, common "problems" faced by elderly people (health degradation due to aging) are:

- Reduced vision or hearing capabilities
- Reduced walking ability (arthritis, osteoporosis)
- Fear of getting lost, getting injured, agoraphobia
- Loneliness and social exclusion

Worldwide, visual impairment is unequally distributed across age groups. More than 82% of all people who are blind are 50 years of age and older, although they represent only 19% of the world's population. Due to the expected number of years lived in blindness (blind years), childhood blindness remains a significant problem, with an estimated 1.4 million blind children below age 15 (http://www.who.int/mediacentre/factsheets/fs282/en/). Hearing loss is the third most common chronic condition reported by elderly people

Figure 1. Most common activities of elderly people classified by gender

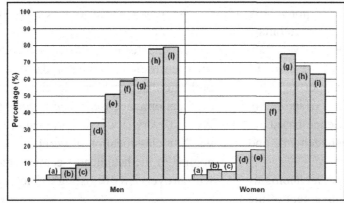

(a)	Go to conferences and concerts
(b)	Go to shows
(c)	Participate in sports activities
(d)	Go to the park, take a walk
(e)	Go to the bar or cafe
(f)	Read
(g)	Go shopping
(h)	Listen to radio
(i)	Assist to elderly association

(Lethbridge-Cejku et al., 2002). The estimated prevalence of significant hearing impairment among people over the age of 65 is approximately 40 to 45 percent and among people over the age of 70 exceeds 83 percent (Cruickshanks et al., 1998). Despite the widespread occurrence of significant hearing loss in the elderly population, only about 20 percent of elderly individuals with significant hearing impairment obtain hearing aids (Kochkin & MarkeTrak, 1999). Moreover, about 30 percent of hearing aid owners are dissatisfied with their instruments (Kochkin & MarkeTrak, 2003), and approximately 16 percent of hearing aid owners report never using their hearing aids (Kochkin & MarkeTrak, 2000). In the study of Prince et al. (1997) it is pointed out that the reduction of walking speed ranges from 0.1-0.7% per year. Moreover, many elderly people are unable to walk faster than 1.4m/s (this is the minimal speed recommended to safely cross an intersection, (Cook & Woollacott, 1995). On the other hand, falls are the first cause of accidental deaths in people over 65 years old. It means nearly the 70% of the accidental deaths in people over 75 (Fuller, 2000). A significant percentage of elderly people are also living alone in their home environment, which gives rise to the feeling of loneliness, social exclusion and eventually, institutionalization as they usually refrain from pursuing their ordinary lives outside the safety of their homes because of fearing to get lost, disoriented, or injured.

In this scenario, wireless technologies offer important means to address problems of elderly people. They provide an elderly person with friendly technological solutions facilitating to pursue the daily activities independently, with dignity and safety. The services provided by wireless technologies range from the possibility to quickly access and collect all medical records of the elderly person (such as problems, medications, past medical history, immunizations, laboratory data, and radiology reports) to elder location tracking and health condition monitoring. All these services contribute to give a continuous medical support to elderly person by providing peace of mind to their families and reducing the burden on professional carers.

AN OVERVIEW OF WIRELESS TECHNOLOGIES

The general term "wireless" refers to numerous forms of transmission that do not use optical fibers or metal wires. Wireless technologies can be grouped in four classes:

- Wireless wide-area networks (WWANs) that allow phones, PDAs and laptops, to exchange data with the Internet;
- Wireless local-area networks (WLANs) that permits devices to be attached without a physical connection;
- Personal area networks (PANs) that allow peripheral devices such as printers and keyboards to be attached to computers without a physical connection.
- Hand-held PDAs that can operate independently with an on-line computer.

Various standards are used to provide wireless transmission in the different applications, including cellular, satellite, infrared line of sight, packet radio, microwave and spread spectrum. Figure 2 shows the principal standards applied for each of the four classes of wireless technologies.

With respect to *Wide-Area Network* class, the standard of 2G, 2.5G, 3G, 3.5G and 4G have different strategic and technological challenges. In particular the biggest challenge of the 2G standard was to involve adapting voice-centric networks to deliver competitive high-speed Internet access and data rates. While 2.5G and 3G networks challenge was to improve performance by offering a high-speed Internet access and full broadband mobility. More recently the 3.5 aimed to enhance the data rate to 3G systems and finally 4G aimed to introduce technologies that provide wireless

Figure 2. Standards classes

TECHNOLOGY CLASS	PRINCIPAL STANDARDS
Wireless Wide Area Networks (W-WANs)	**First Generation (1G analog voice: 1980s)** • AMPS (Advanced Mobile Phone System) • TACS (total Access Communications System) • NMT (Nordic Mobile Telephone) **Second Generation (2G GSM: 1990s)** • GSM (Global System for Mobile) - European Digital Standard • TDMA (Time Division Multiple Access, IS-136) – 1 US digital standard • CDMA (Code Division Multiple Access, IS-95-B) • PDC (Personal Digital Communication) **Intermediate Second Generation (2.5G GPRS)** • HSCSD (High-Speed Circuit Switched Data) • D-AMPS TDMA – Intermediate step to UWC-136 • GPRS (General Packet Radio Service) – evolutionary step from GSM & D-AMPS TDAM to UWC-136 **Third Generation (3G UMTS)** • CDMA Multi Carrier (IS 2000) • CDMA Direct Spread (Wideband CDMA or WCDMA-FDD, frequency-division duplex) • CDMA Time Division Duplex (TDD) or WCDMA-TDD) • TDMA Single Carrier (UWC-136 and EDGE, Enhanced Data Rates for GSM Evolution) • TDMA Multi Carrier (DECT, Digital Enhanced Cordless Telecommunication) • 3GSM (3 Generation GSM) – delivered through EDGE and WCDMA **Intermediate Third Generation (3.5G HSPDA)** • HSUPA • HSOPA **Fourth Generation (4G MBWA)** • OFDM • MIMO
Wireless Local Area Networks (W-LANs)	• IEEE 802.11b (Wi-Fi) • IEEE 802.11a • IEEE 802.11g • IEEE 802.11e • IEEE 802.11n • WEB (Wired Equivalent Privacy) • IEEE 802.1x (Port Based Network Access Control) • TKIP (Temporal Key Integrity Protocol)
Handheld Devices	• WAP (Wireless Application Protocol) – de facto standard for providing Internet communications over the wireless phone system • WTLS (Wireless Transport Layer Security) – the security layer of WAP, functionally equivalent to wired TLS
Personal Area Networks (PANs)	• Bluetooth • UWB • Zigbee • RFID

WAN-type access for nomadic and mobile users with data rates of 20 Mbps or more.

, Considering the *Wireless Local Area Network* class, the first standard to become accepted in the market was 802.11b, which specifies encoding techniques that provide for raw data rates up to 11 Mbps using a modulation technique called Complementary Code Keying and also supports Direct-Sequence Spread Spectrum from the origi-nal 802.11 specification. Afterwards, the 802.11a standard used a more efficient transmission method called Orthogonal Frequency Division Multiplexing that enabled raw data rates up to 54 Mbps. In June 2003, the IEEE ratified 802.11g, combined the best of both worlds: raw data rates up to 54 Mbps on the same radio frequency as the already popular 802.11b. Afterwards, the IEEE 802.11e introduces a so-called hybrid coordination function containing two medium access mechanisms: contention-based channel access and controlled channel access. Finally, the newest WLAN technology is 802.n working in 5GHz frequency, but it is not finalised yet (White Paper, 2006).

About the *Personal Area Networks* class, the Bluetooth was the first standard wireless personal network technology. It is used to links laptops, mobile phones and other portable devices and connectivity to the Internet. The WiMedia Ultra Wide Band (UWB) standard provides high data rates (up to 480 Mb/s) with a range of up to 10 meters. ZigBee is a global standard that addresses the unique needs of remote monitoring & control, and sensory network applications; it enables broad-based deployment of wireless networks with low cost, low power solutions. Finally, the RFID is an Automatic Data Collection technology that uses radio-frequency waves for transferring data between a reader and a movable item to identify, categorize, and track.

Finally, with respect to the *Handheld Devices* class, the A WAP browser provides all of the basic services of a computer based web browser but simplified to operate within the restrictions of a mobile phone, such as its smaller view screen. WAP sites are websites written in, or dynamically converted to, WML (Wireless Markup Language) and accessed via the WAP browser. While WTLS was developed to address the problematic issues surrounding mobile network devices - such as limited processing power and memory capacity, and low bandwidth - and to provide adequate authentication, data integrity, and privacy protection mechanisms.

WIRELESS TECHNOLOGIES IN THE HEALTHCARE

The rapid growth of the standards for wireless technologies extended the potential for exploitation on the healthcare sector. A Kalorama's market study (2007) underlines that the rapid growth of wireless technologies in healthcare sector is driven by demand to enhance healthcare processes. The introduction of wireless technologies in the healthcare environment has led to an increased accessibility to healthcare providers, more efficient tasks and processes and higher quality of healthcare services. At present, healthcare institutions all over the world use a wide range of fragmented wireless systems in numerous applications, by recognising their multiple benefits in terms of improved process efficiencies. For instance, mobile computing solutions, such as cellular 3G and beyond, WiFi and WiMAX, are used by physicians to access and collect patients medical data anywhere and at any time. The present of pervasive computing, consisting of Bluetooth, ZigBee, wireless sensor network and RFID, provides an innovative means for location tracking of patients and for vital parameters transmission.

Starting from these considerations, in the following subsections we classify standards wireless technologies, applied to the healthcare sectors, in three different classes: acquisition wireless technologies, location-tracking wireless technologies and monitoring wireless technologies.

Acquisition Wireless Technologies

With the recent advances of wireless technologies it becomes possible for physicians and care givers to access and collect all medical records of the elderly person (such as problems, medications, past medical history, immunizations, laboratory data, and radiology reports) everywhere and every time. Thanks to a wireless Network (WiFi), physicians have the possibility to utilize small handheld devices to access and collect all elderly person medical information and complete tasks such as dictation and drug prescription, use larger wireless tablets to document encounters and review radiology of reports.

This process allows physicians to collect a wide array of elderly person information, as well as carry out real-time charting in the elderly per-

Figure 3. Wireless access and collection of elderly person medical information

son's electronic medical record. This has given rise to a total change. In fact traditionally the process of accessing and collecting medical information has been paper-based. However, the paper-based system is inefficient for managing enormous amounts of information that can affect care of elderly people. For example:

- medical information may be illegible because it is hand written and poorly organized, making it difficult for physicians to locate the information they need;
- an elderly person who visits more than one health care provider has several medical records that often are not shared with other physicians and/or hospitals. Indeed Information becomes fragmented and this can cause errors in elderly person care;
- physicians must retain a tremendous amount of information about the dose and the frequency the elderly person should receive for instance a particular drug, side effects of the drugs and interactions with other medications or food.
- elderly people with chronic diseases often have to monitor their health. Many times they must wait until their next scheduled visit to share this information with their physician.

The EHR electronic health record (EHR) solution combined with a wireless network allows overcoming all these problems. Collecting and transferring elderly person information

electronically has the potential to reduce clinical errors and improve elderly person safety as well as allowing physicians to communicate more quickly and to identify relevant information more easily. Good EHR wireless systems can improve the cost-effectiveness of health services, reduce duplication and increase efficiency. EHR wireless systems can also make information much more readily accessible to elderly people, allowing them to assume more control over their medical records and thereby become more active in their own care.

However, in order to satisfy all these benefits, EHR wireless systems should have the following characteristics (Mandl at al., 2001):

- *Comprehensiveness*: each system must be able to know what has previously been done, because care is normally provided to an elderly person by different doctors and/ or institutions and in different geographical areas,.
- *Accessibility:* the elderly person must consent to the use of its medical records. Otherwise, if he/she is unconscious, only personal or societal policy must dictate use.
- *Interoperability*: different EHR wireless systems should be able to share records from multiple sources, including physicians' offices, hospital computer systems and/or laboratories.
- *Confidentiality*: the elderly person should have the right to decide who can examine and alter its own medical records.

- *Accountability:* any access to or modification of personal medical record should be recorded and visible to the elderly person.
- *Flexibility:* the elderly person should therefore be able to grant or deny study access to selected personal medical data.

Location-Tracking Wireless Technologies

One of the central challenges in sensor networks for AAL is the position tracking, whose goal is to monitor the movements of elderly people at home. Depending on the desired level of tracking, the elderly person's position can be acquired by using different wireless solutions. These solutions include:

- Location determination using Wireless Local Area Networks (WLANs) (Hatami & Pahlavan, (2005), Yamasaki et al. (2005)). In this case, the received signal strength from one or more WLAN access points installed in house is measured. The location fix is then obtained either with triangulation, using measurements of the perceived signal strength from several access points, or through comparison with pre-stored signal strength values from calibrated points (fingerprinting). Since indoor radio channels suffer from severe multipath propagation and shadow fading, fingerprinting provides higher accuracy (of up to 1-3m) than triangulation.
- Ultra wideband (UWB) systems which exploit bandwidths beyond 1GHz and are able to each accurate estimations of the time of arrival (ToA) of the received signals (Schwarz et al., 2005). UWB signals do not suffer from multipath fading, which is a highly desirable property for accurate ToA estimation in indoor areas reaching as low as 15cm.
- Bluetooth technology such as (Kotanen et al. (2003), Bandara et al. (2004)). Bluetooth was originally developed for short range wireless communication, and can also be employed for locating mobile devices in a certain area that is represented by the range of the device, typically less than 10m.
- RFID-based positioning (Hähnel et al. (2003), Chon et al. (2004)) based on Radio Frequency Identification (RFID) tags installed in infrastructure or fabricated within smart carpets. RFID is a short-range transmission technology that uses radio frequency waves to transfer data between a tag and a reader. Tags can be either active or passive. Passive tags do not send their own signal but use the power of the received signal to send a response back to the reader. The spatial coordinates of the tag itself can be stored to the tag's memory. By reading this location information, equipment with RFID reader can determine its location. Since passive tags are inexpensive, lightweight, and battery free, a grid of tags could be installed permanently into the infrastructure to form a positioning system with no dependency on a centralized database or wireless infrastructure for communications. An RFID based information grid system with a reader integrated into the user's shoe is presented in (Willis & Helal, 2005). The established system helps elderly people to move around independently in the area equipped with the grid of tags.
- Satellite positioning: to a certain extent, satellite positioning can be used indoor as well. The number of satellites within range and their geometry limit the performance of these positioning systems. Signals are either heavily attenuated by the home materials or reflected in as multipath. High Sensitivity GPS (HSGPS) receivers are

able to achieve higher performance than conventional GPS receivers, by using large banks of correlators and digital signal processing to search for GPS signals. Thus, HSGPS receivers are suitable for several (although not all) indoor environments, especially houses with relatively thin walls.

All these wireless solutions combined with camera network allow obtaining semantic information that can be used for understanding daily routine patterns of elderly person at home. In this way, alerts may be generated in cases where abnormal movements are detected or when the camera network detects abnormal situation, e.g. falls (as shown in Figure 4).

This allows detecting if elderly person is falling and afterwards is lying on the ground and at the same time to better providing adapted assistance and preventive care measures.

Monitoring Wireless Technologies

Effective care of elderly people requires an accurate monitoring of their health status. The health monitoring is not only required only for elderly people suffering from acute or chronic diseases, but also for those that living in their home environment needs to receive a continuous medical assistance. The wireless technologies are emerging and are envisioned to be a promising approach for remotely monitoring the health elderly people at home. By using wireless medical sensors (such as heart-rhythm, temperature, oximeter, accelerometer etc.), physicians have the possibility to continuously measure parameters that indicate the state of health of an elderly person.

In particular, the sensors collect vital health parameters from the body of the patient and send these data (in electronic format) to a personal server from where they can be examined by a doctor that can promptly assist the elderly person

Figure 4. Tracking of a falling elderly person

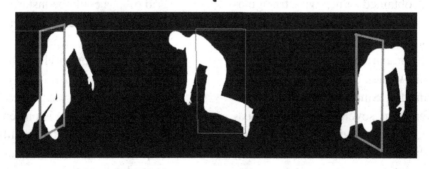

Figure 5. Monitoring wireless technologies

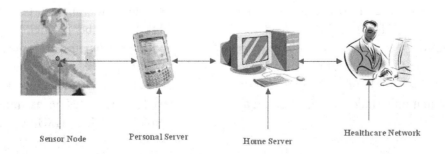

Sensor Node   Personal Server   Home Server   Healthcare Network

if variations of vital parameters occur. Afterwards, the parameters are processed and made ready to be sent to a healthcare network.

The wireless health-monitoring can significantly improve the quality of healthcare and provide elderly people with a comfortable, continuous and pervasive care. Such a wireless health monitoring does not require the physicians to be in close proximity to the elderly person; however, it still provides the same quality of care. It provides a better resource utilization and sharing, reduces doctor's intervention and makes healthcare more affordable. However, wireless sensors have to satisfy several requirements. Fist of all, in order to achieve non-invasive and unobtrusive continuous health monitoring, they have to be lightweight and small. The size and weight of sensors is determined by the size and weight of batteries. Moreover, they must garantee data integrity and meet privacy requirements mandated by the law for all medical devices. Although the advantages of use wireless health-monitoring weighs far more than its disadvantages, there are also some potential threats that have to be considered. The most important limitation is the small screen sizes of the handheld used by physicians to examined data. This does not allow physicians to visualize electronic health records in a single screen. Moreover, the handheld provides very less scope for input; for this reason data entry becomes a trivial process. If physicians need to make a long note of illness and medication of elderly person, it becomes a time consuming process as the speed of data entry and accuracy issues need to be addressed here. Finally, handheld device can be easily hacked, lost or stolen. Hence some form of security must be built into the devices. Another potential threat would be the entry of remote users into the hospitals expert system or mainframe computer. This poses a threat to the privacy and well being of the elderly person.

The following section provides an overview of existing wireless systems for AAL and shows how these systems apply the aforementioned classes of wireless technologies and standards.

AN OVERVIEW OF EXISTING WIRELESS SYSTEMS APPLIED IN THE AAL

Several intelligent wireless systems applied in the AAL have been developed in the past few years. Such systems utilize different wireless technologies to monitor the health and daily activities of elderly people at home. They can provide early warning to medical specialists, record information (in electronic format) that can help to set the cause of a health problem and assist elderly person as soon as possible. The system proposed by Lin et al. (2006) is addressed to elderly people suffering from dementia. The system integrates the technologies of Radio Frequency Identification (RFID), Global System for Mobile communications (GSM), Global Positioning System (GPS), and Geographic Information System (GIS). In particular, the system includes four monitoring areas: (i) the indoor residence monitoring, (ii) the outdoor activity monitoring, (iii) the emergency rescue and (iv) the remote monitoring modes. With respect to the indoor residence monitoring area, the system allows to automatically detect if the elderly person enters or leaves certain specific areas of the home, such as bathroom, kitchen etc. The system is also able to send warning message to the call center, when the elderly person leaves home alone. This allows care provider (or family members) to receive the message immediately, providing sufficient time to prevent the elderly person from danger situations. Considering the outdoor activity monitoring area, the system allows setting the activity area of the elderly person by pushing on the button of the locator. Once the elderly person leaves the detected area, an alarm signal alerts family members via a GSM network. The system is also able to help elderly person that is in an emergency situation. By pressing the emergency rescue button, he/she can send an emergency message to the call center. After the call center receives this message, it examines the transmitted data to identify the elderly person, records the emergency situation, and transmits the geographical data, including elderly person profile and location information, to physicians and family members. Finally, the remote monitoring modes area allows family members to connect to the call center when they want to know the current location of the elderly person. Through the ID authentication, the system automatically reports the current location via periodic location report mode or a single location report mode.

Wang et al. (2006) implemented the I-Living system for assisted living. The system uses various embedded wireless technologies (e.g., sensors, bluetooth-enabled medical devices, actuators, displays, etc.) coordinated under a local intelligence node, called the Assisted Living Hub (ALH) that can be a black box equipped with one or more wireless interface cards (Bluetooth, IEEE 802.11, Infrared or Ultra Wide Band), or with a specialized PC or PDA. These wireless technologies are used for: (i) vital sign measurement, (ii) personal localization, (iii) personal behaviour profiling. The measurement of vital signs (such as the blood pressure glucose level, heart bit rate, etc.) is carried out through Bluetooth that transmits data to the ALH. This allows physicians to monitor health status of elderly person at desirable time granularity. If physicians detect any abnormal health situations, medical instructions can be given before the situations deteriorate. Personal belongings (such as, hearing aids, eyeglasses, etc.) attached with tags can be located through RFID/Ubisense readers. When the elderly person does not find his/her belongings, he/she can use a simple vocal command (through a Bluetooth-enabled headset) to the ALH, which schedules the RFID/Ubisense readers to locate the object. Finally, with respect to personal behaviour profiling, the I-Living system allows monitoring the movement

of elderly person in a privacy preserving manner (without the use of surveillance video cameras). The RFID readers installed in the environment keep track of elderly person location and detect abnormal spatio-temporal movement, without intrusion of privacy.

The INHOME project (http://www.ist-inhome. eu/inhome/Home.php) proposes a system that allows elderly people living in a monitoring home to be assisted by a specialist in case of abnormal events. Two kinds of monitoring activities are performed by the system: (i) activity monitoring and (ii) health monitoring. The activity monitoring refers to elderly person physical activity (frequency and also duration of the movements) and the consequences it has on environment (temperature in a room etc.). For this purpose, sensors node are used which are divided in two categories: (i) infrastructure nodes, which form the ZigBee-based mesh communication network and run a routing protocol to enable multi-hop communications and (ii) sensing nodes, which need to be worn by people and are equipped with an accelerometer. The health monitoring refers to physiological statistics (pulse rate, body temperature etc.) taken by physicians in order to assess the basic body function. There are two communication interfaces: the Bluetooth and the 802.11. The Bluetooth is used to directly transfer the medical information to the system terminal while the 802.11 interface is used when the Bluetooth connectivity is not guaranteed. After acquiring data from the medical device, the terminal sends them through a WLAN communication to a residential gateway that processes the data.

Hanak at al. (2007) proposed a complex wireless and personalized AAL solution, which enables the delivery of integrated functionality that includes: health management, mental monitoring, mood assessment and physical/relaxation exercises. The aim of the authors was "to create an open architecture where home-based and wearable sensors provide data and information to a portable controller (such as a mobile phone, PDA, Internet

Tablet or small factor computer) which not only collects information, but evaluates trends, provides advice on health, diet or workout regiment, and does so via a transparent and redundant data link between the elderly person and his/her caretakers". Starting from this assumption the system uses: (i) a number of healthcare and monitoring devices (placed in the home) connected to a small factor computer via wireless standards and optionally with USB interface; (ii) a mobile computational platform linked with a mobile phone to process sensor data, manage AAL applications and ensure redundant connectivity via 3G and WiFi data networks; (iii) wearable sensors to measure physiological state associated with health and fitness; (iv) WiFi, Bluetooth and 3G mobile connectivity to connect the elderly person with the outside world. In particular, WiFi provides large data files, a high throughput channel capable of delivering real-time video, and interactive services. Bluetooth connects different devices to deliver data to a server. Finally, 3G mobile connectivity allows accessing high data rate services.

MobiHealth Project (http://www.mobihealth. org/) proposes a system, which aims to provide continuous health monitoring of elderly person. The system is based on UMTS and GPRS technologies that, together with the technologies of Body Area Networks (BANs), enable the monitoring of chronic conditions and detection of health emergencies whilst maximizing the mobility of the elderly person. BAN technologies are implemented by using both front-end

supported and self-supporting sensors. In case of front-end supported sensors, multiple sensors share a power supply and data acquisition facilities. Self-supporting sensors have a power supply and facilities for amplification, conditioning, digitization and communication. The hardware platforms to support the system software architecture include both programmable Personal Digital Assistants (PDAs) and mobile phones which serve as Mobile Base Units (MBUs).

The different wireless technologies used by the analysed systems are summarized in Figure 6.

CONCLUSION AND FUTURE WORKS

The chapter provided a classification of wireless technologies in the field of AAL according to three different classes. The first class consists of Acquisition wireless technologies that enable healthcare professionals to access and collect all records of the elderly person (such as problems, medications, past medical history, immunizations, laboratory data, and radiology reports) wherever they are in the country and potentially worldwide. The second class is composed of Location-tracking wireless technologies that are used to track the movement of the elderly person. Finally, the Monitoring wireless technologies enable doctors and carers to continuously monitor the health status of the elderly person providing the transmission of information such as live vital signs. This allows the delivery of related information of the elderly

Figure 6. Wireless technologies used by the analysed systems

WIRELESS TECHNOLOGIES	PROPOSED SYSTEMS				
	Chung-Chih Lin et al.	Wang et al.	INHOME Project	Hanak at al.	MobiHealth Project
RFID	X				
GSM	X				
GPS	X				
802.11		X	X		
BLUETOOTH		X	X	X	
RFID		X			
ZIGBEE			X		
WLAN			X		
3G UMTS				X	X
WIFI				X	
GPRS					X

person to one or more healthcare professionals in reasonable time.

Moreover, several intelligent wireless systems for AAL have been analysed, which included one of more of the aforementioned classes of wireless technologies.

Future work would involve the development of a wireless platform that includes all aforementioned classes of wireless technologies. The platform will represent a friendly technological solution enabling elderly people to pursue their daily activities independently. The functionalities that we intend to implement within the platform are:

- Environment information extraction and representation via audible information by exploiting tracking wireless technologies, such as camera, RFID, Bluetooth and similar near communications field readers.
- Personal and clinical data acquisition by exploiting acquisition and monitoring wireless technologies, such as WiFi, RFID and Bluetooth.

Based on the collection of the user needs and requirements, and the user centric design/implementation methodology, specific interfaces will be chosen to ensure usability by elderly people. The challenge is to implement suitable interfaces that ensure a friendly human-machine interaction and guarantee that all the implemented services are useful.

REFERENCES

Bandara, U., Hasegawa, M., Inoue, M., Morikawa, H., & Aoyama, T. (2004). Design and implementation of a Bluetooth signal strength based location sensing system. In *Proc Radio and Wireless Conference*, 2004, (pp. 319-322).

Chande, H. (2001). *Esperanza de vida y expectativas de salud en la edad avanzada*. Retrieved from http://www.redadultosmayores.com

Chon, H. D., Jun, S., Jung, H., & An, S. W. (2004). Using RFID for Accurate Positioning. In *Proc. GNSS2004*, 2004.

CIS-IMSERSO. (2000). *Study 2.279*. Retrieved from http://www.imsersomayores.csic.es/documentos/documentos/boletinsobreenvejec3ing-01.pdf

Cook, A., & Woollacott, M. (1995). *Motor control, Theory and Practical Applications*. New York: Williams and Wilkins.

Cruickshanks, K. J., Wiley, T. L., Tweed, T. S., Klein, B., Klein, R., Mares-Perlman, J. A., & Nondahl, D. M. (1998). Prevalence of hearing loss in older adults in Beaver Dam, Wisconsin. *American Journal of Epidemiology, 148*(9), 879–886.

Fischer, S., Stewart, T. E., Mehta, S., Wax, R., & Lapinsky, S. E. (2003). Handheld computing in medicine. *Journal of the American Medical Informatics Association, 10*(2), 139–149. doi:10.1197/jamia.M1180

Fuller, G. F. (2000). Falls in the elderly. *American Family Physician, 61*, 2159–2168, 2173–2174.

Hähnel, D., Burgard, W., Fox, D., Fishkin, K., & Philipose, M. (2003). *Mapping and Localization with RFID Technology*. Intel Corporation, 2003.

Hanak, D., Szijarto, G., & Takacs, B. (2007). A Mobile Approach to Ambient Assisted Living. Retrieved June 8, 2008, from http://www.cs.bme.hu/~dhanak/iadis_wac.pdf

Hatami, A., & Pahlavan, K. (2005). A comparative performance evaluation of RSS-based positioning algorithms used in WLAN networks. In *Proc Wireless Communications and Networking Conference, 4*, 2331-2337.

INHOME Project. (n.d.). *An Intelligent Interactive Services Environment for Assisted Living at Home*. Retrieved from http://www.ist-inhome.eu/inhome/Home.php

Kalorama (2007). *Wireless Opportunities in Healthcare*. Kalorama Information.

Kochkin, S., & MarkeTrak, V. (1999). Baby Boomers spur growth in potential market, but penetration rate declines. *Hear J.*, *52*(1), 33–48.

Kochkin, S., & MarkeTrak, V. (2000). Why my hearing aids are in the drawer: The consumers' perspective. *Hear J. Rev.*, *53*(2), 34–42.

Kochkin, S., & MarkeTrak, V. I. (2003). On the issue of value: Hearing aid benefit, price, satisfaction, and brand repurchase rates. *Hearing Rev.*, *10*(2), 12–26.

Kotanen, A., Hannikainen, M., Leppakoski, H., & Hamalainen, T. D. (2003). Experiments on local positioning with Bluetooth. In *Proc ITCC2003*, 2003, (pp. 297-303).

Lethbridge-Cejku, M., Schiller, J. S., & Bernadel, L. (2002). Summary health statistics for U.S. adults: National Health Interview. *Vital Health Stat*, *10*(222), 1–151.

Lin, C.-C., Chiu, M.-J., Hsiao, C. C., Lee, R. G., & Tsai, Y. S. (2006). A A Wireless Healthcare Service System for Elderly with Dementia. IEEE Trans. Infor. Technol. *BioMed, VOL.*, *10*(4), 696–704.

Mandl, K. D., Szolovits, P., & Kohane, I. S. (2001). Public standards and patients' control: How to keep electronic medical records accessible but private. *BMJ (Clinical Research Ed.)*, *322*, 283–287. doi:10.1136/bmj.322.7281.283

MobiHealth Project. (n.d.). *Innovative gprs/umts mobile services for applications in healthcare*. Retrieved from http://www.mobihealth.org/.

Prince, F., Corriveau, H., Hebert, R., & Winter, D. A. (1997). Gait in the elderly. *Gait & Posture*, *5*, 128–135. doi:10.1016/S0966-6362(97)01118-1

Schwarz, V., Huber, A., & Tüchler, M. (2005). *Accuracy of a Commercial UWB 3D Location/Tracking System and its Impact on LT Application Scenarios*.2005 IEEE International Conference on Ultra-Wideband.

Wang, Q., Shin, W., Liu, X., Zeng, Z., Oh, C., Al-Shebli, B., et al. (2006). I-Living: An open system architecture for assisted living. In *Proceedings of the IEEE SMC 2006*.

White Paper. (2006). 802.11n: Next-Generation Wireless LAN Technology. Retrieved from http://www.broadcom.com/docs/WLAN/802_11n-WP100-R.pdf

WHO (World Health Organization). Retrieved from http://www.who.int/mediacentre/factsheets/fs282/en/

Willis, S., & Helal, S. (2005). *A Passive RFID Information Grid for Location and Proximity Sensing for the Blind User*. (Technical Report number TR04-009), University of Florida.

Yamasaki, R., Ogino, A., Tamaki, T., Uta, T., Matsuzawa, N., & Kato, T. (2005). TDOA location system for IEEE 802.11b WLAN. In *Proc Wireless Communications and Networking Conference*, *4*, 2338-2343.

Chapter 8
Healthcare Oriented Smart House for Elderly and/ or Disabled People:
A Case Study

Nicholas S. Samaras
TEI of Larissa, Greece

Costas Chaikalis
TEI of Larissa, Greece

Giorgios Siafakas
TEI of Larissa, Greece

ABSTRACT

Smart houses represent a modern technology which can secure and facilitate our life. The objective of this chapter is to adapt medical sensors to home automated systems, which collect medical data such as blood pressure, heart rate and electrical heart activity for elderly and/or disabled persons. Firstly, the collected data is transferred to a home server and to an external manager for further analysis. Subsequently, data is stored at a database where monitoring is available only for authorized users via a simple web interface. The IEEE 802.15.4 wireless standard has been chosen as the preferred solution for communication in the smart house. Finally, two implementation scenarios of the smart house for an elderly and/or disabled person are simulated using the Custodian software tool. This case study shows that simulating the automation system of a smart house before the implementation is advantageous.

INTRODUCTION AND LITERATURE REVIEW

Smart houses support services which ease and secure people's lives. The applications that a smart house can support are realised by wireless sensors and are divided into the following five categories (Stefanov, Bien, Bang, 2004), (Dewsbury, Taylor, Edge, 2002):

- *Energy management:* Applications which can control the heating and lighting system

DOI: 10.4018/978-1-61520-805-0.ch008

of the house in order to provide the desirable temperature and light.

- *Security and safety:* Applications which can provide security services.
- *Air control services:* Applications which can control the house air quality.
- *Healthcare and health monitoring applications:* Sensors attached on occupant's body collect data about certain biomedical signs. This data is stored, analyzed, evaluated and finally utilised to provide a global view of occupant's health condition.
- *Entertainment:* Applications which can provide entertainment services.

A smart house can help elderly and/or disabled people to have a good quality life and feel safe in their own house. Such a smart house should support healthcare oriented services like medical data collection, data transmission to an external medical manager and data evaluation. Collected medical data represent blood pressure, blood oxygen saturation, body weight, pulse rate and electrical heart activity. Subsequently, data is stored in medical databases, where it is analyzed by medical oriented software. Finally, the system informs a distant medical center in order to manage a possible medical emergency (Stefanov, Bien, Bang, 2004), (Dewsbury, Taylor, Edge, 2002).

The healthcare applications in a smart house are based on lightweight, intelligent medical sensors. These sensors can sense, collect, process and exchange medical data. The network should be wireless in order to give the opportunity to the occupant to move freely and with no restrictions. This type of network represents a Wireless Body Area Network (WBAN), because the sensors are spread over human's body. As it is explained in the following section, the most popular standard for low rate wireless sensor network (WSN) applications is the IEEE 802.15.4 (Gutierrez, 2004), (Gutierrez, Naeve, Callaway, Bourgeois, Mitter, Heile, 2001). The designed smart house system has to be a multi-tier system, divided into three tiers. The 1st tier is composed of sensors that are placed over human's body. The 2nd tier is a personal server that stores, process and manages the collected data. Additionally, a home server may be included in order to store all data. The home server can enable applications to manage any medical emergency situations. Finally, the task of communication with external managers is part of the 3rd tier (Milenkovic, Otto, Jovanov, 2006).

The external managers can be placed in a hospital or in a doctor's office and are responsible for the system and the healthcare management of the smart house occupant. The collected data can be further analyzed and the results can be stored to have a backup and a medical history of the smart house's occupant. The medical devices (sensors) are used to measure parameters such as body temperature, weight, blood pressure, while more complex devices such as electrocardiograms (ECG) are used to check occupant's heart condition. A well known experimental system is MITThril developed at MIT, which is composed of "wearable computing platforms" used for continuous medical data collection and monitoring. One of the most important sensors is ECG which monitors the electrical heart activity in a graphical way. Body temperature and blood pressure are measured by a lightweight sensor, which uses a three-axis movement positioning sensor (Milenkovic, Otto, Jovanov, 2006).

In (Liang, Huang, Jiang, Yao, 2008) a system of wireless smart home sensor network based on the IEEE 802.15.4 standard using Public Switched Telephone Network (PSTN) remote control and a 2.4 GHz radio frequency transceiver is proposed. This work describes the network configuration, the communication protocol and the software/ hardware implementation process. In (Chen, Nugent, Mulvenna, Finlay, Hong, Poland, 2008) the challenge of assisting the inhabitants of a smart house in performing the correct actions at the correct time in the correct place is addressed. Particularly, this work introduces a novel logic-based approach to cognitive modelling based on a highly developed logical theory of actions, namely, Event Calculus. System architecture is presented and the use of the proposed approach through a real world daily activity is demonstrated.

In (Chan, Estève, Escriba, Campo, 2008) a selection of smart home projects is presented, as well as the associated technologies of wearable/implantable monitoring systems and assistive robotics, which are considered to be the components of a smart home environment. Subsequently, in (Jin, Yu, Lai, Feng, 2007) a smart home system prototype is illustrated. It employs an indoor positioning system called Best Beacon Match (BBM) positioning method, which intelligently triggers the proper services for house inhabitants. Zigbee standard is used to implement the prototypes of the components for BBM positioning method. Finally, in (Dewsbury, Clarke, Rouncefield, Sommerville, Taylor, Edge, 2004) the main problems that arise from the design process of a smart house are presented.

In this chapter, sensors are used to collect data in a smart house and transmit it to a server via IEEE 802.15.4 standard. The collected data represents blood pressure and heart rate and each sensor is composed of a platform and a daughter card. The daughter card varies from sensor to sensor, depending on the sensor's application. The platforms to be used are MicaZ, Mica2 and TelosB. These platforms are compatible to the IEEE 802.15.4 standard, they have processing and storage abilities and low power consumption (Crossbow Technology, Inc. MICA2 Datasheet., n.d.), (Crossbow Technology, Inc., n.d.). The collected data is transferred firstly to a home server and then to an external manager for further analysis. Data monitoring is available for authorized users via a web interface, and finally, data is stored in a database at the home server. An early version of the web interface is also implemented. Finally, simulation scenarios and results of a smart house operation are presented using the Custodian simulation tool, which is used for smart house design, including devices and sensors, configur-

ing the properties and functionality to each device (Siafakas, 2008).

SMART HOUSE WIRELESS STANDARD SELECTION

This section presents the wireless standards that can be used in order to simulate a smart house. Generally, wireless technology is more flexible than wired technology, because wireless networks can be easily installed and they are cost effective. Furthermore, maintenance of wireless networks is much easier than maintenance of wired networks. In order to build a smart house, the first step is to choose the network infrastructure (Siafakas, 2008). The main wireless candidate standards to be applied in the design of a smart house are: Wireless Local Area Network (WLAN) standards like IEEE 802.11 family of standards, Third Generation (3G) cellular standards like Universal Mobile Telecommunication System (UMTS) and Wireless Personal Area Network (WPAN) standards like IEEE 802.15.4. WPANs features include ad-hoc network topology with supported data rates up to 250 kbps. The IEEE 802.15.4 standard has low installation cost and maintenance and low energy consumption. Furthermore, WLANs can also be used in smart houses, but due to restrictions in their implementation they are not the preferred solution (Gorday, Hester, Gutierrez, Naeve, Heile, Bahl, Callaway, 2002), (Milenkovic, Otto, Jovanov, 2006), (Gutierrez, 2004), (Huang, Huang, You, Jong, 2007), (Gutierrez, Naeve, Callaway, Bourgeois, Mitter, Heile, 2001), (Liang, Huang, Jiang, Yao, 2008), (Jin, Yu, Lai, Feng, 2007).

In order to select the appropriate wireless standard for our smart house design, the basic requirements are presented below. A person who has sensors on his body must be able to move around the smart house. Therefore, the need for wireless links between sensors and other network devices is necessary. Another requirement is low battery consumption. It is almost impossible to replace the batteries of all the nodes (sensors) in a house frequently. Additionally, the replacement of batteries will raise the maintenance cost of the network. Battery replacement can be very difficult for elderly or disabled persons. Low battery consumption is possible because the sensors may not operate continuously: they enter sleep mode for long periods of time and wake up at specific times per day. For example, a blood pressure sensor does not need to collect data continuously. A sensor may sleep for 99.6% of its operational life according to (Gutierrez, Naeve, Callaway, Bourgeois, Mitter, Heile, 2001).

In the areas of home networking, industry networking, agricultural applications and in automotive industry the throughput requirements are low and use WSNs. Their applications require simple connections between nodes, low data transfer rate and relaxed latency requirements. For example WSNs with medical sensors may be used in medical field, while biomedical sensors may be placed on the human body to collect medical data. In home networking small sensors may be placed inside the house in order to collect data e.g., sun brightness or house temperature (Milenkovic, Otto, Jovanov, 2006), (Huang, Huang, You, Jong, 2007). The wireless ad-hoc sensor standard which achieves all the above requirements, namely low cost, low power consumption, low data rate, easy setup and maintenance is the IEEE 802.15.4 or ZigBee (Gutierrez, 2004), (Xueliang, Cheng, Xingyuan, 2007).

SMART HOUSE SIMULATION USING CUSTODIAN SIMULATION TOOL

Custodian Simulation Tool

Custodian project was developed in order to ease the design and simulation of smart houses. The project is funded by the European Union and is implemented by a consortium of European educational institutes. The initials stand for "Conceptu-

alization for User involvement in Specification and Tools Offering the Delivery of system Integration Around home Networks" (Dewsbury, Taylor, Edge, 2002). Each smart device has many properties which are specified by the system's designer. Different scenarios can be simulated by changing the configuration for each smart device. There is a library of smart devices which can be used by any smart house: each one can be parameterized. The Custodian tool is installed under Microsoft Visio 2000 software, while applications developed by Visual Basic or C++ can be adapted to Microsoft Visio 2000 (Custodian simulation, n.d.), (Martins, Amaral, Santos, Agiannidis, Edge, 2000).

Each smart device has general physical installation details and functions which define its behaviour. Functionality is based on logical conditions which are called states. These logical conditions work as follows: if the value of a state is TRUE then the device is active and participates in the simulation scenario, if the value is FALSE the device is inactive and does not take part in the simulation. This is defined as *Simulation Condition*. If *Simulation Condition* is TRUE, several states that depict the behaviour of the smart devices are active. These logical functions are known as *When Activated* functions. If *Simulation Condition* is FALSE, the *When deactivated* logical function is active. Table 1 presents the functionality of a smart device (Custodian simulation, n.d.), (Martins, Amaral, Santos, Agiannidis, Edge, 2000).

The smart house is based on a template which is provided by the Custodian tool. There are 4 different templates to be used for the design of a smart house. In this chapter we use the *Fully Automated* smart house template. The Custodian Visio2000 stencil and the Custodian Additional Stencil are the group of objects that use this template. Stencil is a library of objects, like sensors and smart devices. There are three ways to activate a smart device. Firstly, the device is activated automatically several times a day. These activations depend on the clock which is used to synchronize the simulation. Secondly, a smart device

Table 1. Device functionality for Custodian simulation tool (Custodian simulation, n.d.)

Device functionality	
Precondition ON	Shows the conditions that should be TRUE before the activation of the smart device. If FALSE the device is inactive.
Precondition OFF	Shows the conditions that should be TRUE before the deactivation of the smart device. If FALSE the device cannot be deactivated.
Simulation Condition	If TRUE the device participates in the simulation (the device is active). If FALSE the device does not participate in the simulation. Multiple simulation conditions for a smart device can coexist and between them one of the logical operands is used.
When Activated	These functions run when the device becomes active, in this case the simulation condition becomes TRUE.
When Deactivated	These functions stop running when the simulation condition becomes FALSE.

may be activated by another device. The *When Activated* functions should be used as *Simulation Condition* for another device, so when a device becomes active another device is activated as well. Thirdly, a device may be activated or deactivated manually: right click on the smart device and turn it ON or OFF (Custodian simulation, n.d.), (Martins, Amaral, Santos, Agiannidis, Edge, 2000).

Smart House Simulation Parameters

The smart house that is used for our simulation model is an apartment, which is approximately 50m² with 5m width and 9m length. The platforms used are Mica2, MicaZ and TelosB. The indoor range of these platforms is 10 – 30m which means that communication between the nodes is supported inside the house. Generally, MicaZ and Mica2 platforms are smaller and lighter than TelosB. TelosB platform can be used as temperature sensor, humidity detector, and light sensor. Mica2 platform uses the 868/916 MHz Industrial Scientific and Medical (ISM) frequency band, while the supported data rate is between 20 and 40 kbps with no interference problems. On the other hand, TelosB and MicaZ platforms use the 2.4 GHz ISM frequency band for their transmissions. The supported data rate is 250 kbps, but the transmissions can be affected by interference (Crossbow Technology, Inc. MICA2 Datasheet., n.d.)., (Crossbow Technology, Inc., n.d.).

The smart devices in the simulation model (e.g. sensors, network devices, actuators) are coloured white when are deactivated and red when activated. There are 5 rooms in this house (living room, bedroom, kitchen, bathroom and corridor) and each of the rooms is presented as a different Microsoft Visio's sheet (Figure 1).

Living Room

The plan of the living room is presented in Figure 2 along with a brief description for each smart device. These devices are: pressure mat, home server, light switches, lights, radiator, open-close window switch, living room window, living room window sensor, living room fan, camera and thermostat (Siafakas, 2008).

The pressure mat is enabled when pressure is applied on it. Therefore, it is placed at the entrance

Figure 1. Smart house simulation

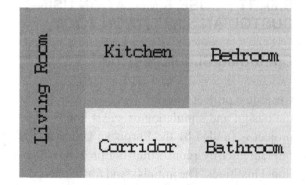

Figure 2. Living room simulation

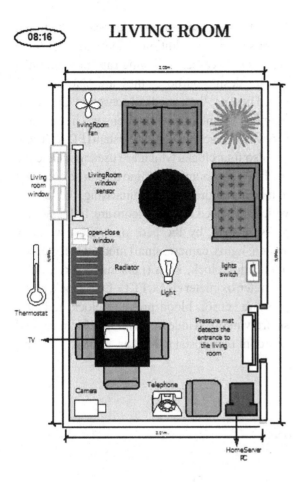

Figure 2. Living room simulation

medical data is pre-processed by the home server and transmitted to an external medical server. The smoke detectors, windows sensors, pressure mats, humidity detectors, the door sensor and the closed-circuit camera all send data to the home server.

The lights are placed in the middle of the living room. They are enabled either by the pressure mat or by the light switch and they are disabled when motion is detected in the corridor, or by the light switch. For this smart device MicaZ platform is used. The heating system of the smart house is based on a clock. There are three time periods during the day and night, that the heating system is enabled. The red colour of the radiator corresponds to the ON condition. The *Simulation Condition* depends on the clock that is responsible for the control of the central heating system. When the *Simulation Condition* is TRUE the radiator is enabled.

The switch is used to open and close the window in the living room. When the switch is turned ON the window opens, otherwise it closes. When it opens the *Simulation Condition* becomes TRUE. If the *Simulation Condition* of the window is FALSE the window is closed. The window sensor is a wireless sensor based on MicaZ platform. It is attached on the window and it is enabled either when the window is opened for a long period of time, or when any vibration is detected. The vibration could mean either a breaking of the glass or an attempt to break into the house through the window. When the sensor becomes active it transmits a message to the home server, which in turn enables the closed-circuit camera and the house alarm. The communication is based on the ZigBee standard.

The fan is enabled when the smoke detector, which is placed in the corridor, detects smoke in the house. In this case the fans in all rooms are activated in order to get rid of the smoke in the house. The smoke may come from the kitchen where the house occupant may have forgotten to turn OFF a cooking appliance. The fan will remain enabled as long as the smoke detector detects

of the living room. When the mat is activated the lights inside the living room are turned ON and a message "someone has entered the living room" is sent to the home server. Turning OFF the lights can be achieved manually, or when any motion is detected in the corridor of the house. For this smart device the MicaZ platform is used.

The home server manages the smart house, and collects and processes the data from the sensors. The data which is stored in a database, may be monitored through a web interface. Furthermore, there are functions which transmit data to external managers. This service is enabled when data is transmitted to the home server from the sensors which are placed inside the house. The transmitted smoke inside the house. For this smart device the MicaZ platform is used. The camera uses a TelosB platform and a web camera is attached to it. The communication between the cameras is based again on ZigBee standard which is supported by the selected platform. The purpose of these cameras is to be enabled by the smoke detectors, window sensors and the door sensor and not for continuous monitoring of the smart house. The recorded video is transmitted and stored to the house server and subsequently it is transmitted to an external manager if necessary. If an emergency situation is detected authorized users may enable the camera circuit to monitor the house or the house occupant. This sensor is based on TelosB platform. It checks the temperature continuously and when the temperature falls under 18°C (64.4°F) the sensor enables the central heating system. The temperature limits can be adjusted as necessary (Siafakas, 2008).

Bedroom

Many bedroom sensors are identical to the living room sensors. In addition to these sensors there are also medical sensors, which are movable units and for design purposes they are placed on the bed. There are three medical sensors: ECG, pulse oximeter and blood pressure sensor. The personal server is a Personal Digital Assistant (PDA). There are also four clocks which are used to enable the medical sensors and to remind the house occupant to take his medication. Summarising, the sensors which are placed in the bedroom are: lights switch, pressure mats by the bed, open-close window switch, lights, camera, smart medicine dispenser, medication clock, PDA (personal server), pulse oximeter, oximeter clock, ECG, ECG clock, blood pressure sensor, blood pressure clock, radiator, smart window, window sensor, bedroom fan and bedroom thermostat (Siafakas, 2008).

Figure 3. Bedroom simulation

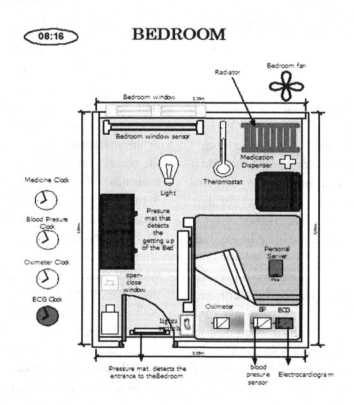

The pressure mats work in the same way as in the living room, namely, they are enabled when somebody steps on them. The mat, which is placed at the door, detects when somebody enters the bedroom. When the pressure mat becomes active, the lights are turned ON automatically and a message is sent to the home server in order to inform the system about the person's position. For this smart device and the bedroom lights switch MicaZ platform is used. Pressure mat 2 (by the bed) becomes active when somebody steps on it. It is placed by the bed where the occupant steps on it when he goes to bed. Again, for this smart device the MicaZ platform is used. For open-close window switch, when the switch is turned ON the window in the bedroom opens, otherwise it closes.

Bedroom lights are enabled either by stepping on pressure mats or by turning the light switch ON. They are turned OFF when a motion is detected in the corridor, or the switch is turned OFF. This smart device and the camera use the MicaZ and TelosB platforms, respectively. Communication between the cameras and the home server are based on the ZigBee standard. The recorded video is transmitted to house server where it is stored, and if necessary, it is transmitted to an external manager.

The smart medication dispenser is a smart device that is used to remind the house's occupant to take his medication. This service is based on a clock that is programmed to enable the smart medicine dispenser certain predetermined times a day and to serve the medicine to the occupant. The medical dispenser informs the occupant for the medication by a sound-light signal. For this smart device MicaZ platform is used. The medication clock is attached on the medicine dispenser and enables the dispenser to serve the medication to the house's occupant. The medication is given on certain times which are determined by the administrator of the medical subsystem of the smart house. The programming of the smart clock is done via the Internet and the house server.

The house server is connected with each external manager via the internet connection of the smart house. The medication clock is programmed to activate the medicine dispenser three times a day and they represent the *Simulation Conditions* for medication clock.

PDA is the manager of the medical sensors. A Personal Area Network (PAN) coordinator is installed on the PDA and synchronizes the sensors' transmissions by sending beacons. The communication between the PDA and the medical sensors is based on the ZigBee standard with transmission frequency at 2.4 GHz. The PDA has a 16 GB Secure digital memory card to store the collected data and a 400 MHz Intel processor. The PDA communicates with the home server using IEEE 802.11g standard. The PDA has the ability to be connected directly to the internet using a General Packet Radio System (GPRS) connection. This implies that the medical services work without any problems even if the smart house's occupant isn't inside the house. This is due to the fact that the PDA is able to store a large amount of data and can transmit it to the external manager or even to the home server via the internet. For this smart device the Mica2 platform is used.

The pulse oximeter is a medical sensor that is based on a MicaZ platform and is used to measure heart rate and blood oxygen saturation. The smart device remains in sleep mode for most of the time and it is activated certain times a day. The activation of the oximeter depends on the oximeter clock. This clock is programmed in accordance to the physicians' suggestions. The oximeter collects the medical data three times a day, it stores it temporarily in the flash memory of the MicaZ platform and then it transmits it to the PDA. Oximeter clock is programmed in order to activate the pulse oximeter at specific time intervals every day. The clock may be set up via the Internet by using the applications resident to the home server. The clock is installed on the PDA and communication between the home server and the PDA is achieved using the IEEE 802.11g standard.

The oximeter clock is enabled three times daily: 8:00 am, 4:00 pm, midnight and each activation lasts for one minute.

The ECG sensor is based on TelosB platform which is compatible with the IEEE 802.15.4 standard. The daughter card uses three electrodes and collects data in order to monitor the electrical activity of the heart. Each ECG lasts for 15 minutes and is activated twice a day. The time in which the ECG becomes active depend on the ECG clock and is programmed by the physicians which are responsible for the smart house's medical applications. The ECG clock manages the ECG sensor in a similar manner as the clocks of the other medical sensors. Blood pressure sensor is based on a MicaZ platform and it is compatible with the ZigBee standard. This sensor measures the blood pressure three times a day and transmits the measurements to the PDA.

Blood pressure clock activates the blood pressure sensor three times per day: 8:01, 16:01 and 24:01. Each active period lasts for 1 minute. The clock is set up by physicians and the settings are patient dependent. The red colour of the radiator means that the heating system is turned ON. The heating management system turns ON the radiators three times a day. The periods that the radiators are active are: 07:00-10:00, 15:00-17:00 and 23:00-01:00. This clock is the *Simulation Condition* of the central heating system. When the *Simulation Condition* is TRUE the radiators are enabled (red), otherwise they are disabled and the colour of the radiators becomes white.

The bedroom window is a smart device, which is managed by a switch on the wall. When the switch is turned ON the window opens, otherwise the window closes. For this smart device the MicaZ platform is used. Window sensor is used for security reasons. The sensor detects when a window is opened for longer than normal periods and detects vibrations of the window. If someone wants to break into the house window vibrations are detected by the sensor. If an earthquake takes place the glasses of the window start to vibrate and

this vibration can also be detected. The window's sensor enables the closed-circuit cameras and informs the home server. This sensor is based on a MicaZ platform which is compatible with IEEE 802.15.4. Bedroom fan has the same properties and functionality as the fan in the living room. Bedroom thermostat temperature sensor monitors the temperature and controls the central heating system and it is based on TelosB platform (Siafakas, 2008).

Kitchen

The smart devices installed in the kitchen support energy management, security and control. Services that monitor the smoke and the humidity levels are supported as well. The level of the water in the kitchen sink is checked by a specific sensor to avoid a possible flood. The window is controlled by a sensor for security reasons and the lights are controlled in order to manage the energy consumption. The following list presents the sensors which are placed in the kitchen (Figure 4): pressure mat, lights switch, open-close window switch, camera, lights, kitchen sink, water level counter, kitchen smoke detector, kitchen humidity detector, kitchen window, kitchen window sensor, kitchen fan, radiator and kitchen thermostat (Siafakas, 2008).

The pressure mat, the kitchen lights, the open-close window switch and the functionalities and platforms are similar as the living room and bedroom. In order to monitor the house in emergency situations, the smart house gives the possibility to authorized users to enable the closed-circuit camera. Also, the kitchen sink is a smart device, which belongs to a subsystem that controls the tap water and is based on TelosB platform.

The water level counter is a sensor which monitors the level of the water in the kitchen sink. If the sensor measures a high water level, it closes the tap and informs the home server. The sensor is attached on the sink and the communication with the home server is based on the ZigBee

Figure 4. Kitchen simulation

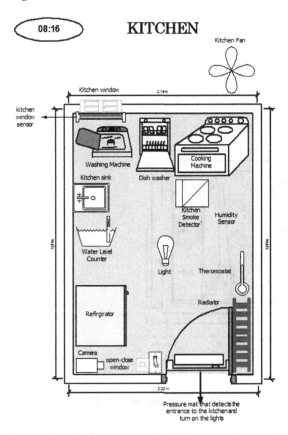

standard. For this smart device TelosB platform is used. The kitchen smoke detector is a sensor that is used to detect smoke inside the kitchen. The sensor is based on a TelosB platform and a daughter card which measures the air quality and clarity. If smoke is detected in the kitchen, the fan is turned ON in order to clean the air, and the closed-circuit camera is enabled and sends a message to the home server for analysis and management. If the alarm system is activated then the smoke detector sends a message to the alarm system to turn it ON.

The kitchen humidity detector measures the level of humidity in the kitchen. High levels of humidity in the kitchen's atmosphere may be caused by a hot water flood, boiling water, or by a radiators leak. High levels of humidity in the house may burden the respiratory status of

a person with asthma. This sensor is based on a TelosB platform and a humidity level counter is attached on the platform as a daughter card. When high humidity levels are detected by the sensor, a message is sent to the home server and the kitchen fan is enabled to clean the atmosphere. Moreover, the closed-circuit camera is activated.

The kitchen window is similar to the other smart windows. Furthermore, the red colour of the radiator means that the heating system is turned ON. The heating management system turns on the radiators three times a day, or when the temperature falls below a certain limit. The periods that the radiators are active are: 07:00-10:00, 15:00-17:00 and 23:00-01:00. This clock represents the *Simulation Condition* of the central heating system. When the *Simulation Condition* is TRUE the radiators are enabled (red), otherwise they are disabled (white). The kitchen thermostat sensor is used to measure the room temperature and if it is bellow the predetermined threshold value (18°C, 64.4°F) the central heating system becomes active. For this smart device TelosB platform is used (Siafakas, 2008).

Bathroom

The smart bathroom supports services such as auto ON and OFF of the lights, entrance detection, humidity detection/control and water level control in the bath. Figure 5 presents the plan of the smart bathroom with the sensors and the rest of the smart devices placed in selected positions. Therefore, the smart devices and the sensors that are used are: pressure mat, lights switch, lights, open-close window switch, camera, smart bathroom sink, radiator, humidity sensor, water, level counter, smart bath, smart bathroom window, window sensor and bathroom thermostat (Siafakas, 2008).

The water level sensor is used to detect the water level in the bathtub. High water level represents a medical emergency situation, such as the fall of an elderly or disabled person inside the bathroom. For this smart device the TelosB platform

Figure 5. Bathroom simulation

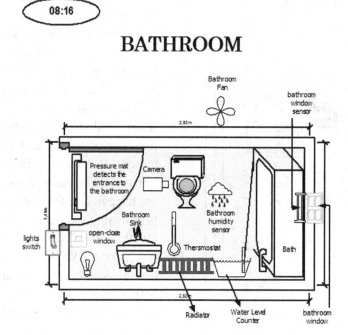

is used. The smart bath is a smart device which is used to setup the water level sensor. For this smart device MicaZ platform is used. The functional description of all other bathroom devices is similar as in the other rooms (Siafakas, 2008).

Corridor

The corridor of the smart house is placed in the middle of house and it provides access to all rooms. Security and safety applications such as house alarm, energy management sensors, thermostat, smart radiator and smoke detection are supported. Figure 6 shows the corridor smart devices and sensors: motion detector, camera, smoke detector, corridor thermostat radiator, lights, house alarm, house alarm switch, second person switch and heating clock (Siafakas, 2008).

The motion detector is a sensor that is composed of a TelosB platform and a digital web camera, which shoots several times a second. A Digital Signal Processor (DSP) is installed on the platform,

which comprises the last two photos to detect any differences. The comparison is done by using an abstraction between these images and if the difference between the images is over a certain threshold value the images are transmitted for further analysis to the home server. The motion detector is placed in the corridor because anyone who wants to move from one room to another inside the house should walk via the corridor. When the sensor is enabled, sends a message to the home server, enables the closed cameras circuit, turns OFF the lights in the other rooms and turns ON the lights in the corridor. The camera is activated by the sensors (windows' sensors, door sensor, smoke detectors), or by an external authorized user by using the home server's applications. The cameras are controlled through the home server using the ZigBee standard. This smart device is based on a TelosB platform.

The central smoke detector is placed in the middle of the house in order to detect smoke coming from everywhere. This sensor whenever

Figure 6. Corridor simulation

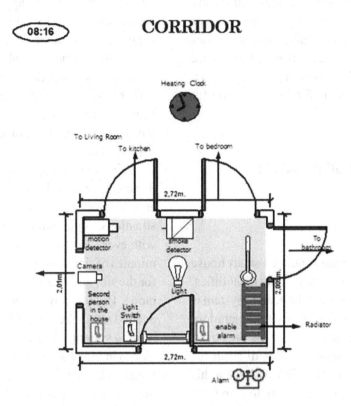

activated it enables the closed-circuit camera and the house alarm, and sends a message to the home server. This too is based on the TelosB platform. Corridor thermostat enables the central heating system, when the temperature falls below 18°C. For this smart device TelosB platform is used. The radiator is either enabled certain times by the heating clock, or by the thermostats in the rooms. For this smart device MicaZ platform is used. The lights turn ON either by the detection of motion in the corridor or by turning the lights switch ON. The lights are turned OFF, when the occupant enters another room or manually when there is no one else inside the house. The house alarm is enabled by the sensors, if an emergency situation is detected. It is based on MicaZ platform, which is ZigBee compatible.

The house alarm switch is a specially designed unit based on a MicaZ platform, it is connected to the house alarm via the IEEE 802.15.4 standard. The switch uses the fingerprints of the house's

occupant to turn ON the alarm, or an eight-character code. The recognition of the fingerprints is based on image processing mechanisms which are installed on MicaZ platform. The second person switch is a smart device which is enabled when another person is inside the house. For security reasons this switch may be turned ON either by the house's occupant or by authorized persons, for example doctors or members of the occupant's family. This switch is turned ON and OFF either by fingerprints' recognition or by an eight-character code. Again, for this smart device MicaZ platform is used.

The heating clock is programmed to enable the heating system of the smart house three periods a day. This clock acts as coordinator for the heating system. It is based on a MicaZ platform, it communicates with the room thermostats via the IEEE 802.15.4 standard and it enables the boiler to heat the house. There is a clock which synchronizes the simulation mechanism: the smart devices and sensors are activated during certain times. The functionality of the objects of this sheet is the same as in *Fully Automated* smart house template. Additionally, there are two more functions which define when day and night start, which are depicted as sun for day and moon for night (Siafakas, 2008).

SMART HOUSE SIMULATION SCENARIOS

Scenario 1

Let us assume that in the simulated smart house lives an old person with many health disabilities. His day starts at 8:00 am and the heating system is turned ON. Every morning he goes to the bathroom and then to the kitchen to prepare his breakfast. Due to his mobility disorders, it is difficult for him to turn ON and OFF the light and due to his mental disabilities he often forgets to turn OFF the lights, or to close the water taps, or even to

turn OFF the cooking appliances. The disabled person must take his medication several times a day, which is difficult for someone with such mental disabilities. He should measure certain vital signs several times daily like blood pressure, blood oxygen saturation and the electrical heart activity. This medical data is collected by a physician, who monitors and controls the disabled person's health.

Scenario 1 corresponds to the simulation of the disabled person's daily routine in a smart house and the way the smart house reacts in different situations. For the simulation the day starts at 6:58 with every 1 minute of real time to be equal to 3 minutes of simulation time. At 6:58 it is still night for the simulation and this is represented by a red moon. The day starts at 7 am and this is represented as a red sun in the Custodian simulation tool. The heating system of the house is enabled at 7:00. As shown in Figures 7 and 8, at 6:58 the radiator and the corridor heating clock are disabled. At 7:07 the heating system is enabled and the radiators remain active up to 10:00 am (Siafakas, 2008).

Figure 7. Heating system deactivated (6:58 am)

Figure 8. Heating system activated (7:07 am)

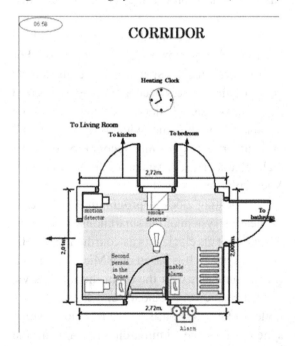

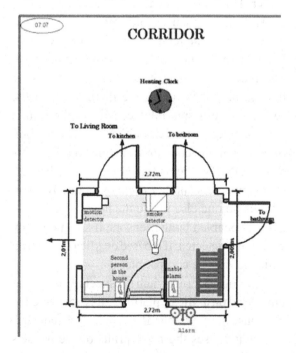

There are medical sensors attached to person's body, which are enabled several times a day due to the physician's instructions who is responsible for the healthcare oriented subsystem of the smart house. The pulse oximeter and blood pressure sensors are enabled at 8:01. It must be mentioned that there are clocks which are responsible for the time that the sensors are active. The sensors transmit the collected data to the PDA for storing and initial processing. These actions can be observed in Figure 9.

At the same time the disabled person gets out of bed when he steps on the pressure mat and the lights are turned ON (Figures 10 and 11).

The disabled person exits the bedroom and passes through the corridor to enter the bathroom. The motion detector in the corridor detects the motion, turns ON the light in the corridor and turns OFF the light in the bedroom. Moreover, motion detector in the corridor enables the closed-circuit camera for security reasons (Figure 12).

The disabled person enters the bathroom by stepping on the bathroom's pressure mat, the light in the bathroom is turned ON and the lights in the corridor are turned OFF. After 10 minutes the disabled person exits the bathroom, the motion detector in the corridor detects the motion, the disabled person enters the kitchen and prepares his breakfast. During breakfast the ECG is enabled and remains active for 15 minutes. As we can see

Figure 10. Enable the pressure mat by the bed

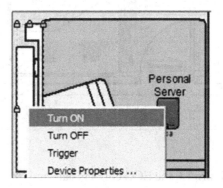

Figure 9. Oximeter and blood pressure sensors activated

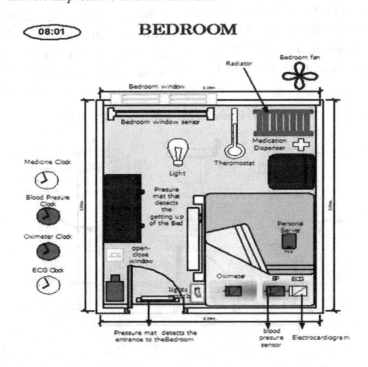

Figure 11. The lighting system is turned on

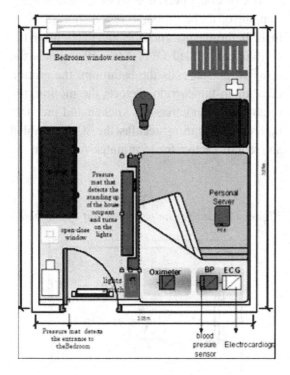

in Figure 13, the ECG collects data and transmits it to the PDA for storing and initial processing.

Subsequently, the disabled person finishes his breakfast and returns to his bedroom. The lights are turned ON and OFF in the same fashion. At 9:00 am it is time for his medication. The medical dispenser becomes active and informs the disabled

person to take his medication either by a voice signal or by a light signal and serves the medicine (Figure 14).

Let us suppose that the disabled person forgot to close the water tab in the kitchen sink. The water level counter detects that the level in the sink is higher than normal and a flood is possible. The sensor becomes active, the water tap closes, the home server is informed and the closed-circuit camera is activated to record the event for detailed analysis (Figure 15).

The smart house is designed to manage emergency situations, which can be medical or not. Emergency situations may be fire, broken window, open door, high humidity levels in the bathroom, water tap that remains open for a long period of time. A house alarm is provided in order to be activated when an emergency situation takes place. For scenario 1 the house alarm isn't turned ON, while in scenario 2 the house alarm is turned ON. Let us suppose that someone breaks the window in the living room and gets into the house. On the window a sensor is attached which can detect vibrations. The window sensor becomes active and it activates the closed-circuit camera and informs the home server of the event. The recorded video is stored in the home server and could be monitored by authorized users to evaluate the event. No one else is informed for the event

Figure 12. Motion is detected in the corridor and the lights are turned on

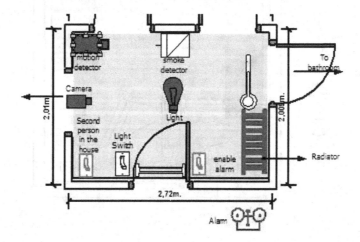

except the external manager. This example involves no house alarm. The results of the simulation scenario 1 using the Custodian simulation tool are listed in Table 2, where for every simulation step the status of the smart house is described. The simulation interval is 30 minutes and the number of steps are 24 (total simulation time 720 minutes) (Siafakas, 2008).

Scenario 2

Scenario 2 is similar to scenario 1, except that the disabled person has enabled the alarm. Therefore, when a sensor detects vibration, the cameras are enabled, the home server is informed and the house alarm is activated. In Figure 16 the alarm is not turned ON, while in Figure 17 the house alarm

is turned ON therefore, when the sensor detects a vibration the house alarm is energized.

Simulation scenario 2 is summarised in Table 3: for specific times the event and the smart house status are presented. The simulation interval in

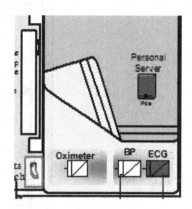

Figure 13. ECG communicates with PDA

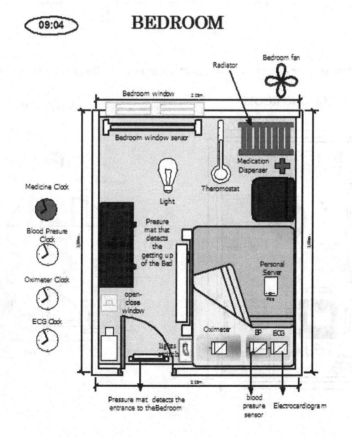

Figure 14. The medication dispenser is activated on specific times

Figure 15. High water level is detected

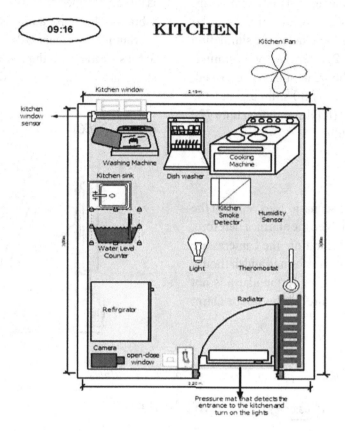

Figure 16. The window sensor detects vibration and the house alarm (in the corridor) isn't turned on

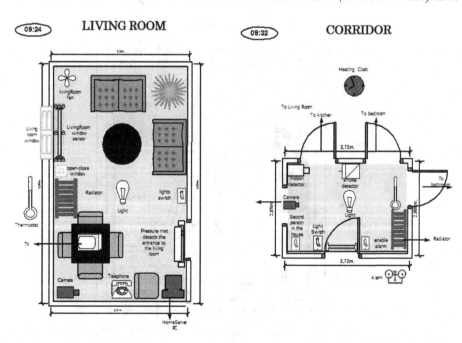

Table 2. Simulation results for scenario 1

Time	Event and smart house status
6:01	It is night and only the home server is activated.
6:31	The same as above.
7:01	The day starts and the central heating system is activated. All the radiators are also activated, as well as the corridor heating clock.
7:31	The central heating system and the home server remain activated.
8:01	The blood pressure sensor and the pulse oximeter are activated for 1 minute. PDA is activated because it stores the data from the sensors and transmits the data to home server.
8:31	Blood pressure and pulse oximeter sensors are deactivated. The central heating system and the home server remain activated. The disabled person gets up from his bed and when he steps on the pressure mat the lights are turned ON. The disabled person passes through the corridor, the motion detector becomes activated, the lights in the corridor are turned ON, the cameras are turned ON and the light in the bedroom turn OFF. Subsequently, the disabled person enters the kitchen the lights are turned ON by stepping on the pressure mat and the lights in corridor are turned OFF. Then, the disabled person enables the cooking appliance to prepare his breakfast.
9:01	The disabled person has left the kitchen. The medication dispenser is activated at 9:00 and remains active up to 9:15. The disabled person takes his medication. He is in the bedroom and lights are turned ON, but he has forgotten to turn OFF the cooking appliance. The smoke detector detects the smoke and enables the fan. The smoke is also detected by the corridor smoke detector. The smoke detectors enable the closed-circuit camera to record the event and the home server informs an external manager to monitor the recorded video. The external manager evaluates the event and informs the fire brigade and an ambulance if necessary.
9:31	The central heating system and the home server remain activated. The disabled person is inside the kitchen, where the lights are turned ON.
10:01	The central heating system is deactivated at 10:00. The home server remains activated. The disabled person turns ON the house alarm system which is placed in the corridor.
10:31	The disabled person moves to bedroom but the lights remain turned ON, because when the disabled person enters the bedroom the pressure mat enabled the light.
11:01	The disabled person is sleeping on his bed and the lights remain turned ON.
11:31	The same as above.
12:01	The disabled person is sleeping. The temperature sensor in the bedroom detects that the temperature has fallen under a certain threshold value. All radiators and the central heating clock are activated.
12:31	The disabled person is still sleeping and the lights remained turned ON. The temperature sensor in the bedroom is deactivated because the temperature is above the threshold value. All radiators and the central heating clock are deactivated.
13:01	The same as above.
13:31	The disabled person has forgotten to close the water tap in the bath. The humidity level in the bathroom increased over a certain threshold value and humidity sensor is activated. The humidity detector enables the fan inside the bathroom and the closed-circuit camera. The recorder video is transmitted to the home server. The humidity detector enables the house alarm and the disabled person wakes up. He goes to the bathroom to see what happens. The lights in the bathroom are turned ON by stepping on the pressure mat. The disabled person closes the water tap in the bath.
14:01	The home server remains activated. The humidity detector isn't activated. The fan and the closed-circuit cameras aren't activated. The disabled person is in the living room where the light is turned ON and the window is opened.
14:31	The disabled person is still in the living room. The light is turned OFF because she had turned them off manually and the window is closed.
15:01	The central heating system is activated at 15:00. The disabled person hasn't left the living room yet.
15:31	The same as above.
16:01	The central heating system remains activated. The blood pressure sensor and the pulse oximeter become active and transmit the data to the PDA. The PDA sends the collected medical data to the home server, which forwards it to an external medical server. The door is opened for a period of time longer than a certain threshold value and the door sensor is activated. The closed-circuit camera is activated and the home server stores the recorded video. The video is monitored by an external user and he may try to close the door or to inform the house's occupant to do so. This depends on the applications installed on the home server.

Table 2. continued

Time	Event and smart house status
16:31	The blood pressure sensor and the pulse oximeter aren't active. The disabled person has entered the bedroom and has turned OFF the light.
17:01	It is night and the home server remains activated. The central heating system isn't activated any more. The medication dispenser is activated at 17:00 and will remain active up to 17:15. The disabled person takes his medication and he is in the bedroom and lights are turned ON.
17:31	The disabled person is in the living room and watches TV. The lights are turned ON because the pressure mat is activated by stepping on it.

Figure 17. The window sensor detects vibration and the house alarm (in the corridor) is turned on

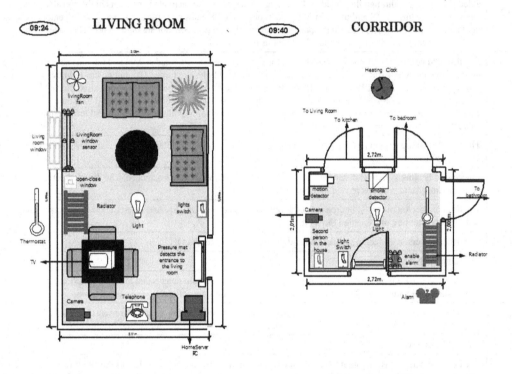

this scenario is 15 minutes, while the number of steps is 24 (total simulation time 360 minutes) (Siafakas, 2008).

MEDICAL DATA MONITORING

A web interface could be designed to monitor the data collected by the medical sensors, i.e. blood pressure, pulse oximeter and ECG. The collected data can be stored in a database, which can be accessed and searched through a web interface. The database would be installed in the home server and the web interface may be used to monitor the data either locally or via the internet. The access to the database via the internet would be allowed only by authorized users. The authorization-authentication mechanism is controlled by the smart house system. The database may be an SQL Server 2005 database which can be implemented for example by Server Explorer of Visual Studio 2005 (Figure 18). The database is composed of two tables: BloodPressure that stores data about

Table 3. Simulation results for scenario 2

Time	Event and smart house status
6:01	It is night and only the home server is activated.
6:16	The disabled person gets up from his bed. He steps on the pressure mat by the bed and the lights are turned ON. He moves to the corridor, the motion detector detects the motion and the light at the corridor is turned ON. The disabled person turns ON the light in the bathroom. The lights in the corridor are turned OFF.
6:31	The lights in the bathroom, corridor and bedroom are turned OFF. The disabled person lies on his bed.
6:46	The same as above.
7:01	The day starts and the central heating system is activated. All the radiators are activated as well as the heating clock in the corridor.
7:16	The central heating system and the home server remain activated. Nothing else is activated inside the house.
7:31	The same as above.
7:46	The same as above.
8:01	The blood pressure sensor and the pulse oximeter are activated for 1 minute at 8:01. The PDA is activated because it stores the data from the sensors and transmits it to the home server.
8:16	The central heating system and the home server remain activated. The blood pressure sensor and the pulse oximeter are deactivated and ECG is activated. The PDA is also activated because it stores the data of the ECG and transmits it to the home server.
8:31	ECG isn't activated any more. At 8:31 am the disabled person gets up from his bed and when he steps on the pressure mat which is placed by the bed the lights are turned ON. The disabled person passes through the corridor and motion detector becomes activated, the lights in the corridor are turned ON, the cameras are turned ON and the bedroom light is turned OFF. The disabled person enters the kitchen the lights are turned ON by stepping on the pressure mat and the lights in corridor are turned OFF. The disabled person enables the cooking appliance to prepare his breakfast.
8:46	The telephone rings and he goes to the living room to answer the call, but the telephone stops ringing when the disabled person is in the corridor. The light in the corridor is turned ON because the motion sensor is activated.
9:01	The disabled person leaves the kitchen. The medication dispenser is activated at 9:00 and remains active up to 9:15. The disabled person takes his medication. He is in the bedroom and the lights are turned ON, but he has forgotten a cooking appliance on. The kitchen smoke detector detects the smoke and enables the fan. The smoke is also detected by the smoke detector in the corridor. The smoke detectors also enable the closed-circuit camera and the home server informs an external manager to monitor the recorded video. The external manager evaluates the event and informs the fire brigade and an ambulance if necessary.
9:16	The central heating system and the home server remain activated. The disabled person sees the smoke and goes to the kitchen. The fans clear the atmosphere inside the house. The smoke detectors are deactivated because the level of the smoke in the house is under a certain threshold value.
9:31	The disabled person is inside the kitchen where the light is turned ON.
9:46	The same as above.
10:01	The central heating system is deactivated at 10:00. The home server remains activated. The disabled person moves to bathroom to wash his hair and turns ON the alarm system which is placed in the corridor.
10:16	The disabled person is inside the kitchen and enables the dishwasher machine and the kitchen light is turned ON.
10:31	The disabled person moves to bedroom and he lied on his bed, but the lights remain turned ON because when he enters the bedroom the pressure mat has enabled the light.
10:46	The same as above.
11:01	The same as above.
11:16	The same as above.
11:31	The same as above.
11:46	The same as above.
12:01	The home server remains activated. The disabled person is sleeping and the lights remain turned ON. The temperature sensor in the bedroom detects that the temperature has fallen under a certain threshold value. All radiators and the central heating clock are activated.

Figure 18. Medical database: blood pressure and heart rate

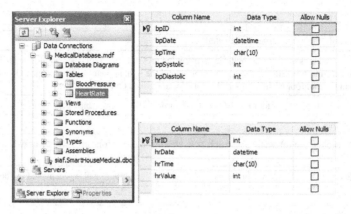

Figure 19. Blood pressure measurements

ID	DATE	TIME	SYS VALUE	DIAS VALUE	ID	DATE	TIME	SYS VALUE	DIAS VALUE
1	8/12/2007	08:02	120	80	48	24/12/2007	00:02	120	70
2	8/12/2007	16:02	140	90	49	24/12/2007	08:02	120	80
3	9/12/2007	00:02	140	100	50	24/12/2007	16:02	150	90
4	9/12/2007	08:02	120	100	51	25/12/2007	00:02	140	90
5	9/12/2007	16:02	100	80	52	25/12/2007	08:02	90	60
6	10/12/2007	00:02	130	90	53	25/12/2007	16:02	120	70
7	10/12/2007	08:02	120	80	54	26/12/2007	00:02	100	70
8	10/12/2007	16:02	130	90	55	26/12/2007	08:02	110	70
9	11/12/2007	00:02	120	80	56	26/12/2007	16:02	140	80
10	11/12/2007	08:02	110	70	57	27/12/2007	00:02	120	90
11	11/12/2007	16:02	100	60	58	27/12/2007	08:02	140	90
12	12/12/2007	00:02	120	80	59	27/12/2007	16:02	160	90
13	12/12/2007	08:02	130	90	60	28/12/2007	00:02	140	90
14	12/12/2007	16:02	140	100	61	28/12/2007	08:02	150	100
15	13/12/2007	00:02	160	100	62	28/12/2007	16:02	170	110
16	13/12/2007	08:02	140	110	63	29/12/2007	00:02	140	100
17	13/12/2007	16:02	130	100	64	29/12/2007	08:02	150	100
18	14/12/2007	00:02	120	90	65	29/12/2007	16:02	120	80
19	14/12/2007	08:02	100	70	66	30/12/2007	00:02	130	80
20	14/12/2007	16:02	120	70	67	30/12/2007	08:02	120	70
21	15/12/2007	00:02	120	80	68	30/12/2007	16:02	140	90
22	15/12/2007	08:02	130	80	69	31/12/2007	00:02	120	90
23	15/12/2007	16:02	130	80	70	31/12/2007	08:02	150	90
24	16/12/2007	00:02	150	90	71	31/12/2007	16:02	120	100
25	16/12/2007	08:02	120	80	72	1/1/2008	00:02	140	100
26	16/12/2007	16:02	110	90	73	1/1/2008	08:02	150	110
27	17/12/2007	00:02	100	80	74	1/1/2008	16:02	140	110
28	17/12/2007	08:02	120	80	75	2/1/2008	00:02	140	100
29	17/12/2007	16:02	130	80	76	2/1/2008	08:02	100	80
30	18/12/2007	00:02	110	70	77	2/1/2008	16:02	90	60
31	18/12/2007	08:02	110	60	78	3/1/2008	00:02	120	80
32	18/12/2007	16:02	110	70	79	3/1/2008	08:02	130	90
33	19/12/2007	00:02	150	100	80	3/1/2008	16:02	150	100
34	19/12/2007	08:02	120	80	81	4/1/2008	00:02	140	110
35	19/12/2007	16:02	140	80	82	4/1/2008	08:02	120	90
36	20/12/2007	00:02	170	110	83	4/1/2008	16:02	160	110
37	20/12/2007	08:02	170	110	84	5/1/2008	00:02	150	110
38	20/12/2007	16:02	180	100	85	5/1/2008	08:02	120	80
39	21/12/2007	00:02	190	100	86	5/1/2008	16:02	130	80
40	21/12/2007	08:02	220	110	87	6/1/2008	00:02	140	70
41	21/12/2007	16:02	200	120	88	6/1/2008	08:02	150	90
42	22/12/2007	00:02	180	110	89	6/1/2008	16:02	120	90
43	22/12/2007	08:02	160	100	90	7/1/2008	00:02	130	100
44	22/12/2007	16:02	150	90	91	7/1/2008	08:02	120	90
45	23/12/2007	00:02	120	90	92	7/1/2008	16:02	140	110
46	23/12/2007	08:02	130	90	93	8/1/2008	00:02	150	110
47	23/12/2007	16:02	120	70	94	8/1/2008	08:02	120	100

blood pressure and HeartRate that stores data about heart rate (Siafakas, 2008).

In order to simulate the way that the web interface monitors the collected data, it is important to import to the database typical values of blood pressure and heart rate for a person with health disabilities. These values are presented in Figures 19 and 20 and are collected by the General Hospital of Thessaly.

DISCUSSION AND CONCLUSION

The aim of this chapter is to demonstrate how computer technology can help persons with health or mental disabilities to live independently. A hot research topic nowadays in computer science is the smart house automation. In an automated house there are services which may help persons with health, mental, or mobility disorders who live alone to have a better quality of life. Additionally, a healthcare oriented subsystem is essential

Figure 20. Heart rate measurements

ID	DATE	TIME	HEART RATE VALUE
1	8/12/2007	08:02	78
2	8/12/2007	16:02	85
3	9/12/2007	00:02	72
4	9/12/2007	08:02	88
5	9/12/2007	16:02	85
6	10/12/2007	00:02	88
7	10/12/2007	08:02	95
8	10/12/2007	16:02	92
9	11/12/2007	00:02	90
10	11/12/2007	08:02	85
11	11/12/2007	16:02	80
12	12/12/2007	00:02	72
13	12/12/2007	08:02	70
14	12/12/2007	16:02	80
15	13/12/2007	00:02	74
16	13/12/2007	08:02	78
17	13/12/2007	16:02	98
18	14/12/2007	00:02	102
19	14/12/2007	08:02	100
20	14/12/2007	16:02	90
21	15/12/2007	00:02	72
22	15/12/2007	08:02	60
23	15/12/2007	16:02	68
24	16/12/2007	00:02	75
25	16/12/2007	08:02	78
26	16/12/2007	16:02	78
27	17/12/2007	00:02	82
28	17/12/2007	08:02	85
29	17/12/2007	16:02	80
30	18/12/2007	00:02	78
31	18/12/2007	08:02	75
32	18/12/2007	16:02	78
33	19/12/2007	00:02	75
34	19/12/2007	08:02	79
35	19/12/2007	16:02	90
36	20/12/2007	00:02	114
37	20/12/2007	08:02	110
38	20/12/2007	16:02	100
39	21/12/2007	00:02	122
40	21/12/2007	08:02	100
41	21/12/2007	16:02	100
42	22/12/2007	00:02	101
43	22/12/2007	08:02	122
44	22/12/2007	16:02	99
45	23/12/2007	00:02	95
46	23/12/2007	08:02	93
47	23/12/2007	16:02	90

ID	DATE	TIME	HEART RATE VALUE
48	24/12/2007	00:02	90
49	24/12/2007	08:02	90
50	24/12/2007	16:02	88
51	25/12/2007	00:02	88
52	25/12/2007	08:02	78
53	25/12/2007	16:02	75
54	26/12/2007	00:02	80
55	26/12/2007	08:02	82
56	26/12/2007	16:02	80
57	27/12/2007	00:02	72
58	27/12/2007	08:02	68
59	27/12/2007	16:02	62
60	28/12/2007	00:02	70
61	28/12/2007	08:02	72
62	28/12/2007	16:02	75
63	29/12/2007	00:02	78
64	29/12/2007	08:02	78
65	29/12/2007	16:02	80
66	30/12/2007	00:02	82
67	30/12/2007	08:02	80
68	30/12/2007	16:02	80
69	31/12/2007	00:02	78
70	31/12/2007	08:02	73
71	31/12/2007	16:02	71
72	1/1/2008	00:02	79
73	1/1/2008	08:02	70
74	1/1/2008	16:02	68
75	2/1/2008	00:02	62
76	2/1/2008	08:02	58
77	2/1/2008	16:02	67
78	3/1/2008	00:02	69
79	3/1/2008	08:02	77
80	3/1/2008	16:02	80
81	4/1/2008	00:02	75
82	4/1/2008	08:02	78
83	4/1/2008	16:02	70
84	5/1/2008	00:02	70
85	5/1/2008	08:02	72
86	5/1/2008	16:02	70
87	6/1/2008	00:02	72
88	6/1/2008	08:02	68
89	6/1/2008	16:02	60
90	7/1/2008	00:02	60
91	7/1/2008	08:02	58
92	7/1/2008	16:02	58
93	8/1/2008	00:02	62
94	8/1/2008	08:02	72

in such a smart house, since elderly and disabled persons face many health problems. There are many wireless standards that can be used for home automation systems, however due to their characteristics, most of them cannot be used in a smart house. The dominant network standard used for smart houses is the IEEE 802.15.4 referred to as ZigBee, which supports wireless networks with low design complexity and energy requirements and it is fairly easy to implement and maintain.

An important aspect in the design of a smart house is to choose the most suitable wireless sensors. Each sensor used in such a system is composed of a platform and a daughter card, connected to the platform. In the automation system of a smart house it is necessary to include a home server which collects all data from the sensors. This server is also the gateway to the internet and has a database installed which is accessed by a web interface. In addition to the home server, a personal medical server should be used to store temporarily and pre-process medical data. This server manages the medical sensors and communicates with the home server to transmit the collected data for further analysis and permanent storage. The medical server usually is a portable device, which stores the data, either when the house's occupant moves away from the house, or when there is a problem with the connection between the home server and the PDA. Thus, it has to be emphasized that the medical server is a crucial part of this system and contributes to the smooth operation of the overall system..

Subsequently, this work showed that a web interface is also necessary. It gives access to authorized users to control and manage the smart house's system and to monitor the collected data. This interface should be connected to the database, which stores all data that is transmitted by the sensors to the home server. The data monitoring is very important for the evaluation of the occupant's health status and the status of the smart house. Authorized users can be either distant users via the internet, or users which access the system locally from the home server. This chapter proposes a simple version of a web interface which monitors medical data.

Future work includes an intelligent system which will manage the water taps. Furthermore, motion sensors may be added in the sink, in the bath so that if any movement is detected, the water tap activates. Light sensors can be added, which will measure the brightness inside the house and turn the lights ON as needed. A medical service that will collect and analyze the values of the blood sugar level will address problems related to diabetic persons. Security of data transmissions is also a very important issue for future work. Additionally, the system must operate with the least possible delay since in many cases the system has to react in real time. This depends on the applications, the sensors and the in-house connections between nodes, as well as the communication between the house and any authorized external user of the system. Thus, real time operation of the system is another important issue for future work. Also, the development of a more sophisticated web interface is of prime importance.

REFERENCES

Chan, M., Estève, D., Escriba, C., & Campo, E. (2008). A review of smart homes – Present state and future challenges. *Computer Methods and Programs in Biomedicine, 1*, 55–81. doi:10.1016/j.cmpb.2008.02.001

Chen, L., Nugent, C., Mulvenna, M., Finlay, D., Hong, X., & Poland, M. (2008). Using Event Calculus for behaviour reasoning and assistance in a smart home. [including Lecture Notes in Artificial Intelligence and Lecture Notes in Bioinformatics]. *Lecture Notes in Computer Science, 5120*, 81–89. doi:10.1007/978-3-540-69916-3_10

Crossbow Technology, Inc. (n.d.). *TelosB Datasheet. Crossbow: Wireless Sensor Networks.* Retrieved from http://www.xbow.com/Products/Product_pdf_files/Wireless_pdf/TelosB_Datasheet.pdf

Crossbow Technology, Inc. MICA2 Datasheet. (n.d.). *Crossbow: Wireless Sensor Networks.* Retrieved from http://www.xbow.com/Products/Product_pdf_files/Wireless_pdf/MICA2_Datasheet.pdf

Crossbow Technology, Inc. MICAz Datasheet. (n.d.). *Cressbow: Wireless Sensor Networks.* Retrieved from http://www.xbow.com/Products/Product_pdf_files/Wireless_pdf/MICAz_Datasheet.pdf

Custodian simulation (n.d.). *Custodian simulation tool homepage.* Retrieved from http://www2.rgu.ac.uk/subj/search/research/sustainablehousing/custodian/home.html

Dewsbury, G., Clarke, K., Rouncefield, M., Sommerville, I., Taylor, B., & Edge, M. (2004). Designing acceptable 'smart' home technology to support people in the home. *Technology and Disability, 15*(3), 191–201.

Dewsbury, G., Taylor, B., & Edge, M. (2002). Designing safe smart home systems for vulnerable people. In *Proceedings of the Health Informatics Conference,* (pp. 65-70).

Gorday, E., Hester, P., Gutierrez, L., Naeve, J. A., Heile, M., Bahl, B., & Callaway, V. (2002, August). Home Networking with IEEE 802.15.4: A Developing Standard for Low-Rate Wireless Personal Area Networks, *IEEE Communications Magazine.*

Gutierrez, J. (2004, September). On the use of IEEE 802.15.4 to enable wireless sensor networks in building automation. In *Proceedings of the 15th IEEE International Symposium on Personal, Indoor and Mobile Radio Communications* (PIMRC, Vol. 3, pp. 1865-1869).

Gutierrez, J. A., Naeve, M., Callaway, E., Bourgeois, M., Mitter, V., & Heile, B. (2001). IEEE 802.15.4: Developing standard for low-power low-cost Wireless Personal Area Networks. *IEEE Network,* (September/October): 2001.

Huang, M.-C., Huang, J.-C., You, J.-C., & Jong, J.-G. (2007, November). The wireless sensor network for home-care system using ZigBee. [IIHMSP]. *IEEE Intelligent Information Hiding and Multimedia Signal Processing, 1,* 643–646.

Jin, M.-H., Yu, C.-H., Lai, H.-R., & Feng, M.-W. (2007). Zigbee positioning system for smart home application. [including Lecture Notes in Artificial Intelligence and Lecture Notes in Bioinformatics]. *Lecture Notes in Computer Science, 4743,* 183–192. doi:10.1007/978-3-540-74767-3_20

Liang, L., Huang, L., Jiang, X., & Yao, Y. (2008). Design and implementation of wireless smart-home sensor network based on ZigBee protocol. In *Proceedings of the International Conference on Communications, Circuits and Systems* (ICCCAS), 2008, (pp. 434-438).

Martins, J. M., Amaral, F. T., Santos, D., Agiannidis, A., & Edge, M. (2000). The Custodian Tool: Simple Design of Home Automation Systems for People with Special Needs. In *Proceedings of the EIB Scientific Conference,* Munich, Germany.

Milenkovic, A., Otto, C., & Jovanov, E. (2006). Wireless sensor networks for personal health monitoring: Issues and an implementation. *Computer Communications Journal, 2006,* 2521–2533. doi:10.1016/j.comcom.2006.02.011

Noury, N., Virone, G., Barralon, P., Ye, J., Rialle, V., & Demongeot, J. (2003). New trends in health smart homes. In *Proceedings of the Healthcom conference,* (pp. 118-127).

Siafakas, G. (2008). *Healthcare oriented smart houses for elderly or disabled persons. MSc thesis*. Department of Informatics & Telecommunications, TEI of Larissa (in collaboration with Staffordshire University, UK).

Stefanov, D. H., Bien, Z., & Bang, W.-C. (2004). The smart house for older persons and persons with physical disabilities: structure, technology arrangements, and perspectives. *IEEE Transactions on Neural Systems and Rehabilitation Engineering, 12*(2), 228–250. doi:10.1109/TNSRE.2004.828423

Xueliang, X., Cheng, T., & Xingyuan, F. (2007). A health care system based on PLC and Zigbee. In *Proceedings of the International Conference on Wireless Communications Networking and Mobile Computing* (WiCom), (pp. 3063-3066).

Chapter 9
Management and Challenges Facing Wireless Sensor Networks in Telemedicine Applications

Ibrahiem Mahmoud Mohamed El Emary
King Abdulaziz University, Saudi Arabia

ABSTRACT

This chapter focuses on the management process of the wireless sensor networks in telemedicine applications. The main management tasks that are reported and addressed covers: topology management, privacy and security issues in WSN management, topology management algorithms, and route management schemes. Also, failure detection in WSN and fault management application using MANNA was presented and discussed. The major challenges and design issues facing WSN management was touched in a separate section. Typical telemedicine interactions involve both store-and-forward and live interaction. Both the traditional live and store-and-forward telemedicine systems provide an extension of healthcare services using fixed telecommunications networks (i.e. non-mobile). Various telemedicine solutions have been proposed and implemented since its initial use some 30 years ago in the fixed network environment using wired telecommunications networks (e.g. digital subscriber line). Technological advancements in wireless communications systems, namely wireless personal area networks (WPANs), wireless local area networks (WLANs), WiMAX broadband access, and cellular systems (2.5G, 3G and beyond 3G) now have the potential to significantly enhance telemedicine services by creating a flexible and heterogeneous network within an end-to-end telemedicine framework. In the future, integrating wireless solutions into healthcare delivery may well come to be a requirement, not just a differentiator, for accurate and efficient healthcare delivery. However, this raises some very significant challenges in terms of interoperability, performance and the security of such systems.

DOI: 10.4018/978-1-61520-805-0.ch009

INTRODUCTION AND CHAPTER OVERVIEW

Telemedicine approach means how to use modern telecommunications and information technologies to provide clinical care to individuals located at a distance, and to support the transmission of information needed to provide that care. It can be sub-divided into 'live' and 'store-and-forward' telemedicine [H S Ng 2006]. Live telemedicine requires the presence of both parties at the same time using audiovisual communications over high-bandwidth and low-latency connections. Almost all specialties of healthcare are able to make use of this kind of consultation, including psychiatric, medical, rehabilitation, cardiology, pediatrics, obstetrics, gynecology and neurology, and there are many peripheral devices which can be attached to computers as aids to an interactive examination. Store-and-forward telemedicine involves the acquisition of data, images and/or video content and transmission of this material to a medical specialist at a convenient time for assessment off line. Many medical specialties rely a great deal on images for assessment, diagnosis and management, and radiology, psychiatry, cardiology, ophthalmology, otolaryngology, dermatology and pathology are some of major services that can successfully make extensive use of the store-and-forward approach [H S Ng 2006].

The advances in the growth of medical sciences, biomedical engineering, communications and information technologies have enabled the growth of telemedicine to provide effective, efficient and improved health care. Medical care generally relies on the face-to-face encounter between patients and doctors. In places where face-to-face encounters are not possible telemedicine links are relied upon to link patients to specialist doctors for consultation for obtaining opinion. The advantages of telemedicine is in providing improved health care to the underprivileged in inaccessible areas, reduce cost and improve quality of health care and more importantly reduce the isolation of specialists,

nurses and allied health professionals. The term telemedicine refers to the use of telecommunications and computer information technologies with medical expertise to facilitate remote health care delivery, medical services to remote areas or across great distances on the globe. It also covers any form of communication between health workers and patients through electronic equipment from remote locations. Telemedicine applications are either based on store and forward or two-way interactive television technology. The store and forward method is used for transferring medical data and digital images from one location to another. Medical data like ECG, heart rate, oxygen saturation, respiratory rate, blood pressure, etc., and images like CT, MRI, ultrasound, etc. Two-way interactive television (IATV) is used when there is a need for a 'face-to-face' consultation between the patient and specialist doctor in another location [Poondi Srinivasan, 2007].

In telemedicine, a typical scenario is two doctors are involved with the patient: a local attending doctor and a remote tele doctor who is engaged to do one or more of a variety of services ranging from tele-consultation, or performing a tele-surgery, as well as tele-diagnosis where a doctor tele-diagnoses a sickness. The concept of telemedicine is not new; an early instance of telemedicine took place in 1959, when a two-way video conferencing link was established using microwaves between University of Nebraska Medical School and a state mental hospital [B. Jeffrey, 1999]. Until the late 1980's, the telemedicine systems were just video conferencing systems with the existing communication infrastructure and they could not provide additional functionality. But in the 1990's the rapid growth of the computer technology enables the telemedicine technology to grow into a more complex and feature-rich service.

The recent advances in telemedicine applications are propelled by two converging trends, which are the advances in Internet and telecommunications technologies and the increasing demand for access to high-quality medical care irrespective of location or geographical mobility. Wireless telemedicine is a new and evolving research area that exploits recent advances in wireless telecommunication networks. The conventional telemedicine systems using the public switched telephone network (PSTN) and Integrated Services Digital Network (ISDN) are available for doctors to deliver the medical care and education remotely. The introduction of wireless telemedicine systems will provide further flexibility, wider coverage and new applications for telemedicine [C. S. Pattichis, 2002]. The wireless telemedicine systems can provide better healthcare delivery, regardless of any geographical barriers, time and mobility constraints [S. Laxminarayan, 2000].

A wireless sensor network (WSN) is a communication network composed of wireless sensor devices. These devices essentially are low cost, low power, multi-functional, small sized and communicate over short distances [A. Akyildiz, 2002]. Typically these devices serve as nodes in a wireless network and are deployed randomly in a given area. Nodes establish connectivity with each other dynamically after deployment and do not follow a pre-determined topology. Therefore WSN are self-organizing in nature and are suitable for health care monitoring, military surveillance, control communication and monitoring disaster areas. One important application of WSN is in remote healthcare monitoring of patients where. Wireless Sensor nodes are placed on patients and thus acquire critical data for remote monitoring by health care providers. Significant amount of research has been done in the area of Wireless Body Area Sensor Networks (WBASN) with many researchers proposing various types of sensor nodes. An example of a wearable health monitoring device that integrates a number of sensor devices onto a wearable motherboard can be found in [K. M. Sungmee Park, 2002]. MIT project called Mithril [J. G. R. DeVaul, 2003], Carnegie Mellon University's e-textile project [J. E. T. Martin, 2003] are a few examples of such systems. Stanford university's lifeguard project

comprise of physiological sensors (ECG/Respiration electrodes, Pulse Oximeter, Blood Pressure Monitor, Temperature probe), a wearable device with built-in accelerometers (CPOD), and a base station (Pocket PC). The CPOD acquires and logs the physiological parameters measured by the sensors.

Several efforts have been made recently to provide an efficient mobile healthcare monitoring system. Authors in [S. Krco, V. Delic, 2003] propose Mobihealth project which is an application of WSN for healthcare monitoring using GSM and UMTS technologies. Researchers in [G. J. Mandellos, 2004] provide solution for emergency healthcare monitoring in ambulances utilizing GSM and Wireless LANs. [M. Rasid, 2005] points out the use of Bluetooth technology for multi channel biomedical signal transmission via GPRS. Thus it is evident that many such projects have been implemented to date; however very little effort has been done to provide security and patient privacy when dealing with WBASNs. Healthcare monitoring systems are traditionally complex systems involving not only data collection using WSN but also data propagation to healthcare provider, large databases and complex expert and knowledge based systems, therefore security and patient privacy is a very sensitive and important issue in design of such systems.

Wireless sensor networks (WSN) consist of many small sensors that are limited in resources, particularly processing power and battery life. There are many challenges associated with sensor networks but the primary challenge is energy consumption. Sensor networks are typically have little human interaction and are installed with limited battery supplies. This makes energy conservation a critical issue in deployed WSNs. All types of networks require monitoring and maintenance. A service that supplies a set of tools and applications that assist a network manager with these tasks is network management. It includes the administration of networks and all associated components. While all networks require some form of network management, different types of networks may stress certain aspects of network management. Some networks may also impose new tasks on network management. There are different types of network management architectures: centralized, hierarchical and distributed. In a centralized approach, one central server performs the role of the network management application. A hierarchical architecture will include multiple platforms, typically one server and several clients, performing network management functions. This type of architecture helps to distribute the functions thus eliminating the bottleneck at the one central server. In order to distribute network management functions even more would be to move to a distributed architecture. This type of network management architecture utilizes multiple peer-to-peer platforms sharing all management tasks. This provides better scalability, availability, reliability and modularity.

WIRELESS SENSOR NETWORKS STRUCTURE

Wireless sensor networks (WSNs) have promised us a new monitor and control model over the distributed computing environment. In general, these networks consist of a large number of sensor nodes densely distributed over the region of interest for collecting information or monitor & track certain specific phenomena from the physical environment. As shown in Figure 1, each sensor node is typically battery-powered, and consists of a processor, sensor, transceiver and other modalities. As sensor nodes are always designed with small dimensions, the size imposes restrictions on its resources (e.g. energy, communication, and processor capacities), and consequently limits sensor nodes to undertake too much complex tasks. In general, sensor nodes are expected to operate autonomously for a long period of time. Because of limited resource, they always split tasks into individual portions, and coordinate with each other to achieve a big objective.

These days, WSNs are likely to operate under very dynamic and critical environment with applications such as environmental monitoring, public safety, medical, transportation and military. Sensor nodes are usually difficult in access because of the geographical locations where they are deployed or the large scale of network. Thus, network maintenance for reconfiguration, recovery from failure or technical problems becomes impractical. In early days, this problem can be ignored as WSNs were supposed to operate cheaply and ready to be disposed. If the system breaks or underperforms, more nodes will be

Figure 1. Basic structure of sensor nodes [Mengjie Yu, 2006]

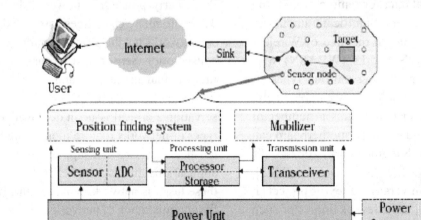

deployed to cover the failure. While, researchers have recently found out that this vision is not always a case within the reach since resource (e.g. the sensor nodes, batteries on which they operate) are not that cheap. In addition, WSN should co-operate with various applications rather than setting up a new network environment. Therefore, WSNs are indeed in need for some sort of management to continuously work without too much human being intervenes.

Management of WSNs is a new research area that only recently started to receive attentions from the research community. It has already presented a set of significant management challenges. The operation of a WSN is greatly affected by different inter-related factors such as network traffic flows, network topologies, and communication protocols. The interactions among those factors are still not clear yet. The environment also imposes a deep impact on the wireless network performance. As a result, the unique features of WSNs make the development of management architecture significantly different enough from traditional computer network. This chapter highlights some management features from current state of researches, which support WSN operation in various aspects [Mengjie Yu, 2006].

NETWORK MANAGEMENT FUNCTIONALITIES

Traditional Networks

Network management of traditional wired networks includes five functional areas, as identified by the International Standards Organization or ISO. These five areas are: fault management, configuration management, security management, performance management and accounting management. Fault management deals with the process of finding problems in the network. This process involves finding the problem, isolating the problem, and fixing the problem if possible. Faults

should be reported in some manner, such as a log file, E-mail message to the network manager, or an alert on the network management system. It may be necessary to prioritize faults that occur in order for the network manager to properly address the problems in a systematic manner [Lisa Frye, 2003]

The process of setting up, monitoring and controlling network devices is configuration management. An inventory of all network devices should be maintained which should include the current configuration of each device. The information about the current network environment should be collected on a periodic basis, either manually or automatic. Reports should be generated that includes this information. A common collection method is called autodiscovery, which is a process that runs on a network management system and will detect all installed network devices and possibly their current configuration. While this process is a good automated tool for current network configuration, it consumes a lot of bandwidth and is not recommended for bandwidth-constrained networks.

Security access to information on the network is security management [Lisa Frye, 2003]. This type of security is different from operating system, physical, or application security. The primary function of security management is controlling access points to critical or sensitive data that is stored on devices attached to the network. Access points to this sensitive data should be identified and secured. Possible risks should be analyzed and then minimized in order to protect the sensitive data. Performance management consists of monitoring network devices and links in order to determine utilization [Lisa Frye, 2003]. Utilization may vary depending on the device and link; it may include such things as CPU load, network card utilization, packet forwarding rate, error rate, or packets queued. Monitoring utilization will help to ensure there is available capacity. Monitoring the network performance will assist in identify current and future bottlenecks and aid in capacity planning. Tracking the utilization of network resources by each user is the goal of accounting management. The primary function of this information is to bill users for their use of the network and its resources [Lisa Frye, 2003]. This is not a common practice but the usage information of each user can assist the network manager in other ways. This information can be used to establish metrics and quotas. The usage information can also help the network manager allocate network resources properly. It is also helpful to see typical user behavior then atypical behavior will be seen and can be addressed. Atypical behavior may indicate a security breach or intrusion or may be an indication of a future device problem.

SENSOR NETWORKS

Network management in sensor networks is comparable to traditional network management. Sensor network management will include the five functional areas identified by ISO, although perhaps in a different manner [Lisa Frye, 2003]. For instance, performance management would also include monitoring to ensure network coverage and connectivity. Security management in sensor networks is difficult due to the ad hoc nature of these networks, the use of wireless communication and the inherent resource limitations of the sensors. One primary goal of network management in sensor networks is that it be autonomous. This is especially important in fault and configuration management. Configuration management includes the self-organization and self-configuration of the sensor nodes. Since WSNs involve very little human intervention after deployment, it is imperative that the areas of fault management be self-diagnostic and self-healing. Another important issue to consider in fault management of WSNs is that a single node failure should not impact the operation of the network, unlike a traditional network device failure causing impact to several users to potentially the entire network.

There are several new functional areas of network management in sensor networks. These new functional areas introduced for network management of WSNs are topology management, energy management and program management. One of these jobs is energy management. Recall that energy conservation is a critical aspect of sensor networks. Saving energy can be done at many different levels and in many different ways and is thus a separate area of network management. The most common way to conserve energy in WSNs is to power off a node when idle, but there have been many proposals in existing algorithms and protocols as well as establishing new protocols in order to be more energy efficient. For example, special MAC protocols and routing protocols are being developed for WSN in order to perform data transmissions using more energy efficient techniques.

Program or code management is another new functional area of network management in WSNs [Lisa Frye, 2003]. The traditional method of updating a program in a sensor node is to attach the node to a programming interface of a laptop or PDA. This is not feasible in many WSN deployments. Transmitting an entire new program version to all sensors in a WSN is not practical as it consumes too much energy and will lead to a short network lifetime. There needs to be a way to transmit minimal packets to all nodes requiring the update while ensuring appropriate nodes receive the update reliably. One solution is to only send the updates to the nodes requiring the update, instead of all nodes in the network. Only sending the part of the code that changed to the nodes is another alternative. There have been several proposals in the area of code update/management and it continues to be an active research area.

There are several key ideas for network management of sensor networks that are not typical in traditional network management [Lisa Frye, 2003]. Again, the fundamental idea is to conserve energy and secondarily, bandwidth. One way to conserve energy and bandwidth is to limit the number of nodes management traffic must travel. One way to accomplish this is to only obtain management information from a portion of the sensors in the network. For example, if there are redundant sensors in one area, retrieving network management information from one node in an area may be sufficient for the task at hand. Many times it is sufficient to have knowledge about regions of the network and not every node in the network.

Another way to conserve energy and bandwidth is to aggregate, process and/or compress network management data prior to sending it to a management station [Lisa Frye, 2003] Several nodes in the network can collect data from neighboring nodes, aggregate the data into one packet and then transmit that packet to the management station. It is also possible to have nodes process management data. By doing this the nodes can determine what data is critical and should be forwarded, thus eliminating the necessity to forward a lot of extraneous data. Management data can be compressed before transmission, much like application data, thus requiring the transmission of less data and conserving both energy and bandwidth. When performing network management of sensor networks, it is critical that only necessary parameters are monitored. Collecting data that is useless or unwanted results in extra traffic, requiring more energy and bandwidth. The network manager should identify only the essential network management tasks and monitor parameters associated with those tasks only. The network manager should also identify less critical data while still maintaining a stable network. While traditional network management is often a centralized application, it is important for network management in sensor networks to be a distributed architecture. Network management should not just be the collection of data from every node with transmission back to the manager node. This will greatly enhance the ability to perform data aggregation and in-network processing, once again reducing energy and bandwidth consumption.

NETWORK MANAGEMENT MODELS AND TYPES

Many networks today are heterogeneous, consisting of different types of devices from different manufacturers. There are also different management models in use, including IETF's SNMP (Simple Network Management Protocol), ISO's CMIP (Common Management Information Protocol), Distributed Management Task Force's (DMTF) Desktop Management Interface (DMI) and DMTF's Web Based Enterprise Management (WBEM) [Lisa Frye, 2003]. With the variety of manufacturers and management models it is a difficult task for a network administrator to manage an organization's network. In order to have one model for network management, the existing models must be merged or mapped into one domain. This requires not only the necessary syntax understanding but it also requires the semantic understanding within each model. An area of research that is looking at mapping all network management models into one, to allow easier management in a heterogeneous environment, ontology.

When related to computer science, ontology is a data model representing a particular domain, including the semantics. Ontologies describe an abstract model of a domain by defining a set of concepts, their taxonomy and interrelation, and the rules that govern these concepts in a way that can be interpreted by machines" [J. E. López de Vergara, 2003]. In order to utilize ontology for network management, the data models from all the management models must be merged into one ontology. This requires mapping rules that will translate the data from each management model. In order to do the mapping, the semantics or meaning of the data must be understood.

Topology Management

The principal issue of WSNs is energy conservation, which is the primary goal of topology management. Another critical goal of topology management, also referred to as topology control, is to ensure network connectivity. There are three basic ideas of topology management in WSNs: topology discovery, sleep cycle management, and clustering. According to [V. Mhatre, 2004], there are six properties that should exist in the topology of WSNs: 1) symmetry, 2) connectivity, 3) spanner, 4) spareness, 5) low degree, and 6) low interference. Consider two nodes in a WSN, x and y. If the network is symmetric, then x is a neighbor of y and vice versa. Two nodes in a network are connected if there is a path, which may be multiple hops, from one node to the other. A network is spanner if the optimal path between two nodes has a cost of c and the optimal path between the same two nodes in the sparse sub-graph of the network is O(c). It is often the case that the two properties, connectivity and sparseness conflict with each other.

Topology Discovery

Topology discovery involves a base station determining the topology or organization of the nodes in the sensor network. The physical connectivity and/or the logical relationship of nodes in the network are reported to the management station which maintains a topology map of the WSN. The base station or network management station will send a topology discovery request to the network. The nodes in the network will respond with its information. There are two basic approaches taken for topology discovery. The first one is a direct approach. In this approach a node will immediately send a response back upon receiving a topology request. The node's response will contain information about that particular node only. The other approach is an aggregated approach in which a node will forward the request but will not respond immediately. Instead, the node will wait until it gets responses to the request from its children. The node will then aggregate all the data received from its children, include its own

information, and then send the response back to its parent or the initiating station.

Sleep Cycle Management

Another idea of topology management is to eliminate redundancy by allowing some redundant nodes to sleep for periods of time. Topology management protocols are used to manage the sleep-wake cycle for nodes. The goal is to conserve energy in each node while continuing to maintain network connectivity. One disadvantage of most sleep cycle management protocols is that many of them trade routing latency for energy conservation. There has been research on the possibility of turning off nodes at the MAC layer when the radio is not being used. Other algorithms have been developed to conserve energy but rely on location or geographic information.

Clustering

The last area of topology management is to organize the nodes into clusters [Lisa Frye, 2003]. This involves arranging the nodes into groups and identifying a leader, or cluster head, for each cluster. This allows a subset of nodes to communicate with the sink nodes, conserving energy in the nodes that no longer must send data to the sinks. Often sink nodes are farther away from many nodes in the network. Clustering abandons these long paths required for communication for smaller hops since nodes will only be communicating with neighbor nodes (except for the cluster heads). Besides energy and bandwidth conservation, there are other advantages of clustering nodes in a WSN. One advantage is that it allows for spatial reuse of resources. If two nodes exist in different non-neighboring clusters, it may be possible for the two nodes to share the same frequency or time slot. It is also beneficial in the face of mobility. When using clustering and a node moves, it is often only necessary to update the information in the nodes sharing a cluster with the mobile node; all nodes in the network will not have to be updated [Lisa Frye, 2003]. Clustering can also facilitate network management and routing since many implementations will only require the cluster head to participate in these functions. In network management, the cluster heads often report the data to the management node on behalf of the entire cluster. Often the cluster heads form the routing backbone for the network.

Privacy and Security Issues in WSN Management

In a healthcare monitoring system, security of data is of utmost importance. From acquiring data from medical measurement sensors, to data transmission over a network, to the data storage and analysis, patient data needs to be protected at all stages. It is therefore important to secure data at physical layer from signal jamming and noise, network layer from routing errors and denial of service and at application layer from unauthorized data manipulation of patient records [Lisa Frye, 2003]. A security consideration for the proposed system in [Lisa Frye, 2003] was classified to three levels of implementation as follows:

Data Privacy at Acquiring Level (Non invasive)

At this level, the Sensor nodes would acquire medical measurement and send these data to the sink device (SD). Also, if there is any data to be sent to any of the sensor nodes such as configuration settings for a sensor, it can be done at this level. Any data that has been acquired must be done in a non-invasive manner and must not be accessed by sensor devices on a different user. This can be achieved by authentication at the MAC layer level for a particular user. When the WSN is deployed, all sensors can be identified and their distinct MAC addresses stored in the sink device [X. Hong, 2004]. Whenever a sensor needs to send some data, it can request connection

by sending a request with its own MAC address. The sink device can identify the incoming request by matching MAC address with the ones stored in its memory.

Data Security at Transmission Level

At this level, all data collected by the SD and is ready to be transmitted was assumed. A users SD is assumed to be roaming in a foreign network and therefore needs to connect to the healthcare provider's device (HD) [G. J. Mandellos, 2004] by either accessing the Home Authentication Server (HAS) or the Foreign Authentication Server (FAS) depending on its current location, either in home network or a foreign network. In either case it will authenticate with the required server using a challenge/ response mechanism by encrypting all correspondence with mutual sharable keys. If the HD allows the user to be registered it will authenticate the session for further data transmission. Figure 2 shows the proposed model by [Lisa Frye, 2003].

Data Security at Healthcare Provider Level

At this level the data is stored in the HD's databases and can be accessed by authorized experts for analysis [S. Krco, 2003]. Application level security can be implemented at this level to guarantee privacy and security.

Security Areas in Transmission

In the proposed model [D.D. Kouvatsa, 2005] a patient is considered to be moving from an area to another physical locality. Therefore a route needs to be established to the healthcare provider's locality. Two cases for providing security in home service were considered, when the user is part of the same network as healthcare provider; and Foreign Service, when the user is the part of a different network as of the healthcare provider.

Figure 2. Secured system models [D.D. Kouvatsa, 2005] HAS: Home Authentication Service, FAS: Foreign Authentication Service CAP: Cell Access point, S1..Si are Sensor devices, SD- Sink Device Arrows show movement direction

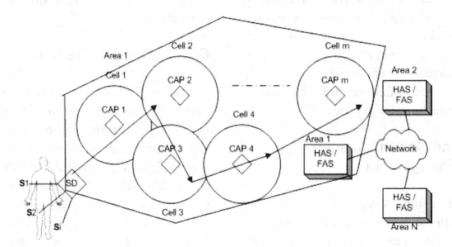

Security in Home Service

In this scenario, the user is part of the same network as of the healthcare provider. To initiate the service user needs to authenticate himself with the home authentication server by sending a service request. The local Cell Access Point (CAP) would forward the request to the Home Authentication Server (HAS). The HAS would generate a challenge request for the user [D.D. Kouvatsa, 2005]. The user will respond to the request, the HAS would authorize access only if the challenge/response mechanism succeeds as shown in Figure.2b. When authenticated the user can establish connection with the healthcare provider.

Security in Foreign Service (Phase: I)

In this scenario the user is not a part of the same network as of the healthcare provider possibly because the user has moved to a different location. A secure route needs to be established for communication to the healthcare provider. For seamless connectivity a Foreign Authentication Server (FAS) exists which provides challenge response condition on behalf of the HAS was assumed.

User sends a request to the local CAP which in turn forwards the request to the FAS. The FAS generates a challenge request on behalf of HAS and sends it back to the user. The user receives the challenge request and responds with a response request. This response request is forwarded by FAS to the HAS in the home network. When the user is authenticated by the healthcare provider a registration and authorization response is generated for FAS. FAS would then send the approval to the user and a secure connection is established

When the user is authenticated by the healthcare provider a registration and authorization response is generated for FAS. FAS would then send the approval to the user and a secure connection is established. Figure 3c shows an example of security in Foreign Service. In case of Sensor devices Si authenticating with the SD, the selected Sensor would send a service request to the SD. SD will create a Challenge Request for Si, which will respond with a response value including the MAC number of the sensor. If the MAC number is matched with pre-set list of MAC numbers, authorization is granted for transmission as shown in Figure 3a.

Figure 3. Authentication in network. (a) Sensor devices authenticating with SD (b) Authentication in Home service (c) Authentication in Foreign Service [D.D. Kouvatsa, 2005] Security in Foreign Service (Phase: II)

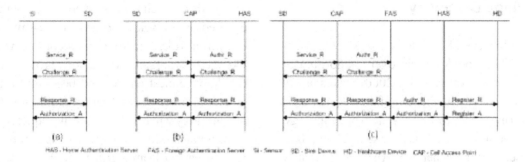

EFFECT OF SECURITY ON QOS

Security services are to provide information secrecy, data integrity and resource availability for users. Information secrecy means to prevent the improper disclosure of information in the communications, while data integrity is to prevent improper modification of data and resource availability is considered to preventing improper denial of services [W. Stallings, 2000].

Role of Challenge / Response Authentication

In a challenge / response based authentication; a user is identified with shared security information (SSI). SSI may include many parameters such as MAC addresses, keys, types of encryption used and various algorithms. An SSI is shared between an authentication server and an SD. At the beginning of a session, as shown in Figure 2b, the HAS sends a challenge value to SD through a CAP(s) for encryption and then verifies the returned value (response value) using a pre-defined encryption / decryption algorithm. In case if the user is roaming in a foreign network as in Figure 2c, the HAS has no information about the users SD. In this case the HAS forwards authentication

responsibilities to the FAS whose sole responsibility is to authenticate a foreign user. The FAS communicates with HAS of adjacent network and forwards the SSI. The HAS of the adjacent network would relay SSI to the local CAP of the HD. If the HD is able to authenticate the users SD, it will update information about the SD and will propagate authentication authorization back to HAS of the local network, which would in turn forward this message to FAS and then back to the user's SD [D.D. Kouvatsa, 2005].

EFFECT ON QOS

Security is an overhead to the existing network QoS measurements therefore it has a strong influence on QoS of a network. QoS metrics such as authentication delay, mobility, cost, call dropping probability and throughput of communication due to authentication overhead has to be affected. Typically authentication delay causes a pause for data transmission which decreases the throughput. Moreover length of keys and complexity of algorithm used also has an adverse effect. Also size of packets transmitted is also increased to include security parameters which affect the payload of messages [D.D. Kouvatsa, 2005].

EXISTING TOPOLOGY MANAGEMENT ALGORITHMS

Topology Discovery

There are several solutions for topology discovery. The Topology Discovery Algorithm or TopDisc [S. Laxminarayan, 2000] makes use of a tree structure, with the root of the tree being the monitoring node, to find the network topology. As the topology request is propagated, neighborhood sets will be generated. Although primarily a topology discovery algorithm, TopDisc creates clusters among the nodes and identify cluster heads in order to report the network topology. This is done by finding the set coverage with a greedy approximation algorithm. The algorithm begins by the monitoring node broadcasting a topology request packet, which will propagate throughout the WSN. TopDisc actually consists of two different versions, both of them node-coloring approaches. The first version, a three color approach, will be discussed first. A white node indicates an undiscovered node, a black node is a cluster head, and a grey node has a neighbor node that is a black node. The algorithm begins with all nodes being white, except for the monitoring node that initiated the topology request. If a white node receives the topology request packet from a black node, then the white node will become a grey node and broadcast the topology request packet. If a white node receives the topology request packet from a grey node, then it will wait a random amount of time. If this node receives the topology request packet from a black node before the time expires, it will become a grey node. However, if this node does not receive the request packet from a black node and the timer expires, it will then become a black node. After a node turns grey or black it will ignore all future topology request packets it receives. All black nodes will report its neighborhood set or member nodes back to the monitoring node [R. Rajaraman, 2002].

The second version of TopDisc uses a four color scheme. White, black and grey are the same as in the first version. There are now also dark grey nodes, which is a discovered node but is not covered by a black node (it is at least two hops away from a black node). This version begins much like the first version, with a node broadcasting a topology request packet and becoming a black node. All other nodes begin as white nodes but become grey when they receive the request packet from a black node. If a white node receives the request packet from a grey node, it will become a dark grey node, indicating it is at least two hops from a black node. After receiving the packet it will start a timer. If this node receives the request packet from a black node before the timer expires it will become a grey node. If the timer expires before another request packet is received by the dark grey node it will become a black node. Again, grey and black nodes ignore any future request packets it may receive [R. Rajaraman, 2002]. TopDisc "works nearly as well as a centralized approach" to topology discovery. There are many possible applications for the use of TopDisc. It can be used to report several network maps, including a connectivity map and a reachability map. TopDisc can also be used to generate an energy model of the network and a usage model.

Another topology discovery algorithm is Sensor Topology Retrieval at Multiple Resolutions or STREAM [C. S. Pattichis, 2002]. This algorithm can return the network topology at different degrees, since different applications may require different topology resolutions. STREAM takes advantage of the Wireless Multicast Advantage, which allows nodes to detect the presence of neighboring nodes by eavesdropping on the communication channel. This allows STREAM to create an approximate topology by getting neighborhood lists from a subset of nodes. STREAM runs in two phases. The first phase is the coloring phase; making use of four colors. A white node is an undiscovered node. A black node is a node in the Minimum Virtual Dominating Set (MVDS) and will send a response to the topology request. A red node is within the specified range of a black node and is considered to be virtually dominated by a black node. A node is blue if it either receives the topology request from a red or blue node or is within the communication range of a black node but not within the specified range of a black node.

The coloring phase begins by a monitoring node sending a topology request packet into the network using controlled flooding. This request packet will contain two parameters, a virtual range and the resolution factor. These two parameters are used to "select a minimal set of nodes required retrieving topology at a desired resolution" [L. B. Ruiz, 2005]. When a white or blue node within the virtual range of a black node receives this request from a black node, it will become a red node. If the node receives the packet from a black node but is not within the virtual range of a black node, it will become a blue node. The node will forward the request and blue nodes will start a timer. If the blue node receives the topology request packet from a black node within its virtual range before the timer expires, it will become a red node. If the timer expires without receiving such a packet, it will become a black node. When a white node receives the topology request packet from a red or blue node, it will become a blue node and start a timer. If this timer expires and the node does not receive a request packet from a black node within its virtual range, it will become a black node. If a node is red or black, it will ignore all future topology request packets it receives. If the network is connected then all nodes at the end of this phase will be either red or black.

The minimal set of nodes required to determine sufficient topology is defined as the Minimum Virtual Dominating Set or MVDS. The greedy approach is used to find the MVDS. Each step chooses the node that will cover the most undiscovered nodes (white nodes) to become a black node. This requires global knowledge of the neighborhood sets. All nodes should be red or black after the coloring phase completes. The second phase is the response phase. All nodes will send their information to its parent black node. Each black node will aggregate the data received from its children. This aggregated data is then forwarded to that black node's parent node. The black nodes will only forward a subset of its neighborhood list. This subset is determined by the resolution factor that was sent in the original topology request packet. STREAM has been shown to be very useful for energy constrained sensor networks. The MVDS is created using a message complexity of N (the number of nodes in the WSN). The retrieval message complexity does not increase as network density increases. The MVDS tree created is optimal in that the responses will travel the minimum number of hops to reach the monitoring node. This algorithm does not require time synchronization. The algorithm makes several assumptions about the WSN. It assumes that channels are error-free. It also assumes that there are no node failures in the network. However, another version of STREAM does exist that can handle channel errors and node failures.

Sleep Cycle Management

There are many different algorithms or protocols that have been developed to help conserve energy in sensor nodes by allowing redundant nodes to sleep. These algorithms determine which nodes are redundant and then selecting a subset of these nodes to sleep for a time period. After the sleep period is over, the nodes must wake-up and participate in the network again. Managing this sleep-wake cycle is the responsibility of these algorithms. One of these topology management algorithms is Sparse Topology and Energy Management or STEM [C. Schurgers, 2002], [C. Schurgers, 2002]. A node will spend a majority of its time monitoring data but a node's radio must only be turned on when the node must forward data. Since the radio is the largest consumer of energy, turning it off when not needed will conserve energy. When there is no data to forward STEM will put the node to sleep (turn of its radio) in order to conserve energy. The more time a network spends in monitoring state, the more energy STEM can save. STEM adds a second radio to the sensor nodes. The primary radio is used for receiving and forwarding messages. The second radio is a low duty cycle radio and is only used to send "wakeup messages". These are messages that are periodically sent to neighbor nodes letting them know that a node must communicate with it. A node will periodically wake up to see if another node is trying to communicate with it. If a node is trying to communicate with it, the node will wake up and receive the communication. If a node is not trying to communicate with it, the node will go back to sleep. Since collisions will occur, a node will also wake up if it is in listening mode and hears a collision. The primary problem with STEM is that it sacrifices latency. If a node must communicate with another node, and that other node is sleeping, then the node must wait before sending its data. This delay in forwarding data is very critical in some applications.

Geographic Adaptive Fidelity or GAF [Y. Xu, S. Bien, 2003], [Y. Xu, J. Heidemann, 2005] is a localized, distributed topology management algorithm that allows nodes to sleep to conserve energy. GAF uses location information, typically from a GPS device, to organize redundant nodes into groups. Some of the redundant nodes will be put to sleep. GAF will divide the network area into virtual grids. A virtual grid is "defined such that, for two adjacent grids A and B, all nodes in A can communicate with all nodes in B and vice versa". [Y. Xu, S. Bien, 2003] since all nodes in adjacent grids can communicate with each other the nodes in these two grids are equivalent to the routing protocol. Nodes are in a sleeping, discovery or active state. All nodes begin in the discovery state where it will send out discovery message and receive replies back in order to determine the nodes in its same grid. The node will then enter the active state. The node will stay in active state for

a specified period of time and will then go back to the discovery state. If a node determines that it is a redundant node for the routing protocol, it will enter the sleeping state for a specified period of time. When a node's timer expires it will transition from the sleeping state to discovery state. Redundant nodes take turns sleeping and are determined which one must remain active by a ranking procedure. This procedure can be random or selected by an algorithm in order to achieve better energy conservation. There are several drawbacks to GAF. First, it requires location information. GAF guesses at connectivity instead of directly measuring it thus requiring more nodes to remain awake than may be necessary. This algorithm is completely independent of the routing algorithm used. This means that GAF may allow a node to sleep even if that node is actively participating in routing. This may cause interruptions in communication and increase the latency.

Cluster-based Energy Conservation or CEC [Y. Xu, J. Heidemann, 2005] is an algorithm based on GAF although it could also be classified as a clustering algorithm. CEC will directly measure the network connectivity, thus not requiring location information and finding redundancy in the network more accurately. Since CEC is more accurate at identifying redundant nodes it conserves more energy than GAF. CEC will organize nodes into overlapping clusters. A cluster is created by grouping nodes that are at most two hops from each other. The node in the cluster that has the most residual energy will select itself to be the cluster head. This is done by exchanging messages among all nodes in the cluster. The cluster head is one hop from all other nodes in the cluster. The role of cluster head is rotated among all nodes in the cluster so all nodes have a chance to sleep and conserve energy. Since the clusters overlap, some nodes will be members of multiple clusters. These nodes are gateway nodes and will connect the clusters preserving network connectivity. CEC does not perform will if the network topology changes frequently. After all cluster heads and gateway nodes are determined, the rest of the nodes in the clusters are considered redundant. These redundant nodes are put to sleep to conserve energy. After a specified amount of time, these nodes will wake up and cluster heads will once again be selected.

Naps [B. P. Godfrey, 2004] were developed in order to conserve energy while still maintaining a connected network. This algorithm is based on network density and will allow some nodes to nap while others are awake and participating in the network. The set of nodes that are awake is changed so that all nodes will have a chance to nap and save energy. The Naps algorithm is based on broadcasting a message. At the start of a time period, for a given node, that node will broadcast a HELLO message. It will then listen for HELLO messages from its neighbors. When it receives a specified number of HELLO messages from neighbors, determined by a threshold that is a parameter to Naps, then that node will nap for the remainder of its time period. If the node does not hear the specified number of HELLO messages then it must remain awake for the duration of that time period. Naps is a simple algorithm and do not require information that many other algorithms require, such as location information. Naps can be used by any application that requires network connectivity for a specified target density. It can adapt to dynamic changes in network topology. It has been shown to conserve energy, especially at high densities. Naps is "an algorithm that maintains good connectivity and energy conservation while scaling to very high node densities without using location information" [B. P. Godfrey, 2004]. One disadvantage of Naps is that it compromises the agility of the network since some nodes nap for periods of time. There are two big assumptions made by Naps, one is that all messages can be reliably delivered to any node and the other is that there are no collisions.

Adaptive Naps for Failed Nodes

One of the assumptions of the Naps algorithm is that messages can be reliably delivered to any node. This may not be possible if a node fails, which is likely to occur due to the dynamic nature of sensor networks. Most sensor networks will see nodes added, deleted or moved changing the network topology and affecting the functionality of clustering algorithms, including Naps. The Naps algorithm was modified in order to be adaptive to node failures [B. P. Godfrey, 2004]. If a node fails, it will no longer be part of the sensor network so other nodes must compensate. There are several ways that compensation for failed nodes can be accomplished. Some possibilities include introducing new nodes into the network, moving nodes from areas of higher density to the area of the failed node, or increasing the energy of nodes near the failed node. Simulations were done to compare the original Naps with the modified Naps. As expected, since the modified algorithm introduced node failures, the original Naps algorithm outperformed the modified version of the Naps algorithm. However, when a neighbor node is selected to compensate for the failed node, this modified version of the Naps algorithm outperforms the original version. The version of the modified Naps algorithm that selected the neighbor node at random performed either the same or slightly better than the version that selected the neighbor node with the most residual energy. This indicates that the node selected to compensate for the failed node is not a critical decision.

Clustering

There are many clustering algorithms that exist today and more being developed. These algorithms can be classified in many different ways, such as requiring location information or not. Some algorithms are distributed, some centralized. There are many different ways the algorithms form clusters, from using node id, node degree (number of neighbors), and location information. The algorithms can be classified according to whether they are single-hop or multi-hop networks within the clusters. If the clusters are in a single-hop network, then the member nodes will communicate directly with the cluster head in a single hop. If member nodes are allowed to use multiple hops to reach the cluster head, then it is a multi-hop network. 1) Single-hop Clustering Algorithms: One of the most successful and studied clustering algorithms is LEACH [W. R. Heinzelman, 2000]. The main design objective of LEACH is to guarantee a certain network lifetime while minimizing energy consumption. This is done by ensuring that all nodes die (run out of energy) at about the same time which extends the network lifetime and leaves very little energy left in nodes when the network dies. It can be configured so that nodes die at about the same time by rotating the role of the cluster head and basing cluster head selection partly on remaining energy. LEACH does both of these things. Heinzelman et al. [W. R. Heinzelman, 2000] has shown that LEACH "successfully distributes the energy-usage among the nodes in the network such that the nodes die randomly and at essentially the same rate".

The operation of LEACH is broken up into rounds with each round consisting of two phases, the setup phase and the steady state phase. The setup phase is when the nodes organize themselves into clusters. A node decides to be a cluster head for that round independent of all other nodes in the network. The node will select a random number and if that number is less than the threshold value then the node will become a cluster head. The threshold value is based on the suggested percentage of cluster heads for that round (determined a priori), the number of times the node has already been a cluster head and the amount of residual energy in the node. The cluster head will broadcast an advertisement message indicating that it is a cluster head. A non-cluster head node will join the cluster of which it received the strongest advertised signal from the cluster

head. The non-cluster head node will send a join request to the cluster head and will then join that cluster. The steady state phase is the normal data collection and routing. Cluster members send the data to its cluster head. The cluster head will fuse all the data received from its member nodes and then transmit one message to the base station, containing the data for its cluster.

LEACH is a flexible and self-adaptive algorithm. It uses TDMA at the cluster-head level, making that transmission efficient. Communication within clusters is done by using CDMA, with neighboring clusters using different codes preventing interference between clusters. LEACH is robust to node failures since most node failures will not affect the overall network operation. There are several disadvantages to LEACH. One is the fact that all cluster heads must broadcast an advertisement message to all nodes in its communication radius. Another downfall is that all cluster heads must transmit data to the base station, which is single hop but may be a long distance. There is also a large overhead necessary to form the clusters. There are several implementations of LEACH. One implementation is a partially distributed architecture requiring some input from the base station. In this version, base station performs the initial selection of cluster heads and will compute the percentage of nodes that should be cluster heads each round (the best results are seen when optimal percent of nodes are cluster heads). A completely distributed version of LEACH requires no input from the base station with all decisions being performed by the nodes locally. LEACH can also be extended to be hierarchical, so that cluster heads communicate with a higher-level cluster head instead of directly with the base station. M-LEACH [V. Mhatre, 2004] is an implementation of LEACH for multi-hop networks, where a node is multiple hops from its cluster head.

ABCP or Access-Based Clustering Protocol designed the clustering operation from a protocol point of view. It defines the message formats, describes how a node responds. It can be configured so that nodes die at about the same time by rotating the role of the cluster head and basing cluster head selection partly on remaining energy. LEACH does both of these things. Heinzelman, et. al. [W. R. Heinzelman, 2000] has shown that LEACH "successfully distributes the energy-usage among the nodes in the network such that the nodes die randomly and at essentially the same rate". The operation of LEACH is broken up into rounds with each round consisting of two phases, the setup phase and the steady state phase. The setup phase is when the nodes organize themselves into clusters. A node decides to be a cluster head for that round independent of all other nodes in the network. The node will select a random number and if that number is less than the threshold value then the node will become a cluster head. The threshold value is based on the suggested percentage of cluster heads for that round (determined a priori), the number of times the node has already been a cluster head and the amount of residual energy in the node. The cluster head will broadcast an advertisement message indicating that it is a cluster head. A non-cluster head node will join the cluster of which it received the strongest advertised signal from the cluster head. The non-cluster head node will send a join request to the cluster head and will then join that cluster. The steady state phase is the normal data collection and routing. Cluster members send the data to its cluster head. The cluster head will fuse all the data received from its member nodes and then transmit one message to the base station, containing the data for its cluster. LEACH is a flexible and self-adaptive algorithm. It uses TDMA at the cluster-head level, making that transmission efficient. Communication within clusters is done by using CDMA, with neighboring clusters using different codes preventing interference between clusters. LEACH is robust to node failures since most node failures will not affect the overall network operation.

There are several disadvantages to LEACH. One is the fact that all cluster heads must broadcast an advertisement message to all nodes in its communication radius. Another downfall is that all cluster heads must transmit data to the base station, which is single hop but may be a long distance. There is also a large overhead necessary to form the clusters. There are several implementations of LEACH. One implementation is a partially distributed architecture requiring some input from the base station. In this version, base station performs the initial selection of cluster heads and will compute the percentage of nodes that should be cluster heads each round (the best results are seen when optimal percent of nodes are cluster heads). A completely distributed version of LEACH requires no input from the base station with all decisions being performed by the nodes locally. LEACH can also be extended to be hierarchical, so that cluster heads communicate with a higher-level cluster head instead of directly with the base station. M-LEACH [V. Mhatre, 2004] is an implementation of LEACH for multi-hop networks, where a node is multiple hops from its cluster head.

ABCP [T.-C. Hou, 2001] or Access-Based Clustering Protocol designed the clustering operation from a protocol point of view. It defines the message formats, describes how a node responds cluster formation. A big problem with ABCP is that it does not rotate the role of cluster heads. If a node becomes a cluster head, it will consume more energy than member nodes since it must transmit data to the base station, and die before most of the other nodes. This algorithm also does not consider residual energy when selecting a cluster head.

Another request-response with first-come-first-serve selection for cluster formation is ABEE [X. Hong, 2004] or Access-Based Energy Efficient cluster algorithm. This algorithm is very similar to ABCP but is based primarily on location. "The most direct factor that the clustering protocol can affect energy is the distance between the nodes to the cluster head" [X. Hong, 2004]. The protocol consists of several states that a node can be in at any given time: idle node sate, member node state and cluster head state. When a node is turned on it enters the idle node state. The node will obtain its current position, possibly from a GPS device. The node will then broadcast a REQ_TO_JOIN message and wait for response messages from cluster heads. If it receives responses, it will join the cluster of the first response it received by sending a response back to the cluster head. If the node does not receive a response, it will become a cluster head.

After joining a cluster the node will transition to the member node state. In this state a node will periodically send a message to the cluster head informing the cluster head of its present location. The node will also receive periodic messages from its cluster head. The member node may also receive messages from other cluster heads. When it does, it will compute the distance to that cluster head. If that cluster head is closer, it will inform its current cluster head that it is leaving that cluster and send a message to the new cluster head that it is joining its cluster. The cluster head state is the node responsible for maintaining the cluster formation. It will periodically broadcast a message indicating its current position. This will allow its member nodes to calculate their distance to the cluster head. It will also allow member nodes of other clusters to join this cluster if it is closer to the node. When the cluster head receives a message from a node wanting to join the cluster, it will send an acknowledgement message back to the node. If the distance between a cluster head and another cluster head is within a specified threshold then the two clusters will merge. In order for the two clusters to merge, the cluster head merging will send a message to all its member nodes informing them of the new cluster head. ABEE will try to balance the residual energy in all the nodes by periodically rotating the role of the cluster head. The new cluster head is selecting by treating the "whole cluster as an entity and each node stands

for particles with equal mass to form the entity" [X. Hong, 2004].

The best cluster head is the node that is at the mass center of the cluster. This is done by the cluster head collecting all location information from the member nodes, which is done by each member node periodically sending its location information to the cluster head. The cluster head will then use the location information to select the cluster that is the closest to the mass center of the cluster to be the next cluster head. As previously mentioned, the role of the cluster head is rotated, which is beneficial. Data sent from member nodes to cluster heads is fused before being sent to the base station. This algorithm has one benefit over some of the other algorithms in that it merges clusters that have cluster heads very close to each other. This will help to better distribute the clusters uniformly. There are two major drawbacks to ABEE. First, when selecting cluster heads it uses location information and does not consider residual energy in nodes. Since cluster head selection is based on location, the location information of all nodes must be known. This requires some form of location device, like a GPS, or some other form of determining a node's location.

ABEE improves the lifetime of the network when compared to ABCP. According to [X. Hong, 2004] there is "a 92.3% lifetime enhancement" over the ABEE protocol and "around a 50% gain in the lifetime of the network coverage". Topology and Energy Control Algorithm or TECA [M. Busse, 2006] will cluster nodes based on one-hop neighbors. Each node will create a neighbor list and measure the link qualities of these neighbors. It will then become a passive node, still listening to transmissions and maintaining neighbor lists. If a passive node is not a member of a cluster, then it will become a cluster head candidate. The node will broadcast this information, plus its node id, residual energy and one-hop neighbor list, to its one-hop neighbors. Based on all one-hop neighbor information, the node with the most residual energy will become a cluster head. This information will be broadcast and all one-hop neighbors will become members of that cluster. If a passive node hears a broadcast from at least two cluster heads, then it will become a bridge candidate. Certain bridge candidates will become bridge nodes, joining neighboring clusters, based on the link quality, residual energy and total number of bridge nodes. After a specified time period, all passive nodes (those not selected to be cluster heads or bridge nodes) will sleep while the cluster heads and bridge nodes remain active. After another specified time period, nodes will wake up in order to select new cluster heads and bridge nodes. TECA allows clusters to be created so cluster heads are not geographically close to each other. The algorithm rotates the role of the cluster head and considers residual energy in selecting the cluster head, which helps prolong the life of the nodes. One of TECAs primary advantage over other clustering algorithms is the use of bridge nodes to preserve network connectivity. 2) Multi-hop Clustering Algorithms: In order to lower the overhead of cluster formation in LEACH, a new algorithm was proposed, PEGASIS [M. Ye, 2005] or Power-Efficient GAthering in Sensor Information Systems. The key idea f PEGASIS it to form a chain among the nodes and take turns transmitting the data to the base station. This allows each node to communication only with a close neighbor, thus consuming less energy.

PEGASIS will begin by forming a chain among all the nodes in the network. The chain can be formed either by the base station computing the chain or broadcasting this information to all the nodes or by using the greedy algorithm. In PEGASIS, the farthest node from the base station begins and the nodes form the chain using the greedy algorithm. After the chain is constructed, each node will transmit its data to the next node in the chain. Each node will fuse the data it receives with its own data and then forward the data to the next node. One node, the leader for that round, will then transmit all the fused data to the base station. The nodes will take turns transmitting data to the base station, thus evenly distributing the energy load among all nodes. There are only a few nodes in the chain that may not take a turn transmitting to the base station. If a node has a relatively distant neighbor, it will consume more energy than the other nodes to transmit it data to its neighbor. These nodes will not take a turn being the leader. There are several assumptions in the PEGASIS algorithm. First, it assumes that all nodes have global knowledge of the network. This allows them to create the best chain using the greedy algorithm and each node will know its neighbor nodes. It also assumes that all nodes employ the greedy algorithm and that the radio channel is symmetric. There are several advantages of PEGASIS. Since nodes only receive and transmit to its neighbors, and they form a chain, each node will only transmit and receive one packet of data in each round. PEGASIS is also robust to node failures. When a node fails, the chain will simply be reconstructed with the remaining nodes. In addition, only one node transmits to the base station in each round. The primary advantage of PEGASIS over LEACH is less overhead in forming the chain compared to the cluster formation in LEACH. According to [M. Ye, 2005] PEGASIS is approximately two to three times better than LEACH, depending on the network size. The major disadvantage of PEGASIS is that it does not consider residual energy when selecting the leader node in each round. This may be added in a future implementation of the algorithm. Another clustering algorithm is the Energy Efficient Clustering Scheme or EECS [M. Ye, 2005]. The goals were to create a fully-distributed, load-balancing clustering algorithm that had little overhead. It is very much like LEACH but attempts to better balance the load among the clusters and cluster heads. In EECS, there is only one cluster head within a certain range with a high probability.

During network deployment the base station will broadcast a message to all nodes in the network. This message is sent at a specific power level which allows the nodes to calculate their approximate distance to the base station. By knowing their distance to the base station, it allows the nodes to determine what power level they must use in order to communicate with the base station when they are cluster heads. The distance from each node to the base station is also used to help balance the load among cluster heads. The base station will periodically broadcast a message to all nodes for synchronization purposes. The first phase is a cluster head election phase in which a constant number of nodes are elected to be candidate cluster heads. Nodes will broadcast a message within a certain radius with its calculated probability of being a cluster head and become a candidate node. If a candidate node hears a broadcast from another node within its radius and that node has more residual energy, then the candidate node will stop trying to be a cluster head. If the candidate node does not hear any broadcasts from other candidate nodes, or if no other candidate node has more residual energy, then that node will become a cluster head. This process produces a near uniform distribution of cluster heads. The load is then balanced among cluster heads in the cluster formation phase. Each cluster head will broadcast a message indicating it is a cluster head. The decision of which cluster a non-cluster head node should join is primarily based on the distance metric. It will base its decision on its distant to the cluster head, the cluster head's distance to the base station, and a weight metric.

EECS rotates the role of the cluster head so that nodes will all consume all their energy at about the same time. The cluster heads will also fuse the data it receives from its member nodes before transmitting the data to the base station, which is a single hop from all cluster heads. According to [M. Ye, 2005], the control overhead across the network is O(n). This chapter also indicated that EECS will prolong the network lifetime over 35% when compared to LEACH. The energy utilization rate is also better in EECS because "EECS always achieves the well distrib-

uted cluster heads while considering the residual factor; further, we consider to balance the load among the cluster heads with weighted function" [M. Ye, 2005]. The energy efficient hierarchical clustering algorithm [S. Bandyopadhyay, 2003] is a distributed algorithm. It assumes the sensors are distributed in a homogenous spatial Poisson process. The initial algorithm was extended to create a hierarchy of clusters where cluster heads send their data to cluster heads in the next higher level of the hierarchy. Each sensor in the network will select a probability for which it should become a cluster head. This node is considered a volunteer cluster head and will advertise itself as a cluster head. This advertisement will be forwarded to all nodes that are a certain number of hops from the volunteer cluster head sending the advertisement. All nodes that receive an advertisement from a volunteer cluster head, and is not itself a cluster head, will join the cluster of the closest cluster head. Any node that is not a member of a cluster and is not already a cluster head will become a forced cluster head.

The energy efficient hierarchical clustering algorithm will fuse all data received from member nodes at the cluster head. No location information is required and time synchronization is also not required. "The proposed algorithm leads to significant energy savings". [S. Bandyopadhyay 2003] The energy savings increases as the network density increases. There are two different ways this algorithm does load balancing among the clusters. Both are done by re-running the clustering algorithm. It can either be re-run periodically or when triggered by cluster head because its remaining energy has fallen below a threshold. The primary problems with this algorithm are in the selection of cluster heads. First, the role of cluster heads is not rotated, unless the clustering algorithm is re-run. Also, when selecting a node to become a cluster head the residual energy is not a consideration. LLC [J. Kim, 2005] or Low-energy Localized Clustering is a clustering algorithm for heterogeneous networks. The network using LLC is a two-tiered network consisting of one tier that is cluster heads and a lower tier consisting of sensor nodes. In this algorithm the cluster heads are determined prior to network deployment.

Cluster heads are devices that have more processing power and more initial energy. When deployed the sink node will know the location of all deployed cluster heads. This algorithm consists of two phases, an initial phase and the cluster radius control phase. The initial phase is done to help conserve energy in the cluster head nodes. While these nodes do have more energy than typical sensor nodes they still have a limited amount of energy. The cluster heads will create a triangle and determine a cluster radius decision point or CRDP. The cluster radius control phase will adjust the cluster radius, once again to conserve energy in cluster heads. The "cluster radius of three points involving construction of a triangle can be dynamically controlled by using the CRDP as a pivot point" [J. Kim, 2005]. LLC considers two different types of cluster radius control algorithms. These are the Non-Linear Programming or NLP based approach and the Vector Computation (VC) based approach. The LLC algorithm requires the location information of all nodes. It also does not rotate the role of the cluster head since cluster heads are pre-determined and are more powerful devices. Overlapped clustering area is minimized when using the LLC algorithm. It also "outperforms traditional clustering approaches in the aspect of the sensor network lifetime" [J. Kim, 2005]. It also consumes less energy than traditional clustering algorithms. This was an introduction to some existing clustering algorithms. Others exist and others are being developed as the research continues.

Topology Controlled Data Compression Algorithm

Another energy-conserving technique for WSNs is data compression. Sending large amounts of data from sensor nodes to the base station is very

energy-draining. In order to conserve some of the valuable energy, data compression can be used. Before sending data from a node, the data is first compressed, requiring less data to be transmitted. One method of data compression is Distributed Source Coding (DSC) which can compress the data from multiple sensors. This is done by using a correlation value which is basically the difference between two sensor readings. A sensor will then use this correlation value, encode the data using the difference between its actual reading and the correlation value, and only send the encoded data. The receiver will decode the data received based on the correlation value and the correlated data. This will require fewer bits for transmission than if the node sent the actual data sensed.

In order to get the best compression ratio, thus sending the fewest amounts of data, the correlation value should be as small as possible. This is the result of having nodes that are sensing similar values to use each other for the encoding. The best way to get nodes to use closely correlated nodes is to group nodes together based on their sensed data. A recent research project modified the centralized version of LEACH (LEACH-C) and instead of grouping nodes based on location as LEACH-C does, the modified version groups nodes based on the sensed data. An initial sensor reading is obtained and sent to the base station. The base station will then determine the best way to group nodes so that all clusters will have the smallest possible correlation value. This will allow all nodes in each cluster to have small correlation values and transmit a small amount of data by encoding it using DSC.

Route Management Scheme

To utilize the limited energy or power of the sensor nodes here, network architecture for the monitoring and routing management of the sensor networks was proposed. To define the architecture we have to follow a route group formation algorithm. In the proposed system model, two types of sensors were defined: agent sensor and isolate sensor. Those sensors which have a direct communication with the base station are called 'agent' sensors. And sensors which are out of the communication range from the base station or which cannot receive the radio signal from the base station due to obstacles are called 'isolate' sensors. The agent sensors act as hops for the route of the isolate sensors. Unlike the proposed network architecture forms groups for the isolate sensors where each group contain at most one agent sensor. Moreover based on the residual energy an agent sensor can be a hop for a certain maximum number of isolate sensors to route their data to the base station and vice versa. In this case the initialization phase is almost like the approach used in [Mohammad Younis, 2003]. The only difference that is made here is for the route group formation approach.

Initialization Phase

Like [Mohammad Younis, 2003], in the initialization phase each base station send a beacon message to the deployed sensor nodes. Actually it wants to assess the quality of its communication link to other sensors. As a result the sensor which has direct communication to the base station collects the information of those sensors that cannot reach the base station directly. After the initial radio signal transmission each sensor can have the following information:

- Agent Sensor (A): If it has a direct communication link to the base station.
- Isolate Sensor (I): If the sensor has a link to an agent sensor but not direct to the base station.
- Neighbor List (N): It is the set of sensors which are within the transmission range of a sensor.
- Hop List (H): It is the set of sensors which are agent sensors but within the transmission range of a Sensor.

Route Management Algorithm

In this section, route management algorithm shown in the following algorithm was proposed [Mohammad Younis, 2003]. Isolate sensors are organized in a group where each group contain one agent sensor. All agent sensor have a direct link to the base station so for them hop communication via agent is not needed. Each isolate sensors are included in a group and their route has been set up by the route (I, A) function.

Route management algorithm [l. B. Ruiz, 2003]

```
Algorithm (A, I)
1. for each isolate sensor Ij
calculate the cardinality of Hop
list(H)
end for
2. Sort isolate sensors I in a
non decreasing order of Hop List
(H)
3. for all agent sensor Aj
set agent_id(Aj)= 0
end for
4. for each isolate sensor Ij
if (Cardinality(H)==1)
set agent_id(Ij)= Only reachable
Agent(Aj)
add Ij to group_list(Aj)
set route (I,Aj)
else if (Cardinality(H)>1)
for each Agent Aj in the Hop
list (H)
calculate res_energy(Aj)
end for
if (Agent(Aj)has highest res_
energy(Aj)
&& group_list(Aj)< MAX)
set agent_id(Ij)= Agent(Aj)
add Ij to group_list(Aj)
set route (I,Aj)
else if(Agent(Aj)has highest
res_energy(Aj)&& group_list(Aj)=
```

```
MAX)
remove Aj from Neigbour List(Ij)
repeat step 4 for Ij
end for
```

Figure 4 represents a scenario for the proposed sensor network route management model [Mohammad Younis, 2003]. Here four groups each have an agent sensor along with maximum three isolate sensors. Each group contains MAX four sensors including an agent sensor was considered.

FAILURE DETECTION IN WIRELESS SENSOR NETWORKS

WSNs are embedded in applications to monitor the environment and sometimes, act upon it. In applications where we are interested in the conditions of the environment at all times (subject to some discretization, of course), sensor nodes will be programmed to sense and send back their measurements at regular intervals or continuously. These networks are called programmed and continuous, respectively. In other applications (probably a large class of them), we are only interested in hearing from the network when certain events occur. We call these networks event-driven networks. On the other hand, when the network is able to answer to queries of the observers, we refer to this network as on demand [S. Marti, 2000]. Configuring the network as event-driven is an attractive option for a large class of applications since it typically sends far fewer messages. This is translated into a significant energy saving, since message transmissions are much more energy-intensive when compared to sensing and (CPU) processing. For instance, if the application is temperature monitoring, it could be possible just to report data when the temperature of the area being monitored goes above or below certain thresholds.

In terms of failure detection, event-driven networks present challenges not found in continuous networks. Under normal conditions, the observer of a continuous network receives sensing data at regular intervals. This stream of data not only delivers the content we are interested in, but also works as an indicative of the network operation quality. If data are received from every single node, then it knows that all is well (of course, assuming that the messages are authenticated, and cannot be spoofed). If, however, the management

Figure 4. Routing management model [Mohammad Younis, 2003]

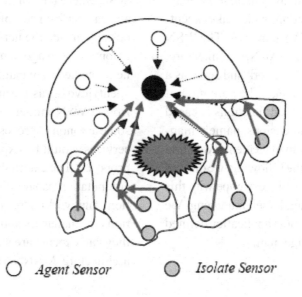

○ *Agent Sensor*   ◉ *Isolate Sensor*

application stops receiving data from certain nodes or entire regions of the network, it can not distinguish if a failure has occurred or if no application event has occurred. Leveraging precisely on this indication, and supposing that nodes periodically send messages to the base station, Staddon et al. [S. Marti, 2000] proposed a scheme for tracing failed nodes in continuous sensor networks. Their scheme takes advantages of periodic transmission of sensor reports to do the tracing. Because we consider event-driven networks, their solution is not directly applicable.

In [S. Marti, 2000], it is proposed a scheme where nodes police each other in order to detect faults and misbehavior. More specifically, nodes listen-in on the neighbor it is currently routing to, and can determine whether the message it sent was forwarded. If the message was not forwarded, the node concludes that its neighbor has failed and chooses a new neighbor to route to. Unfortunately, this scheme does not help in cases in which an entire region is compromised. In our work, we study the problem of failure detection for an event-driven WSN and propose a fault management solution using some management services, management functions, and WSN models which are part of the MANNA architecture [S. Marti, 2000]. In MANNA management services for WSNs are defined. These management services are performed by a set of functions which take executing conditions from the WSN models. The WSN models, as defined in the MANNA architecture, represent the states of the network and serve as a reference for the management. The definition of the management services and functions is based on three management dimensions, namely management functional areas, management levels, and WSN functionalities. In the following, we discuss how the MANNA architecture can cope with this kind of network promoting its self managing. We also describe the management application defined for providing fault management.

Fault Management Application Using MANNA

In order to evaluate the fault management capabilities of the management solution proposed, an application that monitors an environment to collect temperature data has been simulated [L. B. Ruiz, 2003]. An event-driven WSN has been considered. This network as being heterogeneous and hierarchical was supposed [L. B. Ruiz, 2003]. The sensor nodes only disseminate data when the temperature of the area being monitored goes above or below certain thresholds. In a hierarchical network, nodes are grouped into clusters and there is a special node called cluster-head. In a heterogeneous network, the cluster-heads have more resources and, thus, are more powerful than the common-nodes. Furthermore, they are responsible for sending data to a base station (BS). The BS also communicates with the observer, which is a network entity or a final user that wants to have information about data collected from the sensor nodes. In our implementation, the management agents execute in the cluster-heads where aggregation of management and application data is performed. This mechanism decreases the information flow and energy consumption as well. A manager is located externally to the WSN where it has a global vision of the network and can perform complex tasks that would not be possible inside the network. In this work we use automatic management services and functions, i.e., executed by management entities (manager or agent) invoked as a result of information acquired from a WSN model. The computational cost of some autonomic process (automatic management services) could be expensive to the architecture proposed. The external manager then extends the computation capabilities avoiding the consumption of network energy to carry out this task. Locations for managers and agents, and the functions they can execute are suggested by the functional architecture. MANNA architecture also proposes two other architectures: physical and information. More details can be found in [L. B. Ruiz, 2003].

In terms of the management functional areas and management levels, some functions depend for the fault management in the network and network element management levels as the network functionality have been implemented. The fault management in the network element level involves only the detection because it is probably difficult to restore a node to its normal condition. The main management services executed in this work are coverage area maintenance service and failure detection service. A partial list of the management functions employed in the experiments, in no particular order, is: monitored area definition, node distribution, node self-test, node localization discovery, self-organization, network operating parameters configuration, topology map discovery, aggregation, energy map generation, management operation schedule, node operating state control, node administrative state control, coverage area map generation, control density and audit map generation. Some WSN models were used [L. B. Ruiz, 2003], such as: network topology map (represents the actual topology map and the reachability of the network); residual energy map (represents the remaining energy in a node or in a network); sensing coverage area map (describes the actual sensing coverage map of the sensor elements); communication coverage area map (describes the present communication coverage map from the range of transceivers); cost map (represents the cost of energy necessary for maintaining the desired performance levels); audit map (describes the actual (security or safe) of the sensor elements which have been attacked). The management application is divided into two phases: installation and operation. The installation phase occurs as soon as the nodes are deployed in the network. In this phase, each node sends out its position in the area and reports it to the agent located in the cluster-head. The agent aggregates the information received from the nodes in the group and sends a LOCATION TRAP of its local-

ization to the manager. The common-nodes also inform their energy level that the agent aggregates in an ENERGY TRAP sent to the manager. The management application builds all needed WSN models based on both local information and data sent by the agents, i.e., the WSN topology map model and the WSN energy model. These two models are used to build the WSN coverage area model, which the manager uses to monitor the sensing and communication coverage area.

In the operation phase, while the sensor nodes are performing their functions, i.e., collecting and sending temperature data, management activities take place. Among them, energy level monitoring plays a central role. Each node checks its energy level and sends a message to the agent whenever there is a state change. This information is transmitted to the manager via another ENERGY TRAP. Any information the agent receives is recorded in its MIB. The manager can, then, recalculate the energy and topology maps, as well as the coverage area, which characterizes the coverage area maintenance service. Also, operations can be sent to the agents in order to execute the failure detection management service. The manager sends GET operations in order to retrieve the node state. The GET-Responses are used to build the WSN audit map. If an agent or a node does not answer to a GET operation, the manager consults the energy map to verify if it has residual energy. If so, the manager detects a failure and sends a notification to the observer. In this way, MANNA architecture provides failure detection in event-driven WSN. In the next section we describe the experiments conducted in order to evaluate MANNA's performance as a solution for failure detection.

CHALLENGES AND DESIGN ISSUES

The primary goal of many WSN protocols and algorithms is energy conservation. This is true of topology management algorithms. Energy conservation is one of many design goals that should be considered when designing or evaluating topology management algorithms. Along with conserving energy among the nodes, the algorithm should minimize the energy required for running. While doing this, another primary goal is to maximize the network lifetime. Many times these two goals work concomitantly [J. E. López de Vergara, 2003]. If the algorithm can be distributed and not centralized, it would be beneficial. This would lessen the communications required. Also, there are often multiple sinks or base stations, so nodes only have to communicate with the closest one. Having a centralized solution might require some nodes to communicate long distances.

The maintenance overhead of the algorithm should be kept to a minimum. This would require less energy consumption for the algorithm. It would also require less processing power, which is often limited as well in sensor nodes. If the algorithm can be developed requiring no location information or time synchronization, that would be advantageous. Requiring such information again requires additional communication [J. E. López de Vergara, 2003]. The protocol or algorithm should be developed so it is robust to node mobility and node failures. Many applications or sensor node deployment have node mobility; some by design and some just by the nature of the application (nodes may shift or move accidentally. WSNs are prone to node failures. This may be due to running out of energy, hardware failures or simply the node being destroyed due to harsh conditions. The algorithm will be more successful if it is robust to node failures.

SUMMERY AND CONCLUSION

Network management is a critical function in all types of networks. In a traditional wired network, network management is typically a centralized architecture with a primary server controlling most network management functions. There are five primary functional areas of traditional network management: fault management, configuration management, security management, performance management and accounting management. Wireless sensor networks are networks consisting of many sensor nodes, which are constrained by power and energy. Network management is critical in WSNs but is more practical implemented as a distributed architecture, with different tasks being performed by different nodes in the network. There may still be a primary base station or sink that collects and stores the network management data. The functional areas for network management in WSNs include the five functional area of traditional network management plus the following areas: energy management, program or code management, and topology management. There are three primary tasks of topology management. These tasks are to determine the network topology, allow some nodes to sleep and management when nodes sleep, and cluster the nodes of the network. There are several existing algorithms that have been developed in each of these areas of topology management with research in each area ongoing.

REFERENCES

Akyildiz, A. (2002). A Survey on Sensor Networks. *IEEE Communications Magazine*, 102–114. doi:10.1109/MCOM.2002.1024422

Bandyopadhyay, S., & Coyle, E. *(2003). An Energy Efficient Hierarchical Clustering Algorithm for Wireless Sensor Networks". IEEE INFOCOM 2003. In* Proceedings of the Twenty-Second Annual Joint Conferences of the IEEE Computer and Communications Societies. *Volume 3, pp.1713- 1723.*

Busse, M., Haenselmann, T., & Effelsberg, W. *(2006). TECA: a Topology and Energy Control Algorithm for Wireless Sensor Networks. In* Proceedings of the International Symposium on Modeling, Analysis and Simulation of Wireless and Mobile Systems *(MSWiM '06). Torremolinos, Malaga, Spain. ACM*

DeVaul, J. G. R., et al. *(2003). Applications and Architecture. In* Proceedings of the 7th IEEE International Symposium on Wearable Computers, *(pp. 4-11).*

Galego, J. (2005). Performance Analysis of Multiplexed Medical Data Transmission for Mobile Emergency Care over UMTS Channel. *IEEE Transactions on Information Technology in Biomedicine, 9*(1), 13–22. doi:10.1109/TITB.2004.838362

Godfrey, B. P., & Ratajczak, D. (2004). *Naps: Scalable, Robust Topology Management in Wireless ad hoc Networks. ISPN '04.* Berkeley, CA: ACM.

Heinzelman, W. R., Chandrakasan, A., & Balakrishnan, H. *(2000). Energy-Efficient Communication Protocol for Wireless Microsensor Networks. In* Proceedings of the 33rd Annual Hawaii International Conference on System Sciences.

Hong, X., & Liang, Q. *(2004). An Access-Based Energy Efficient Clustering Protocol for ad hoc Wireless Sensor Network. In* Proceedings of the 15th IEEE International Symposium on Personal, Indoor and Mobile Radio Communications, *(PIMRC 2004, Volume: 2. pp.1022- 1026).*

Hou, T.-C., & Tsai, T.-J. (2001). An Access-Based Clustering Protocol for Multihop Wireless ad hoc Networks. *IEEE Journal on Selected Areas in Communications, 19*(7), 1201–1210. doi:10.1109/49.932689

Jeffrey, B., & Ringel, M. (1999). *Telemedicine and the Reinvention of Healthcare.* New York: McGraw-Hill.

Kim, J., Kim, S., Kim, D., & Lee, W. (2005). *Low-Energy Localized Clustering: An Adaptive Cluster Radius Configuration Scheme for Topology Control in Wireless Sensor Networks. In* Proceedings of the IEEE 61st Vehicular Technology Conference, *(VTC 2005, Volume: 4. pp. 2546- 2550).*

Krco, S., & Delic, V. *(2003). Personal Wireless Sensor Network for Mobile Health Care Monitoring. In* Proceedings of IEEE TELSIKS 2003, *Serbia Montenegro, (pp.471-474).*

Laxminarayan, S., & Istepanian, R. H. (2000). Unwired e-Med: The Next Generation of Wireless and Internet Telemedicine Systems. *IEEE Transactions on Information Technology in Biomedicine, 4,* 189–193.

Lindsey, S., & Raghavendra, C. S. *(2002). PEGASIS: Power-Efficient Gathering in Sensor Information Systems. In* Proceedings of the IEEE Aerospace Conference.

López de Vergara, J. E., et al. *(2003). Semantic Management: Application of Ontologies for the Integration of Management Information Models. In* Proceedings of the Eighth IFIP/IEEE International Symposium on Integrated Network Management, *Colorado Springs.*

Mandellos, G. J., et al. *(2004). A Novel Mobile Telemedicine System for Ambulance Transport Design and Evaluation. In* Proceedings of the 26th Annual International Conference of the IEEE EMBS, *San Francisco, (pp. 3080-3083).*

Marti, S. Giuli, T. J. Lai, K., & M. Baker (2000), "Mitigating Routing Misbehavior in Mobile ad hoc Networks". In ACM Mobicom, pp. 255-265

Martin, J. E. T., Jones, M., & Shenoy, R. *(2003). Towards a Design Framework for Wearable Electronic Textiles. In* Proceedings of the 7th IEEE International Symposium on Wearable Computers, *(pp. 190-199).*

Mhatre, V., & Rosenberg, C. *(2004). Homogeneous Vs Heterogeneous Clustered Sensor Networks: a Comparative Study. In* Proceedings of the IEEE International Conference on Communications, *(Volume 6, pp.3646-3651 Vol.6)*

Ng, H. S. (2006). Wireless Technologies for Telemedicine. *BT Technology Journal, 24*(2). doi:10.1007/s10550-006-0050-9

Pattichis, C. S. (2002). Wireless Telemedicine Systems: an Overview. *IEEE Antennas & Propagation Magazine, 44*, 143–153. doi:10.1109/MAP.2002.1003651

Rajaraman, R. (2002). Topology Control and Routing in ad hoc Networks: a Survey. *ACM SIGACT News, 33*(2), 60–73. doi:10.1145/564585.564602

Rasid, M., & Woodward, B. (2005). Bluetooth Telemedicine Processor for Multichannel Biomedical Signal Transmission via Mobile Cellular Networks. *IEEE Transactions on Information Technology in Biomedicine, 9*(1). doi:10.1109/TITB.2004.840070

Ruiz, L. B. Nogueira, J. M. S. and Loureiro, A. A. (2003). MANNA: A Management Architecture for Wireless Sensor Networks". IEEE Communications Magazine, 41(2):116{125

Ruiz, L. B. (2005). On the Design of a Self-Managed Wireless Sensor Network. *IEEE Communications Magazine*, 95–102. doi:10.1109/MCOM.2005.1497559

Schurgers, C., Tsiatsis, V., Ganeriwal, S., & Srivastava, M. (2002). Optimizing Sensor Networks in the Energy-Latency-Density Design Space. *IEEE Transactions on Mobile Computing, 1*(1). doi:10.1109/TMC.2002.1011060

Schurgers, C., Tsiatsis, V., Ganeriwal, S., & Srivastava, M. (2002). Topology Management for Sensor Networks: Exploiting Latency and Density. In *Proceedings of MOBIHOC '02*, Lausanne, Switzerland: ACM.

Srinivasan, P. (2007). Store and Forward Applications in Telemedicine for Wireless IP Based Networks. *Journal of Networks, 2*(6).

Stallings, W. (2000). *Network Security Essentials, Applications and Standards*. Upper Saddle River, NJ: Prentice Hall.

Sungmee Park, K. M., & Jayaraman, S. *(2002). The Wearable Motherboard: a Framework for Personalized Mobile Information Processing (PMIP). In* Proceedings of 39th ACM/IEEE Design Automation Conference, *(pp. 170- 174).*

Xu, Y. *Bien, S. Mori, Y. Heidemann, J., & Estrin, D. (2003).* Topology Control Protocols to Conserve Energy in Wireless ad hoc Networks *(Technical Report 6), University of California, Los Angeles, Center for Embedded Networked Computing*

Xu, Y., Heidemann, J., & Estrin, D. *(2005). Geography-Informed Energy Conservation for ad hoc Routing. In* Proceedings of the 7th annual international conference on Mobile computing and networking. *Rome, Italy. (pp. 70 – 84).*

Ye, M. Li, C., Chen, G., & Wu, J. (2005). EECS: An Energy Efficient Clustering Scheme in Wireless Sensor Networks". 24th IEEE International Performance, Computing, and Communications Conference, (IPCCC 2005). pp. 535- 540.

Younis, M., et al(2003). Architecture for Efficient Monitoring and Management of Sensor Networks, *(MMNS, LNCS)*

KEY TERMS AND DEFINITIONS

Autodiscovery: It is a common collection method which is a process that runs on a network management system and will detect all installed network devices and possibly their current configuration. While this process is a good automated tool for current network configuration, it consumes a lot of bandwidth and is not recommended for bandwidth-constrained networks.

Distributed Source Coding (DSC): An approach that compress the data from multiple sensors. This is done by using a correlation value which is basically the difference between two sensor readings.

Geographic Adaptive Fidelity (GAF): A localized, distributed topology management algorithm that allows nodes to sleep to conserve energy. GAF uses location information, typically from a GPS device, to organize redundant nodes into groups. Some of the redundant nodes will be put to sleep. GAF will divide the network area into virtual grids.

Healthcare Monitoring Systems: Are traditionally complex systems involving not only data collection using WSN but also data propagation to healthcare provider, large databases and complex expert and knowledge based systems, therefore security and patient privacy is a very sensitive and important issue in design of such systems.

MANNA Management Services for WSNs: These management services are performed by a set of functions which take executing conditions from the WSN models. The WSN models, as defined in the MANNA architecture, represent the states of the network and serve as a reference for the management. The definition of the management services and functions is based on three management dimensions, namely management functional areas, management levels, and WSN functionalities.

Network Management: It is the processes that exert five functional areas on networks to achieve certain quality of service, as identified by the International Standards Organization or ISO. These five areas are: fault management, configuration management, security management, performance management and accounting management. Fault management deals with the process of finding problems in the network. This process involves finding the problem, isolating the problem, and fixing the problem if possible. Faults should be reported in some manner, such as a log file, E-mail message to the network manager, or an alert on the network management system.

Ontologies: Describe an abstract model of a domain by defining a set of concepts, their taxonomy and interrelation, and the rules that govern these concepts in a way that can be interpreted by machines.

Store-and-Forward Telemedicine: It is an approach that involves the acquisition of data, images and/or video content and transmission of this material to a medical specialist at a convenient time for assessment off line.

Telemedicine: The term telemedicine refers to the use of telecommunications and computer information technologies with medical expertise to facilitate remote health care delivery, medical services to remote areas or across great distances on the globe. It also covers any form of communication between health workers and patients through electronic equipment from remote locations. Telemedicine applications are either based on store and forward or two-way interactive television technology. The store and forward method is used for transferring medical data and digital images from one location to another. Medical data like ECG, heart rate, oxygen saturation, respiratory rate, blood pressure, etc., and images like CT, MRI, ultrasound, etc. Two-way interactive television (IATV) is used when there is a need for a 'face-to-face' consultation between the patient and specialist doctor in another location.

Wireless Sensor Network (WSN): Is a communication network composed of wireless sensor devices. These devices essentially are low cost, low power, multi-functional, small sized and communicate over short distances. Typically these devices serve as nodes in a wireless network and are deployed randomly in a given area. Nodes establish connectivity with each other dynamically after deployment and do not follow a pre-determined topology. Therefore WSN are self-organizing in nature and are suitable for military surveillance, control communication and monitoring disaster areas. Wireless sensor networks (WSNs) have promised us a new monitor and control model over the distributed computing environment. In general, these networks consist of a large number of sensor nodes densely distributed over the region of interest for collecting information or monitor & track certain specific phenomena from the physical environment.

Chapter 10
Security in Smart Home Environment

Georgios Mantas
University of Patras, Greece

Dimitrios Lymberopoulos
University of Patras, Greece

Nikos Komninos
Athens Information Technology, Greece

ABSTRACT

This chapter presents the concept of Smart Home, describes the Smart Home networking technologies and discusses the main issues for ensuring security in a Smart Home environment. Nowadays, the integration of current communication and information technologies within the dwelling has led to the emergence of Smart Homes. These technologies facilitate the building of Smart Home environments in which devices and systems can communicate with each other and can be controlled automatically in order to interact with the household members and improve the quality of their life. However, the nature of Smart Home environment, the fact that it is always connected to the outside world via Internet and the open security back doors derived from the household members raise many security concerns. Finally, by reviewing the existing literature regarding Smart Homes and security issues that exist in Smart Home environments, the authors envisage to provide a base to broaden the research in Smart Home security.

INTRODUCTION

Over the last decades the Smart Home development is a continuously evolving field that faces exceptional challenges. However, the recent advances in information and communications technologies have led the Smart Home development in a good level of maturity. A Smart Home is a living environment that incorporates the appropriate technology, called Smart Home technology, to meet the resident goals of comfort living, life safety, security and efficiency (Ricquebourg et al., 2006; Pohl & Sikora, 2005; Jiang, Liu, & Yang, 2004; Friedewald, Da Costa, Punie, Alahuhta, & Heinonen, 2005).

DOI: 10.4018/978-1-61520-805-0.ch010

Smart home technology achieves these goals building an environment which consists of a variety of home systems. A Smart Home encompasses four types of Smart Home systems; Home Appliances, Lighting and Climate Control system, Home Entertainment system, Home Communication system and Home Security System (Pohl & Sikora, 2005; Valtchev, Frankov, & ProSyst Software AG, 2002). Each of the above systems is characterized by different requirements (e.g. data rate, distance) based on the applications that supports. Thus, different physical media are appropriate for different Smart Home systems. In a Smart Home, the physical media that can be used by the Smart Home systems are the following: the existing wiring, a new wiring and the air. The existing wiring refers to the existing electrical wiring, the existing telephone wiring and the existing coax cabling. A new wiring requires installation of new cabling in the walls and the air refers to wireless networking (Pohl & Sikora, 2005; Jiang et al., 2004; Valtchev et al., 2002; Adams, 2002; Zahariadis, 2003).

In spite the fact that there is a high level of complexity and heterogeneity because of the various communication media and network protocols, the Smart Home systems are integrated into a well structured network, called Smart Home internal network. This integration is achieved using a central node, called residential gateway (RG), which serves as a bridge between the internal network of the Smart Home environment and the Internet. The residential gateway represents the intelligent control of a Smart Home as it manages the systems and connects them to the outside Internet world (Pohl & Sikora, 2005; Valtchev et al., 2002; Adams, 2002; HGI, 2006).

However, the heterogeneous and dynamic nature of the Smart Home internal network, the fact that it is always connected to the Internet and the fact that the household members usually open security back doors unintentionally are factors that create many security challenges in a Smart Home environment. For that reasons, security is a critical issue in Smart Home environment. The principal idea behind secure Smart Home is to preserve occupant privacy (improper eavesdropping or tampering of information) and not to allow service interference (e.g. blocking home network services) (Jeong, Chung, & Choo, 2006; Herzog et al., 2001; Thomas & Sandhu, 2004; Wang, Yang, & Yurcik, 2005; Schwiderski-Grosche, Tomlinson, Goo, & Irvine, 2004; He, 2002).

The notion of providing security in Smart Home environments relies on the maintenance of six essential properties; Confidentiality, Integrity, Authentication, Authorization, Non-repudiation and Availability. Confidentiality, Integrity, Authorization, Non-repudiation and Availability play very important roles in ensuring of Smart Home internal network security. However, Authentication can be considered as the first step in the pyramid of a security mechanism (Jeong, et al., 2006; Komninos, Vergados, & Douligeris, 2007a; Thomas & Sandhu, 2004; Schwiderski-Grosche et al., 2004; He, 2002; Bergstrom, Driscoll, & Kimball, 2001).

Following the introduction, this chapter is organized as follows. Firstly, in the second section, the concept of the Smart Home and its main components are presented. Furthermore, an overview of the main Smart Home systems is given and the role of the residential gateway in the Smart Home environment is discussed. The third section is devoted to the current Smart Home networking technology. In the fourth section, the security requirements that should be satisfied in a Smart Home are described. The fifth section concentrates on the factors that affect the security in a Smart Home environment. In the sixth section, security threats for the Smart Home internal network are discussed. In the seventh section, existing security technologies that provide security features in Smart Homes are described. Finally, the eighth section concludes the chapter.

Figure 1. Smart home concept

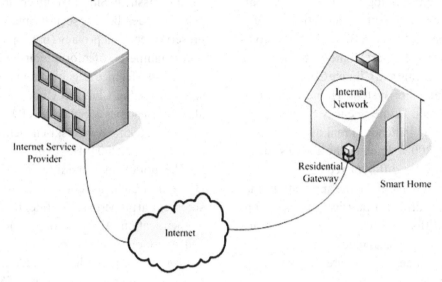

SMART HOME CONCEPT

It is very important to determine the main components of the Smart Home architectural model in order to be able to understand the factors that raise security breaches in a Smart Home environment as well as realize security technologies that can be applied to minimize the risk of security attacks. Smart Home can be considered that consists of three main components; the internal network, the external network and the residential gateway. These three components are presented in the Figure 1.

The internal network is the basis of a Smart Home and can consist of wired and wireless networks. The internal network of a Smart Home incorporates a combination of different communication media and protocols in order to support a number of Smart Home systems that simplify the residents' life and improve their quality of life. The external network of a Smart Home includes Internet and the service provider which is in charge to provide services over Internet to the household members. Finally, residential gateway (RG) is an always connected device located in a Smart Home and plays a very important role in bridging the internal network of the Smart Home and the outside world (Ricquebourg et al., 2006; Pohl & Sikora, 2005; Valtchev et al., 2002; Zahariadis, 2003; HGI, 2006; Delphinanto, 2003).

Smart Home Systems

The Smart Home internal network can integrate a variety of Smart Home systems, which provide a convenient and safe environment to the household members, as well as help them to perform their household tasks effectively. Smart Home systems can be classified into four categories (Figure 2): Home Appliances, Lighting and Climate Control system, Home Entertainment System, Home Communication System and Home Security System (Pohl & Sikora, 2005; Valtchev et al., 2002; Friedewald et al., 2005; Zahariadis, 2003; Delphinanto, 2003).

Home Appliances, Lighting and Climate Control System

Home Appliances, Lighting and Climate Control system consists of three subsystems. The Home Appliances Control subsystem monitors and

Figure 2. Smart home systems

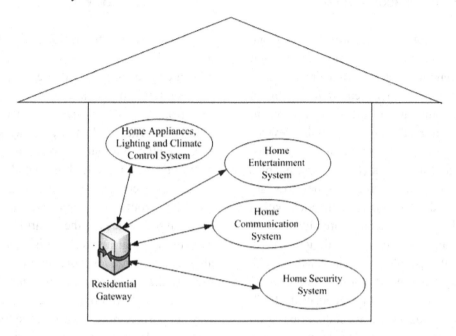

controls the power outlets in Smart Home. Thus, based on this subsystem, the habitat is able to monitor the power consumption as well as switch off power outlets separately. Furthermore, the Home Appliances Control subsystem can include smart appliances that communicate with each other and the outside Internet world making habitat's daily life more comfortable and enjoyable. The Lighting Control subsystem consists of switches, lights and sensors. This subsystem monitors the intensity of light as well as the activities of the occupants in a smart domestic environment. Based on these factors the Lighting Control subsystem adapts lighting of intelligent inhouse ambient. Finally, the Climate Control subsystem includes the functions of heating, ventilating, and air-conditioning. This subsystem monitors and controls temperature and humidity in a Smart Home environment providing healthy conditions within. Additionally, Lighting and Climate Control subsystem reduces costs for heating, cooling and lighting by smart energy management helping the homeowner to save money (Pohl & Sikora, 2005; Valtchev et al., 2002; Friedewald et al., 2005; Zahariadis, 2003; Delphinanto, 2003).

Home Entertainment System

Home Entertainment system provides the connection and communication of audio and video appliances over broadband networks serving distribution of high fidelity audio signal and high quality digital video. An Entertainment system can be consisted of a home theater, projection systems, plasma or LCD screens, a multi-channel surround sound system, satellite and digital television channels, video on demand systems, gaming consoles, a central media server, a central control system as well as a multi room audio video system for full audio and visual distribution. Digital audio is distributed from MP3 files, Internet radio and the home media server throughout the system to every room in the Smart Home. Furthermore, digital video content is distributed from the broadband connection, DVDs, PCs and the home media server to any video screen in the smart environment (Pohl & Sikora, 2005; Teger, Waks, & System Dynamics Inc., 2002; Valtchev et al., 2002; Han, Park, Jeong, & Park, 2006; Friedewald et al., 2005; Zahariadis, 2003; Delphinanto, 2003).

Home Communication System

Home Communication system provides telephone services such as conventional voice services and video conferencing calls as well as incorporates the intercommunication system of an intelligent inhouse environment for calling from room to room. Furthermore, this system contains devices such as PCs, printers, scanners, mobile phones, personal digital assistants (PDAs) and enables them to communicate with each other, to share information and a broadband connection within the Smart Home. Thus, tenants are able to chat, send emails and share data (e.g. digital photos, video) with other people in any place in the world. Finally, this system supports telecommuting for the residents (Pohl & Sikora, 2005; Teger et al., 2002; Valtchev et al., 2002; Han et al., 2006; Friedewald et al., 2005; Zahariadis, 2003; Delphinanto, 2003).

Home Security System

Home Security system encompasses identification mechanisms such as biometric recognition, voice recognition and face recognition, RFID tokens and smart cards that provide access control. Moreover, this system includes notification mechanisms such as burglar alarms that allow immediate reaction. Also, surveillance mechanisms such as CCTV can be part of Home Security system for monitoring in a Smart Home. What is more, there are solutions such as vibration shock sensors, glass-break sensors, for the detection of an intruder to a habitat. Furthermore, there are systems which use lights that automatically switch on and off giving the impression that someone is at home. Additionally, Home Security System comprises electro-mechanical door locks, electric windows and door shutters. Finally, health and well-being monitoring for disabled and elderly people as well as children can be part of this system (Pohl & Sikora, 2005; Teger et al., 2002; Valtchev et al., 2002; Han et al., 2006; Friedewald et al., 2005; Zahariadis, 2003; Delphinanto, 2003).

Residential Gateway

In a Smart Home, the residential gateway is a network device which integrates all the different networking technologies that exist in the Smart Home internal network as well as provides access from the internal network to Internet and vice versa. The residential gateway serves as a single point of internal network convergence and distribution of both LAN-initiated and WAN-initiated services. The residential gateway enables switching, routing and inter-working functions between the devices of the Smart Home systems over the internal network. This network device also supports high level distribution of advanced multimedia services over Internet broadband connectivity. Furthermore, the residential gateway supports remote control of the Smart Home systems and home appliances (Ricquebourg et al., 2006; Pohl & Sikora, 2005; Valtchev et al., 2002; Adams, 2002; Zahariadis, 2003; HGI, 2006).

Due to the variety of access network technologies, the residential gateway is able to interface with the majority of wired or wireless broadband access networks (e.g. ADSL, broadband mobile phone network, satellite link etc.). Different WAN side interfaces types can be provided by a residential gateway, but only one interface is supported at a time. Additionally, the residential gateway is able to support wired/wireless LAN interfaces towards the internal network since there are a lot of wired (HomePlug, HomePNA, Ethernet, IEEE 1394 and USB) and wireless (IEEE 802.11, Bluetooth, Zigbee and HiperLAN) networking technologies in a Smart Home. Moreover, the residential gateway provides QoS management to support services of different types at the same time. Besides, the residential gateway contains the rules for classification, queuing and priority field mappings (Zahariadis, 2003; HGI, 2006).

Furthermore, a residential gateway enables functionalities related to security of the Smart Home environment. It provides protection for the household members from unauthorized attacks and intrusions. Thus, a residential gateway encompasses a variety of security features such as firewalls, authentication mechanisms, authorization mechanisms and intrusion detection mechanisms (Kim, Lee, Han, & Kim, 2007; Zahariadis, 2003; HGI, 2006).

SMART HOME NETWORKING TECHNOLOGY

Smart Home internal network is based on various communication media and protocols (Figure 3). It is a combination of wired and wireless networks, since various transmission mediums, such as telephone lines, power lines, radio communication and wired cables are used in order to transmit signal throughout the Smart Home environment (Ricquebourg et al., 2006; Jiang et al., 2004; Teger et al., 2002; Valtchev et al., 2002; Zahariadis, 2003; HGI, 2006; Delphinanto, 2003). Thus, the security threats in the internal network include those derived from both wired networks and wireless networks.

Smart Home networks can be organized into three categories: existing wired networks, new wired networks and wireless networks (Figure 3). Existing wired networks reuse the existing in-home wiring, which consists of electrical wiring, telephone wiring and coaxial cabling, to transfer data. New wired networks require special cabling to distribute high-speed data and video throughout the dwelling. Finally, wireless networks use the air as transmission medium and offer solutions with "no wires" requirements (Teger et al., 2002; Valtchev et al., 2002; Zahariadis, 2003; HGI, 2006; Delphinanto, 2003).

Wired networks provide more security compared to wireless networks, since they cannot be as easily tapped. It is easy for an adversary to intercept the signal or to disturb the normal operation of a wireless network, because of the fact that wireless technologies cannot control the transmission range. Furthermore, the dynamism and mobility provided by wireless networks yield more chances for adversaries to exploit vulnerabilities of the network invisibly (Schwiderski-Grosche et al., 2004; Komninos, Vergados, & Douligeris, 2007c; Krishnamurthy, Kabara, & Anusas-amornkul, 2002; Zahariadis, 2003; HGI, 2006).

Figure 3. Smart home networking technologies

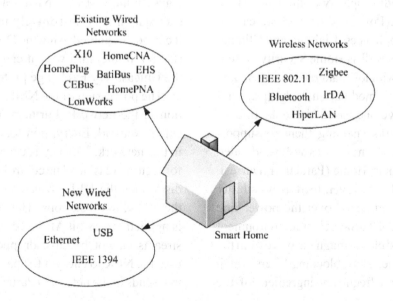

Existing Wired Networks

Existing wired network technology is directly applicable to new and old houses as rewiring of the buildings is not required. The major limitations of this networking technology include the networks' structure and the interference from the original operation of the network. Based on existing wiring of a home, Powerline networks, Phoneline networks as well as Coaxial networks can be developed to satisfy the needs of the household members (Jiang et al., 2004; Teger et al., 2002; Valtchev et al., 2002; Zahariadis, 2003; HGI, 2006; Delphinanto, 2003).

Powerline Networks

Powerline networking makes use of the existing electrical wiring, which is already used to provide power to home appliances and lights. The main target of Powerline networking is to connect devices to each other and to Internet plugging them directly into AC wall outlets in a Smart Home. However, based on the current Powerline technologies, we need to add an adapter to each device before it is plugged into an outlet. Currently Powerline networks support low speed connections (50 Kbps to 350 Kbps) because of the small bandwidth capacity of the wire. Thus, in a Smart Home Powerline networking can be used in Home Appliances, Lighting and Climate Control system as well as Home Security system for applications with low data rate requirements. Furthermore, new modulation techniques and technologies have increased the data rate of Powerline networks enabling them to support multimedia applications such as audio and video streaming in a Smart Home (Paruchuri, Durresi, & Ramesh, 2008). However, there is possibility that the transmitted signal over the power line network leaks out of the Smart Home environment through the leaked electromagnetic wave from the electric power line. Thus, blocking filters which block off the high frequency ingredient of the

signal should be installed in the power line communication network (Nishi, Morioka, & Sakurai, 2005). The main communication protocols for Powerline networks are HomePlug, X10, BatiBus, CEBus, LonWorks, and EHS (Jiang et al., 2004; Teger et al., 2002; Zahariadis, 2003; HGI, 2006; Delphinanto, 2003).

HomePlug is the major standard for Powerline communication. It is a simple-to-use, Ethernet-class standard and is created by the HomePlug Powerline Alliance. There are four versions of HomePlug standard. The first version, HomePlug 1.0, supports connections with data rate at 14Mbps. The second version, HomePlug 1.0 Turbo, runs at 85Mbps. The third version, HomePlug AV designed for HDTV and VoIP applications runs at 189Mbps. Finally, the last version, HomePlug Command and Control, operates at low data rate and is suitable for applications of Home Appliances, Lighting and Climate Control system (Adams, 2002; Zahariadis, 2003; HGI, 2006; Delphinanto, 2003).

Furthermore, HomePlug AV protocol forms virtual private LANs using cryptographic isolation. When a virtual private network is formed, a Network Membership Key (NMK) is distributed to all station of this network. The distribution of the NMK to all stations may take place with three ways. In the first way, NMK can be provided to each station by he host directly. In the second way, it can be distributed using the Device Access Key (DAK). In the third way, it can be passed using the Unicast Key Exchange protocol.

The possession of the NMK defines each station in the network. Furthermore, another key, called Network Encryption Key (NEK), is used in this network. This key is changed periodically for security reasons. The controller of the network distributes the NEK, which is encrypted using the NMK, to all stations. The encryption which is applied is 128-bit AES to ensure that the data streams cannot be eavesdropped. Each station uses the NEK to encrypt the payloads of the data that sends in the network (Paruchuri et al., 2008).

Phoneline Networks

Phoneline networking provides an easy and inexpensive way to connect devices for sharing data, peripherals and a high-speed Internet access throughout a Smart Home using the registered phone jacks and the existing in-home telephone cabling without affecting the telephone service. Phoneline networking requires the installation of a network adapter, which supports the phone-line protocols, to each device that the user wants to connect to the Phoneline network. Then, the user connects the network adapter of the device to the telephone outlet with a standard telephone cable. In contrast to Powerline networks and coaxial networks which require physical isolation or data encryption to prevent eavesdropping, Phoneline networks do not use any method for ensuring security as they are not shared (Björklund, 2007).

HomePNA is the main industry standard for Phoneline networking and provides an additional communication channel over the existing telephone line (Jiang et al., 2004; Teger et al., 2002; Valtchev et al., 2002; Zahariadis, 2003). HomePNA is an Ethernet-based standard and is developed by the Home Phoneline Networking Alliance. Recently, there are a lot of vendors that comply with this standard. There are three versions of HomePNA, the HomePNA 1.0 providing data rate at 1 Mbps, the HomePNA 2.0 running at 10 Mbps and the HomePNA 3.0 operating at 100 Mbps. Therefore, Phoneline networks can handle applications of Home Communication system and Entertainment system that include applications with high data rate requirements (Adams, 2002; Zahariadis, 2003; HGI, 2006; Delphinanto, 2003).

Coaxial Networks

Coaxial networking makes use of coaxial cabling which is normally used for distribution of radio and TV signal in a residence. Coaxial networks are characterized by large bandwidth capabilities and can support applications of Home Communication system and Home Entertainment system (Teger et al., 2002; Valtchev et al., 2002; Zahariadis, 2003; HGI, 2006). The major standard for this technology is HomeCNA, which is developed by the Home Cable Network Alliance. However, Coaxial networking represents the minority of in-home networks for existing buildings because of small use of coaxial cabling (Adams, 2002; Zahariadis, 2003; Delphinanto, 2003). In Coaxial networks, physical isolation as well as encryption are required to avoid eavesdropping on network traffic (Björklund, 2007).

New Wired Networks

New wired networks or structured wiring networks provide high performance connectivity and high reliability. Thus, this type of in-home networks can support applications of Home Communication system, Home Entertainment system and Home Security system. The main disadvantage of new wired networks is that they can not be installed or extended easily in an existing home or apartment because of their wiring requirements. Running new data cables inside the walls of an existing brick or stone home is not an affordable solution. However, it is a good idea to run the wiring throughout the house while it is being built. The most common communication standards of new wired networking are Ethernet, IEEE 1394 and USB (Jiang et al., 2004; Valtchev et al., 2002; Zahariadis, 2003; HGI, 2006).

Ethernet or IEEE 802.3 is the most widespread wired-LAN standard for PCs and workstations. Ethernet is a mature technology characterized by simplicity in installation and configuration. This standard can support a plethora of services such as TCP/IP based data, voice and video applications in a Smart Home and is supported by a lot of vendors. In 1985, the first version, Ethernet (10Base), was defined and run at a data rate of 10 Mbps. After ten years, the second version, Fast Ethernet (100Base), was published and run at 100 Mbps. The third version, Gigabit Ethernet

(10000Base), works at 1Gbit/s. Finally, the last version, 10Gigabit Ethernet, operates at 10Gbit/s (Adams, 2002; Zahariadis, 2003; HGI, 2006; Delphinanto, 2003).

Ethernet has a number of vulnerabilities that affect the network security. The main weakness is the fact that all stations in a local network share the same physical channel. Thus, an attacker can easily eavesdrop on transmitted traffic as what a station sends over the network can be received simultaneously by all the other stations of the network. Furthermore, Ethernet standard does not provide any mechanism for verification of message sender's identity or verification of message integrity. Therefore, an adversary can generate fraudulent data and insert them in the network traffic or he/she can obtains messages that are being exchanged between two legitimate communicating parties and retransmit them later as an authorized entity. These two weaknesses can be addressed dividing the Ethernet LAN in the Smart Home into sub-networks using bridges (Khoussainov & Patel, 2000).

Wireless Networks

Wireless networking is a very attractive solution for Smart Home networking providing simple installation, high flexibility and high data rate. Additionally, wireless networking does not include the cost of rewiring as well as the challenges of the existing wiring networks. What is more, wireless networks can be expanded easily in a home environment according to household members' needs. Wireless networks are used to satisfy requirements for mobility, ad hoc networking, relocation as well as coverage of areas hard to wired local area networks. Consequently, there are many applications areas for wireless networks. However, wireless networks sometimes have line-of-sight requirements and limited coverage. They can be used in all types of Smart Home systems, from Home Appliances, Lighting and Climate Control system to Communication, Entertainment and Security

systems. There are a lot of residential wireless networking standards but the most dominant are IEEE 802.11, Bluetooth (IEEE 802.15.1), Zigbee (IEEE 802.15.4), and HiperLAN (Ricquebourg et al., 2006; Jiang et al., 2004; Teger et al., 2002; Valtchev et al., 2002; Adams, 2002; Zahariadis, 2003; HGI, 2006; Delphinanto, 2003).

IEEE 802.11

IEEE 802.11 is a set of standards and is considered as the most widespread standard for wireless local area networks worldwide. In 1999, IEEE published 802.11a and 802.11b. IEEE 802.11b is the slowest and least expensive standard. In 2002, 802.11g was published to extend the IEEE 802.11b data rates to 54Mbps operating in the 2.4GHz band. Its range is around 50 meters. Right now, 802.11g is the most popular flavor of 802.11 for in-home networks because of its speed and reliability. Finally, IEEE 802.11n is the newest standard that is widely available and improves speed (140 Mbps) and range, but, it still in draft form (Adams, 2002; Zahariadis, 2003; HGI, 2006; Delphinanto, 2003).

Security in IEEE 802.11 standards is provided using Wired Equivalent Privacy (WEP), Wi-Fi Protected Access (WPA) and Wi-Fi Protected Access 2 (WPA2). WEP was the first security mechanism providing confidentiality, access control and data integrity in wireless communication. WEP uses RC4 encryption algorithm to protect the transmitted data. However, WEP is the most unsecured mechanism of these three, as it has a number of vulnerabilities. Transmitted packets can be easily captured and forged by attackers. Furthermore, WEP uses static keys which are rarely changed by users. WPA is a security mechanism created in response to the known serious weaknesses of WEP. WPA is a subset of the 802.11i standard. Similar to WEP, WPA uses RC4 as its encryption method. However, the strongest of these three security mechanisms is WPA2 which is based on the full 802.11i standard. This mechanism uses Advanced Encryption Standard (AES) as encryption method and provides better security than WEP and WAP (Krishnamurthy et al., 2002; Björklund, 2007; Komninos & Mantas, 2009).

Bluetooth

Bluetooth (IEEE 802.15.1) is an open standard specification that enables short-range (10cm – 10m) wireless connections for a wide range of portable and/or fixed devices. The older Bluetooth 1.0 has a maximum data rate at 1 Mbps while the newest Bluetooth 2.0 can handle up to 3Mbps. Bluetooth enabled devices communicate through short-range, ad hoc networks called piconets. Piconets are established dynamically and automatically as Bluetooth devices enter and leave radio proximity. Furthermore, Bluetooth technology supports both data and voice transmission simultaneously (Ricquebourg et al., 2006; Adams, 2002; Zahariadis, 2003; HGI, 2006; Delphinanto, 2003).

Bluetooth implements several authentication and data encryption mechanisms to provide security. The Bluetooth authentication scheme uses a challenge response method. The Bluetooth encryption scheme encrypts the payloads of the transmitted packets using a stream cipher E_0. Furthermore, any pair of Bluetooth enabled devices that desire to communicate with each other should generate a session key, called link key, using a combination of an initialization key, the device MAC address and the Personal Identification Number (PIN). However, Bluetooth has a number of weaknesses which can be exploited by adversaries to obtain keys and the PIN numbers, depending on how session initialization of the communication standard is performed (Krishnamurthy et al., 2002; Hager & Midkiff, 2003).

Zigbee

Zigbee (IEEE 802.15.4) is a wireless standard of data transmission allowing the communication of device to device with low cost as well as low data rates and low power consumption. It replaces wired solutions with low data rates requirements. Zigbee can operate at 2.4 GHz with a basic bit rate of 250Kbps. Zigbee is suited for house-oriented applications such as applications of Home Appliances, Lighting and Climate Control system as well as Home Security system (Ricquebourg et al., 2006; Adams, 2002; HGI, 2006; Delphinanto, 2003).

Zigbee security is based on a centralized infrastructure providing a central control on security of the network. There is a centralized trust entity that is trusted by all nodes in the network and is responsible for distribution of keys and admission control of nodes requesting to access to the network. Each network can not have more than a single centralized trust entity and each device can be associated to only one centralized trust entity. However, this entity can be considered as a single point of failure and can be a security vulnerability of the network which can be exploited by malicious attackers.

Furthermore, Zigbee standard proposes three types of keys; link key, network key and master key. Link key is shared between any two devices and is used to secure their communication. Network key is a common key for all devices and is shared among all devices in the network. Network key is used to secure all broadcast communications in the network. Master key is pre-installed or derives from the centralized trust entity and is used to generate the link keys.

Additionally, Zigbee standard provides data freshness, data integrity, authentication and encryption. Data freshness is achieved using counters which are reset every time a new key is generated. Data integrity is provided by Message Authentication Codes. Network level authentication and device level authentication are provided using the common network key and the link keys respectively. Finally, Zigbee proposes 128-bit AES encryption using the common network key for network encryption and the link keys for device encryption (Baronti et al., 2007).

HiperLAN

HiperLAN is a wireless LAN standard published by European Telecommunications Standard Institute (ETSI). There are two versions; HiperLAN 1 and HiperLAN 2. HiperLAN 1 was published in 1996 and its maximum data rate is 23.5Mbps. HiperLAN 2 was published in 2000 and can handle up to 54Mbps data rate. The basic services that two versions can support are data, audio and video transmission (Zahariadis, 2003; Delphinanto et al., 2003).

HiperLAN uses schemas for mutual authentication of mobile devices, encryption of data and exchange of encryption keys. HiperLAN standard proposes five authentication mechanisms based on the challenge response approach providing mutual authentication between mobile devices and the access point. Furthermore, HiperLAN uses the DES and 3DES algorithms for data encryption. Finally, the exchange of encryption keys is based on the Diffie-Hellman protocol. In spite the fact that HiperLAN has several relatively strong security mechanisms, there are a lot of vulnerabilities (Casole, 2002).

SECURITY REQUIREMENTS IN SMART HOME

Having presented the concept of a Smart Home and described the networking technologies used to implement its systems, the security requirements for a Smart Home environment are identified. The main security objectives that a Smart Home environment must fulfil are Confidentiality, Integrity, Authentication, Authorization, Non-repudiation and Availability (Jeong et al., 2006; Herzog et al., 2001; Kim et al., 2007; Schwiderski-Grosche et al., 2004; Kangas, 2002; He, 2002; Bergstrom et al., 2001; Komninos et al., 2007c).

Confidentiality is concerned with preventing unauthorized access to certain information. In an attack at confidentiality, an adversary may use services providing information about the Smart Home's status in order to enable indirect surveillance of resident's activities in a Smart Home environment (Komninos et al., 2007a; He, 2002; Bergstrom et al., 2001; Komninos et al., 2007c; Krishnamurthy et al., 2002). Confidentiality can be achieved using symmetric cryptographic ciphers (i.e. block or stream ciphers).

Integrity is a security service that provides prevention of unauthorized modification of information. Integrity ensures that data have not been changed, destroyed or lost during any process, such as transfer, storage or retrieval. In other words, Integrity ensures that data are consistent and correct. Integrity can be compromised by a malicious attacker who eavesdrops on the traffic to or from the internal network of a Smart Home and tampers data. Integrity can be provided using a Message Authentication Code (MAC) (Herzog et al., 2001; Bergstrom et al., 2001; Komninos et al., 2007c; Krishnamurthy et al., 2002).

Authentication is a security service related to verification of an entity based on a password or a shared secret key between the communicating parties. Authentication allows one entity to verify the identity of another entity. There are two types of authentication; entity authentication and message authentication. Entity authentication verifies the validity of the claimed identity of each entity. In other words, entity authentication confirms the identities of communicating parties. On the other hand, message authentication verifies that a message derives from the claimed entity. In a Smart Home environment, a lot of authentication mechanisms are required for user-to-device, user-to-internal network, device-to-device, device-to-internal network and user-to-service provider authentications. An adversary may pretend to be another legitimate user or entity in order to obtain critical information regarding home users or access Smart Home environment services (Jeong et al., 2006; Komninos et al., 2007a; Schwiderski-Grosche et al., 2004; Bergstrom et al., 2001;

Komninos et al., 2007c; Krishnamurthy et al., 2002; Komninos & Mantas, 2009).

Authorization is the process that determines the user's access rights on a device or a network resource and what a device is allowed to do within the Smart Home environment. Authorization can also provide different access levels to guarantee that entities can only access and perform operations on network resources that they are authorized for. The devices of the Smart Home internal network can be categorized into two types; home devices and foreign devices. Regarding the home devices, the authorization mechanism is based on home user's access rights on the devices. Regarding foreign devices, the owner of each device delegates certain access rights to foreign users who have to pay when they wish to use them. However, an adversary can use forged authorizations to perform prohibited actions in a Smart Home environment (Schwiderski-Grosche et al., 2004; Bergstrom et al., 2001; Komninos et al., 2007c; Krishnamurthy et al., 2002).

Non-repudiation corresponds to a security service providing protection against denial of involvement in an action. For instance, Non-repudiation prevents both sender and receiver from denying of a transmitted message or access to services. This service is similar to a signature by the author or recipient of a document in real life. Furthermore, this service can not prevent an entity from repudiating having performed a particular action. However, it can provide proof (i.e. proof of commitment, resource use, obligation, data origin) that can be stored and used later by a trusted third party in order to resolve disputes that arise in cases that an action is repudiated by one of the entities participated in the action. Non-repudiation can be provided using digital signatures based on public key encryption cryptosystems (Schwiderski-Grosche et al., 2004; He, 2002; Komninos et al., 2007c; Krishnamurthy et al., 2002; Stallings, 2005).

Availability ensures that network services and resources (i.e. bandwidth) are available and protected against events impacting the network such as malicious attacks. Especially, the Smart Home internal network is exposed to direct denial of service attacks, since it is exposed to Internet directly. What is more, disaster recovery solutions are included in this service since the internal network is exposed to a variety of attacks that lead to the loss or reduction of availability (He, 2002; Komninos et al., 2007c; Krishnamurthy et al., 2002;).

FACTORS AFFECTING THE SECURITY IN SMART HOME

Security is a crucial and critical issue in a Smart Home environment. Many home users are concerned about unauthorized access into their home and about privacy of their data. However, it is not a trivial task to provide security in the Smart Home environment because of its heterogeneous nature, dynamic nature, the fact that it is always connected to Internet as well as the open security back doors derived from the household members (Jeong et al., 2006; Herzog et al., 2001; Thomas & Sandhu, 2004; Wang et al., 2005; Haque & Ahamed 2006; Schwiderski-Grosche et al., 2004; He, 2002; Ziegler, Mueller, Schaefer, & Loeser, 2005).

Smart Home internal network is an extremely heterogeneous network since it consists of a vast range of different devices, applications and communication technologies as we have already described. In a Smart Home, there are many devices such as light switches, white appliances, sensors, cameras, TVs, phones, PCs, and PDAs, with very different capabilities and requirements, and communicate with each other via wired and wireless networks (Wang et al., 2005; Schwiderski-Grosche et al., 2004; Ziegler et al., 2005). Consequently, the deployment of security mechanisms depends on the device capabilities and requirements. The capabilities of devices vary widely in terms of memory storage, battery power and computational capability (Haque & Ahamed 2006; Krishnamurthy et al., 2002). There are devices such as PCs that can easily handle complex computations and support security features. However, there are devices such as the handset of a cordless phone that they do not have the appropriate computational power because of their limited resources (i.e. memory storage, battery power and computational capability). These devices usually provide no protection or they may able to support only simple security mechanisms (Krishnamurthy et al., 2002). Thus, exploiting these devices, intruders can compromise residential networks. Furthermore, not all devices require the same level of security. It can vary from low level to high level. Different security mechanisms should be implemented depending on the requirements of each device.

Moreover, the applications supported of Smart Home Systems are also diverse. There are applications that support different types of data such as audio, video signals and low date rate sensor information, with different features. Thus, each application has security schemes that should be optimal for it. Applications that support high data rate services (e.g. multimedia applications) require security mechanisms that do not increase delay or jitter. On the other hand, applications that support low data rate services (e.g. over a sensor network) can be constrained to use complex security schemes because of power consumption (Haque & Ahamed 2006; Schwiderski-Grosche et al., 2004; Krishnamurthy et al., 2002).

Additionally, having presented the Smart Home networking technology in section "Smart Home Networking Technology", it is clear that the internal network of a Smart Home is a completely heterogeneous network which integrates a number of different communication technologies. Each of Smart Home networking technologies has its own features and security weaknesses. For instance, wireless technologies can be easily tapped because of their broadcast nature. An attacker can intercept the signal or disturb the normal operation of a wireless communication.

On the other hand, wired technologies provide higher levels of security inherently.

In a Smart Home environment, there are also a lot of wireless devices, supporting a wide range of services, which join and leave the internal network completely arbitrarily, forming an extremely volatile ad hoc subnetwork. This ad hoc subnetwork is extremely dynamic and changes from time to time. Thus, the topology of the internal network is dynamic, which means that the required security mechanisms should be reconfigured dynamically every time that the topology is changed without home user's intervention (Thomas & Sandhu, 2004; Wang et al., 2005; Haque & Ahamed 2006; Schwiderski-Grosche et al., 2004; Krishnamurthy et al., 2002). Otherwise, the internal network suffers from several security vulnerabilities. However, the deployment of security mechanisms in an ad hoc network is a challenging issue because of its inherent dynamic nature. Thus, the security solutions regarding the ad hoc networking should be based on dynamic security mechanisms with sufficient intelligence in order to prevent security breaches.

Additionally, the expansion of the Smart Home internal network to the outside world via Internet creates many network security problems, as it is exposed to a variety of cyber attacks such as DoS attacks, malicious software, eavesdropping and so on (Jeong et al, 2006; Herzog et al., 2001; Kim et al., 2007; Kangas, 2002; Bergstrom et al., 2001). In contrast to dial up connections to Internet, Smart Home high-speed connections provide constant connectivity to Internet, which implies static IP address. The fact that the IP address does not change makes the internal network to be easily hacked, since attackers have a lot of time to guess the IP address and hack the connected devices (Herzog et al., 2001). Moreover, the internal network is subjected to all legacy security attacks of an open network since it is accessible from Internet.

First of all, malicious attackers can cause havoc in a Smart Home environment as they can intercept and modify remotely transmitted messages of networks (i.e. Powerline network, Phoneline network, wireless networks) that comprise the internal network of the Smart Home. Furthermore, malicious attackers might compromise the internal network and use it to launch attacks against other networks covering their tracks. Adversaries can also use the computing power and the resources of the compromised internal network for Denial of Service attacks against other Internet nodes. Furthermore, adversaries might gain access over Internet to confidential information of the household members eavesdropping on their Internet traffic. For example, sniffing messages of e-banking transactions, adversaries can get credit card numbers or they can learn about the behavior of the household members. Also, they can get the locking mechanism password of the home in order to burglarize it (Herzog et al., 2001; Bergstrom et al., 2001).

Thus, due to the heterogeneity of devices, applications and communication technologies in a Smart Home environment, the dynamic nature of the Smart Home internal network as well as the fast permanent connection to the outside world, there is not a single security solution that is able to provide all required security services in order to decrease the risk of security attacks. Consequently, the challenges for security insurance can be addressed with a diversity of security mechanisms, protocols and services that should be integrated and managed in the Smart Home internal network.

Finally, the household members are another factor that makes a Smart Home environment vulnerable to a rich variety of security threats. Most of the household members are usually non-professionals in networking as well as network security field. However, they usually build the internal network without participation of security professionals. Thus, there are always security weaknesses in the internal network which can be exploited by intruders. Additionally, household members often abuse their privileges raising many security issues. Furthermore, in many cases, home users consider that the appropriate security measures are complicated and they are not willing to follow them because of low usability. Besides, there are cases that residents do not use security protection or follow security policies because either they do not care about security or they are not able to understand completely the threats that they are faced with (Thomas & Sandhu, 2004; Wang et al., 2005; He, 2002).

SECURITY THREATS IN SMART HOME

Smart Home security threats can be derived from the factors described in section "Factors Affecting the Security in Smart Home" and they usually attempt to compromise one or more of the security requirements for a Smart Home environment presented in section "Security Requirements in Smart Home". These threats are mainly classified into internal and external threats.

Internal Threats

Internal threats stem from within the trusted Smart Home internal network. However, they are not given the attention they deserve compared with external attacks. Internal threats can be derived from inappropriate network construction and configuration, incomplete security plan and software pitfalls.

Inappropriate Smart Home internal network construction and configuration of network enabled devices create many security breaches in a Smart Home environment. It is very important the professional design and implementation of the internal network. Additionally, it is a very critical issue the correct configuration and set up of network devices (e.g. servers), user devices (laptops, PDAs) and firewalls. Otherwise, a wrongly configured device can raise security risks. However, for a non-professional home user, the correct construction and configuration can be an extremely difficult and daunting task.

Furthermore, there are not complete security policies in a Smart Home environment. Any home user (young children, people lacking security skills) is allowed to use any device and access any service. Besides, any resident can change the Smart Home internal network since he\she can modify the configuration of network equipment, add or remove network devices from the internal network as well as install or uninstall software of network devices. Additionally, the security features of the Smart Home environment can be modified intentionally or unintentionally by any home user. Also, there are cases that the home users abuse their privileges (e.g. frequently changing systems' settings, downloading uncertified software). Thus, a lot of security holes for intruders can be raised when the home user does not follow security policies properly. Finally, another fact that poses many security threats to the internal network is the use of software with security pitfalls (Wang et al., 2005; He, 2002).

External Threats

Smart Home internal network is subject to a lot of security threats derived from outside malicious nodes. The types of the external threats are classified based on the way the information is compromised. There are two generic types of threats: passive and active attacks.

In passive attacks, the intruder intends to gain unauthorized access to information that is being transmitted without modifying it. The detection of passive attacks in a communication is not easy, since the intruder does not change the messages that are being exchanged between the sender and the receiver. Passive attacks can be either eavesdropping or traffic analysis (He, 2002; Komninos et al., 2007c, Stallings, 2005). These two passive attacks are described below.

Eavesdropping allows an intruder to monitor the home user traffic (e.g. telephone conversation, email message) between the Smart Home internal network and the outside world without

the consent of the communicating parties. This traffic may contain confidential information that the residents do not want to disclosure it to unauthorized third parties. Eavesdropping is the most widely identified security problem in open networks and is an attack on confidentiality of the Smart Home internal network.

Traffic analysis is a subtler passive attack as it allows an adversary to deduce information observing the traffic pattern of a communication that is taking place between one communicating party located in the Smart Home environment and one located in the outside world. Using traffic analysis, the adversary is able to infer sensitive information (e.g. home user's location, passwords) from the messages that are being exchanged even when they are encrypted and they can not be decrypted. In traffic analysis attack, the greater the number of observed messages, the more information can be extracted.

In active attacks, the adversary intends to tamper the information or generate fraudulent data into the Smart Home internal network. Active attacks can result in severe losses for the home users. The main types of active attacks are masquerading, replay, message modification, denial of service and malicious codes (He, 2002; Komninos et al., 2007c, Stallings, 2005).

In masquerading attack, an intruder gains certain unauthorized privileges pretending to be another legitimate user or entity. The intruder may impersonate an authorized home user or entity and access to the Smart Home internal network remotely in order to get sensitive information or obtain services. This attack is often combined with others attacks such as replay attack.

In replay attack, an adversary firstly obtains messages that are being exchanged between two legitimate communicating parties and retransmit them later as an authorized entity. The adversary may capture a copy of a valid service request sent from a device in the Smart Home environment, store it and then replay it in order to access the service that the home user is authorized to.

Message modification takes place when an unauthorized entity modifies contents of a legitimate message by deleting, adding to, or changing it. Furthermore, in this attack, an adversary can also create delays to some messages or change their order producing unauthorized effect. Message modification can take place when an adversary intents to hijack the communication between two authorized entities, alter a software so that it performs maliciously or change values in a data file. This attack can result in a DoS attack and is an attack on integrity.

Denial of service attack is used in cases that an adversary intents to make a network unavailable to users or reduce the availability of network services. The adversary can send countless messages to the Smart Home internal network in order to overload its resources with traffic. Thus the authorized users are not able to access the services of the home network. Additionally, the adversary can send a tremendous amount of messages to servers and devices connected to Internet so as to block the internal traffic transmitted via wired or wireless networks inside the Smart Home.

Malicious codes are software threats that cause adverse affects to the Smart Home internal network exploiting its vulnerabilities. Malicious codes are used to modify, destroy or steal data as well as allow unauthorized access. Malicious codes can be classified into two categories. The first category includes those (i.e. Trap doors, viruses, logic bombs and Trojan horses) that need a host program. They are parts of programs that can not exist independently of some actual application software. The second category consists of those (i.e. worms and zombies) that are self-contained programs and can be scheduled and run by the operating system. Furthermore, malicious codes can be categorized on those that do not replicate and those that do. The former are parts of programs that are to be activated when the host program is invoked in order to perform a specific function. The latter contains parts of programs or independent programs that when they are executed they produce one or more copies of themselves in order to be activated later on the same system or another system.

Each of the malicious code has different threat to network security as they have their own characteristics. Malicious codes are distributed combining network communication and multiple attacking methods. They are distributed via emails, web pages, instant communication tools, software pitfalls, etc. The security threats of malicious codes have the highest risk in a Smart Home environment compared to corporation networks due to lack of home user's awareness about network security and data protection.

SECURITY TECHNOLOGIES FOR SMART HOMES

The most essential security technologies for making a Smart Home internal network secure are authentication and authorization mechanisms. Both mechanisms are required in order to restrict any malicious entity from accessing the Smart Home internal network. Furthermore, use of firewalls is another intrusion prevention mechanism that is important to increase security in Smart Home environment. However, intrusion prevention mechanisms alone are not sufficient for the Smart Home internal network because of its complexity and heterogeneity. Therefore, the use of intrusion detection systems (IDS) is also required.

Authentication Mechanisms

Authentication process includes entity authentication and message authentication. Entity authentication ensures the authenticity of the entity and message authentication verifies that the received message derives from the right sender. There are mechanisms for entity authentication as well as message authentication.

Entity authentication mechanisms support two processes; identification process and verification process. In identification process, an entity (e.g. home user) requests access to a network claiming a certain identity based on an identifier. The verification process is based on three approaches; proof by knowledge, proof by possession and proof by property (Kim et al., 2007; Kangas, 2002; Komninos & Mantas, 2008, 2009).

The proof by knowledge approach takes into consideration what the user knows. This approach usually checks a secret password or an identifier (ID) of the user that request access. The authentication mechanisms based on this approach called ID-password-based authentication mechanisms. The proof by possession approach depends on what the user possesses. This approach is based on the ownership of a smart card that should be connected during the login process. The authentication mechanisms that follow this approach called smart card-based authentication mechanisms. The proof by property approach is based on what the user is. In this approach, the verifier measures certain biometrics properties (e.g. fingerprint, iris, retina) of the user. The authentication mechanisms based on this approach called biometric-based authentication mechanisms.

Additionally, the entity authentication mechanisms can be divided into two categories; authentication mechanisms for intra-domain, and authentication mechanisms for inter-domain (Kim et al., 2007). In contrast to Intra-domain authentication mechanisms taking place in the Smart Home environment, inter-domain authentication mechanisms are applied out of the Smart Home environment. Authentication mechanisms for intra-domain include the authentication mechanisms based on proof by knowledge, proof by possession and proof by property approaches.

However, authentication mechanisms for inter-domain include the authentication mechanisms based on proof by knowledge and proof by possession approaches. Authentication mechanisms using biometric information are not used for inter domain authentication. It happens because once biometric information is disclosed to malicious attackers the user can not exchange the exposed biometric information for new one as the modification of human body is very difficult. Thus, it results in serious privacy violation in cases that biometric information is revealed. Consequently, it is not logical to use biometric-based authentication mechanisms in applications that require biometric information to be transferred over Internet (Kim et al., 2007; Yun-kyung, Hong-il, & Hyung-kyu, 2006).

Message authentication mechanisms are achieved using public key cryptosystems and digital signatures (Kangas, 2002). In public key cryptosystems, each communicating party has a pair of keys. One is used for encryption and the other for decryption. The key used for encryption is known to everyone and is referred to as public key. On the other hand, the key used for decryption remains secret and is known as private key. The private key and the public key are related mathematically. But, the private key can not be derived from the public key in a reasonable amount of time. In public key cryptosystems, the sender encrypts a message with the recipient's public key and only the entity (i.e. recipient) with the corresponding private key can decrypt the encrypted message (Stallings, 2005). Furthermore, digital signatures are used in public key cryptosystems. Digital signatures are produced using sender's private key. A message signed with sender's private key can be verified by the entity that knows the sender's public key.

In a Smart Home Environment, the authentication mechanism challenges the home user to provide his unique information (e.g. password, smartcard, fingerprint). If the authentication mechanism can verify that the shared secret was presented correctly, the home user is authenticated directly. Furthermore, a home user is required to be authenticated only one time to access any network resource or service. If the authentication does not succeed, this leads to rejection or termination of the access and the creation of a report to a security management center. Furthermore, there are cases that the home user desires to access a remote application server which performs its own authentication. In these cases, the user is identified by the residential gateway and it does the required authentication with the remote server instead of the user. It is happens because the residential gateway has an authentication mapping function, which achieves mapping between authentication mechanisms for intra-domain and authentication mechanisms for inter-domain (Kim et al., 2007).

Authorization Mechanisms

The purpose of authorization is to control the authenticated entity's access rights on network services and resources. Additionally, authorization contributes to reduce the harmful consequences of exposure to malicious accesses. Thus, authorization mechanisms are used to determine what level of access a particular authenticated entity should have on network services and resources in a Smart Home environment. For authorization within the Smart Home internal network, the existing authorization mechanisms can be used. The existing authorization mechanisms can be classified into three categories; server-based authorization mechanisms, peer-to-peer authorization mechanisms and certificate-based authorization mechanisms (Kim et al., 2007; Kangas, 2002).

Server-based authorization mechanisms are used in client-server communication model. In this mechanism, the server generates and keeps authorization rules. Server-based authorization mechanism is the simplest authorization mechanism.

Peer-to-peer authorization mechanisms are based on peer-to-peer communication service model. In this mechanism, a peer manages the authorization rules or requires help of a designated authorization server. This mechanism is more complicated than the server-based authorization mechanism because of a number of constraints such as database maintenance and hardware specifications of peer's machine.

Finally, certificate-based authorization mechanisms refer to authorization infrastructures, where Authorization Certificates (ACs) are used for authentication and access control simultaneously. AC establishes authorization access rights between a subject and a resource (Kim et al., 2007; Kangas, 2002; Stallings, 2005).

All the above three categories of authorization mechanisms use an Access Control List (ACL) schema or a Role-based Access Control (RBAC) schema. Access Control List (ACL) schema includes a list of permissions attached to an object. ACL establishes relationships between subjects (i.e. entities) and objects (i.e. resources). ACL determines the entity allowed to access the object and what operations are allowed to be performed on the object. ACL schema defines access rights of entities to the resources in terms of write, read and execute permissions. First of all, when an entity requests to perform an operation on an object, the list is checked in order to decide whether to proceed with the operation or not. ACL schema includes two models; discretionary and mandatory. In discretionary access control model, the owner of an object is able to have full control access to the object. In mandatory access control model, the authorization mechanism enforces restrictions that override the permissions stated in the ACL. Role-based Access Control (RBAC) schema is a newer alternative approach to discretionary access control model and mandatory access control model. In Role-based Access Control (RBAC) schema, an intermediate component, called role, is used between a subject and a resource (Kim et al., 2007; Kangas, 2002; Stallings, 2005).

Intrusion Prevention: Firewalls

A firewall is a hardware device or software running on another device which inspects the information passing through it in order to prevent unauthorized Internet entities from accessing private networks connected to Internet. A firewall examines all network traffic entering or leaving the private network and blocks the network traffic that does not conform to a defined set of rules based on security criteria (Stallings, 2005; HGI, 2006).

The firewall techniques used in order to control the network traffic are packet filtering, proxy service and stateful inspection. In packet filtering method, firewall analyzes packets, entering or leaving the private network, against a set of filters and accepts or discards them based on user-defined rules. Firewall provides a private network with the capability to perform coarse-grain filtering on IP and TCP/UDP headers, including IP addresses, port numbers and acknowledgment bits. However, in this method it is difficult for the user to configure the firewall. Furthermore, this method is vulnerable to IP spoofing attack.

In proxy service method, firewall retrieves all information entering and leaving the private network and then sends it to the requesting entities. Thus, firewall hides the true IP addresses of the private networks devices from malicious adversaries.

In stateful inspection method, firewall monitors the state of network connections (i.e. TCP, UDP) passing across it and stores information (i.e. IP addresses, ports sequence numbers, etc.) about them in a state table. Thus, filtering decisions are based on the information that has been stored based on the prior packets that have passed through the firewall. Firewall is able to distinguish legitimate packets for different types of connections. Thus, only packets matching a known connection state are accepted by the firewall. However, firewalls that follow the stateful inspection technique are not very efficient for applications that include IP addresses and TCP/UDP port information in the payload. To have higher level of security, firewalls should combine packet filtering with application gateways. Application gateways recognize the specific packets and analyze their payloads in order to obtain the required information and make policy decisions (Stallings, 2005; HGI, 2006).

All the above firewall techniques are not competitors. A Smart Home environment can employ all of them together to provide defence in depth. As we have already discussed in section "Smart Home Concept", the residential gateway is the official access point to the Smart Home internal network. All traffic transmitted from Internet to the internal network or to Internet from the internal network passes through the residential gateway. Thus, a firewall can be installed on the residential gateway in order to block all unauthorized accesses or suspicious data. The installed firewall monitors and analyzes all traffic between the internal network and Internet to decide whether it corresponds to the criteria of the Smart Home security policy.

Intrusion Detection

Intrusion detection is used as a second line of defence to protect the Smart Home internal network because once an intrusion is detected, a response can then take place to minimize damages. In case that an intruder succeeds in his attack over the Smart Home internal network, intrusion detection systems (IDS) can detect this attack and stop the activities of the intruder. In the Smart Home internal network, both Network-based IDS and host-based IDS can be used. Network-based IDS are used in wired networks where traffic monitoring takes place at switches, routers and gateways. However, host-based IDS are used in ad hoc networks where there are not such traffic concentration points. Host-based IDS are concerned with what is happening on each individual node of the ad hoc network (Komninos, Vergados, & Douligeris, 2007b; Komninos & Douligeris, 2009).

Intrusion detection techniques are classified into two categories; misuse detection and anomaly detection. Misuse detection technique requires audit data for analysis and compares these data to already known attack patterns stored in large databases. In cases that any comparison between the audit data and the known attack patterns results in a match, an intrusion alarm is set. The main advantage of misuse detection technique is the fact that it can accurately and efficiently detect instances of known attacks. However, this technique is not able to detect the newly invented attacks.

On the other hand, anomaly detection technique is based on statistical behaviour. Anomaly detectors look for behaviour that deviates from normal network activity. First of all, this technique requires the collection of audit data for analysis. Then, the audit data is transformed to a format statistically comparable to the profile of a user generated dynamically and updated based on the user's usage. In cases that any comparison between the audit data and the user's profile results in a deviation that crosses a set threshold, then an intrusion alarm is activated. The main advantage of anomaly detection technique is that it can detect unknown or new intrusion without requiring prior knowledge of the intrusion. The main disadvantage of this technique is that it may not be able to describe what the attack is (Stallings, 2005; Komninos & Douligeris, 2009).

CONCLUDING REMARKS

In this chapter, we have presented the concept of the Smart Home itself as well as its systems and the used networking technologies in order to perceive the security issues of Smart Homes. However, Smart Home security is of extreme importance since it affects the privacy of the household members. Thus, a variety of important security issues in Smart Home environments were discussed. Especially, the security objectives of a Smart Home as well as the main factors that increase the level of difficulty to provide security in a Smart Home environment were described. Furthermore, the threats that intend to compromise the security requirements were examined. Finally, existing security mechanisms that provide security features in a Smart Home environment were presented.

In a lot of cases, most of the home users are not security-aware enough to realize the implica-

tions of Smart Home environments. However, the importance of Smart Home security is going to be raised in the future because of the increasing complexity and heterogeneity of the Smart Home internal networks and the increasing use of remote working habits of the home users. Thus, there are requirements that should take place in order to reduce the risks of security attacks in a Smart Home environment. First of all, the main requirements for ensuring security in a Smart Home environment are the correct network design and construction as well as the correct configuration of network devices (e.g. firewalls, servers etc.) by professionals in networking and network security. Furthermore, operating systems and application software should be installed or configured correctly. Moreover, the correct creation of complete security policies is obligated. Security policies specify the home user's privileges and responsibilities. Additionally, user's privileges should be restricted to avoid security breaches. Finally, the correct installation and use of a reliable virus defense system is required.

REFERENCES

Adams, C. E. (2002). Home area network technologies. *BT Technology Journal*, *20*(2), 53–72.

Baronti, P., Pillai, P., Chook, V. W. C., Chessa, S., Gotta, A., & Hu, Y. F. (2007). Wireless sensor networks: A survey on the state of the art and the 802.15.4 and ZigBee Standards. *Computer Communications*, *30*(7), 1655–1695.

Bergstrom, P., Driscoll, K., & Kimball, J. (2001). Making Home Automation Communications Secure. *IEEE Computer*, *34*(10), 50–56.

Björklund, H. F. (2007, March). *Wiring Devices and Technologies in Home Environment*. Paper presented at the TKK T-110.5190 Seminar on Internetworking.

Casole, M. (2002). WLAN security – Status, Problems and Perspective. In *Proceedings of European Wireless 2002*. Florence Italy.

Delphinanto, A., Huiszoon, B., Rivero, D.S., Hartog, F., Boom, H., Kwaaitaal, J., & Wijk, P. (2003). *Home Networking Technologies Overview and Analysis*. Residential Gateway Environment, Deliverable D3.1.

Friedewald, M., Da Costa, O., Punie, Y., Alahuhta, P., & Heinonen, S. (2005). Perspectives of ambient intelligence in the home environment. *Telematics and Informatics - Elsevier, 22*(3), 221-238.

Hager, C., & Midkiff, S. (2003). An Analysis of Bluetooth Security Vulnerabilities. In *Proceedings of Wireless Communications and Networking Conference* (pp. 1825-1831). New Orleans, LA.

Han, I., Park, H., Jeong, Y., & Park, K. (2006). An Integrated Home Server for Communication, Broadcast Reception, and Home Automation. *IEEE Transactions on Consumer Electronics, 52*(1), 104–109.

Haque, M., & Ahamed, S. I. (2006). Security in Pervasive Computing: Current Status and Open Issues. *International Journal of Network Security, 3*(3), 203–214.

He, G. (Spring 2002). *Requirements for Security in Home Environments*. Paper presented at Residential and Virtual Home Environments – Seminar on Internetworking, HUT TML Course T-110.551.

Herzog, A., Shahmehri, N., Bednarski, A., Chisalita, I., Nordqvist, U., Saldamli, L., et al. (2001). Security Issues in E-Home Network and Software Infrastructures. In *Proceedings of the 3rd Conference on Computer Science and Systems Engineering in Linköping* (pp. 155-161). Norrköping, Sweden.

Home Gateway Initiative (HGI) (2006). Home Gateway Technical Requirements: Release 1.

Jeong, J., Chung, M., & Choo, H. (2006). Secure User Authentication Mechanism in Digital Home Network Environments. In Sha, E., Han, S.-K., Xu, C.-Z., Kim, M. H., Yang, L. T., & Xiao, B. (Eds.), *Embedded and Ubiquitous Computing* (pp. 345–354). Springer.

Jiang, L. Liu, D., & Yang, Bo. (2004). SMART HOME RESEARCH. In *Proceedings of the Third International Conference on Machine Learning and Cybernetics* (pp. 659-663). Shanghai.

Kangas, M. (Autumn 2002). *Authentication and Authorization in Universal Plug and Play Home Neworks*. Paper presented at Ad Hoc Mobile Wireless Networks – Research Seminar on Telecommunications Software, HUT TML – Course T-110.557.

Khoussainov, R., & Patel, A. (2000). LAN security: problems and solutions for Ethernet networks. *Computer Standards & Interfaces, 22*(3), 191–202.

Kim, G. W., Lee, D. G., Han, J. W., & Kim, S. W. (2007). Security Technologies Based on Home Gateway for Making Smart Home Secure. In Denko, M. (Eds.), *Emerging Directions in Embedded and Ubiquitous Computing* (pp. 124–135). Springer.

Komninos, N., & Douligeris, C. (2009). LIDF: Layered intrusion detection framework for ad-hoc networks. *Journal in Ad Hoc Networks, 7*(1), 171–182.

Komninos, N., & Mantas, G. (2009). Intelligent Authentication and Key Agreement Mechanism for WLAN in e-Hospital Applications. In Feng, J. (Ed.), *Wireless Networks: Research Technology and Applications)*. Nova Science Publishers Inc.

Komninos, N., & Mantas, G. (2008). Efficient Group Key Agreement & Recovery in Ad Hoc Networks. In *Proceedings of the 2nd IET International Conference on Wireless, Mobile & Multimedia Networks* (pp. 25-28). Beijing, China.

Komninos, N., Vergados, D., & Douligeris, C. (2007a). Authentication in a Layered Security Approach for Mobile Ad Hoc Networks. *Journal in Computers & Security, 26*(5), 373–380.

Komninos, N., Vergados, D., & Douligeris, C. (2007b). Detecting Unauthorized and Compromised Nodes in Mobile Ad-Hoc Networks. *Journal in Ad Hoc Networks, 5*(3), 289–298.

Komninos, N., Vergados, D., & Douligeris, C. (2007c). Multifold Authentication in Mobile Ad-Hoc Networks. *International Journal of Communication Systems, 20*(12), 1391–1406.

Krishnamurthy, P., Kabara, J., & Anusasamornkul, T. (2002). Security in Wireless Residential Networks. *IEEE Transactions on Consumer Electronics, 48*(1), 157–166.

Nishi, R., Morioka, H., & Sakurai, K. (2005). Trends and Issues for Security of Home-Network Based on Power Line Communication. In *Proceedings of the 19ᵗʰ International Conference on Advanced Information Networking and Applications* (pp. 655-660).

Paruchuri, V., Durresi, A., & Ramesh, M. (2008). Securing Powerline Communications. In *Proceedings of the IEEE International Symposium on Power Line Communications and Its Applications* (pp. 64-69). Jeju city, Jeju Island.

Pohl, K., & Sikora, E. (2005). Overview of the Example Domain: Home Automation. In Pohl, K., Böckle, G., & van der Linden, F. J. (Eds.), *Software Product Line Engineering Foundations, Principles and Techniques* (pp. 39–52). New York: Springer.

Ricquebourg, V., Menga, D., Durand, D., Marhic, B., Dalahoche, L., & Logé, C. (2006). The Smart Home Concept: our immediate future. In *Proceedings of the 1ˢᵗ IEEE International Conference on E-Learning in Industrial Electronics.*

Schwiderski-Grosche, S., Tomlinson, A., Goo, S. K., & Irvine, J. M. (2004). Security Challenges in the Personal Distributed Environment. In *Proceedings of IEEE 60ᵗʰ Vehicular Technology Conference.* Los Angeles.

Stallings, W. (2005). *Cryptography and Network Security Principles and Practices.* Upper Saddle River, NJ: Prentice Hall.

Teger, S., & Waks, D. (2002). *System Dynamics Inc* (pp. 114–119). End-User Perspectives on Home Networking. IEEE Communications Magazine.

Thomas, R. K., & Sandhu, R. (2004). Models, Protocols, and Architectures for Secure Pervasive Computing: Challenges and Research Directions. In *Proceedings of the Second IEEE Annual Conference on Pervasive Computing and Communications Workshops.*

Valtchev, D., & Frankov, I., & ProSyst Software AG. (2002). Service Gateway Architecture for a Smart Home. *IEEE Communications Magazine,* 126–132.

Wang, J., Yang, Y., & Yurcik, W. (2005). Secure Smart Environments: Security Requirements, Challenges and Experiences in Pervasive Computing. In *Proceedings of NSF Pervasive Computing Infrastructure Experience Workshop.*

Yun-kyung, L., Hong-il, J., & Hyung-kyu, L. (2006). Secure Biometric Recognition method in Home Network. In *Proceedings of the 32ⁿᵈ Annual Conference of the IEEE Industrial Electronics Society* (pp. 3745-3749). Paris.

Zahariadis, T. B. (2003). *Home Networking Technologies and Standards.* New York: Artech House.

Ziegler, M., Mueller, W., Schaefer, R., & Loeser, C. (2005). Secure Profile Management in Smart Home Networks. In *Proceedings of the 16ᵗʰ International Workshop on Database and Expert Systems Applications.* Copenhagen, Denmark.

Chapter 11
The Concept of Interoperability for AAL Systems

Lamprini T. Kolovou
University of Patras, Greece

Dimitrios Lymberopoulos
University of Patras, Greece

ABSTRACT

e-Health considers the healthcare environment as an electronic workspace where different Medical Information Systems (MIS) supports the automation of information processing, the exchange of medical and administrative data and the automation of medical workflow. AAL systems are MISs of special purposes that use wireless technology to provide healthcare to citizens. By their nature AAL systems are totally distributed, they include various medical and other users' devices and the mobility of people increases their complexity and creates advanced requirements for the communication of data. Effectiveness and functionality of AAL premise interoperability at all levels of communication. In this chapter the definitions of interoperability are examined and how these are specialized for the healthcare area as well. In addition, the applied technologies and some significant issues that regard interoperability are analyzed.

1 INTRODUCTION: OVERVIEW OF AAL SYSTEMS

The most significant feature of Ambient Assisted Living (AAL) systems is *mobility* of patients that is supported by wireless devices, which's basic characteristics are: they are associated with a particular person and applications can be targeted to that individual; their owners take them wherever they are; they offer direct links to vital informa-

tion and caregivers and to peer groups that can provide social support; they are essentially small computers that can capture, store and process information.

When talking about AAL systems, we are talking about wireless medical applications. There are two major categories of wireless applications in the area of healthcare: applications for monitor physiological functions and send the information to physicians; applications that provide information and feedback directly to patients, thus

DOI: 10.4018/978-1-61520-805-0.ch011

encouraging them to pay attention to and take o more active role in managing their health.

Applications of first category rely in sensors that are portable, wearable or implantable. Communications for these applications are typically "upstream". Applications of second category are primarily "downstream" although more advanced applications may involve two-way communication. Most of them are based on test messaging using short message service of cell phones. Latest applications use multimedia message service or two-way video.

2 DEFINING INTEROPERABILITY

2.1 The General Definition

At the very top of an '*interoperability* scale' are three levels, each one subdivided: functional, syntactic, and semantic. Full sharing of information requires that the two top levels of interoperability are reached: functional and syntactic interoperability: the ability of two or more systems to exchange information (so that it is human readable by the receiver); semantic interoperability: the ability for information shared by systems to be understood at the level of formally defined domain concepts (so that the information is computer processable by the receiving system).

To make interoperability clearly described, the terms of *interfacing* and *integration* have to be defined. The distinction between interfacing, integration and interoperability is extremely important.

Interface: a boundary at which interaction occurs between two systems, processes, etc. An interface defines how to access an object.

Integration: combination of diverse application entities into a relationship which functions as a whole.

Interoperability: a state which exists between two application entities when, with regard to a specific task, one application entity can accept data from the other and perform that task in an appropriate and satisfactory manner without the need for extra operator intervention.

This definition of interoperability, in its mention of a specific task, usefully distinguishes interoperability from integration. It also brings precision and operational meaningfulness to the IEEE and ISO definition of interoperability namely

"the ability of two or more systems to exchange data, and to mutually use the information that has been exchanged"

2.2 Interoperability in E-Health

The most known definitions of interoperability for healthcare systems are of three international organizations, CEN, IEE and HIMSS. These examine interoperability from different perspectives:

- HIMSS describe the dimensions that comprise a more expansive notion of interoperability
- CEN defines a broad array of user-driven interoperability functional profiles
- IEEE analyses the modules of an interoperability's functional model

Studying these definitions, a common area of interoperability in e-Health is defined as presented in Table 1.

2.3 HIMSS Definition

The HIMSS Integration and Interoperability Steering Committee (I&I) (formed in September 2004) attempted to develop an interoperable definition of interoperability that the entire healthcare industry could agree to. Starting from the general definition, I&I concerned interoperability as "the ability of health information systems to work together within and across organizational boundaries in order to advance the effective delivery of healthcare for

Table 1. The levels of interoperability in healthcare

HIMSS	IEEE	CEN
Uniform movement of healthcare data	Data communication	Information profiles
Uniform presentation of data	Information model	
Uniform user controls	System administration and confidentiality	IT infrastructure profiles
Uniform safeguarding data security and integrity		
Uniform protection of patient confidentiality	Applications, services and agents model	
Uniform assurance of a common degree of system service quality	Uniform user's environment	Workflow profiles
	User application interface	
	Applications" data management	

individuals and communities". The I&I further definition at least answers the question "what is the goal of interoperability?», which leaded to a deeper description of interoperability that considers interoperation from six dimensions.

The interoperability dimensions that comprise a more expansive notion of interoperability according to I&I include:

1. Uniform movement of healthcare data from one system to another such that the clinical or operational purpose and meaning of the data is preserved and unaltered

2. Uniform presentation of data, enabling disparate stakeholders to use different underlying systems to have consistent presentation of data when doing so is clinically or operationally important.

3. Uniform user controls, to the extent that a stakeholder is accessing a variety of underlying systems, and the contextual information and navigational controls are presented consistently and provide for consistent actions in AAL relevant systems.

4. Uniform safeguarding data security and integrity as data moves from system to system such that only authorized people and programs may view, manipulate, create, or alter the data.

5. Uniform protection of patient confidentiality even as stakeholders in different organiza-

tions access data that has been exchanged across systems, particularly in order to prevent unauthorized access to sensitive information by people who should not, or do not, need to know.

6. Uniform assurance of a common degree of system service quality (e.g., reliability, performance, dependability, etc.), so that stakeholders who rely on a set of interoperable systems can count on the availability and responsiveness of the overall system as they perform their jobs.

2.4 IEEE Definition

In 1996 IEEE introduced a reference model for interoperability concept in the area of e-Health. This reference model is work of sub-committee of Clinical Information Systems and describes the individual dimensions of interoperability with eight (8) levels. Each level defines a set of procedures that should be supported by the e-Health environment, in order to provide interoperability between the various medical information systems (MIS).

The levels of reference model are the followings:

1. *Data communication.* The procedures of this levels support: (a) the common structure of exchanged information and (b) the common interface for the communication of MISs.

2. *Information model.* The procedures of this level cover the semantic interoperability concept. The information model defines the major entities and terms of the 'enterprise' environment and ensures that these entities, the terms and the 'clinical' procedures (medical actions) have a common meaning for AAL communicating MISs.

3. *System management and confidentiality.* It covers the interoperability issue from the operational point of view and supports the management of the different MISs with an integrated manner. The procedures of this level are: (a) programs software monitoring; (b) users' rights administration; (c) authentication and authorization mechanisms; (d) improvement and extension of MISs; (e) error handling.

4. *Common user environment.* This level contains procedures that define: (a) the parameters for users' common 'working' environment and (b) services for integrated use of different MISs (e.g. a unique access point).

5. *Application user interface.* The procedures of this level support a common methodology for the presentation of information and common mechanisms for the interaction between the users and the graphical user interface.

6. *Application model, services & agents.* This level assigns the policy that is followed by MISs for data process and includes:
   ◦ Model for uses' data validation that is activated for every transaction between the users and the MISs
   ◦ Services that provide common tools (at application level) for the use of MISs and information's exchange
   ◦ Agents that perform data processing, relate the applications of different MISs and automate the individual users' processes and the combinational workflow of these processes

7. *Application data management.* The procedures of this level supports: (a) data storage, (b) processes for data communication, (c) application of information model's (level 2) constraints for semantic integration of applications.

8. *Application system characteristics.* This level is diversified by the previous levels and expresses a different option of interoperability, as describes parameters as functionality, safety and confidentiality and control.

2.5 CEN Definition

The CEN/ISSS e-Health Focus Group workingroup produced a report for current and future issues about interoperability in the area of e-Health. That report focuses on standardization and analyzes interoperability from the practical and operational point of view. The definition of interoperability is approached by three levels as following described.

The first level defines two forms of interoperability, the 'reactive' and the 'proactive'.

- Reactive interoperability is achieved with AAL these alterations, adaptations and extensions that should be followed by MISs, in order to implement suitable interfaces between them and create an interoperable environment.

- Proactive interoperability is achieved with the integration and unification of AAL standards that are used in the area of e-Health, ensuring the interoperable communication of MISs, without implementing further communication interfaces for each of them.

The second level describes the interoperability issues in the context of e-Health as follows:

- The effective communication and exchange of information is achieved by combinational use of advanced technologies of IT and the standards for messaging and security.

- Customization and cost for implementation of new MISs have to be the minimal.
- Special mechanisms should be implemented for integrated use of different standards, in order to eliminate the ambiguous 'translation' of the information that is exchanged between different MISs.
- MISs have to provide their services with a common manner as to support effective healthcare.
- The MISs of global market have to be interoperable independent on their vendors (standards-compliant products).
- Common assesses methodologies for MISs should be available for effectiveness and interoperability estimation.

In the third level of this analysis the requirements that arise from the above stated issues are abstracted in three functional profiles which are:

- Infrastructure profiles: they provide secure and safe infrastructure for data exchange and sharing of information, supporting functional and syntactic interoperability.
- Information profiles: they provide common information models, archetypes' mechanisms and encoding systems supporting the semantic interoperability.
- Workflow profiles: they are 'build' upon the previous profiles and support the active collaboration of MISs and the provision of added-value services for the users.

2.6 Standardization and Interoperability

Interoperability is achieved by using standardization in a proper and efficient manner. *Standards*

provide the rules and recommendations, based on which a process is implemented. Whereas there are many standards available from organizations which might meet the needs of applications and networks, there can be no guarantees that standards will interwork unless proven in practical applications and/or pilots.

2.7 Interoperability for AAL Systems

"Ambient Assisted Living" (AAL) systems aim:

- to extend the time people can live in their preferred environment by increasing their autonomy, self-confidence and mobility
- to support maintaining health and functional capability of the elderly individuals,
- to promote a better and healthier lifestyle for individuals at risk
- to enhance the security, to prevent social isolation and to support maintaining the multifunctional network around the individual
- to support carers, families and care organizations
- to increase the efficiency and productivity of used resources in the ageing societies

Interoperability for these systems should provide the necessary means:

- to establish the interworking of health organizations and cross-border communication to support the mobile citizen
- to exchange interoperable information structures and also integrating point of care medical and test devices
- to create an inventory of those standards that are necessary to achieve these business requirements
- to provide ease of use and plug-and-play device interactions and re-configurability

3 FUNCTIONAL LEVEL

At functional level, the technologies for developing wireless interoperable applications and the employed standards for the transmission of information are essential to be defined.

3.1 Wireless Application Protocol (WAP)

WAP is not a protocol, but rather a suite of open international protocols for application layer network communications, aimed to standardize the way that wireless devices can be used for Internet access, including e-mail, the World Wide Web, newsgroups, and instant messaging. Devices that use WAP are interoperable. WAP also aims at bridging the gap between the variety of mobile bearers' services and basic Internet protocols such as TCP/IP and HTTP, the HyperText Transfer Protocol commonly used to access Web pages over the fixed Internet.

A WAP browser provides AAL of the basic services of a computer based web browser but simplified to operate within the restrictions of a mobile phone, such as its smaller view screen. WAP sites are websites written in, or dynamically converted to, WML (Wireless Markup Language) and accessed via the WAP browser.

The architecture of a system that supports WAP services consists of: a WAP gateway; the HTTP web server; the WAP compatible device. WAP gateway acts as mediator between Cellular device and HTTP or HTTPS web server. WAP gateway routes requests from the client to an HTTP (or Web) server. The WAP gateway can be located either in a telecom network or in a computer network. HTTP server receives the request from WAP gateway and processes it and finally sends the output to the WAP gateway, which in turn sends this information to the WAP device using the wireless network. Wap device is part of the wireless network that sends the WAP request to the WAP gateway, which in turn translates WAP requests to WWW requests. After receiving the response from the HTTP Web Server, WAP Gateway translates Web responses into format that is manageable by the WAP client and sends it to the WAP Device.

The goals that WAP meets are the following:

- Independent of wireless network standard
- Open to all
- Will be proposed to the appropriate standards bodies
- Applications scale across transport options
- Applications scale across device types
- Extensible over time to new networks and transports

3.1.1 Short Message Service (SMS)

SMS is a globally accepted wireless service that enables the transmission of alphanumeric messages between mobile subscribers and external systems, such as electronic mail, paging and voice mail systems.

The point-to-point SMS provides a mechanism for transmitting short messages to and from wireless handsets. The service makes use of a short message service center (SMSC), which acts as a store-and-forward system. The wireless network provides for the transport of short messages between the SMSC and the handsets. In contrast to existing text message transmission services the service elements are designed to provide guaranteed delivery of text messages to the destinations.

A distinguishing characteristic of the service is that the active mobile handset is able to receive or submit a short message at any time, independent of whether or not a voice data call is in progress. SMS also delivers the short message by the network and temporary failures are identified. The short message is stores in the network until the destination becomes available.

SMS is characterized by out-of-band packet delivery and low-bandwidth message transfer. Initial applications of SMS focused on eliminating alphanumerical pagers by permitting two-way general-purpose messaging and notifications services, primarily for voice mail. As technology and network matured, a variety of services were introduced, including electronic mail and fax integration, paging integration, interactive banking and information services such as stock quotes. Wireless data applications include downloading of subscriber identity module (SIM) cards for activation, debit and profile=editing purposes.

The benefits of SMS to the service provider are as follows:

- Increased call completion on wireless and wire-line networks by leveraging the notification capabilities of SMS
- An alternative to alphanumeric paging services
- Enabling wireless data access to corporate users
- Provision of value-added services such as e-mail, voice mail and fax mailing integration; reminder service;
- Provision of key administrative services

The benefits of SMS to subscribers center on convenience, flexibility and seamless integration of messaging services and data access. From this perspective, the benefit is to use the handset as an extension of the computer. SMS also eliminates the need for sepeerate devices for messaging, as services can be integrated into a single wireless device – the mobile terminal.

3.2 IEEE 802.11 Protocol

IEEE 802.1X is an IEEE Standard for port-based Network Access Control ("port" meaning a single point of attachment to the LAN infrastructure). It is part of the IEEE 802.1 group of networking protocols. It provides an authentication mechanism to devices wishing to attach to a local area network (LAN), either establishing a point-to-point connection or preventing it if authentication fails.

It is used for most wireless 802.11 access points and is based on the Extensible Authentication Protocol (EAP).

An 802.11 LAN is based on a cellular architecture where the system is subdivided into cells. Each cell, called basic service set (BSS) is controlled by a base station, called Access Point (AP). Even though that a wireless LAN may be formed by a single cell, with a single AP, most installations are formed be several cells, where Access Pints are connected through some kind of backbone that is called distribution system (DS), typically Ethernet, and in some cases wireless itself.

The whole interconnected wireless LAN including the different cells, their respective APs and DS, is seen to the upper layers of the OSI model, as a single 802 network and called as Extended Service Set (ESS). A typical 802.11 LAN with the components is described in Figure 1.

3.3 Wi-Fi Systems

Wireless Fidelity (Wi-Fi) is a universal wireless networking technology that utilizes radio frequencies to transfer data. Wi-Fi allows for high speed Internet connections without the use of cables or wires. Wi-Fi is based on the IEEE 802.11 family of standards and is primarily a local area networking (LAN) technology designed to provide in-building broadband coverage. Current Wi-Fi systems based on IEEE 802.11a/g support a peak physical-layer data rate of 54Mbps and typically provide indoor coverage over a distance of 100 feet. Wi-Fi has become the defacto standard for last feet broadband connectivity in homes, offices, and public hotspot locations. Systems can typically provide a coverage range of only about 1,000 feet from the access point. Wi-Fi offers remarkably higher peak data rates than do 3G systems, primarily since it operates over a larger 20MHz bandwidth but Wi-Fi systems are not designed to support high-speed mobility.

One significant advantage of Wi-Fi over WiMAX and 3G is the wide availability of ter-

Figure 1. Typical 802.11. LAN

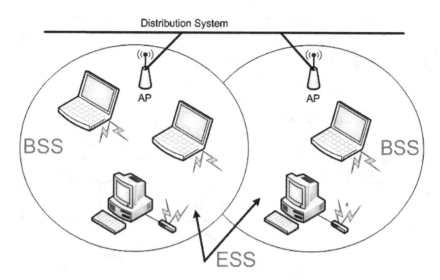

minal devices. Wi-Fi interfaces are now being built into a variety of devices, including personal data assistants (PDAs), cordless phones, cellular phones and laptops.

Wi-Fi systems are half duplex shared media configurations where AAL stations transmit and receive on the same radio channel and employees Carrier Sense Multiple Access with Collision Avoidance protocol (CSMA/CA) for media access and Distributed Control Function (DCF) that is a mechanism for collision avoidance.

The working concept of a Wi-Fi system employees three items:

- Radio signals: Radio Signals are the keys which make Wi-Fi networking possible. These radio signals transmitted from Wi-Fi antennas are picked up by Wi-Fi receivers that are equipped with Wi-Fi cards.
- Wi-Fi Card which fits in user's device: It connects the user's device to the antenna for a direct connection to the internet and it can be external or internal, meaning that a Wi-Fi card can be installed in the device or have it externally connect.

- Access Points (hotspot): A Wi-Fi hotspot is created by installing an access point to an internet connection. When a Wi-Fi enabled device, such as a Pocket PC, encounters a hotspot, the device can then connect to that network wirelessly.

Wi-Fi technology is sluggishly adopted basically via the compatibility and interoperability problems that arise. That is due to the lack of standardization, harmonization and certification between the different versions of 802.11 versions (e.g. 802.11a and 802.11b).

Nowadays, the focus in wireless is shifting to the wide area. WiMax, short for Worldwide Interoperability for Microwave Access, is defined in IEEE 802.16 standards is designed to deliver a metro area broadband wireless access (BWA) service, and is being promoted by the WiMax Forum. WiMAX is similar wireless system to Wi-Fi, but on a much larger scale and at faster speeds.

3.4 Positioning

Positioning regards the ability to determine the location of a mobile device and it is significant

Figure 2. Wi-Fi working concept

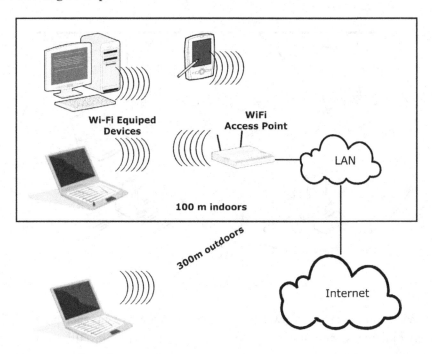

because *location* suggests context. Additionally, to delivering information about a user's physical setting, a valuable piece of information in its own right, location implies an individual's current tasks and goals. A great number of location systems have already been created, which may be divided in two main classes: satellite positioning, referred to as GPS (Global Positioning System) and network-based positioning, referred to as GPS-less positioning.

GPS systems can operate effectively mostly in outdoor clear space environments, where the signal strengthens from at least three satellites are high. Due to the main disadvantage of the system and to get better performance there has been developed a number of extensions of GPS system that base on building or using add-on infrastructure components: mobile networks employed to send through additional information to GPS receivers give birth to Assisted GPS systems, terminal stations that receive additional correction signal and forward it to GPS receivers

are used in Differential GPS systems. Improved techniques increase accuracy up to few meters, and some -even to few millimeters. Indoor GPS technique is based on generating a GPS to allow compatibility with GPS receivers with minimal adaptation to simulated signal.

The network-based positioning class may in turn be subdivided by infrastructure into three subclasses:

- Positioning in cellular networks (GSM networks, CDMA networks, and other brands): it is derived a broad range of algorithms such as cell identification, enhanced observe time difference, direction or angle of arrival, uplink time difference of arrival, absolute time of arrival, differential time of arrival, mobile terminal positioning over satellite and others.
- Positioning in wireless LAN (Local Area Network): it is based on wireless LAN infrastructure and uses the measurements

of signal strength (abbreviated as SS) of wireless LAN access points or bridges to compute physical location of the target device (PDA, laptop) equipped with WLAN card – network adapter. It is mostly useful in indoor environments, where GPS techniques fail to perform up to application requirements. However, it may also work for outdoor environments.

- Positioning in ad hoc sensor networks: it is based on sensor networks and uses short distance signal propagations to determine mobile user's location with accuracy up to the coverage of short-range signal-emitter

Satellite positioning systems can be classified by some other features such as whether they provide physical information about location or symbolic information, whether they are used outdoor or indoor, or how they are separated by the scale, ranging from the worldwide systems to single-room systems. In addition, positioning systems differ in technology used, which is in a way dependant on underlying infrastructure, defining the GPS and WLAN (wireless local-area network) positioning systems. From this point of view, further classification can be determined according to the network topology, the communication topology and the signal strength propagation model for WLAN positioning systems and the signal measurements, the reference point, the mobility of receiver and the time response for GPS positioning systems.

3.4.1 Bluetooth and Bluetooth ULP

3.4.1.1 Bluetooth
Bluetooth is a short-range wireless communications technology for connecting portable devices while maintaining security at high levels. The Bluetooth specifies a uniform structure for a wide range of devices to connect and communicate each other.

The *Bluetooth* data transport system follows a layered architecture that covers the four lowest layers and employees the associated protocols defined by the *Bluetooth* specification as well as a common service layer protocol, the service discovery protocol (SDP). The generic access profile (GAP) specifies the profile requirements.

In order an application to support Bluetooth additional services are required and higher layer protocols that are defined in the *Bluetooth* specification.

The lowest layer of the architecture of Bluetooth data transport system is the physical channel. At this layer, a number of types of physical channels are defined. AAL Bluetooth physical channels are characterized by an RF frequency combined with temporal parameters and restricted by spatial considerations. Two Bluetooth enabled devices use a shared physical channel for communication. To achieve this their transceivers need to be tuned to the same RF frequency at the same time, and they need to be within a nominal range of each other.

For improve efficiency and support legacy, the Bluetooth transport architecture sub-divides the logical layer, distinguishing between logical links and logical transports. This sub-division provides a general and commonly understood concept of a logical link that provides an independent transport between two or more devices. The logical transport sub-layer is required to describe the inter-dependence between some of the logical link types, mainly for reasons of legacy behavior.

3.4.1.2 Bluetooth ULP (Wibree)
Wibree is optimized for sending limited amount of data as this ensures a long battery life. It has a range of several hundred meters that allow it to be used for sensors around a typical house, making it equally applicable for personal devices and fixed, assisted living sensors.

Wibree's main application is to provide an ultra low power radio within the 2.4GHz band. Low power is always determined in large part by the application – the longer a device is active, and the more data it transmits, the shorter its battery life will be.

This low power is achieved by designing a radio and protocol that lets the radio stay asleep. It can wake activated quickly, when it will broadcast its requirement to transfer data on a number of advertising channels across the spectrum. The receiving device, acknowledges the message and tell the sending device which channel to send its data on. It will then acknowledge receipt of this data, at which point both can be inactivated again. The whole process lasts less than three or four milliseconds.

One of the most important features about Wibree is that it is quickly embedded into a wide range of mobile phones. That allows the phone to act as a gateway for information, transmitting it back over the network to an internet based monitoring service.

3.5 xG Networks

All technologies presented previously are utilized in order to provide with interoperable manner specific services to the users of a wireless network. To have a complete view of the 'scene' the evolution of the wireless telecommunication networks is presented below.

0G phones, standing for the 1st generation of mobile phones, were satellitephones developed for boats mainly - but anyone could get one in one's car in the beginning of the 90s for several thousand dollars. Networks such as Iridium, Global Star and Eutelsat were truly worldwide (although for physical reasons, think of a satellite as a fixed point above the equator, some Northern parts of Scandinavia aren't reachable), and everybody thought at that time that satellite phones would become mainstream products as soon as devices got smaller and cheaper. This vision proved wrong when the GSM concretely came to life in 1990/1991 in Finland.

1G: Firstly, there were analog GSM systems that existed for a few years. And then came the digital systems.

2G: this generation of mobile telecommunications is the most widespread technology in the world and uses Global System for Mobility (GSM).

General Packet Radio Service is a 2.5G network that supports data packets

2.5G: the demand for higher data rates has led to the development of so-called "2G+" or "2,5G" systems. For the GSM technology, the first step has been General Packet Radio Service (GPRS) which offers packet switched transmission at bit rates of about 40 kb/s by allocating several time slots of a frame to the same data transmission.

2.75G: this generation uses Enhanced Data GSM Environment (EDGE), which is a pretty recent standard and allows for downloading information faster.

3G: The ITU has deployed a lot of efforts to define a family of systems, called 3G systems, which provide high data rate to offer multimedia services. Under the name International Mobile Communications – 2000 (IMT-2000), these systems have been designed for use in the frequency bands selected by the World Radio Conference (WRC) in the year 1992. The this generation uses the Universal Mobile Telecommunications Standard (UMTS). Aimed at enabling long expected videoconferencing. Its other name is 3GSM, which expresses that UMTS is 3 times better than GSM.

3.5G or 3G+: this generation uses High-Speed Downlink Packet Access (HSDPA). This protocol supports better data rates and it is 6 times faster than UMTS (up to 3.6 Mbytes/sec).

4G: it still is a research lab standard. 4G should be exactly a seamless concept that is cost effective, simple, operable and personalized according to the users' needs. It should support the shift from technology-centric to user-centric concepts and should provide with an interoperable and seamless manner access "anywhere, anytime, anyhow and always-on". With 4G data rates are expected to reach 100 Mbytes/sec.

4 SYNTACTIC LEVEL

Syntactic interoperability is related with the use of data communication (or *messaging*) standards. The understanding of this requires the presentation of how "message" is defined for e-Health, what is the messaging standard, which are these standards and how they are used.

4.1 How "Message" Is Defined In Healthcare

A message is a set of data that are encoded with specific rules. The general structure of a message includes a 'header' that consists of addressing information and the 'payload', where the block of real data is hosted (Figure 3).

In the area of healthcare, in its simplest case, a message is a sequence of characters that are encoded according to the employed messaging standard. The rules of the standard define the order of the characters into the message, the algorithm for the separation and distinction of the cells of the header and of the payload and the meaning of predefined data in specific cells of the message. In a more complex form, the message includes specific fields for multimedia content and special characters, for the data processing from the sender and the receiver.

Figure 3. Message general structure

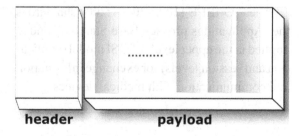

header   **payload**

4.2 What Healthcare Messaging Standards Provide

The main purpose of messaging standards in e-Health is approached by three contradictory definitions that describe that the messaging standards:

- "specify the way that clinical or other data of MISs are structured in form of messages and are transferred from one MIS to others. They define the type, the structure and the order of data ensuring compatibility among the different MISs"
- "allow the performance of such processes that provide transactions' integration during the communication of different MISs"
- "define the structure and content of data that can be exchanged between systems, as well as the policies and procedures that guide the exchange"

4.3 Which Are These Standards and How Should Be Used

Various standardization organizations and committees in the area of e-Health have proposed messaging standards that are established by the developers of MISs and they have been accepted by e-Health community. The most known messaging standards are following presented.

4.3.1 HL7

Health Level Seven was created in 1987 and goals to provide messaging standards for the exchange, administration and integration of clinical data. The HL7 standard and its versions, provide a set of rules for: the structure of the messages; encoding; the events that trigger messages' exchange; the types of the messages; the types of data that are connected to the triggering events; the proposed sequence of messages during a sessions between two communicating entities.

4.3.2 NEMA

The American College of Radiology (ACR) and the National Electrical Manufacturers Association (NEMA) created in 1983 a committee that intended to specify a standard for: the communication of digital medical images; the implementation and extension of communication and archive system; the creation of database systems for hosting diagnostic information that is distributed to various archiving systems.

This standards, called as Digital Imaging and Communications in Medicine (DICOM) have been established for the communication of medical images and includes rules that specify: the semantic of a special set of commands and the related with them information; the semantic of services, files' structures and information catalogues for supporting off-line communication; processes for network applications; processes for new services implementation.

4.3.3 CEN/TC 251

The European Committee for Standardization (Comité Européen de Normalisation — CEN) supports the introduction of new messaging standards by the means of various working groups. Specifically, the Technical Committee (TC) 251 works on messaging standards for the interoperable communication of different MISs.

The ENV 1613 messaging standard, known as "Messages for exchange of laboratory information" is used for transferring requests for laboratory examinations and the allocation of respective medical reports, in the form of messages. The types of the messages that this standard defines, cover AAL the types of laboratory examinations and the individual objects that are used are specified by the "Domain Information Model".

4.3.4 ANSI

The American National Standards Institute (ANSI) created a the Accredited Standards Committee (ASC) X12 in 1979 to propose, maintain, translate, publish and support of national standards of organizations American National Standards and UN/EDIFACT. These standards support the electronic data interchange (EDI).

The ASC X12N Interactive Healthcare Claim/ Encounter (IHCLME) supports billing processes and facilitates the interaction of various MISs with proper information systems via network services.

EDIFACT standard is a general-purpose standard that has been established in the area of MISs and is used for the electronic interchange of information at enterprise-level.

The NCPDP standard has been proposed by National Council for Prescription Drug Programs (NCDPD) and provides specific structures of messages for validation and service of medical prescriptions.

4.3.5 ISO/TC 215

The Technical Committee 'Health Informatics of ISO (ISO/TC 215) was created in 1998 and targets on the standardization for achieving compatibility and interoperability between heterogeneous MISs, in order to eliminate the repetition of information.

ISO 17432:2004 provides an internet service for supporting Web-access to DICOM persistent objects. It employees HTML and XML languages, utilizes HTTP/HTTPs protocols and basically, uses the 'unique identifiers' that DICOM defines for imaging examinations.

The ISO/IEEE 11073-20101:2004 standard is the 'Applications profiles-Base Standard' and is applied in the upper levels of OSI model (application and session levels) for exchange information and communication with medical devices.

4.3.6 IEEE

The Institute of Electrical and Electronic Engineers (IEEE) (created in 1963) was come into play on standardization area in United States through IEEE Standards Association (IEEE-SA).

The MEDIX standard was produced by a working group of IEEE and it is based on object-oriented methodology. This standard supports the presentation of AAL types of medical data and specifies the requirements that regard the application level of OSI model for the communication with medical devices through a "Medical Information Bus".

4.3.7 Syntactic Interoperability Issues

In that interoperability level the issues arise due to three factors: a) the lack of a unique interchange format, b) the use of various, overlapping and incompatible data communication standards and c) the different implementations of these standards. The above factors can be addressed by either enforcing a single standard or by introducing compatibility mechanisms for the existing standards. In both cases, the problem should be handled from a standardization point of view. Although these factors create syntactic interoperability problems, their existence is essential to implement viable MISs within an open healthcare enterprise environment.

Hitherto, the syntactic interoperability is achieved by means of communications servers that follow the middleware approach. The core functionality of these servers contains 'translation' of AAL exchanged MISs' messages. Each server's implementation focuses on the translation of specific messaging standards, e.g. HL7 v2.3 – to – HL7 v3.0. This approach leads to strict structures that prevent the reusability of each server and affect the communication architecture of each MIS. An effective way to achieve syntactic interoperability is the specification of a common reference model for the implementation of such servers as to achieve the integration and interoperable communication of MISs without interfering in their own architectures.

5 SEMANTIC LEVEL

A common usage of the term "semantic interoperability in eHealth" is:

"Semantic interoperability implies that the structure of the 'documents' is interpretable, and that their content is understandable. Making this content understandable sometimes requires that the keys for its correct and safe interpretation, such as the terminological systems used, are identified and easily available"

The functional and the syntactic interoperability ensure that the related systems the means for exchanging information are available and this is done efficiently. To fully achieve the interoperable communication systems must 'understand' the exchanged information with the same way. Furthermore, the aim here is not only exchanging data and information but reuse and process the data more intelligently. Semantic interoperability is essential for automatic computer processing, which will enable the implementation of advanced clinical applications. In fact, healthcare delivery deals basically with information and knowledge management and in terms of clinical information dissemination.

However, semantic interoperability is not an "all or nothing" concept. The degree of semantic interoperability depends on the level of the agreement between sender and receiver regarding the terminology and the content of archetypes and ontologies to be used.

5.1 The Concept of 'Ontology'

Ontologies play a significant role in defining the high-level commonalities in heterogeneous systems' requirements. An ontology can assist organizations in accepting standard definitions. Likewise, an ontology can lead to more successful open source applications by identifying negotiated design principles and standards and lastly, an ontology can assist in the description of the platform independent model. Ontology for medical applications is concerned "with the principled definition of healthcare classes and the relations among them".

In am more general concept, the term "ontology" can be defined as an explicit specification of conceptualization. Ontologies capture the structure of the domain, which includes the model of the domain with AAL its possible restrictions. The conceptualization describes knowledge about the domain, not about the particular state of affairs in the domain. Ontologies specify than this conceptualization by using particular modeling language and particular terms. Formal specification is required in order to be able to process ontologies and operate on ontologies automatically. In order to understand in communication, ontologies must be shared between the agents of the different systems.

5.2 The Concept of 'Archetype'

An archetype is an original model on which something is patterned or based. More precisely, archetypes are documents that control the clinical content of data stored. An archetype pattern is a "high-level abstraction of a generalized solution that can be implemented and applied to solve problems that are common to different health solutions. Archetype patterns have the potential to offer a cohesive, integrated framework for ontology development. They have the potential to deliver decentralized, modular, loosely coupled and reusable ontologies by acting as a gateway to standards and providing an intermediate step in development.

A key benefit of archetypes is that they are created by the healthcare professionals who have the real knowledge and expertise of the clinical

data requirements. Archetypes allow the clinical knowledge in a software system to be changed without becoming involved in programming (creating software) and without disturbing the existing software installation. This means that there is a relatively simple means for the clinical knowledge to be changed and extended without AAL the delays, cost and risk associated with software upgrades. Another key benefit of Archetypes is that they help to drive the standardization of clinical data. This is achieved due to archetypes allow both professionals and MISs to share clinical knowledge in a convenient and commonly defined way.

Defining an archetype internally, three major components are specified as follows:

- A record of a clinical session or a clinical document that is submitted as a single unit comprises a composition. The electronic record of a patient is a collection of compositions
- A group of clinical data values form a coherent Observation, Evaluation or Instruction using an entry
- That clinical data that can be captured is defined as data values

By using a system based on archetypes, professionals can manage with an efficient and a fine way what clinical data they wish to capture in the medical records of the patients.

5.3 Terminology Standards

First step for semantic interoperability is using the proper 'terminology standards'. These standards support the convergence towards a common framework for formal representation, and eventually the development and maintenance of a multilingual clinical reference terminology. The SNOMED and ASTM E2457 – 07 standards are following described, will a variety of standards are used, such as 'Read', CTV3, ICD10, etc.

5.3.1 Systematized Nomenclature of Medicine

The Systematized Nomenclature of Medicine (SNOMED) is considered to be the most comprehensive multilingual clinical healthcare terminology globally.

SNOMED CT aims to improve patient care through the development of systems to accurately record health care encounters. Ultimately, patients will benefit from the use of SNOMED CT, for building and facilitating communication and interoperability in electronic health data exchange. SNOMED CT was originally created by the College of American Pathologists by combining SNOMED RT and a computer based nomenclature and classification known as Clinical Terms Version 3, formerly known as Read Codes Version 3, which was created on behalf of the UK Department of Health and is Crown copyright.

SNOMED CT is a clinical healthcare terminology and a resource with comprehensive, scientifically-validated content. It is essential for electronic health records because it cans cross-map to other international standards and it is already used in more than fifty countries.

The basic objective of any SNOMED CT translation is to provide accurate representations of SNOMED CT concepts in way that is understandable, usable, and safe. Translations must be concept-based, as term-to-term translations usually yield literal expressions that are often meaningless. Instead, the translator analyzes each concept based on the position within the hierarchy, the descriptions, and relationships to other concepts before deciding on the most meaningful translation of a concept.

SNOMED CT is continuously updated to meet the needs of users around the world and for this purpose it is now collaborates with a number of significant standardization organizations, such as DICOM, HL7, ISO and X12 (Accredited Standards Committee).

5.3.2 ASTM E2457-07

ASTM E2457-07 terminology is intended to specify with proper documentation the principal concepts, and their associated terms, that are utilized in the healthcare information domain and AAL of its specialized subdomains. This terminology can be employed to AAL areas of healthcare about which information is kept or utilized. It is intended to complement and utilize those concepts already identified by other national and international standards organizations. It identifies alternate accepted terms for the same concept and its elected term. Its terms clarify and simplify usage in the dialog and documentation about the concepts, processes and data that are used to schedule, conduct and manage AAL phases of healthcare. This standard does not address AAL of the safety concerns, associated with its use. It is the responsibility of the user of this standard to establish appropriate safety and health practices and determine the applicability of regulatory limitations prior to use.

6 MARKUP LANGUAGES

'Markup languages' is an essential part when talking about interoperability for network (and especially internet) medical applications and more significant for wireless applications. Here, the most important languages are presented.

6.1 Handled Device Markup Language (HDML)

The Handheld Device Markup Language (HDML) is a markup language intended for display on-handheld computers, information appliances, smartphones, etc.. It was originally developed in about 1996 by Unwired Planet, the company that became Openwave. HDML was submitted to W3C (www.w3.org)for standardization, but was not turned into a standard. Instead it became an important influence on the development and standardization of WML, which then replaced HDML in practice. It uses Openwave's Handheld Device Transport Protocol (HDTP), instead of WAP.

HDML is similar to HTML, but of different purpose. HDML is used for wireless and handheld devices with small displays, like PDA, mobile phones and so on.

Phones access HDML sites with the following way: Once the URL is typed into the browser of the phone, it sends a request to Openwave's UP.Link gateway. The gateway sends an HTTP request to the Web server. The Web servers return the page via HTTP back to the Openwave UP.Link gateway. The gateway sends the data via HDTP to the wireless carrier's network and finally to the phone.

HDML and the Openwave gateway are most popular throughout North America. In Europe, WML and the Nokia WAP gateway and browser are the emerging standard. However, some versions of Openwave browsers do interpret basic WML.

6.2 HyperText Markup Language (HTML)

HTML is the *lingua franca* for publishing hypertext on the World Wide Web. HTML has been developed with the vision that AAL manner of devices should be able to use information on the Web It is a non-proprietary format based upon SGML, and can be created and processed by a wide range of tools, from simple plain text editors to sophisticated authoring tools. It is the language that AAL computers can 'understand. It uses tags to structure the text into headings, paragraphs, lists, hypertext links etc. W3C's statement of direction for HTML is given on the HTML Activity Statement.

HTML gives authors the means to:

- Publish online documents with headings, text, tables, lists, photos, etc.

- Retrieve online information via hypertext links
- Design forms for conducting transactions with remote services, for use in searching or submit information
- Include multimedia content in their documents

The problems/limitations that HTML arises are:

- The presented content is not signaled semantically
- The structure of the documents is not recognized similarly by AAL browsers
- It is difficult to isolate the significant information
- Advanced search engines are not easily supported

6.3 Extensible Markup Language (XML)

Extensible Markup Language (XML) –a W3C Recommendation– is a simple, very flexible text format derived from Standard Generalized Markup Language (SGML) [ISO 8879]). Originally designed to meet the challenges of large-scale electronic publishing, XML is also playing an increasingly important role in the exchange of a wide variety of data on the Web and elsewhere.

XML describes a class of data objects called XML documents and partially describes the behavior of computer programs which process them. By construction, XML documents are conforming SGML documents. XML documents are made up of storage units called entities, which contain either parsed or unparsed data. Markup encodes a description of the document's storage layout and logical structure. XML provides a mechanism to impose constraints on the storage layout and logical structure.

By the means of XML data are easily separated from HTML and data sharing, data transport and platform changes are simplified. The design goals for XML are:

- XML be straightforwardly usable over the Internet
- XML support a wide variety of applications
- XML be compatible with SGML
- It is easy to write programs which process XML documents
- The number of optional features in XML is to be kept to the absolute minimum, ideally zero
- XML documents are human-legible and reasonably clear
- The XML design is prepared quickly
- The design of XML is formal and concise
- XML documents is easy to create
- Terseness in XML markup is of minimal importance

A lot of new languages are created with XML.

- XHTML the latest version of HTML
- WSDL for describing available web services
- WAP and WML as markup languages for handheld devices
- RSS languages for news feeds
- RDF and OWL for describing resources and ontology
- SMIL for describing multimedia for the web

6.4 Extensible HyperText Markup Language (XHTML)

The Extensible HyperText Markup Language (XHTML) 1.0 was created shortly after HTML 4.01 to help the transition of hypertext to a new generation of mark-up languages for text. XHTML is a family of current and future document types and modules that reproduce, subset, and extend HTML, reformulated in XML. XHTML Family document types are AAL XML-based, and ulti-

mately are designed to work in conjunction with XML-based user agents. Strict, Transitional, and Frameset XHTML 1.0 is the basis for a family of document types that subset and extend HTML.

XHTML is used applying a special process, "Modularization". XHTML Modularization is decomposition of XHTML 1.0, and by reference HTML 4, into a collection of abstract modules that provide specific types of functionality. These abstract modules are implemented using the XML Document Type Definition language, but an implementation using XML Schemas is expected. The rules for defining the abstract modules, and for implementing those using XML DTDs, are defined by W3C documents. The well-defined elements that are produced employing this process can be combined and extended by document authors, document type architects, other XML standards specifications, and application and product designers to make it economically feasible for content developers to deliver content on a greater number and diversity of platforms. By specifying a standard, either software processes can autonomously tailor content to a device, or the device can automatically load the software required to process a module.

6.5 Wireless Markup Language (WML)

WML is a free and extensible Webdesigner's off-line HTML generation toolkit for Unix, distributed under the GNU General Public License (GPL v2). WML internally consists of nine independent languages. The main idea of WML is a sequential filtering scheme where each language provides one of nine processing passes. So WML reads an input file, applies passes 1-9 (or optionally only the passes specified) and finally produces one or more output files.

Wireless Markup Language is a lot like HTML in that it provides navigational support, data input, hyperlinks, text and image presentation, and forms. WML ships with an already written set of include files which define additional higher-level functionality. WML is not a closed toolbox; it is only the core upon which a special HTML generation environment is based. WML documents are XML documents that validate against the WML Document Type Definition. The W3C Markup Validation service (validator.w3.org) can be used to validate WML documents (they are validated against their declared document type).

Mobile devices are moving towards support for greater amounts of XHTML and even standard HTML as processing power in handsets increases. These standards are concerned with formatting and presentation. They do not however address cell-phone or mobile device hardware interfacing in the same way as WML.

7 SPECIAL ISSUES

One of the most challenging aspects is finding solutions that reconcile users' demand for highly personalized services with their desire of privacy. There is a fine line between the presenting users with useful services that are relevant to their location and preferences and bombarding them with annoying location-sensitive ads. Organizations are attempting to define standards that will help preserve the privacy of wireless users and prevent spamming and also provide services with high quality.

7.1 Users' Service Quality

For creating an integrated environment, where AAL applications work and collaborate with an interoperable manner as a whole, the communication of these systems is not enough. Interoperability not only means 'communication', 'exchange of information' and 'understanding of data', but also to provide AAL users of AAL MISs with services of the same high quality, which is translated to effectiveness, usability and reliability.

For developers and ICT community the challenge is to enrich MISs with new and advanced services and make them available to the public and healthcare professionals too. The main concerns while implementing and using AAL systems are:

- Users have access to lower telecommunication bandwidth and experience high error rates while communicating
- Cheap wireless devices nay not be able to support AAL wireless services such as fast information retrieval
- Screen size dictates the web browsing and the user experience is not the same way as in desktop environment
- Limited computational power of wireless devices do not allow full performance of applications
- The network must be able to support connection admission control, so that traffic stream is guaranteed a service according to its requirement
- The technology must be able to differentiate between various traffic types and service them according to parameters needed for acceptable transfer across a network
- The technology must be able to support real-time traffic management
- The technology must be able to support congestion control

Apart from technology and network issues, quality of service is totally connected with the designation of the provided services, the environment through which these are available to the users, the application interfaces and interaction workflow between the users and the systems. AAL these, should be answered with accuracy, ensuring that the users will access the services of AAL systems, through an integrated and user-friendly environment efficiently.

7.2 Security Issues

Security is an issue that is studied in detail in a separated chapter of this book. Nevertheless, security is a very significant issue when we are talking about interoperability mechanisms, because various information systems exchange and commonly share clinical data or other information, as content or context of patients' medical records. The combination of interoperability and security help to increase acceptance of ambulatory monitoring technology, while at the same time lowering cost of these systems through vendor competition. Besides, security is a significant and distinct level of interoperability according to AAL three definitions of interoperability, presented in 2.2.

Security should be ensured at AAL levels of the communication and transferring of data. Any time wireless technology is used to transmit personal information, that information must be strongly protected to guard against unauthorized access to the contents of the signal. A wireless-equipped device connected to a network can serve as an illicit entry point for the entire network if it is not properly set up. To prevent data leakage from wireless access points it is vital to secure the entire network, rather than only specific devices. For example, when cellular phones and PDAs are used to transmit or store e-mail or instant messages, they can pose risks. The users must be sure that these devices operate in a secure manner. Security features include encryption of transmissions, password protection and automated data wiping. Where embedded chip devices collect or use personal information, it must be ensured that encryption or similar strong security measures are in place. The information systems to which the devices are connected should provide 'end-to-end' security for personal information.

Furthermore, security must be ensured from applications side too. Developers have to implement special mechanisms for protecting data bases and archiving systems against access by unauthorized users. Also, specific policies must be designed and employed from medical applications in order to determine the communication schemes between the various MISs, their roles during the sessions and the type of information that they will exchange.

REFERENCES

8021AB. (2005). Station and Media Access Control Connectivity Discovery. IEEE Computer Society.

W3C (n.d.). *Technical Reports and Publications.* Retrieved from www.w3.org

A compilation of IEEE standard computer glossaries. (1990). *IEEE STD 610.12, and IEEE Standard Computer Dictionary.* New York: IEEE.

Accelerating the movement toward standards-based interoperability in healthcare. (1996). *Clinical Information Systems Subcommittee of the IEEE-USA* Medical Technology Policy Committee.

Aguilar, A. (2005). *Semantic Interoperability in the Context of e-Health.* CDH Seminar. Retrieved from http://m3pe.org/seminar/aguilar.pdf

Cavoukian, A. (2007, August). *Fact Sheet, "Wireless Communication Technologies, Safeguarding Privacy & Security".* Infrmation and Privacy Commissioner / Ontario, August 2007 subconscious

Current and future standardization issues in the e-Health domain: Achieving interoperability (2005). *CEN/ISSS e-Health Standardization Focus Group*, CEN, 2005

Digital Imaging and Communications in Medicine (DICOM). (2004). *Part I: Introduction and overview.* New York: National Electrical Manufacturing Association, PS3.1-2004, 2004

Gavrilovska, L. M., & Atanasovski, V. M. (2007, June). Interoperability in Future Wireless Communications Systems: A Roadmap to 4G. *Microwave Review, 13*(1).

HL7. (n.d.). *Final guide*. Retrieved from www.hl7.org

Huff, S. M. (1998). Clinical data exchange standards and vocabularies for messages. *Journal pf American Medical Informatics Association, AMIA Annual fall Symposium Supplement*, 1998

IEEE. 1073 (n.d.). *Standard for medical devices communications*. Retrieved from www.hipaanet.com

Interoperability definition and background. (2005). *Healthcare Information and Management Systems Society*.

Kim, K. (2005). *Clinical Data Standards in Health Care: Five Case studies*. Sacramento: California Health Foundation.

Nanda, P., & Fernades, R. C. (2007). Quality of service in Telemedicine. In *Proceedings of the First IEEE, International Conference on the Digital Society*, 2007.

Salaur, L. (2005*). Building a Commodity Location-based Service at Botanic Garden of University of Freiburg*, (Master Thesis), University of Freiburg.

Wireless Short Message Service. (2007). *The International Engineering Consortium*. Web OriForum Tutorials.

KEY TERMS AND DEFINITIONS

E-Health: By the means of Information and Communications Technology supports the automation of medical workflow inbound and outbound healthcare enterprises. In a broader sense, the term characterizes 'an attitude' and a commitment for networked, global thinking, to improve health care locally, regionally, and worldwide.

IEEE: The Institute of Electrical and Electronic Engineers is a non-profit organization. IEEE is the world's leading professional association for the advancement of technology.

Integration: Combination of diverse application entities into a relationship which functions as a whole. It requires interoperability to be implemented.

Interface: A boundary at which interaction occurs between two systems, processes, etc. An interface defines how to access an object.

Interoperability: State which exists between two application entities when, with regard to a specific task, one application entity can accept data from the other and perform that task in an appropriate and satisfactory manner without the need for extra operator intervention. It requires interfaces to be implemented.

Medical Information Systems (MIS): Are considered as all applications and information systems that are implemented to provide healthcare services inbound and outbound healthcare enterprises. They use Information and Communications technology in order to support the automation of medical workflow and the processing and exchange of data. They are part of e-Health.

Messaging: It is the creation, storage, exchange, and management of objects of communication, which are called 'messages'. In e-Health, messages can include medical or administrative information that are transferred between the various applications and embed textual or multimedia data.

Service Quality: Refers to a number of inter-related factors that are related with the operation of employed systems and infrastructure, the ability of identifying and facing problems quickly and systematically, the possibility of establishing valid and reliable service performance measures and the measurement of users' satisfaction and other performance outcomes.

Chapter 12
A Strategic Approach to E-Health Interoperability Using E-Government Frameworks

Thanos Papadopoulos
University of Southampton, UK

Spyros Angelopoulos
The University of Warwick, UK

Fotis Kitsios
University of Macedonia, Greece

ABSTRACT

E-government projects have a breadth of impact that extends far beyond their respective context. However, current e-Government methodologies and models used are only tailored to specific requirements. Despite the use of interoperability in e-government, there has been a paucity of literature on adapting e-government frameworks in the healthcare context and in e-health in particular. Aiming to fill this gap, this chapter justifies why interoperability frameworks currently used in e-government may be useful in e-health. Therefore, this study attempts to address the issues faced by surveying the models consisting of effective practices in e-Government IT integration management, as well as IT support. The overall aim of this chapter is to conduct a critical analysis of well-established e-Government models and frameworks. Understanding e-Government integration project management will ultimately help in the development of an effective practice model, which will improve e-Government implementation.

INTRODUCTION

This chapter is concerned with the adaptation of e-government interoperability frameworks in the context of e-health. Most governments around the globe released their e-government strategies dur-

ing the last decade. Their own framework policies, covering security, and confidentiality as well as delivery channels supported these e-government strategies. The European Union has set up different initiatives in the area of e-government within the limits of its powers in the domain of Public Administration (Alabau, 2004). One of such policies was the interoperability policy (CEC, 2002; OECD, 2003).

DOI: 10.4018/978-1-61520-805-0.ch012

However, despite the use of interoperability in e-government, there has been a paucity of literature on adapting e-government frameworks in the healthcare context and in e-health in particular. Aiming to fill this gap, this chapter justifies why interoperability frameworks currently used in e-government may be useful in e-health.

The chapter is organised as follows: after a thorough discussion on interoperability frameworks and their application in e-government, the healthcare context is presented and the usefulness of these frameworks in e-health is explained. The chapter concludes by presenting future research avenues.

INTEROPERABILITY FRAMEWORKS

Interoperability is "the ability to exchange information and mutually to use the information which has been exchanged" (CEC, 1991). An interoperability framework aims at referencing the basic technical specifications that all agencies relevant to the e-government strategy implementation should adopt. This interoperability framework should enable, at least, the interoperability between IS from different agencies in order to provide services to citizens and businesses in an integrated way.

A Government Interoperability Framework (GIF) is one way to achieve e-Government interoperability. A GIF is a set of standards and guidelines that a government uses to specify the preferred way that its agencies, citizens and partners interact with each other. As noted by Guijarro (2007), a GIF includes: "the basic technical specifications that all agencies relevant to the e-Government strategy implementation should adopt." A GIF normally includes:

- Context
- Implementation and compliance regimes
- Technical content
- Process documentation.

Principles indicate the priorities of government in terms of ICT development. These principles guide the development of the GIF and become the criteria for choosing standards. Many of the GIFs recognized seven similar key principles as described below:

- Interoperability
- Market support
- Security
- Scalability
- Reusability
- Openness
- Privacy

According to Guijarro (2009) interoperability frameworks in Europe have shown up "as a key tool for interoperability in the deployment of e-Government services", both at national as well as European level. They are initially focused on technical interoperability, but recently inclusion of semantic in the interoperability frameworks started.

The main issue of an interoperability framework is the integration of a wide variety of legacy software applications. This has always created a costly and time-consuming IT challenge and has led the Business Integration to focus on the concepts of Service Oriented Architecture (SOA) (Channabasavaiah, Holley, & Tuggle, 2004) as well as Event Driven Architecture (Sadtler, Crabtree, Cotignola, & Michel, 2004). These two models enable process level integration allowing the automatic communication among sub-components of heterogeneous systems, rather than a simple data transfer between different systems.

Governments are adopting solutions based on SOAs to solve their business integration problems according to e-government plans, new technologies and market developments. Governments Agencies that want to operate in real time and realise the zero-latency must adopt event-driven architecture, message-oriented middleware and publish-subscribe communication (Baldoni, Con-

Figure 1. e-GIFs in European Union (Gatautis, 2009)

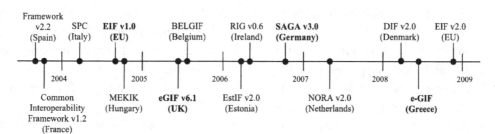

tenti, Piergiovanni, & Virgillito, 2003). Embracing Event-driven architecture is in fact essential to synchronize data without batch processing and redundant manual entry.

Event-driven and Service-oriented architectures are compatible but distinct concepts, each one with its inherited advantages and disadvantages. One of the critical issues arising now is finding more efficient and effective ways of designing, developing and deploying Web services (WSAT, 2001) based systems; more importantly, moving beyond the basic point-to-point Web services communications to broader application of these technologies to enterprise-level processes. The challenge is to extend the Web services and SOA vision with the emerging Enterprise Service Bus model that provides a standards-based integration layer using the Even-driven architecture. Messages are made available and delivered to all the subscribers in a timely manner.

Nowadays, building an e-Government Interoperability Framework must oppose the tendency to "reinvent the wheel" and requires examination and extended review of related research and standardization efforts (Guijarro, 2007) in the UK, Germany, Greece and other EU countries (Figure 1 and Table 1).

The following section enumerates and discusses eight major initiatives being carried out by governmental agencies in the context of interoperability, which have produced the corresponding interoperability frameworks. The frameworks that are discussed in the following sections are: the British e-Government Interoper-

ability Framework, The French ADAE, the German Standards for e-government Applications, the Danish e-Government Interoperability Framework, the Federal Enterprise Architecture Framework, the Esthonian Interoperability Framework and last but not least, the Greek e-Government Interoperability Framework. The study has been based on the analysis of the publicly available documents. An important difference of these various frameworks relate to enforcement. The e-GIF reflects a higher level of enforcement than CCI, SAGA, and DIF. e-GIF is mandatory, whereas CCI, SAGA and DIF are recommendations and guidelines (Guijarro, 2007).

e-GIF: The British Interoperability Framework

The heart of British strategy for ensuring IT supports the business transformation of government

Table 1. Interoperability Frameworks adapted from Guijarro (2007)

Framework	Agency	Country	Year
e-GIF	eGU	UK	2005
CCI	ADAE	France	2003
SAGA	KDSt	Germany	2003
DIF	ITST	Denmark	2005
IDABC AG	IDABC	EU	2004
EAG	CIOC	USA	2002
Greek e-GIF	COI	Greece	2008
EIF	MEAC	Esthonia	2006

is the e-GIF (e-Government Interoperability Framework). This transformation is about delivering better and more efficient public services. The e-Government Unit (eGU) contributes to this through the e-GIF and also by supporting joined-up service delivery, sharing best practice and putting the citizen at the centre of government's work. The British e-GIF specification has been led by:

- Interoperability
- Scalability
- Openness
- Market support
- International standards

The value of interoperable systems, and the benefits of the standards-based approach exemplified in the e-GIF, is becoming widely recognised by the private sector. This has led to calls to adopt the policy, or a similar tool, to further increase efficiency and enable new and exciting services to be developed across different sectors. E-GIF mandates specifications and policies for any cross-agency collaboration and for e-government service delivery. It covers four areas (eGU, 2005):

- Interconnectivity
- Content management
- Data integration
- E-services access

In the eGIF, the Technical Standards Catalogue was initially regarded as a part of High Level Architecture, together with other high-level models. Both the catalogue and the models served as a reference in the requirements, design and implementation of e-government services. The role was played with the help of reusable elements such as patterns, components and resources (eEnvoy, 2001). The set of high-level models that comprised the High Level Architecture can be regarded as part of an e-government enterprise architecture. Within the eGIF, two initiatives are relevant for content management metadata:

- eGov Metadata Standards (eGMS), which lays down the elements, refinements and encoding schemes to be used by government officers when creating metadata for their information resources or when designing search systems for ISs (eGU, 2005).
- Integrated Public Sector Vocabulary (IPSV) structured thesaurus of administrative activities both at central and local governments. IPSV was setup initially for use within the eGMS and it enhances the Government Category List (GCL) (FEAPMO, 2005).
- IPSV is a truly semantic initiative, whereas eGMS deals mainly with syntactic issues. The e-GIF contains a Technical Standard Catalogue, which is revised and updated every six months.

The e-GIF is parted by:

- The Framework itself that covers policy statements of high-level, technical policies and management as well as implementation and compliance regimes
- The Registry that covers the e-GMS and GCL, the Government Data Standards Catalogue, Extensible Markup Language (XML) schemas and the Technical Standards Catalogue.

The French ADAE

E-government is now seen as the only way of building a government working to serve citizens, businesses and associations. The services prepared in this context must bring together the State, regional authorities and public bodies in the health and welfare sector to enable users of government services, or the intermediaries assisting them to claim their rights more quickly and more simply and receive personalized information from the administration through the medium of their choice, and must improve administrative problem-solving in conditions of proven security.

Although France is well known for the high quality of its public websites, its e-government services are quite average in comparison with those of its European and international neighbours. Recent technological advances, the appropriation by the civil service and political decision-makers of ICT tools, the expectations by users of government services of a real simplification of administrative formalities, and the budget restrictions hampering government departments add up to an outstanding opportunity to engage in a massive job of building up e-government. The major aim of the national e-government programme is to decide on the gradual setting up of the provision of the services citizens, the professions and civil servants are entitled to expect, supported by an e-government developed coherently and with coordination.

The French attempt has been under the "Agence pour le Développement de l'Administration Électronique" (ADAE), which published "Le Cadre Commun d'Intéroperabilité" (CCI) in 2002. It comprises the recommendations for strengthening public electronic systems coherence and for enabling multi-agency electronic service delivery (ADAE, 2003). ADAE has been very active in the development of reusable information resources and has set up the Antalia project that provides services to central and local governments as well as businesses and citizens in order locate reusable reference resources. The user would be able to find nomenclatures, guides, data models, and XML schemas.

Outstanding developments have certainly taken place in some sectors, but online services are far from being the norm in France that they are or soon will be in neighbouring countries, and the fact that these initiatives have not been coordinated means that existing administrative complexity is simply replicated, with the multiplication of unnecessary expenditure. Several structures have

been set up at ministerial or inter-ministerial level to handle matters relating to e-government, but there has been no overall coordination.

The government therefore intends to enable citizens and professionals to have tools and services, which will enable them to exercise their rights more simply and completely.

- Decentralised storage of data
- Identification in interdepartmental relations
- Online user identification
- The personal space: control by the user of the transmission of his or her data in administrative online procedures
- Better exercise of the right of access by public and professionals to the data gathered by the administration.

The Government has decided to continue discussions in order to draw up the outlines of this new form of user/administration relationship, and in particular:

- To define the legal environment which will make it possible to set up a "pact of trust" in e-government while respecting our basic principles of public freedoms and monitoring the transparency and rationalisation of exchanges
- To stipulate the legal guarantees linked with the use of trusted third parties, in particular when setting up personal spaces
- To confirm the relevance of the identity federation solutions under consideration.

The strategic plan and the accompanying action plan reflect great ambitions. The protagonists of e-government, strongly attached to the durability of public service French-style, have done their utmost to achieve all these ambitions. However, they must ensure the appropriation of users and technological developments, which are sometimes unforeseeable and must, therefore, be able to overhaul the initial projects they had decided on. One important aspect is to give visibility to all those involved, in the short, medium and long term. This is how France makes its voice heard more clearly in Europe.

German Standards and Architectures for e-Government Applications

There are other European and German projects in the field of e-government. The "Document Management and Electronic Archiving in Electronic Courses of Business" (DOMEA) concept (KBsT, 2005a) is the basis of the German Government for meeting the objective of a paperless office.

DOMEA introduces the concepts and criteria that should lead to paperless offices in the administrations. The three-pieced modular structure of DOMEA consists of documents, records and files. In contrast to our solution the issues of hierarchical process execution and security in the distributed process execution is not addressed. Germany's Federal Government Co-ordination and Advisory Agency for IT in the Federal Administration (KBSt), published the SAGA framework (Standards and Architectures for e-Government Applications) in 2003. SAGA is guideline that serves as an orientation aid for decision-makers in the e-government teams in German administrations (KBSt, 2003).

Within the SAGA defined by the German Federal Ministry of the Interior, regulations on standards, procedures, methods and also products for the modern IT-evolution are provided (KBsT, 2005b). Standards are divided into different categories (mandatory, recommended, under observation and rejected). SAGA also proposes applications like the "Government Site Builder". This application is a Content Management System (CMS) whose Document Management component offers versioning on change; write-locks and the possibility to use meta-data for documents. However, the "Government Site Builder" was

not designed for the work with cross-authority process execution.

In SAGA, moving from task-oriented to process-oriented administration appears today as the key challenge to overcome. Regarding the current version of the SAGA, the Reference Model of Open Distributed Processing (RM-ODP) is not well used since standards are not appropriately associated to viewpoints and there are many aspects not yet established. Finally, SAGA partially has too much "German / Bund Flavor" and there is not sufficient internationalization at European Union level (Charalabidis, Lampathaki, & Stassis, 2007). Further lessons learnt from the experience with SAGA suggest that:

Standards and technologies to be followed should be proposed in an eGIF, yet a determination on certain technologies is not necessary for achieving interoperability and should not be integrated in eGIFs since variety guarantees continuous innovation and competition and prevents market foreclosure

A bottom-up approach needs to be adopted covering equally all the viewpoints of the RM-ODP: technology, information, and enterprise, computational and engineering. Creating patterns of standard processes and data models for similar services must be pursued

The continuous revisions of the eGIF must be balanced between adding the latest developments and experiences and its being characterized as too complex and overregulated.

Danish e-Government Interoperability Framework

In order to achieve the goals for e-Government, such as efficiency, improving levels of services and cost-cutting, public servants must use IT in an optimal way. This is not achieved through local initiatives spread across the public sector and a national set of guidelines as well as strategic initiatives is needed. The Interoperability Framework is one initiative toward harmonizing the use of technologies throughout the Danish administration. The Danish e-Government Interoperability Framework was initially intended to become a guideline for public agencies in their attempt to develop IT plans as well as projects.

The Danish Government compiled the Danish e-Government Interoperability Framework (DIF) in 2004 collaborating with a committee whose aim is the facilitation as well as coordination of IT related initiatives (DIF, 2004). DIF has been compiled in accordance with the European Interoperability Framework (EIF) and offers a set of guidelines, technical standards as well as policies, which outlines the government's policy on how to achieve interoperability. The framework is targeted at any authority that request to interoperate with other national authorities or abroad with the EU and its member countries. The rationale behind the focus on interoperability is that a contribution towards better interoperability can reach a number of objectives:

- Efficiency
- Usefulness
- Transparency
- Provide assistance in local decisions relating to IT
- Make it easier to ensure coherency and optimization locally.

These objectives can be reached by making use of the possibilities provided by e-Government initiatives. An optimal progress can only be achieved by using common standards throughout the public sector. It is the objective of the DIF to contribute to this task of standardization. In the e-Government project and thus in the framework, the term "standard" is used in a broader sense meaning a set of recommendations which might originate from a "de jure" standard, a "de facto" standard or from a standard especially designed for a given purpose.

Across the Danish Government a collaboration to achieve consensus on standards, specifications and technologies has been established. The aim is to agree upon which standards to use throughout the public sector. As mentioned earlier, the committee representing government, regions and local governments of Denmark is a central player in this collaboration. The IT Architecture Committee and the XML Committee acknowledge their views on standards, specifications and technologies in the DIF. Those standards are core elements relevant across the government and domain elements relevant within a specific domain only.

The following assumptions outline the recommendations by the interoperability framework:

- Use open standards
- Incorporate existing standards in a broader context
- Stimulate the re-use of already established standards
- Re-design administrative processes in order to make the best use of offered technology.
- Coordinate and manage the initiative.

The purpose of such a framework is the jurisdiction for which it was introduced. They need to address issues that do not necessarily play a role at the national level. This means that if the scope of a national interoperability framework is beyond the country's borders, attention must be paid to surmount the transnational obstacles.

The DIF addresses various aspects of standards, specifications and technologies to support the task of implementing e-Government and for this purpose the document has been divided into these categories:

- User Interfaces
- Document and Data Interchange
- Web-based Services
- Content Management and Metadata Definition

- Data Integration
- Identity Management
- Interconnectivity
- Operations
- Business area specific standards

The framework provides an overview of the IT standards set by the national public administration. Three top-level categories are used:

- Technical standards
- Data standards
- Process standards.

The technical standards have so far been the mainstay of the framework. The process standards describe common approaches and guidelines for processes, and are a relatively new area in the work on e-government standardisation.

As a step in the consolidation and dissemination of the framework, it has been decided to clearly state how the content of the website can be used. The Danish interoperability framework is known as a "best practice" for such frameworks and is subject to increasing attention from countries, which have no such framework. The IT Architecture Committee has therefore decided to make the framework available through a Creative Commons license, hereby making the content available and open for all to reuse while also pointing out that the IT Architecture Committee holds the intellectual property rights to the framework.

European Interoperability Framework

The EU equivalent of a national framework for interoperability is the European Interoperability Framework (EIF). Within the European Commission, the Directorate-General Enterprise & Industry published the IDABC Programme (Interoperable Delivery of European e-Government Services to public Administrations, Business and Citizens) in 1999 (IDABC, 2004). It takes advantage of the opportunities offered by ICTs to:

- Support and empower the delivery of cross-border public sector services to citizens and businesses across Europe.
- Improve efficiency as well as collaboration between European public administrations.

IDABC is a Community Programme that pioneered the use of IT in public administrations and facilitated the transition from paper-based to electronic exchanges across Europe. The primary objective of IDABC was to enhance the exchange of information among the different community policy departments.

Moreover, IDABC provides funding to projects that address the policy requirements and improve cooperation between administrations across the continent. Public sector administrators are represented in the IDABC programme's management committee and in many expert groups.

By using state-of-the-art ICTs, developing common solutions and services and by providing a platform for the exchange of good practice between public administrations, IDABC consists a common ground for discussions about interoperability, pinpointing which interoperability issues should be addressed when implementing pan-European e-government services. It, however, avoids prescribing any concrete architecture or standard catalogue. The EU's EIF and the supporting IDABC Architecture Guidelines (2004) are intended to address the interoperability of pan-European e-Government services (PEGS). Its scope includes A2A, A2C, and A2B (where "A" stands for "Administration", "C" for "Citizens" and "B" for "Business"). The EIF identifies three types of PEGS interactions:

- Direct interaction between citizens or enterprises of one Member State with administrations of other Member States and/or institutions
- Data exchange across Member States as to resolve cases that citizens or busi-

nesses may have with their own public administration.

- The exchange of data between various EU institutions or agencies, or between an European Union institution or agency as well as one or more administrations of Member States.

The EIF's recommendations are quite high level, whereas the related IDABC Architecture Guidelines (2004) are very low level, thereby leaving a large gap between these two sets of specifications. The impact of the EIF so far appears to have been rather modest, in part, because PEGS have not yet appeared in significant numbers. Nevertheless, the EIF is referenced frequently in national interoperability frameworks, most of which at least claim the intention of complying with it (Charalabidis, Lampathaki, & Stassis, 2007; Malotaux, van der Harst, Achtsivassilis, & Hahndiek, 2007; Rothenberg, Botterman, & van Oranje-Nassau, 2008).

Federal Enterprise Architecture Framework

E-Government initiatives require a flexible, comprehensive framework that supports designing, development of planning requirements, as well as building major systems. This is essential if the Federal Government is to:

- Leverage IT investments and avoid duplication of infrastructure
- Link business processes via shared and protected IS
- Encourage dissimilar business processes, services as well as activities that lie beyond the boundaries of the respective Agency.

In the United States of America, the Federal Chief Information Officers Council (CIOC) issued the Federal Enterprise Architecture Framework (FEAF) in 1999 (CIOC, 1999). To leverage FEAF

guidance in e-government implementation, the Federal CIOC endorsed the E-government Enterprise Architecture Guidance (CIOC EAG) in 2002, for guiding the e-government projects across the federal government (CIOC, 2002).

The idea behind FEA was the identification of potential opportunities, to make processes simpler as well as to unify workflows across the agencies and within the lines of business of the public sector. The outcome of this effort was a more citizen-centered government, which will maximize technology investments in order to better achieve the outcomes of its mission. This approach also increased the potential for meaningful collaboration by clearly identifying opportunities where shared elements of e-government solutions might occur.

The Federal Enterprise Architecture (FEA) is a function-driven framework for describing the business operations of the Federal Government independent of the Agencies that perform them. The Federal Enterprise Application Framework (FEAF), provides several approaches, models, as well as definitions for communicating the overall organisation and relationships of architecture components that are needed for the development and maintenance of the FEA. This Guidance was developed in accordance with the basic principles and structure defined in the FEA and FEAF. It identifies a core set of e-government architectural concepts and pragmatic examples for e-government Initiatives across the Federal Government. The FEAF defined, and the Federal CIO Council adopted, principles that govern and represent the criteria against which all potential investment and architectural decisions are weighed. The FEAF principles are summarized here in order to emphasize their applicability and importance to this e-government guidance:

- Standards
- Investments
- Data Collection
- Security

- Functionality
- Information Access
- Proven Technologies
- Privacy

The FEAF defined, and the Federal CIO Council adopted, a four layer, segmented structure for defining the Federal Enterprise Architecture. The models in this guidance associated with the Business, Performance, Data, and Application Architectures are primarily conceptual descriptions to establish a baseline of effective e-government architectural concepts and a common vocabulary. The models and standards associated with the Technology Architecture present more pragmatic guidance and examples for e-government Initiatives.

Business Architecture presents the evolving Federal Enterprise Architecture Business Reference Model that systematically identifies the business functions of the Federal Government. This model is provided for context and the guidance does not attempt to define business architectures or e-government processes for specific functions or organisations. Data Architecture development was not practical in the timeframe available for this initial guidance. Instead, the Data Architecture section provides initial guidance on areas such as the use of XML, which are key to e-government solutions.

Application Architecture defines the major application components common to e-government solutions, and includes two models:

- The Conceptual Model provides the bridge between the business view of the Business Reference Model and the systems view of the remaining models
- The Interoperability Model describes the common technical components of an e-government solution and how they interoperate within and across e-government solutions

Technology Architecture provides more pragmatic implementation guidance for e-government Initiatives in the form of:

- Example Technical Models for major components of an e-government solution
- E-government Technical Reference Model
- Starter set of voluntary industry standards that should be understood and considered by e-government Initiatives.

The FEA includes a Performance Reference Model (PRM) that provides common outcome and output measures throughout the Federal Government. The Interoperability Model describes the primary application components supporting the Conceptual/Process Model and how they interoperate within and across e-government solutions. This includes interoperability at the user, data, and application levels. The Interoperability Model reflects commonly found industry representations, embracing industry standards and best practices.

Many components of the e-government Interoperability Model will be required for all e-government Initiatives. However, the business requirements of each e-government Initiative will determine which components are most critical or central to that initiative. e-government Initiatives should identify the critical components for their business requirements and ensure that those components are robustly supported in their architecture.

eG-Cooperative Framework

Castellano, Pastore, Arcieri, Summo, and Bellone de Grecis (2005) present a framework, which enables the cooperation of applications across different Government Agencies in order to supply new added value services tailored to citizens and business needs. Moreover it promotes an internal process reengineering realised by integrating legacy governmental applications. The framework is based on the Enterprise Service Bus (ESB) model and on the Web Services technology. Finally, their study describes the architecture of the prototypal framework and a case study of a single desk for businesses. They describe an open standard framework following the Italian National Center for Information Technology in the Public Administration (CNIPA) standards and complies with the relevant developments around EU as well as the rest of the world. The framework improves G2C interactions by supplying a single access point, built around the life events of citizens.

As main result the framework is able to supply to citizens and businesses, services built around the events of their life as a process composed by activities executed by more eG-Domains. To achieve this goal the framework is based on two ESB. The first is the backbone for inter-GAs cooperation while the second realises intra-GAs service integration. Moreover, by adopting open and widespread standards, the proposed Framework founds the reduction of costs and risk associated with deploying major IT projects. Moreover it aligns government with the rest of industry.

The eG-Domain represents all the computing resources, networks, applications and data that belong to a specific Government Agency. The communication in this network is managed by the eG-Bus. Each eG-Domain is connected to the eG-Bus through the eG-Gate. The eG-Bus provides a common, standard-based infrastructure for application connectivity and process orchestration (Von Huizen, 2003) among different eG-Nodes. It is the middleware that:

- Transforms message formats between consumer and provider
- Routes requests to correct service provider
- Converts transport protocol between consumer and provider
- Ensure a secure communication.

The eG-Domain main interactions are requiring/providing a service and communicating/

processing an event in order to supply "events of life" services as a process composed by activities executed by one or more intra and extra Domain services.

To realise the integration among GAs different resources the eG-Domain architecture is based on the ESB model. The main components in this architecture are:

- eG-DomainBus: it is the middleware able to establish the communication among the different services present in the GA.
- eG-Gate: it realises the connection between the eG-Domain and the eG-Bus.
- eG-Services: they are services present in the GA provided by databases, legacy applications, portals and workflow engines. Each eG-Service is mapped into a Web Service.

Greek e-Government Interoperability Framework

The Greek attempt on an e-Government Interoperability Framework (Greek e-GIF, 2008) has been the cornerstone of the national strategy for transition and adjustment of the requirements of modern times and is directly related to European directions and objectives. The Greek e-GIF aims to support effectively at Central, Regional as well as Local level and contribute to the achievement of interoperability at the level of IS, procedures as well as data. The Framework is consisted by the following:

- The Certification Framework for Public Administration web sites
- The Interoperability Framework between IS and e-Government transaction services of public administration
- The Digital Authentication Framework
- The Documentation Model.
- Four Project Units part the e-GIF:

- Developing of Framework for e-Government Services
- Design Data Standards and XML Schema
- Development of Educational Materials and organisation of Seminars
- Coordination of bodies and Specialized Services.

This project has been designed in order to study the Service Framework and the development of interoperability standards. The e-government agencies policies in interoperability have been scrutinized in order to identify common treats in the creation and maintenance of their interoperability frameworks. Interoperability frameworks have shown up as a key tool for interoperability in the deployment of e-government services. Although they initially focused on technical interoperability, inclusion of semantics in the interoperability frameworks started recently. The inclusion is still at early stages: the interoperability frameworks are mainly dealing with syntax issues, but increasingly tackling specific issues in semantics, namely ontologies.

The new Hellenic e-Government Service Provision and Interoperability Framework introduces a new system that will interact with e-Government portals and back-office applications, guiding their evolution and ensuring interoperability by design, rework or change. The implementation addresses a number of key issues, such as (Chalabidis et al., 2007):

- Development of unified governmental data models
- Specification of truly interoperable, one-stop governmental services
- Definition of standards and rules
- Adoption of protection, security and authentication mechanisms and arrangement of the corresponding legal issues
- Change management procedures and customization techniques for applying the

findings to the specific public administration needs and demands.

The initial application of the Greek eGIF, as well as the evolutions of the German and UK eGIF's are indicating that new perspectives should be taken into consideration from now on, analysed as following (Vitkauskaite & Gatautis, 2008):

- Importance and adequate effort should be put in defining standard electronic services for businesses and citizens, thus providing clear examples to administrations and service portal developers
- The paper-based specification should give way to system-based presentation of the framework, incorporating service descriptions, data definitions, certification schemes and application metrics in a common repository
- Organisational interoperability issues should be supported by a more concrete methodology of how to transform traditional services to electronic flows.

The collaboration among European e-Government Interoperability Frameworks is particularly beneficial for the ongoing frameworks, since it ensures that lessons from the pioneers' experience are learnt and that the same mistakes will not be repeated.

In the near future the Hellenic gambit will conduct research on the distinct frameworks complementing its first release, publication of XML Schemas based on Core Components methodology, initial training of key staff within administrations and extension of the system in order to encourage stakeholders to engage themselves and build synergies across the public sector in a truly interdisciplinary way (Sourouni, Lampathaki, Mouzakitis, Charalambidis, & Askounis, 2008).

The Estonian IT interoperability Framework

One of the main objectives of the Estonian ICT policy is to make state IS citizen-oriented as well as service-based. IS need to be integrated into a single logical whole serving the population and different organisations. To this end, it is necessary to set clear rules and agreements, and to use common middleware.

The Estonian IT interoperability framework (EIF, 2006) is parted by standards as well as guidelines aimed that ensure the integration of IS in a single logical whole, in order to provide services for public administration institutions, enterprises and citizens both in the national and the European context. It gives a systematic overview of the positive trends in the development of the Estonian state IS. The cornerstones of the state IT architecture are the following:

- Technical interoperability
- Security
- Openness
- Flexibility
- Scalability

Although the functioning of state IS is targeted at achieving the same rationality as the private sector, sharp differences between the state and the private sector remain. It is not the state's aim to provide services under a certain cost, but to ensure their expediency. It is presumed that in the nearest future, IS will enable to perform several operations from one and the same place. Same indicators as that of the private sector cannot measure the efficiency of public sector ISs. In terms of integrated service provision, public sector ISs has to serve as pathfinders for private sector ISs. Participation through public procurement in the development of state ISs and satisfying the needs of the state as a whole poses a considerable challenge for the Estonian IT sector. The Estonian IT interoperability framework serves as:

- A guidance for those elaborating concepts for country-wide ISs
- A guidance for IT project managers in the public administration for elaborating concepts for the IS of their institutions
- An aid in the organisation of public procurements.

The aim of the IT interoperability framework is to increase public sector efficiency in Estonia by improving the quality of services provided to citizens and enterprises both at the Estonian and the EU level. The specific objectives of the framework are the following:

- To facilitate and, consequently, implement the transformation of institution-based public administration into a service-centred one, where all citizens can communicate with the state without knowing anything about its hierarchical structure and division of roles
- To reduce public sector IT expenses through a wide use of centrally developed solutions
- To improve the interoperability of new IT projects through a co-ordinated use of centrally developed infrastructure, middleware and open standards
- To improve the co-ordination and management of state ISs and to accelerate the development of IT solutions
- To contribute to the co-development of the state IS
- To allow autonomous development for all systems within the principles of organisational, semantic and technical interoperability
- To ensure free competition in the area of public procurement.

The logical components of the state IS are the following:

- IS
- The administration system for the state IS together with its services catalogue
- The state-administered citizen IT environment
- Support systems and rules.

IT experts representing the central and the local government agencies as well as organisations from the third and the private sector have elaborated the framework. The work of the expert group was led by the Department of State IS of the Ministry of Economic Affairs and Communications (MEAC) together with private sector specialists.

ADAPTING E-GOVERNMENT FRAMEWOKRS TO E-HEALTH

E-health can be perceived as the application of information and communication technologies (ICT) across the whole range of functions that affect healthcare, from diagnosis to follow-up. It suggests one of the innovations since the advent of modern medicine and public health measures like sanitation and clean water (Silber, 2003).

The use of new technologies has included for instance communications infrastructure for disease prevention and health maintenance, evidence-based medicine and drug databases for professional and patient purposes (*ibid*). However, literature (Kitsios, Papadopoulos, & Angelopoulos, 2009) has suggested that no e-Health universal implementation framework exists. The scope of research, choice of criteria and methodology followed in existing studies has been also heavily criticised (Silber, 2003).

Apart from the insufficiency of literature on establishing a common "language" for implementing e-Health, there seem to be specific enablers or barriers that play an important role to its widespread diffusion. The barriers may be cultural and related to the complex nature of the healthcare context, political, technical and economic. The various

sectors of the health care system have traditionally been characterised by different stakeholders and regulation- and financing mechanisms. Indeed, the implementation of Health policy initiatives is based on a complex series of interactions between the centre –inner context– and periphery –outer context– come to the foreground, each one of which attempts to influence the other (Papadopoulos & Merali, 2009). Circulars, consultative documents and White Papers are the main means through which the governments attempt to promote policies and change –and in our case, e-Health– but these policies are due to be locally interpreted and accordingly adapted by pressure groups and stakeholders (Ham, 2004). Furthermore, the vertical organisational structure of healthcare organisations according to discipline, knowledge, people, and location versus the horizontal way of providing care to patients render the task of collaboration, development, and implementation of e-health a challenging process (Aguilar, 2006; SMFT, 2003).

In such a context, interoperability is suggested as the sustainable way to assist partners acting in various locations, taking under consideration their different expertise, agendas, cultures and languages; by using information systems from different vendors, it enables all stakeholders to "collaborate harmoniously to deliver quality healthcare to meet the technical demands for the successful support of complex healthcare processes, modern healthcare enterprise architectures must achieve and implement interoperability in all the healthcare domains. Interoperability, which may be expressed using functional, syntactic, or semantic methods, it is necessary to provide information dissemination for all areas in healthcare" (Aguilar, 2006).

Since there is need for interoperability in e-health, the aforementioned frameworks suggested for e-government come to the foreground. The reason for the use of the specific frameworks is threefold: firstly, both e-health and e-government are both based on the need for secure and high speed connectivity; secondly, they are based on building trust amongst the various public organisations (e-government) and citizens, who prefer services and information tailored to their needs and requirements; and thirdly, they need to consider the needs and interests of users and citizens, which should be better integrated into the implementation and adaptation processes (Kitsios, Angelopoulos, & Zannetopoulos 2008). Therefore, the similar complexities entailed in both e-government and e-health when aiming towards interoperability in which various players are entailed as well as the occurring technical and political challenges render the interoperability frameworks in e-government helpful guides in establishing interoperability in the e-health domain (Aguilar, 2006).

CONCLUSION

This chapter explored the various interoperability frameworks for e-government and suggested that the complexities entailed in e-health and e-government advocate towards the use of e-government interoperability frameworks in e-health context.

This chapter does not stand out as a critical literature review of interoperability frameworks but discusses adequately the most important frameworks used and makes a case for their use in e-health. The deployment of e-health requires systems aimed at interoperability between local, regional, and national healthcare. More studies, hence, need to be conducted exploring factors necessary for establishing interoperability between e-health systems successfully and securing the provision of seamless services to patients.

REFERENCES

ADAE. (2003). Le Cadre Commun d'Int'eroperabilit'e version 2.1 Retrieved from http://www.adae.gouv.fr/article.php3?id article=219

Aguilar, A. (2006). Semantic Interoperability in the Context of e-Health. Retrieved from http://www.antonio-aguilar.com/files/papers/ehealth_aguilar.pdf

Alabau, A. (2004). The European Union and its eGovernment development policy. Fundacio´n Vodafone. Retrieved from http://www.upv.es/~lguijar/socinfo/publicaciones_f.htm

Angelopoulos, S., Kitsios, F., & Babulac, E. (2008). From e to u: Towards an innovative digital era. In Kotsopoulos, S., & Ioannou, K. (Eds.), *Heterogeneous Next Generation Networking: Innovations and Platforms* (pp. 427–444). Hershey, PA: Idea Group Publishing.

Baldoni, R., Contenti, M., Piergiovanni, S. T., & Virgillito, A. (2003). Modelling Publish/Subscribe Communication Systems: Towards a Formal Approach. In *Proc. of 8th IEEE International Workshop on Object-oriented Real-time Dependable Systems*, Guadalajara, Mexico.

Castellano, M., Pastore, N., Arcieri, F., Summo, V., & Bellone de Grecis, G. (2005). An E-Government Cooperative Framework for Government Agencies. In *Proc. Of 38th International Conference on System Sciences, Hawaii*, 5(5): 121c.

CEC. Commission of the European Communities (1991). *Council Directive 91/250/EEC of 14 May 1991 on the legal protection of computer programs.*

CEC. Commission of the European Communities (2002). *eEurope 2005: An information society for all.* An Action Plan to be presented in view of the Sevilla.

Channabasavaiah, K., Holley, K., & Tuggle Jr. E.M. (2004). Migrating to a service-oriented architecture, IBM. Retrieved from ibm.com/developerworks/webservices/library/ws-migratesoa/

Charalabidis, Y., Lampathaki, F., & Stassis, A. (2007). *A Second-Generation e-Government Interoperability Framework. 5th Eastern European eGov Days 2007 in Prague.* Austrian Computer Society.

CIOC. Federal Chief Information Officer Council (1999). *Federal Enterprise Architecture Framework, version 1.1.*

CIOC. Federal Chief Information Officer Council (2002). *E-Gov Enterprise Architecture Guidance, draft-version 2.0.*

DIF. Danish e-Government Interoperability Framework. (2004). Retrieved from http://standarder.oio.dk/English

eEnvoy. Office of the e-Envoy (2001). *e-Services Development Framework, version 1.0.*

eGU, e-Government Unit. (2005), *e-Government Interoperability Framework, version 6.1.*

Estonian Interoperability Framework, E. I. F. (2006). Retrieved from http://www.epractice.eu/files/media/media_890.pdf

FEAPMO. Federal Enterprise Architecture Project Management Office, FEA Consolidated Reference Model Document. (2005). Retrieved from http://www.whitehouse.gov/omb/egov/documents/CRM.PDF.

Gatautis, R., Kulvietis, G., & Vitkauskaite, E. (2009). Lithuanian eGovernment Interoperability Model. Retrieved from http://internet.ktu.lt/lt/mokslas/zurnalai/inzeko/62/1392-2758-2009-2-62-38.pdf

Guijarro, L. (2005). Policy and practice in standards selection for e-government interoperability frameworks. In *Proc. of EGOV 2005 Conference*, pp. 163–173, Copenhaguen (Denmark).

Guijarro, L. (2007). Interoperability frameworks and enterprise architectures in e-government initiatives in Europe and the united states. *Government Information Quarterly*, 24(1), 89–101.. doi:10.1016/j.giq.2006.05.003

Guijarro, L. (2009). Semantic interoperability in e-Government initiatives [Dimensions of the efficiency of public-private partnership. Inzinerine Ekonomika-Engineering.]. *Computer Standards & Interfaces*, 1(31), 174–180. doi:10.1016/j.csi.2007.11.011

Ham, C. (2004). *Health Policy in Britain* (5th ed.). New York: Palgrave.

IDABC. Enterprise DG (2002). *Architecture Guidelines for trans-European Telematics Networks for Administrations, version 6.1*, Brussels.

IDABC. Enterprise & Industry DG (2004a). *Architecture Guidelines for transEuropean Telematics Networks for Administrations, version 7.1*, Brussels.

IDABC. Enterprise & Industry DG (2004b). *European Interoperability Framework for pan-European e-government services, version 1.0*, Brussels.

KBSt. (2003). Standards and Architectures for e-Government Applications, version 2.0. Retrieved from http://www.kbst.bund.de/SAGA

KBsT. Federal Government Co-ordination and Advisory Agency (2005a*). SAGA-Standards and Architectures for e-Goverment Applications, version 2.1*, Schriftenreihe der KBSt 82.

KBsT. Federal Government Co-ordination and Advisory Agency (2005b). *DOMEA concept. Document Management and Electronic Archiving in Electronic Courses of Business, Organisational Concept 2.0*, Schriftenreihe der KBSt 74.

Kitsios, F., Angelopoulos, S., & Zannetopoulos, I. (2008). Innovation and e-government: an in depth overview on e-services. In Kotsopoulos, S., & Ioannou, K. (Eds.), *Heterogeneous Next Generation Networking: Innovations and Platform* (pp. 415–426). Hershey, PA: Idea Group Publishing.

Kitsios, F., Papadopoulos, T., & Angelopoulos, S. (2009). A roadmap to the introduction of pervasive Information Systems in healthcare. In Lazakidou, A., Siassiakos, K., & Ioannou, K. (Eds.), *Wireless Technologies for Ambient Assisted Living and Health Care: Systems and Applications*. Hershey, PA: Idea Group publishing.

Malotaux, M., van der Harst, G., Achtsivassilis, J., & Hahndiek, F. (2007). *Preparation for Update European Interoperability Framework 2.0: Final report.*

OECD. Organisation for Economic Co-operation and Development. (2000). Annual Report 2000. Retrieved from http://www.oecd.org/dataoecd/30/59/1842666.pdf

OECD. Organisation for Economic Co-operation and Development. (2003). *The e-Government Imperative*, OECD e-Government Studies, France.

Papadopoulos, T., & Merali, Y. (2009). Stakeholder dynamics during process innovation implementation in healthcare: Lean Thinking in a hospital of UK National Health Service. *International Journal of Healthcare Technology and Management, 10*(4/5), 303–324..doi:10.1504/IJHTM.2009.030453

Rothenberg, J., Botterman, M., & van Oranje-Nassau, C. (2008). *Towards a Dutch Interoperability Framework: Recommendations to the Forum Standaardisatie*. RAND Corporation.

Sadtler, C., Crabtree, B., Cotignola, D., & Michel, P. (2004). *Patterns: Broker Interactions for Intra- and Inter-enterprise* (pp. 47–53). International Technical Support Organization.

SFMT. (2003). *Structured Architecture for Medical Business Activities (SAMBA)*. Swedish Federation for Medical Informatics.

Silber, D. (2003). The *case for eHealth. Presented at the European Commission's high-level conference on eHealth May 22/23*

Sourouni, A.-M. Lampathaki, F., Mouzakitis, S., Charalabidis, Y., & Askounis, D. (2008). Paving the way to egovernment transformation: interoperability registry infrastructure development. In *Proc. of EGOV 2008 Conference*, pp. 340-351, Turin (Italy).

The Greek e-GIF. (2008). *The Greek e-GIF*. Retrieved from http://egif.epu.ntua.gr

Vitkauskaitė, E., & Gatautis, R. (2008*). E-Government interoperability issues in Lithuania. In Proc of 8th International Conference on Electronic Business*, pp. 80–87, Hong Kong.

Von Huizen, G. (2003). *Time to get on the bus: A standards-based foundation for the connected enterprise* (pp. 8–15). Dallas: Business Integration Journal, Business Integration Journal Press.

WSAT. Web Service Architecture Team. (2001). *Web Services Conceptual Architecture, IBM*. Retrieved from http://www.ibm.com/software/solutions/webservices/pdf/wsca.pdf

Compilation of References

A compilation of IEEE standard computer glossaries. (1990). *IEEE STD 610.12, and IEEE Standard Computer Dictionary.* New York: IEEE.

Abel, D. J., Taylor, K., Ackland, R., & Hungerford, S. (1998). An exploration of GIS architectures for Internet environments. *Computers, Environment and Urban Systems, 22*(1), 7–23. doi:10.1016/S0198-9715(98)00016-7

Abowd, D., & Mynat, D. (2000). Charting past, present and future research in Ubiquitous computing. *AC Transactions on Computer-Human Interaction, 7*(1), 29–58. doi:10.1145/344949.344988

Accelerating the movement toward standards-based interoperability in healthcare. (1996). *Clinical Information Systems Subcommittee of the IEEE-USA* Medical Technology Policy Committee.

ADAE. (2003). Le Cadre Commun d'Int'eroperabilit'e version 2.1 Retrieved from http://www.adae.gouv.fr/article.php3?id article=219

Adams, C. E. (2002). Home area network technologies. *BT Technology Journal, 20*(2), 53–72.

Aggarwal, C. (Ed.). (2007). *Data Streams: Models and Algorithms.* New York: Springer.

Aguilar, A. (2005). *Semantic Interoperability in the Context of e-Health.* CDH Seminar. Retrieved from http://m3pe.org/seminar/aguilar.pdf

Aguilar, A. (2006). Semantic Interoperability in the Context of e-Health. Retrieved from http://www.antonio-aguilar.com/files/papers/ehealth_aguilar.pdf

Ahmed, A. A., Shi, H., & Shang, Y. (2003). A Survey on Network Protocols for Wireless Sensor Networks. In *Proc. of International Conference on Information Technology: Research and Education* (ITRE'03), (pp. 301 – 305).

Ajzen, I. (1991). The theory of planned behaviour. *Organizational Behavior and Human Decision Processes, 50,* 179–211. doi:10.1016/0749-5978(91)90020-T

Ajzen, I., & Fishbein, M. (1980). *Understanding attitudes and predicting social behaviour.* Englewood Cliffs, NJ: Prentice-Hall.

Akyildiz, I., Su, W., Sankarasubramaniam, Y., & Cayirci, E. (2002). A survey on Sensor Networks. *IEEE Communications Magazine, 40*(8), 102–114. doi:10.1109/MCOM.2002.1024422

Alabau, A. (2004). The European Union and its eGovernment development policy. Fundacio´ n Vodafone. Retrieved from http://www.upv.es/~lguijar/socinfo/publicaciones_f.htm

Andrews, J. G., Ghosh, A., & Muhamed, R. (2007). *Fundamentals of WiMAX: Understanding Broadband Wireless Networking.* Upper Saddle River, NJ: Prentice Hall.

Angelopoulos, S., Kitsios, F., & Babulac, E. (2008). From e to u: Towards an innovative digital era. In Kotsopoulos, S., & Ioannou, K. (Eds.), *Heterogeneous Next Generation Networking: Innovations and Platforms* (pp. 427–444). Hershey, PA: Idea Group Publishing.

Astro Teller. (1994).Turing completeness in the language of genetic programming with indexed memory. In *Proceedings of the 1994 {IEEE} World Congress on Computational Intelligence,* 1, IEEE Press. Retrieved from http://dgpf.sourceforge.net/documents/006-2006-07-17-kuvs_paper.pdf

Avancha, S. (2003). *Wireless Sensor Networks.* Boston: Kluwer Academic/Springer Verlag Publishers.

Babulak, E. (2005a). Automated Environment via Cyberspace. In *Proceedings of the International Conference on Applied Computing* (IADIS), Algarve, Portugal.

Babulak, E. (2005b). Quality of Service Provision Assessment in the Healthcare Information and Telecommunications Infrastructures. Accepted for publication in the *International Journal of Medical Informatics.*

Baldoni, R., Contenti, M., Piergiovanni, S. T., & Virgillito, A. (2003). Modelling Publish/Subscribe Communication Systems: Towards a Formal Approach. In *Proc. of 8th IEEE International Workshop on Object-oriented Real-time Dependable Systems,* Guadalajara, Mexico.

Bandara, U., Hasegawa, M., Inoue, M., Morikawa, H., & Aoyama, T. (2004). Design and implementation of a Bluetooth signal strength based location sensing system. In *Proc Radio and Wireless Conference,* 2004, (pp. 319-322).

Bandyopadhyay, S., & Coyle, E. *(2003). An Energy Efficient Hierarchical Clustering Algorithm for Wireless Sensor Networks". IEEE INFOCOM 2003. In* Proceedings of the Twenty-Second Annual Joint Conferences of the IEEE Computer and Communications Societies. *Volume 3, pp. 1713 - 1723.*

Baritchi, A., Cook, D., & Holder, L. *(2000), Discovering structural patterns in telecommunications data. In* Proceedings of the Thirteenth Annual Florida AI Research Symposium *(pp. 82-85).*

Baronti, P., Pillai, P., Chook, V. W. C., Chessa, S., Gotta, A., & Hu, Y. F. (2007). Wireless sensor networks: A survey on the state of the art and the 802.15.4 and ZigBee Standards. *Computer Communications, 30*(7), 1655–1695.

Bergstrom, P., Driscoll, K., & Kimball, J. (2001). Making Home Automation Communications Secure. *IEEE Computer, 34*(10), 50–56.

Berreti, D. (1998). Default set of BSS Parameters for Cosmote Network and set of BSS parameters for umbrella cells, Nokia Productivity Services. *Technical Report, Nokia Telecommunications, 7.8.1998,* (pp. 2-16).

Bhargava, A., & Zoltowski, M. (2003). Sensors and wireless communication for medical care. In *Proc. 14th International Workshop on Database and Expert Systems Applications,* (pp. 956–960).

Biegel, G., & Cahill, V. (2004). A Framework for Developing Mobile, Context-aware Applications. In *Proceedings of the Second IEEE International Conference on Pervasive Computing and Communications* (PerCom04), IEEE Computer Society.

Björklund, H. F. (2007, March). *Wiring Devices and Technologies in Home Environment.* Paper presented at the TKK T-110.5190 Seminar on Internetworking.

Black, J. P., Segmuller, W., Cohen, N., Leiba, B., Misra, A., Ebling, M. R., & Stern, E. (2004). Pervasive Computing in Health Care: Smart Spaces and Enterprise Information Systems. In MobiSys Workshop on Context, Boston Massachusetts, USA.

Bohn, J., Gaertner, F., & Vogt, H. (2003). Dependability Issues of Pervasive Computing in a Healthcare Environment. Proceedings of the First International Conference on Security in Pervasive Computing.

Bonabeau, E., Dorigo, M., & Theraulaz, G. (1999). *Swarm Intelligence: From Natural to Artificial Systems, Santa Fe Institute Studies in the Sciences of Complexity.* New York: Oxford University Press.

Borriello, G., Stanford, V., Naranayaswami, C., & Menning, W. (2007). Pervasive Computing in Healthcare. [Editorial]. *IEEE Pervasive Computing / IEEE Computer Society [and] IEEE Communications Society, 6*(1), 17–19. doi:10.1109/MPRV.2007.11

Boulis, A., & Srivastava, M. B. (2003), "Node-level Energy Management for Sensor Networks in the Presence of Multiple Applications," in Proc. IEEE PerCom Conf.

Bulusu, N., et al. (2001). Scalable coordination for wireless sensor networks: Self-configuring localization systems. In *Proc. of the 6th International Symposium on Communication Theory and Applications* (ISCTA'01), Ambleside, UK

Busse, M., Haenselmann, T., & Effelsberg, W. *(2006). TECA: a Topology and Energy Control Algorithm for Wireless Sensor Networks. In* Proceedings of the International Symposium on Modeling, Analysis and Simulation of Wireless and Mobile Systems *(MSWiM '06). Torremolinos, Malaga, Spain. ACM*

Callon, M. (1986). Some elements in sociology of translation: domestication of the scallops and fishermen of St. Brieuc Bay. In Law, J. (Ed.), *Power, action and belief* (pp. 196–233). London: Routledge.

Cam, H., Ozdemir, S., Nair, P., & Muthuavinashippan, D. (2003). (in press). ESPDA [IEEE Sensor, Toronto, Canada]. *Energy-Efficient and Secure Pattern Based Data Aggregation for Wireless Sensor Networks.*

Camp, J. D., & Knightly, E. W. (2008). The IEEE 802.11s Extended Service Set Mesh Networking Standard. *IEEE Communications Magazine*, 46.

Casole, M. (2002). WLAN security – Status, Problems and Perspective. In *Proceedings of European Wireless 2002*. Florence Italy.

Castellano, M., Pastore, N., Arcieri, F., Summo, V., & Bellone de Grecis, G. (2005). An E-Government Cooperative Framework for Government Agencies. In *Proc. Of 38th International Conference on System Sciences, Hawaii, 5*(5): 121c.

Cavoukian, A. (2007, August). *Fact Sheet, "Wireless Communication Technologies, Safeguarding Privacy & Security"*. Infrmation and Privacy Commissioner / Ontario, August 2007 subconscious

CEC. Commission of the European Communities (1991). *Council Directive 91/250/EEC of 14 May 1991 on the legal protection of computer programs.*

CEC. Commission of the European Communities (2002). *eEurope 2005: An information society for all*. An Action Plan to be presented in view of the Sevilla.

Chakravorty, R. (2006). A programmable service architecture for mobile medical care. In *Proceedings of the 4th Annual IEEE International Conference on Pervasive Computing and Communications Workshops (PerCom '06)*, Pisa, Italy, (pp. 532–536).

Chan, M., Estève, D., Escriba, C., & Campo, E. (2008). A review of smart homes – Present state and future challenges. *Computer Methods and Programs in Biomedicine, 1*, 55–81. doi:10.1016/j.cmpb.2008.02.001

Chande, H. (2001). *Esperanza de vida y expectativas de salud en la edad avanzada*. Retrieved from http://www.redadultosmayores.com

Channabasavaiah, K., Holley, K., & Tuggle Jr. E.M. (2004). Migrating to a service-oriented architecture, IBM. Retrieved from ibm.com/developerworks/webservices/library/ws-migratesoa/

Charalabidis, Y., Lampathaki, F., & Stassis, A. (2007). *A Second-Generation e-Government Interoperability Framework. 5th Eastern European eGov Days 2007 in Prague*. Austrian Computer Society.

Chen, L., Nugent, C., Mulvenna, M., Finlay, D., Hong, X., & Poland, M. (2008). Using Event Calculus for behaviour reasoning and assistance in a smart home. [including Lecture Notes in Artificial Intelligence and Lecture Notes in Bioinformatics]. *Lecture Notes in Computer Science, 5120*, 81–89. doi:10.1007/978-3-540-69916-3_10

Chen, G., & Kotz, D. (2000). A survey of context-aware mobile computing research, Technical Report TR2000-381, Department of Computer Science, Dartmouth College.

Chon, H. D., Jun, S., Jung, H., & An, S. W. (2004). Using RFID for Accurate Positioning. In *Proc. GNSS2004*, 2004.

CIOC. Federal Chief Information Officer Council (1999). *Federal Enterprise Architecture Framework, version 1.1.*

CIOC. Federal Chief Information Officer Council (2002). *E-Gov Enterprise Architecture Guidance, draft-version 2.0.*

CIS-IMSERSO. (2000). *Study 2.279.* Retrieved from http://www.imsersomayores.csic.es/documentos/documentos/boletinsobreenvejec3ing-01.pdf

Conner, S. W., Kruys, J., Kyeongsoo, K., & Zuniga, J. C. (2006). *IEEE 802.11s Tutorial.* Retrieved February, 03, 2009, from http://www.ieee802.org/802_tutorials/06-November/802.11s_Tutorial_r5.pdf

Cook, A., & Woollacott, M. (1995). *Motor control, Theory and Practical Applications.* New York: Williams and Wilkins.

Cortes, C., Pregibon. (2001). D. Signature-based methods for data streams. *Data Mining and Knowledge Discovery, 5*(3), 167–182. doi:10.1023/A:1011464915332

Cortes, C., & Pregibon, D. *(1998), Giga-mining. In* Proceedings of the Fourth International Conference on Knowledge Discovery and Data Mining *(pp. 174-178). New York: AAAI Press.*

Cox, K., Eick, S., & Wills, G. (1997). Visual data mining: Recognizing telephone calling fraud. *Data Mining and Knowledge Discovery, 1*(2), 225–231. doi:10.1023/A:1009740009307

Crossbow Technology, Inc. (n.d.). *TelosB Datasheet. Crossbow: Wireless Sensor Networks.* Retrieved from http://www.xbow.com/Products/Product_pdf_files/Wireless_pdf/TelosB_Datasheet.pdf

Crossbow Technology, Inc. MICA2 Datasheet. (n.d.). *Crossbow: Wireless Sensor Networks.* Retrieved from http://www.xbow.com/Products/Product_pdf_files/Wireless_pdf/MICA2_Datasheet.pdf

Crossbow Technology, Inc. MICAz Datasheet. (n.d.). *Cressbow: Wireless Sensor Networks.* Retrieved from http://www.xbow.com/Products/Product_pdf_files/Wireless_pdf/MICAz_Datasheet.pdf

Cruickshanks, K. J., Wiley, T. L., Tweed, T. S., Klein, B., Klein, R., Mares-Perlman, J. A., & Nondahl, D. M. (1998). Prevalence of hearing loss in older adults in Beaver Dam, Wisconsin. *American Journal of Epidemiology, 148*(9), 879–886.

Current and future standardization issues in the e-Health domain: Achieving interoperability (2005). *CEN/ISSS e-Health Standardization Focus Group*, CEN, 2005

Custodian simulation (n.d.). *Custodian simulation tool homepage.* Retrieved from http://www2.rgu.ac.uk/subj/search/research/sustainablehousing/custodian/home.html

Czarniawska, B., & Sévon, G. (Eds.). (2005). *Global Ideas: How Ideas, Objects and Practices Travel in the Global Economy.* Malmö: Liber & Copenhagen Business School Press.

Daftari, A., Mehta, N., Bakre, S., & Sun, X. H. (2003). *On design framework of context aware embedded systems.* Chicago: Monterey Workshop.

Daniilidis, A. (2007). IEEE *802.11s Wireless Mesh Networks.* Retrieved March 23, 2009 from http://ece-classweb.ucsd.edu/winter10/ece287/homework/802.11s_tutorial.pdf

Davis, F. (1989). Perceived Usefulness, Perceived Ease of Use, and User Acceptance of Information Technology. *Management Information Systems Quarterly, 13,* 319–340. doi:10.2307/249008

Davis, F., Bagozzi, R. P., & Warshaw, P. R. (1989). User Acceptance of computer technology – A comparison of two theoretical models. *Management Science, 35,* 982–1003. doi:10.1287/mnsc.35.8.982

De Sa, M., Carrico, L., & Antunes, P. (2007). Ubiquitous Psychotherapy. *IEEE Pervasive Computing / IEEE Computer Society [and] IEEE Communications Society, 6*(1), 20–27. doi:10.1109/MPRV.2007.23

Deb, B., Bhatnagar, S., & Nath, B. (2004). STREAM: Sensor Topology Retrieval at Multiple Resolutions. *Kluwer Journal of Telecommunications Systems, 26*(2), 285–320. doi:10.1023/B:TELS.0000029043.27689.3f

Deb, B., Bhatnagar, S., & Nath, B. (2001). A Topology Discovery Algorithm for Sensor Networks with Applications to Network Management. (Tech. Rep. DCS-TR-441), East Rutherford, NJ: Rutgers University

Deb, S. B. B., & Nath, B. (2002). *A Topology Discovery Algorithm for Sensor Networks with Applications to Network Management.* (Tech. rep. DCSTR-441), Dept. of Computer Science, Rutgers Univ.

Delphinanto, A., Huiszoon, B., Rivero, D.S., Hartog, F., Boom, H., Kwaaitaal, J., & Wijk, P. (2003). *Home Networking Technologies Overview and Analysis.* Residential Gateway Environment, Deliverable D3.1.

DeVaul, J. G. R., et al. *(2003). Applications and Architecture. In* Proceedings of the 7th IEEE International Symposium on Wearable Computers, *(pp. 4-11).*

Devitt, A., Duffin, J., & Moloney, R. *(2005), Topographical proximity for mining network alarm data.* In Proceedings of the 2005 ACM SIGCOMM Workshop on Mining Network Data *(pp. 179-184). New York: ACM Press.*

Dewsbury, G., Clarke, K., Rouncefield, M., Sommerville, I., Taylor, B., & Edge, M. (2004). Designing acceptable 'smart' home technology to support people in the home. *Technology and Disability, 15*(3), 191–201.

Dewsbury, G., Taylor, B., & Edge, M. (2002). Designing safe smart home systems for vulnerable people. In *Proceedings of the Health Informatics Conference,* (pp. 65-70).

Dey, A. K., Abowd, G. D., & Salber, D. (2001). A conceptual framework and a toolkit for supporting the rapid prototyping of context-aware applications. *Human-Computer Interaction, 16,* 97–166. doi:10.1207/S15327051HCI16234_02

Dickson, K. Chiu, W. & Leung, H. (2005). Towards ubiquitous tourist service coordination and integration: a multi-agent and semantic web approach. In *Proceedings of the 7th international conference on Electronic commerce ICEC 05.* ACM Press

DIF. Danish e-Government Interoperability Framework. (2004). Retrieved from http://standarder.oio.dk/English

Digital Imaging and Communications in Medicine (DICOM). (2004). *Part I: Introduction and overview.* New York: National Electrical Manufacturing Association, PS3.1-2004, 2004

Dimitriadou, E., Ioannou, K., Panoutsopoulos, I., Garmpis, A., & Kotsopoulos, S. (2005). Priority to Low Moving Terminals in TETRA Networks. *WSEAS Transactions on Communications, 11*(4), 1228–1236.

Dix, A., Finlay, J., Abowd, G. D., & Beale, R. (2004). *Human-Computer Interaction.* Upper Saddle River, NJ: Prentice Hall.

Dunlop, J. (1999). *Digital Mobile Communications and the TETRA System.* New York: John Wiley & Sons.

eEnvoy. Office of the e-Envoy (2001). *e-Services Development Framework, version 1.0.*

eGU, e-Government Unit. (2005), *e-Government Interoperability Framework, version 6.1.*

Erdogan, A., Cayirci, E., & Coskun, V. (2003). Sectoral Sweepers for Sensor Node Management and Location Estimation in Adhoc Sensor Networks. In *Proc. IEEE MILCOM Conf.*

Estonian Interoperability Framework, E. I. F. (2006). Retrieved from http://www.epractice.eu/files/media/media_890.pdf

Ezawa, K. *Norton (1995), S. Knowledge discovery in telecommunication services data using Bayesian network models. In* Proceedings of the First International Conference on Knowledge Discovery and Data Mining; *Montreal Canada. Menlo Park, CA: AAAI Press.*

Fawcett, T., & Provost, F. (1997). Adaptive fraud detection. *Data Mining and Knowledge Discovery, 1*(3), 291–316. doi:10.1023/A:1009700419189

Fawcett, T., & Provost, F. (2002). Fraud Detection. In Klosgen, W., & Zytkow, J. (Eds.), *Handbook of Data Mining and Knowledge Discovery* (pp. 726–731). New York: Oxford University Press.

Fawcett, T., & Provost, F. *(1999), Activity monitoring: Noticing interesting changes in behavior. In* Proceedings of the Fifth ACM SIGKDD International Conference on Knowledge Discovery and Data Mining, *53-62. New York: ACM Press.*

FEAPMO. Federal Enterprise Architecture Project Management Office, FEA Consolidated Reference Model Document. (2005). Retrieved from http://www.whitehouse.gov/omb/egov/documents/CRM.PDF.

Fischer, S., Stewart, T. E., Mehta, S., Wax, R., & Lapinsky, S. E. (2003). Handheld computing in medicine. *Journal of the American Medical Informatics Association, 10*(2), 139–149. doi:10.1197/jamia.M1180

Fishbein, M., & Ajzen, I. (1975). *Belief, Attitude, Intention and Behavior: An Introduction to Theory and Research.* Reading, MA: Addison-Wesley.

Fok, C., Roman, G., & Lu, C. (2005). Mobile Agent Middleware for Sensor Networks: An Application Case Study. In *Proc. IEEE ICDCS Conf.*

Friedewald, M., Da Costa, O., Punie, Y., Alahuhta, P., & Heinonen, S. (2005). Perspectives of ambient intelligence in the home environment. *Telematics and Informatics - Elsevier, 22*(3), 221-238.

Fuller, G. F. (2000). Falls in the elderly. *American Family Physician, 61*, 2159–2168, 2173–2174.

Funk, J. L. (1998). Competition between regional standards and the success and failure of firms in the world-wide mobile communication market. *Telecommunications Policy, 22*(4/5), 419–441. doi:10.1016/S0308-5961(98)00024-X

Galego, J. (2005). Performance Analysis of Multiplexed Medical Data Transmission for Mobile Emergency Care over UMTS Channel. *IEEE Transactions on Information Technology in Biomedicine, 9*(1), 13–22. doi:10.1109/TITB.2004.838362

Gandon, F., & Sadeh, N. (2004). Semantic Web Technologies to Reconcile Privacy and Context Awareness, *Web Semantics Journal, 1*(3).

Garlan, D., Siewiorek, D., Smailagic, A., & Steenkiste, P. (2002). Project Aura: Towards Distraction-Free Pervasive Computing. *IEEE Pervasive Computing / IEEE Computer Society [and] IEEE Communications Society, 1*(2), 22–31. doi:10.1109/MPRV.2002.1012334

Gatautis, R., Kulvietis, G., & Vitkauskaite, E. (2009). Lithuanian eGovernment Interoperability Model. Retrieved from http://internet.ktu.lt/lt/mokslas/zurnalai/inzeko/62/1392-2758-2009-2-62-38.pdf

Gavrilovska, L. M., & Atanasovski, V. M. (2007, June). Interoperability in Future Wireless Communications Systems: A Roadmap to 4G. *Microwave Review, 13*(1).

Getoor, L., & Diehl, C. P. (2005). Link mining: A survey. *SIGKDD Explorations, 7*(2), 3–12. doi:10.1145/1117454.1117456

Ghumman, S. A. (2009). *Security in Wireless Mesh Networks (Master's Thesis in Computer Network Engineering, School of Information Science, Computer and Electrical Engineering, Halmstad University, 2009).* Retrieved August 13, 2009, from http://hh.diva-portal.org/smash/get/diva2:306340/fulltext01

Glass, S., Portmann, M., & Muthukkumarasamy, V. (2008). Securing Wireless Mesh Networks. *IEEE Internet Computing Magazine, 12*(4).

Godfrey, B. P., & Ratajczak, D. (2004). *Naps: Scalable, Robust Topology Management in Wireless ad hoc Networks. ISPN '04.* Berkeley, CA: ACM.

Gorday, E., Hester, P., Gutierrez, L., Naeve, J. A., Heile, M., Bahl, B., & Callaway, V. (2002, August). Home Networking with IEEE 802.15.4: A Developing Standard for Low-Rate Wireless Personal Area Networks, *IEEE Communications Magazine.*

Gu, T., Wang, X. H., Pung, H. K., & Zhang, D. Q. (2004). An Ontology-based Context Model in Intelligent Environments. In *Proceedings of Communication Networks and Distributed Systems Modeling and Simulation Conference.* San Diego.

Guijarro, L. (2007). Interoperability frameworks and enterprise architectures in e-government initiatives in Europe and the united states. *Government Information Quarterly*, *24*(1), 89–101..doi:10.1016/j.giq.2006.05.003

Guijarro, L. (2009). Semantic interoperability in e-Government initiatives [Dimensions of the efficiency of public-private partnership. Inzinerine Ekonomika-Engineering.]. *Computer Standards & Interfaces*, *1*(31), 174–180. doi:10.1016/j.csi.2007.11.011

Guijarro, L. (2005). Policy and practice in standards selection for e-government interoperability frameworks. In *Proc. of EGOV 2005 Conference*, pp. 163–173, Copenhaguen (Denmark).

Gutierrez, J. A., Naeve, M., Callaway, E., Bourgeois, M., Mitter, V., & Heile, B. (2001). IEEE 802.15.4: Developing standard for low-power low-cost Wireless Personal Area Networks. *IEEE Network*, (September/October): 2001.

Gutierrez, J. (2004, September). On the use of IEEE 802.15.4 to enable wireless sensor networks in building automation. In *Proceedings of the 15th IEEE International Symposium on Personal, Indoor and Mobile Radio Communications* (PIMRC, Vol. 3, pp. 1865-1869).

Hager, C., & Midkiff, S. (2003). An Analysis of Bluetooth Security Vulnerabilities. In *Proceedings of Wireless Communications and Networking Conference* (pp. 1825-1831). New Orleans, LA.

Hähnel, D., Burgard, W., Fox, D., Fishkin, K., & Philipose, M. (2003). *Mapping and Localization with RFID Technology*. Intel Corporation, 2003.

Ham, C. (2004). *Health Policy in Britain* (5th ed.). New York: Palgrave.

Han, J., Altman, R. B., Kumar, V., Mannila, H., & Pregibon, D. (2002). Emerging scientific applications in data mining. *Communications of the ACM*, *45*(8), 54–58. doi:10.1145/545151.545179

Han, I., Park, H., Jeong, Y., & Park, K. (2006). An Integrated Home Server for Communication, Broadcast Reception, and Home Automation. *IEEE Transactions on Consumer Electronics*, *52*(1), 104–109.

Hanak, D., Szijarto, G., & Takacs, B. (2007). A Mobile Approach to Ambient Assisted Living. Retrieved June 8, 2008, from http://www.cs.bme.hu/~dhanak/iadis_wac.pdf

Haque, M., & Ahamed, S. I. (2006). Security in Pervasive Computing: Current Status and Open Issues. *International Journal of Network Security*, *3*(3), 203–214.

Harrisson, D., & Laberge, M. (2002). Innovation, identities and resistence: The social construction of innovation. *Journal of Management Studies*, *39*(4), 497–521. doi:10.1111/1467-6486.00301

Hatami, A., & Pahlavan, K. (2005). A comparative performance evaluation of RSS-based positioning algorithms used in WLAN networks. In *Proc Wireless Communications and Networking Conference, 4*, 2331-2337.

Hayes, T. L., Pavel, M., Larimer, N., Tsay, I. A., & Nutt, J. (2007). Simultaneous assessment of multiple individuals. *IEEE Pervasive Computing / IEEE Computer Society [and] IEEE Communications Society*, *6*(1), 36–43. doi:10.1109/MPRV.2007.9

He, G. (Spring 2002). *Requirements for Security in Home Environments*. Paper presented at Residential and Virtual Home Environments – Seminar on Internetworking, HUT TML Course T-110.551.

Hedetniemi, S. M., Hedetniemi, S. H., & Liestman, A. (1988). A Survey of Gossiping and Broadcasting in Communication Networks. *Networks*, 18.

Heinzelman, W. R., Kulik, J., & Balakrishnan, H. (1999). Adaptive Protocols for Information Dissemination in Wireless Sensor Networks. In *Proc. ACM MobiCom '99*, Seattle, WA.

Heinzelman, W., Chandrakasan, A., & Balakrishnan (2000). Energy-Efficient Communication Protocol for Wireless Micro-Sensor Networks. In *Proc. of the 33rd Annual Hawaii International Conf. on System Sciences*, (pp. 3005- 3014).

Held, A., Buchholz, S., & Schill, A. (2002). Modelling of Context Information for Pervasive Computing Applications. In *Proceedings of the 6th World Multiconference on Systemics, Cybernetics and Informatics*. Orlando, FL.

Herzog, A., Shahmehri, N., Bednarski, A., Chisalita, I., Nordqvist, U., Saldamli, L., et al. (2001). Security Issues in E-Home Network and Software Infrastructures. In *Proceedings of the 3rd Conference on Computer Science and Systems Engineering in Linköping* (pp. 155-161). Norrköping, Sweden.

Hiertz, G., Max, S., Zhao, R., Denteneer, D., & Berlemann, L. (2007). *Principles of IEEE 802.11s*. Retrieved February 05, 2009 from http://user.cs.tu-berlin.de/~hornant/ieee_802_11s/ 04428715.pdf

Hill, S., Provost, F., & Volinsky, C. (2006). Network based marketing: Identifying likely adopters via consumer networks. *Statistical Science, 21*(2), 256–276. doi:10.1214/088342306000000222

HL7. (n.d.). *Final guide*. Retrieved from www.hl7.org

Hoblos, K. G. Staroswiecki, M., & Aitouche, A. (2000). *Optimal Design of Fault Tolerant Sensor Networks*. IEEE Int'l. Conf. Cont. Apps., Anchorage, AK, (pp. 467-72)

Holger, K., & Andreas, W. (2003). *A short Survey of Wireless Sensor Networks*. (TKN Technical Report) TKN-03-018, Berlin.

Home Gateway Initiative (HGI) (2006). Home Gateway Technical Requirements: Release 1.

Hong, D., Chiu, D. K. W., & Shen, V. Y. (2005). Requirements elicitation for the design of context-aware applications in a ubiquitous environment. In *Proceedings of the 7th international conference on Electronic commerce ICEC 05*. ACM Press. Jackson, J., & Murphy, P. (2006). Clusters in regional tourism: An Australian case. *Annals of Tourism Research, 33*(4), 1018–1035.

Hong, D., & Rappaport, S. (1986). Traffic model and performance analysis for cellular mobile radio telephone systems with prioritized and non prioritized handoff procedures. *IEEE Trans., VT-35*, 77–92.

Hong, X., & Liang, Q. *(2004). An Access-Based Energy Efficient Clustering Protocol for ad hoc Wireless Sensor Network. In* Proceedings of the 15th IEEE International Symposium on Personal, Indoor and Mobile Radio Communications, *(PIMRC 2004, Volume: 2. pp.1022-1026).*

Hou, T.-C., & Tsai, T.-J. (2001). An Access-Based Clustering Protocol for Multihop Wireless ad hoc Networks. *IEEE Journal on Selected Areas in Communications, 19*(7), 1201–1210. doi:10.1109/49.932689

Hsin, C., M. Liu (2006), "A Two-Phase Self-Monitoring Mechanism for Wireless Sensor Networks. *Journal of Computer Communications special issue on Sensor Networks, 29*(4), 462–476.

Huang, M.-C., Huang, J.-C., You, J.-C., & Jong, J.-G. (2007, November). The wireless sensor network for home-care system using ZigBee. [IIHMSP]. *IEEE Intelligent Information Hiding and Multimedia Signal Processing, 1*, 643–646.

Huff, S. M. (1998). Clinical data exchange standards and vocabularies for messages. *Journal pf American Medical Informatics Association, AMIA Annual fall Symposium Supplement*, 1998

IBM. (2003). *An Architectural Blueprint for Autonomic Computing*. IBM and Autonomic Computing. Retrieved from http://www.redbooks.ibm.com/redbooks/pdfs/sg246635.pdf

IDABC. Enterprise & Industry DG (2004a). *Architecture Guidelines for transEuropean Telematics Networks for Administrations, version 7.1*, Brussels.

IDABC. Enterprise & Industry DG (2004b). *European Interoperability Framework for pan-European e-government services, version 1.0*, Brussels.

IDABC. Enterprise DG (2002). *Architecture Guidelines for trans-European Telematics Networks for Administrations, version 6.1*, Brussels.

IEEE. 1073 (n.d.). *Standard for medical devices communications*. Retrieved from www.hipaanet.com

IEEE. 802.16d-2004.(2004).*Standard for Local and metropolitan area networks*. IEEE

IEEE. 802.16e-2005. (2005).*Standard for Local and metropolitan area networks (Amendment 2)*. IEEE

INHOME Project. (n.d.). *An Intelligent Interactive Services Environment for Assisted Living at Home*. Retrieved from http://www.ist-inhome.eu/inhome/Home.php

Intanagonwiwat, C. Estrin, D., & Gonvindan, R. (2001). *Impact of Network Density on Data Aggregation in Wireless Sensor Networks*. In Proc. IEEE ICDCS Conf.

Intanagonwiwat, C., Govindan, R., & Estrin, D. Heidemann, J., & Silva, F. (2003), "Directed Diffusion for Wireless Sensor Networking," IEEE/ACM Transactions on Networking, vol. 11, pp. 2-16

Interoperability definition and background. (2005). *Healthcare Information and Management Systems Society*.

Ioannou, K., Louvros, S., Panoutsopoulos, I., Kotsopoulos, S., & Karagiannidis, G. (2002). Optimizing the Handover Call Blocking Probability in Cellular Networks with High Speed Moving Terminals. *IEEE Communications Letters*, *6*(10). doi:10.1109/LCOMM.2002.802048

Iyer, R., & Kleinrock, L. (2003). *QoS Control for Sensor Networks*. Presented at the IEEE International Communications Conference (ICC'03), Anchorage, AK, May 11-15.

Jafari, R., Dabiri, F., Brisk, P., & Sarrafzadeh, M. (2005). CustoMed: A power optimized customizable and mobile medical monitoring and analysis system. In *Proceedings of ACM HCI Challenges in Health Assessment Workshop in Conjunction with Proceedings of the Conference on Human Factors in Computing Systems (CHI '05)*, Portland, OR.

Jea, D., & Srivastava, M. B. (2006). A remote medical monitoring and interaction system, In *Proceedings of the 4th International Conference on Mobile Systems, Applications, and Services (MobiSys '06)*, Uppsala, Sweden, June 2006.

Jeffrey, B., & Ringel, M. (1999). *Telemedicine and the Reinvention of Healthcare*. New York: McGraw-Hill.

Jennings, N. R., Faratin, P., Lomuscio, A. R., Parsons, S., Sierra, C., & Wooldridge, M. (2002). Automated negotiation: prospects, methods and challenges. *International Journal of Group Decision and Negotiation*, *10*(2), 199–215. doi:10.1023/A:1008746126376

Jeong, J., Chung, M., & Choo, H. (2006). Secure User Authentication Mechanism in Digital Home Network Environments. In Sha, E., Han, S.-K., Xu, C.-Z., Kim, M. H., Yang, L. T., & Xiao, B. (Eds.), *Embedded and Ubiquitous Computing* (pp. 345–354). Springer.

Jiang, L. Liu, D., & Yang, Bo. (2004). SMART HOME RESEARCH. In *Proceedings of the Third International Conference on Machine Learning and Cybernetics* (pp. 659-663). Shanghai.

Jin, M.-H., Yu, C.-H., Lai, H.-R., & Feng, M.-W. (2007). Zigbee positioning system for smart home application. [including Lecture Notes in Artificial Intelligence and Lecture Notes in Bioinformatics]. *Lecture Notes in Computer Science*, *4743*, 183–192. doi:10.1007/978-3-540-74767-3_20

Kalorama (2007). *Wireless Opportunities in Healthcare*. Kalorama Information.

Kangas, M. (Autumn 2002). *Authentication and Authorization in Universal Plug and Play Home Neworks*. Paper presented at Ad Hoc Mobile Wireless Networks – Research Seminar on Telecommunications Software, HUT TML – Course T-110.557.

Kaplan, H., Strauss, M., & Szegedy, M. *(1999), Just the fax—differentiating voice and fax phone lines using call billing data. In* Proceedings of the Tenth Annual ACM-SIAM Symposium on Discrete Algorithms *(pp. 935-936). Philadelphia, PA: Society for Industrial and Applied Mathematics.*

Karl, H., & Willig, A. (2003). *A Short Survey of Wireless Sensor Networks. (Technical Report)*. Telecommunication Networks Group, Technische Universität Berlin.

Kay, J., & Frolik, J. (2004). Quality of Service Analysis and Control for Wireless Sensor Networks. In *Proc. of the 21st International Conf. on Mobile Ad-Hoc and Sensor Systems* (MASS'04), pp. 359-368, Fort Lauderdale, FL.

KBSt. (2003). Standards and Architectures for e-Government Applications, version 2.0. Retrieved from http://www.kbst.bund.de/SAGA

KBsT. Federal Government Co-ordination and Advisory Agency (2005a*). SAGA-Standards and Architectures for e-Goverment Applications, version 2.1*, Schriftenreihe der KBSt 82.

KBsT. Federal Government Co-ordination and Advisory Agency (2005b). *DOMEA concept. Document Management and Electronic Archiving in Electronic Courses of Business, Organisational Concept 2.0*, Schriftenreihe der KBSt 74.

Khoussainov, R., & Patel, A. (2000). LAN security: problems and solutions for Ethernet networks. *Computer Standards & Interfaces, 22*(3), 191–202.

Kientz, J. A., Hayes, G. R., Westeyn, T. L., Starner, T., & Abowd, G. D. (2007). Pervasive computing and autism: assisting caregivers of children with special needs. *IEEE Pervasive Computing / IEEE Computer Society [and] IEEE Communications Society, 6*(1), 28–35. doi:10.1109/MPRV.2007.18

Kim, K. (2005). *Clinical Data Standards in Health Care: Five Case studies*. Sacramento: California Health Foundation.

Kim, G. W., Lee, D. G., Han, J. W., & Kim, S. W. (2007). Security Technologies Based on Home Gateway for Making Smart Home Secure. In Denko, M. (Eds.), *Emerging Directions in Embedded and Ubiquitous Computing* (pp. 124–135). Springer.

Kim, J., Kim, S., Kim, D., & Lee, W. *(2005). Low-Energy Localized Clustering: An Adaptive Cluster Radius Configuration Scheme for Topology Control in Wireless Sensor Networks. In* Proceedings of the IEEE 61st Vehicular Technology Conference, *(VTC 2005, Volume: 4. pp. 2546- 2550)*.

Kim, T. H., & Hong, S. (2003). Sensor Network Management Protocol for State-Driven Execution Environment. In *Proc. ICUC Conf*.

Kitsios, F., Angelopoulos, S., & Zannetopoulos, I. (2008). Innovation and e-government: an in depth overview on e-services. In Kotsopoulos, S., & Ioannou, K. (Eds.), *Heterogeneous Next Generation Networking: Innovations and Platform* (pp. 415–426). Hershey, PA: Idea Group Publishing.

Kitsios, F., Papadopoulos, T., & Angelopoulos, S. (2009). A roadmap to the introduction of pervasive Information Systems in healthcare. In Lazakidou, A., Siassiakos, K., & Ioannou, K. (Eds.), *Wireless Technologies for Ambient Assisted Living and Health Care: Systems and Applications*. Hershey, PA: Idea Group publishing.

Klemettinen, M., Mannila, H., & Toivonen, H. (1999). Rule discovery in telecommunication alarm data. *Journal of Network and Systems Management, 7*(4), 395–423. doi:10.1023/A:1018787815779

Kochkin, S., & MarkeTrak, V. (1999). Baby Boomers spur growth in potential market, but penetration rate declines. *Hear J., 52*(1), 33–48.

Kochkin, S., & MarkeTrak, V. (2000). Why my hearing aids are in the drawer: The consumers' perspective. *Hear J. Rev., 53*(2), 34–42.

Kochkin, S., & MarkeTrak, V. I. (2003). On the issue of value: Hearing aid benefit, price, satisfaction, and brand repurchase rates. *Hearing Rev., 10*(2), 12–26.

Kohn, L. T., & Corrigan, J. (2000). (eds). *To Err Is Human: Building a Safer Health System*. National Academy Press, 2000. Available at: http://books.nap.edu/books/0309068371/html/index.html

Komninos, N., & Douligeris, C. (2009). LIDF: Layered intrusion detection framework for ad-hoc networks. *Journal in Ad Hoc Networks, 7*(1), 171–182.

Komninos, N., Vergados, D., & Douligeris, C. (2007a). Authentication in a Layered Security Approach for Mobile Ad Hoc Networks. *Journal in Computers & Security, 26*(5), 373–380.

Komninos, N., Vergados, D., & Douligeris, C. (2007b). Detecting Unauthorized and Compromised Nodes in Mobile Ad-Hoc Networks. *Journal in Ad Hoc Networks, 5*(3), 289–298.

Komninos, N., Vergados, D., & Douligeris, C. (2007c). Multifold Authentication in Mobile Ad-Hoc Networks. *International Journal of Communication Systems, 20*(12), 1391–1406.

Komninos, N., & Mantas, G. (2009). Intelligent Authentication and Key Agreement Mechanism for WLAN in e-Hospital Applications. In Feng, J. (Ed.), *Wireless Networks: Research Technology and Applications). Nova Science Publishers Inc.*

Komninos, N., & Mantas, G. (2008). Efficient Group Key Agreement & Recovery in Ad Hoc Networks. In *Proceedings of the 2nd IET International Conference on Wireless, Mobile & Multimedia Networks* (pp. 25-28). Beijing, China.

Korkea-aho, M. (2000). Context-aware application surveys, available at: http://users.tkk.fi/~mkorkeaa/doc/context-aware.html

Kotanen, A., Hannikainen, M., Leppakoski, H., & Hamalainen, T. D. (2003). Experiments on local positioning with Bluetooth. In *Proc ITCC2003*, 2003, (pp. 297-303).

Kourouthanassis, E., P., Giaglis, M., G., & Vrechopoulos, A. P. (2007). Enhancing user experience through pervasive information systems: The case of pervasive retailing. *International Journal of Information Management, 27,* 319–335. doi:10.1016/j.ijinfomgt.2007.04.005

Kraus, S. (2001). *Strategic Negotiation in Multiagent Environments*. Cambridge, MA: The MIT Press.

Krco, S., & Delic, V. *(2003). Personal Wireless Sensor Network for Mobile Health Care Monitoring. In* Proceedings of IEEE TELSIKS 2003, *Serbia Montenegro, (pp.471-474).*

Krishnamachari, B. (2003). On the Complexity of Distributed Self-Configuration in Wireless Networks. Kluwer Academic Springer Publishers. *Telecommunication Systems, 22*(1-4), 33–59. doi:10.1023/A:1023426501170

Krishnamurthy, P., Kabara, J., & Anusas-amornkul, T. (2002). Security in Wireless Residential Networks. *IEEE Transactions on Consumer Electronics, 48*(1), 157–166.

Kropft, P. (2002). What is Pervasive Computing. Series of Lecture notes.

Kulik, J., Heinzelman, W. R., & Balakrishnan, H. (2002). Negotiation-base protocols for Disseminating Information in Wireless Sensor Networks. *Wireless Networks, 8,* 169–185. doi:10.1023/A:1013715909417

Kwang-Cheng Chen, J., & de Marca, R. B. (2008). *Wiley Mobile WiMAX.* New York: Wiley-IEEE Press. doi:10.1002/9780470723937

Kyriacou, E., Pavlopoulos, S., Koutsouris, D., Andreou, A., Pattichis, C., & Schizas, C. (2001). Multipurpose Health Care Telemedicine System. In *Proceedings of the 23rd Annual International Conference of the IEEE/EMBS*, Istanbul, Turkey.

Lassila, P. (2006). *Performance Challenges in Wireless Mesh Networks*.Retrieved January 15, 2009, from http://www.netlab.tkk.fi/tutkimus/abi/publ/ist2006-lassila.pdf

Latour, B. (2005). *Reassembling the Social: An Introduction to Actor-Network-Theory*. Oxford: Oxford University Press.

Latour, B., & Woolgar, S. (1986). *Laboratory Life: The Construction of Scientific Facts*. Chichester: Princeton University Press.

Latour, B. (1987). *Science in Action: How to Follow Scientists and Engineers through Society*. Milton Keynes: Open University Press.

Laxminarayan, S., & Istepanian, R. H. (2000). Unwired e-Med: The Next Generation of Wireless and Internet Telemedicine Systems. *IEEE Transactions on Information Technology in Biomedicine, 4,* 189–193.

Lee, K. J., & Seo, Y. H. (2006). A pervasive comparison shopping business model for integrating offline and online marketplace, Proceedings of the 8th international conference on Electronic commerce: The new e-commerce: innovations for conquering current barriers, obstacles and limitations to conducting successful business on the internet ICEC 06. ACM Press.

Lee, K. J., Ju, J., & Jeong, J. M. (2006). Mobile and pervasive commerce track: A payment & receipt business model in U-commerce environment, Proceedings of the 8th international conference on Electronic commerce: The new e-commerce: innovations for conquering current barriers, obstacles and limitations to conducting successful business on the internet ICEC 06. ACM Press.

Lethbridge-Cejku, M., Schiller, J. S., & Bernadel, L. (2002). Summary health statistics for U.S. adults: National Health Interview. *Vital Health Stat, 10*(222), 1–151.

Liang, L., Huang, L., Jiang, X., & Yao, Y. (2008). Design and implementation of wireless smart-home sensor network based on ZigBee protocol. In *Proceedings of the International Conference on Communications, Circuits and Systems* (ICCCAS), 2008, (pp. 434-438).

Liebowitz, J. (1988). *Expert System Applications to Telecommunications*. New York: John Wiley & Sons.

Lin, Y., Jan, I., Ko, P., Chen, Y., Wong, J., & Jan, G. (2004). A wireless PDA-based physiological monitoring system for patient transport. *IEEE Transactions on IT in Biomedicine, 8*(4), 439–447. doi:10.1109/TITB.2004.837829

Lin, C.-C., Chiu, M.-J., Hsiao, C. C., Lee, R. G., & Tsai, Y. S. (2006). AA Wireless Healthcare Service System for Elderly with Dementia. IEEE Trans. Infor. Technol. *BioMed, VOL., 10*(4), 696–704.

Lindsey, S., & Raghavendra, C. S. *(2002). PEGASIS: Power-Efficient Gathering in Sensor Information Systems. In* Proceedings of the IEEE Aerospace Conference.

Liu, W., Zhang, Y., Lou, W., & Fang, Y. (2004). Managing Wireless Sensor Network with Supply Chain Strategy. In *Proc. IEEE QSHINE Conf.*

López de Vergara, J. E., et al. *(2003). Semantic Management: Application of Ontologies for the Integration of Management Information Models. In* Proceedings of the Eighth IFIP/IEEE International Symposium on Integrated Network Management, *Colorado Springs.*

Louis Lee, W., Datta, A., & Cardell-Oliver, R. (2006). *WinMS: Wireless Sensor network-Management system, An Adaptive Policy-based Management for Wireless Sensor Networks* (Tech. Rep. UWA-CSSE-06-001), The University of Western Australia.

Lukkari, J., Korhonen, J., & Ojala, T. (2004). SmartRestaurant: mobile payments in context-aware environment, Proceedings of the 6th international conference on Electronic commerce ICEC 04. ACM Press. Mark Weisers Vision, retrieved February 3, 2005, from Ubiq Website: http://www.ubiq.com/hypertext/weiser/SciAmDraft3.html

Malotaux, M., van der Harst, G., Achtsivassilis, J., & Hahndiek, F. (2007). *Preparation for Update European Interoperability Framework 2.0: Final report.*

Mandellos, G., Lymperopoulos, D., Koukias, M., Tzes, A., Lazarou, N., & Vagianos, C. (2004). A Novel Mobile Telemedicine System for Ambulance Transport: Design and Evaluation. In *Proceedings of the 26th Annual International Conference of the IEEE EMBS*, San Francisco, pp. 3080-3083.

Mandl, K. D., Szolovits, P., & Kohane, I. S. (2001). Public standards and patients' control: How to keep electronic medical records accessible but private. *BMJ (Clinical Research Ed.), 322*, 283–287. doi:10.1136/bmj.322.7281.283

Mani, D., Drew, J., Betz, A., & Datta, P. *(1999), Statistics and data mining techniques for lifetime value modelin. In* Proceedings of the Fifth ACM SIGKDD International Conference on Knowledge Discovery and Data Mining *(pp. 94-103). New York, NY: ACM Press.*

Marti, S. Giuli, T. J. Lai, K., & M. Baker (2000), "Mitigating Routing Misbehavior in Mobile ad hoc Networks". In ACM Mobicom, pp. 255-265

Martin, J. E. T., Jones, M., & Shenoy, R. *(2003). Towards a Design Framework for Wearable Electronic Textiles. In* Proceedings of the 7th IEEE International Symposium on Wearable Computers, *(pp. 190-199).*

Martins, J. M., Amaral, F. T., Santos, D., Agiannidis, A., & Edge, M. (2000). The Custodian Tool: Simple Design of Home Automation Systems for People with Special Needs. In *Proceedings of the EIB Scientific Conference*, Munich, Germany.

Masand, B., Datta, P., Mani, D., & Li, B. (1999). CHAMP: A prototype for automated cellular churn prediction. [Apologize]. *Data Mining and Knowledge Discovery*, *3*(2), 219–225. doi:10.1023/A:1009873905876

Menezes, A. J., van Oorschot, P. C., & Vanstone, S. A. (1997). *Handbook of Applied Cryptography*. Boca Raton: CRC Press.

Mhatre, V., & Rosenberg, C. *(2004). Homogeneous Vs Heterogeneous Clustered Sensor Networks: a Comparative Study. In* Proceedings of the IEEE International Conference on Communications, *(Volume 6, pp. 3646-3651 Vol. 6)*

Milenkovic, A., Otto, C., & Jovanov, E. (2006). Wireless sensor networks for personal health monitoring: Issues and an implementation. *Computer Communications Journal*, *2006*, 2521–2533. doi:10.1016/j.comcom.2006.02.011

Min, R., et al. (2001). Low Power Wireless Sensor Networks. In *Proceedings of International Conference on VLSI Design*, Bangalore, India

MobiHealth Project. (n.d.). *Innovative gprs/umts mobile services for applications in healthcare*. Retrieved from http://www.mobihealth.org/.

Motorola White Paper on WiMAX. (2007). *D vs. E, Motorola*: The advantages of 802.16e over 802.16d. Motorola. Retrieved from http://www.motorola.com/staticfiles/Business/Solutions/Industry%20Solutions/Service%20Providers/Wireless%20Operators/Wireless%20Broadband/wi4%20WiMAX/_Document/StaticFile/WiMAX_E_vs._D__White_Paper.pdf

Nanda, P., & Fernades, R. C. (2007). Quality of service in Telemedicine. In *Proceedings of the First IEEE, International Conference on the Digital Society*, 2007.

Ng, H. S. (2006). Wireless Technologies for Telemedicine. *BT Technology Journal*, *24*(2). doi:10.1007/s10550-006-0050-9

Nishi, R., Morioka, H., & Sakurai, K. (2005). Trends and Issues for Security of Home-Network Based on Power Line Communication. In *Proceedings of the 19th International Conference on Advanced Information Networking and Applications* (pp. 655-660).

Noble, B., Satyanarayanan, M., Narayanan, D., Tilton, T., Flinn, J., & Walker, K. (1997). Agile application-aware adaptation for mobility, in: Proceedings of the 16th ACM SOSP.

Norman, D. A. (1999). *The Invisible Computer: Why Good Products Can Fail, the Personal Computer Is So Complex, and Information Appliances Are the Solution*. The MIT Press.

Noury, N., Virone, G., Barralon, P., Ye, J., Rialle, V., & Demongeot, J. (2003). New trends in health smart homes. In *Proceedings of the Healthcom conference*, (pp. 118-127).

OECD. Organisation for Economic Co-operation and Development. (2000). Annual Report 2000. Retrieved from http://www.oecd.org/dataoecd/30/59/1842666.pdf

OECD. Organisation for Economic Co-operation and Development. (2003). *The e-Government Imperative*, OECD e-Government Studies, France.

Orwat, C., Graefe, A., & Faulwasser, T. (2008). Towards pervasive computing in health care – A literature review. *BMC Medical Informatics and Decision Making*, *8*(26).

Papadopoulos, T., & Merali, Y. (2009). Stakeholder dynamics during process innovation implementation in healthcare: Lean Thinking in a hospital of UK National Health Service. *International Journal of Healthcare Technology and Management*, *10*(4/5), 303–324..doi:10.1504/IJHTM.2009.030453

Paruchuri, V., Durresi, A., & Ramesh, M. (2008). Securing Powerline Communications. In *Proceedings of the IEEE International Symposium on Power Line Communications and Its Applications* (pp. 64-69). Jeju city, Jeju Island.

Passos, R. M., Coelho, C. J. N., Loureiro, A. A. F., & Mini, R. A. F. (2005). Dynamic Power Management in Wireless Sensor Networks: An Application-Driven Approach. In *Proc. of the 2nd Annu. Conference on Wireless On-demand Network Systems and Services* (WONS '05), (pp. 109 – 118)

Pattichis, C., Kyriacou, E., Voskarides, S., Pattichis, M., Istepanian, R., & Schizas, C. (2002). Wireless Telemedicine Systems: An Overview. *IEEE Antennas and Propagation, 44*(2), 143–153. doi:10.1109/MAP.2002.1003651

Pavlopoulos, S., Kyriacou, E., Berler, A., Dembeyiotis, S., & Koutsouris, D. (1998). Novel emergency telemedicine system based on wireless communication technology—AMBULANCE. *IEEE Transactions on Information Technology in Biomedicine, 2*(4), 261–267. doi:10.1109/4233.737581

Perillo, M., & Heinzelman, W. B. (2003). Providing Application QoS through Intelligent Sensor Management. In *Proc. IEEE SNPA Conf.*

Perrig, A., et al. (2004). Security in wireless sensor networks," Communications of the ACM (CACM), *Wireless sensor networks, Special Issue: Wireless sensor networks, 47*(6), 53-57.

Pike, R., Presotto, D., Dorward, S., Flandrena, B., Thompson, K., Trickey, H., & Winterbottom, P. (1995). Plan 9 from Bell Labs. *Computing Systems, 8*(3), 221–254.

Pohl, K., & Sikora, E. (2005). Overview of the Example Domain: Home Automation. In Pohl, K., Böckle, G., & van der Linden, F. J. (Eds.), *Software Product Line Engineering Foundations, Principles and Techniques* (pp. 39–52). New York: Springer.

Prince, F., Corriveau, H., Hebert, R., & Winter, D. A. (1997). Gait in the elderly. *Gait & Posture, 5*, 128–135. doi:10.1016/S0966-6362(97)01118-1

Rajaraman, R. (2002). Topology Control and Routing in ad hoc Networks: a Survey. *ACM SIGACT News, 33*(2), 60–73. doi:10.1145/564585.564602

Rajaravivarma, V., Yang, Y., & Yang, T. (2003). An Overview of Wireless Sensor Network and Applications. In *Proc. of the 35th Southeastern Symposium on System Theory*, (pp. 432-436).

Ramanathan, N., Kohler, E., & Estrin, D. (2005). Towards a Debugging System for Sensor Networks. *International Journal of Network Management, 15*(4), 223–234. doi:10.1002/nem.570

Ramanathan, N., & Yarvis, M. (2005). A Stream-oriented Power Management Protocol for Low Duty Cycle Sensor Network Applications. In Proc. IEEE EmNetS-II Workshop

Rasid, M., & Woodward, B. (2005). Bluetooth Telemedicine Processor for Multichannel Biomedical Signal Transmission via Mobile Cellular Networks. *IEEE Transactions on Information Technology in Biomedicine, 9*(1). doi:10.1109/TITB.2004.840070

Ricquebourg, V., Menga, D., Durand, D., Marhic, B., Dalahoche, L., & Logé, C. (2006). The Smart Home Concept: our immediate future. In *Proceedings of the 1st IEEE International Conference on E-Learning in Industrial Electronics.*

Romer, K., & Mattern, F. (2004). *The Design Space of Wireless Sensor Networks* (pp. 54–61). IEEE Wireless Communications.

Roset, S., Murad, U., Neumann, E., Idan, Y., & Pinkas, G. *(1999), Discovery of fraud rules for telecommunications—challenges and solutions. In* Proceedings of the Fifth ACM SIGKDD International Conference on Knowledge Discovery and Data Mining*; pp.409-413. New York: ACM Press.*

Rosset, S., Neumann, E., & Eick, U., & Vatnik. (2003). Customer lifetime value models for decision support. *Data Mining and Knowledge Discovery, 7*(3), 321–339. doi:10.1023/A:1024036305874

Rothenberg, J., Botterman, M., & van Oranje-Nassau, C. (2008). *Towards a Dutch Interoperability Framework: Recommendations to the Forum Standaardisatie.* RAND Corporation.

Roussos, G. (2003). Appliance design for pervasive computing. *IEEE Pervasive Computing / IEEE Computer Society [and] IEEE Communications Society*, *2*(4), 75–77.

Ruiz, L. B., Braga, T. R. M., Silva, A., Assuncao, H. P., Nogueira, J. M. S., & Loureiro, A. A. F. (2005). On the Design of a Self- Managed Wireless Sensor Network. *Communications Magazine, IEEE*, *43*(8), 95–102. doi:10.1109/MCOM.2005.1497559

Ruiz, L. B., Nogueira, J. M., & Loureiro, A. A. F. (2003). MANNA: A Management Architecture for Wireless Sensor Networks. *IEEE Communications Magazine*, *41*(2), 116–125. doi:10.1109/MCOM.2003.1179560

Ruiz, L. B., Silva, F. A., Braga, T. R. M., Nogueira, J. M. S., & Loureiro, A. A. F. (2004). On Impact of Management in Wireless Sensors Networks. In *Proc. of the 9th IEEE/ IFIP Network Operations and Management Symposium* (NOMS' 04) vol. 1, pp. 657 - 670, Seoul, Korea

Ruiz, L. B., Siqueira, I. G., Oliveira, L. B., Wong, H. C., Nogueira, J. M. S., & Loureiro, A. A. F. (2004). Fault Management in Event-Driven Wireless Sensor Networks. In *Proc. ACM MSWiM Conf*. Retrieved from http://telegraph.cs.berkeley.edu/tinydb/tinydb.pdf, 2005.

Ruta, M., Noia, T. D., Sciascio, E. D., Piscitelli, G., & Scioscia, F. (2007). Session M5: e-business systems and applications: RFID meets bluetooth in a semantic based u-commerce environment, Proceedings of the ninth international conference on Electronic commerce ICEC 07. ACM Press.

Sadtler, C., Crabtree, B., Cotignola, D., & Michel, P. (2004). *Patterns: Broker Interactions for Intra- and Inter-enterprise* (pp. 47–53). International Technical Support Organization.

Salaur, L. (2005*). Building a Commodity Location-based Service at Botanic Garden of University of Freiburg*, (Master Thesis), University of Freiburg.

Salvi, A. B., & Sahai, S. (2002). Dial m for money, Proceedings of the 2nd international workshop on Mobile commerce WMC 02. ACM Press.

Sargeant, P. (2008). *White Paper on WiMAX*: The Promise of WiMAX. *Motorola*. Retrieved from http://www.motorola.com/staticfiles/Business/B2B_Internationalization_Patni/_Documents/White%20Papers/Static%20Files/The_Promise_of_WiMAX_WP.pdf?pLibItem=1&keywords=White%20papers&localeId=252.

Sarker, S., Sarker, S., & Sidirova, A. (2006). Understanding business process change failure: an actor-network perspective. *Journal of Management Information Systems*, *23*(1), 51–86. doi:10.2753/MIS0742-1222230102

Sasisekharan, R., Seshadri, V., & Weiss, S. (1996). Data mining and forecasting in large-scale telecommunication networks. *IEEE Expert*, *11*(1), 37–43. doi:10.1109/64.482956

Scheermesser, M., Kosow, H., Rashid, A., & Holtmann, C. (2008). User acceptance of pervasive computing in healthcare: Main findings of two case studies. Second International Conference on Pervasive Computing.

Schilit, B. N., Adams, N., & Want, R. (1994). Context-aware computing applications, In IEEE Workshop on Mobile Computing Systems and Applications, pp. 85-90, Santa Cruz, CA, US.

Schmalstieg, D., & Reitmayr, G. (2005). The World as a User Interface: Augmented Reality for Ubiquitous Computing. Central European Multimedia and Virtual Reality Conference 2005 (CEMVRC 2005), Prague, Czech Republic.

Schurgers, C., Tsiatsis, V., Ganeriwal, S., & Srivastava, M. (2002). Optimizing Sensor Networks in the Energy-Latency-Density Design Space. *IEEE Transactions on Mobile Computing*, *1*(1). doi:10.1109/TMC.2002.1011060

Schurgers, C., Tsiatsis, V., Ganeriwal, S., & Srivastava, M. (2002). Topology Management for Sensor Networks: Exploiting Latency and Density. In *Proceedings of MOBIHOC'02*, Lausanne, Switzerland: ACM.

Schwarz, V., Huber, A., & Tüchler, M. (2005). *Accuracy of a Commercial UWB 3D Location/Tracking System and its Impact on LT Application Scenarios.* 2005 IEEE International Conference on Ultra-Wideband.

Schwiderski-Grosche, S., Tomlinson, A., Goo, S. K., & Irvine, J. M. (2004). Security Challenges in the Personal Distributed Environment. In *Proceedings of IEEE 60ᵗʰ Vehicular Technology Conference.* Los Angeles.

SFMT. (2003). *Structured Architecture for Medical Business Activities (SAMBA).* Swedish Federation for Medical Informatics.

Shade, B. (2001). Increased Productivity Through E-Manufacturing, by Cahners Business Information.

Shafer, S., Krumm, J., Brumitt, B., Meyers, B., Czerwinski, M., & Robbins, D. (1998). *The new easyliving project at microsoft research.* Gaithersburg, Maryland: In DARPA / NIST Smart Spaces Workshop.

Shah, R. C., & Rabaey, J. M. (2002). Energy Aware Routing for Low Energy Ad Hoc Senso Networks. In *Proceedings of IEEE Wireless Communications and Networking Conference* (WCNC), Orland, FL

Shen, C. Srisathapornphat, C., & Jaikaeo, C. (2001). *Sensor Information Networking Architecture and Applications.* IEEE Personal Communication. (pp. 52-59).

Shi, E., & Perrig, A. (2004). *Designing Secure Sensor Networks* (pp. 38–43). IEEE Wireless Communications.

Siafakas, G. (2008). *Healthcare oriented smart houses for elderly or disabled persons. MSc thesis.* Department of Informatics & Telecommunications, TEI of Larissa (in collaboration with Staffordshire University, UK).

Silber, D. (2003). The *case for eHealth. Presented at the European Commission's high-level conference on eHealth May 22/23*

Sinha, A., & Chandrakasan, A. (2001). Dynamic power management in wireless sensor networks. *Design and Test of Computers, IEEE, 18*(2), 62–74. doi:10.1109/54.914626

Song, H. Kim, D. Lee, K., & Sung, J. (2005). Upnp-Based Sensor Network Management Architecture. In *Proc. ICMU Conf.*

Sourouni, A.-M. Lampathaki, F., Mouzakitis, S., Charalabidis, Y., & Askounis, D. (2008). Paving the way to egovernment transformation: interoperability registry infrastructure development. In *Proc. of EGOV 2008 Conference*, pp. 340-351, Turin (Italy).

Srinivasan, P. (2007). Store and Forward Applications in Telemedicine for Wireless IP Based Networks. *Journal of Networks, 2*(6).

Stajano, F. (2002). *Security for Ubiquitous Computing.* Wiley press. doi:10.1002/0470848693

Stallings, W. (2000). *Network Security Essentials, Applications and Standards.* Upper Saddle River, NJ: Prentice Hall.

Stallings, W. (2005). *Cryptography and Network Security Principles and Practices.* Upper Saddle River, NJ: Prentice Hall.

Stavroulakis, P. (2007). *TErrestrial Trunked RAdio - TETRA: A Global Security Tool (Signals and Communication Technology.* Berlin, Germany: Springer.

Stefanov, D. H., Bien, Z., & Bang, W.-C. (2004). The smart house for older persons and persons with physical disabilities: structure, technology arrangements, and perspectives. *IEEE Transactions on Neural Systems and Rehabilitation Engineering, 12*(2), 228–250. doi:10.1109/TNSRE.2004.828423

Sun, S., Su, C., & Ju, T. (2005). A study of consumer value-added services in mobile commerce: focusing on domestic cellular phone companies in Taiwan, China, Proceedings of the 7th international conference on Electronic commerce ICEC 05. ACM Press.

Sungmee Park, K. M., & Jayaraman, S. *(2002). The Wearable Motherboard: a Framework for Personalized Mobile Information Processing (PMIP). In* Proceedings of 39th ACM/IEEE Design Automation Conference, *(pp. 170- 174).*

Swan, J., & Scarbrough, H. (2005). The politics of networked innovation. *Human Relations, 58*, 913–943. doi:10.1177/0018726705057811

Teger, S., & Waks, D. (2002). *System Dynamics Inc* (pp. 114–119). End-User Perspectives on Home Networking. IEEE Communications Magazine.

The Greek e-GIF. (2008). *The Greek e-GIF*. Retrieved from http://egif.epu.ntua.gr

Thomas, R. K., & Sandhu, R. (2004). Models, Protocols, and Architectures for Secure Pervasive Computing: Challenges and Research Directions. In *Proceedings of the Second IEEE Annual Conference on Pervasive Computing and Communications Workshops*.

Tilak, S., Abu-Ghazaleh, N., & Heinzelman, W. (2002). A taxonomy of Wireless Micro-senor Network Models. *ACM SIGMOBILE. Mobile Computing and Communications Review, 6*(2), 28–36. doi:10.1145/565702.565708

Tilak, S. Abu-Ghazaleh, N. B., & Heinzelman, W. (2002). Infrastructure tradeoffs for sensor networks. In Proc. *ACM WSNA Conf.*

Tolle, G., & Culler, D. (2005). Design of an Application-Cooperative Management System for Wireless Sensor Networks. In *Proc. EWSN*

Tolmie, P., Pycock, J., Diggins, T., MacLean, A., & Karsenty, A. (2002). *Unremarkable Computing*. Xerox Research Centre Europe.

Townsend, C., & Arms, S. (2004). *Wireless Sensor Networks: Principles and Applications*. Williston, VT: Micro Strain Inc.

Turon, M. (2005). Mote-View: A Sensor Network Monitoring and Management Tool," in Proc. IEEE EmNetS-II Workshop

Tynan, R., Marsh, D., O'Kane, D., & O'Hare, G. M. P. (2005). Agents for wireless sensor network power management. In *Proc of International Conference workshops on Parallel Processing* (ICPP '05) Workshops, (pp. 413-418).

Valtchev, D., & Frankov, I., & ProSyst Software AG. (2002). Service Gateway Architecture for a Smart Home. *IEEE Communications Magazine*, 126–132.

van de Kar, E. (2005). The design of a mobile information and entertainment service on a UMTS testbed, Proceedings of the 7th international conference on Electronic commerce ICEC 05. New York: ACM Press.

Varshney, U. (2006). Patient monitoring using infrastructure oriented wireless LANs. *International Journal of Electronic Healthcare, 2*(2), 149–163.

Varshney, U. (2006). Using wireless technologies in healthcare. *Int. Journal on Mobile Communications, 4*(3), 354–368.

Varshney, U. (2005). Pervasive healthcare: applications, challenges and wireless solutions. *Communications of the AIS* 16.

Viera, M. A. M. Viera, L. F. M. Ruiz, L. B. Loureiro, A. A. F. Fernandes, A. O. Nogueira, J. M. S. (2003). Scheduling Nodes in Wireless Sensor Networks: A Voronoi Approach. In *Proc. of the 28th Annual IEEE International Conference on Local Computer Networks* (LCN '03), (pp.423 – 429), 20-24.

Vitkauskaitė, E., & Gatautis, R. (2008*). E-Government interoperability issues in Lithuania. In Proc of 8th International Conference on Electronic Business*, pp. 80–87, Hong Kong.

Von Huizen, G. (2003). *Time to get on the bus: A standards-based foundation for the connected enterprise* (pp. 8–15). Dallas: Business Integration Journal, Business Integration Journal Press.

W3C (n.d.). *Technical Reports and Publications*. Retrieved from www.w3.org

Wade, E., & Asada, H. (2007). Conductive-Fabric Garment for a Cable-Free Body Area Network. *IEEE Pervasive Computing / IEEE Computer Society [and] IEEE Communications Society, 6*(1), 52–58. doi:10.1109/MPRV.2007.8

Wan, C.-Y., Eisenman, S. B., & Campbell, A. T. (2003). CODA: COngestion Detection and Avoidance in Sensor Networks. In *Proc. ACM SenSys Conf.*

Wan, C.-Y., Eisenman, S. B., Campbell, A. T., & Crowcrof, J. (2005). Siphon: Overload Traffic Management using Multi-radio Virtual Sinks in Sensor Networks. In *Proc. ACM SenSys Conf.*

Wang, H., Cao, J. and Zhang, Y. (2007). *Access control management for ubiquitous computing. Future Generation Computer Systems*, accepted for publication in Future Generation Computer Systems journal.

Wang, H., Cao, J., & Zhang, Y. (2006). Ubiquitous computing environments and its usage access control. In *Proceedings of the First International Conference on Scalable Information Systems, INFOSCALE*. Hong Kong: ACM Press.

Wang, J., Yang, Y., & Yurcik, W. (2005). Secure Smart Environments: Security Requirements, Challenges and Experiences in Pervasive Computing. In *Proceedings of NSF Pervasive Computing Infrastructure Experience Workshop.*

Wang, Q., Shin, W., Liu, X., Zeng, Z., Oh, C., Al-Shebli, B., et al. (2006). I-Living: An open system architecture for assisted living. In *Proceedings of the IEEE SMC 2006.*

Wang, Y., van de Kar, E., & Meijer, G. (2005). Designing mobile solutions for mobile workers: lessons learned from a case study. In *Proceedings of the 7th international conference on Electronic commerce ICEC 05.* New York: ACM Press.

Warneke, B., & Pister, K. S. J. (2002, September). MEMS for Distributed Wireless Sensor Networks. In *Proc. of 9th International Conf. on Electronics, Circuits and Systems.* Dubrovnik, Croatia.

Watson, R. T. (2000). U-commerce: the ultimate. *Ubiquity, 1*(33). ACM Press.

Watson, R. T. (2004). *Data management: Databases and Organizations 4th edition.* New York: Willey press.

Wei, C., & Chiu, I. (2002). Turning telecommunications call details to churn prediction: A data mining approach. *Expert Systems with Applications, 23*(2), 103–112. doi:10.1016/S0957-4174(02)00030-1

Weise, T., & Geihs, K. (2006). *DGPF - An Adaptable Framework for Distributed Multi- Objective Search Algorithms Applied to the Genetic Programming of Sensor Networks.* The 2nd International Conference on Bioinspired Optimization Methods and their Applications, Ljubljana, Slovenia

Weiser, M. (1991). The computer for the 21st century. *Scientific American, 265*(3), 66–75. doi:10.1038/scientificamerican0991-94

Weiser, M. (1996). *Open House, Web magazine of the Interactive Telecommunications Program of New York University.* Appeared in March, 1996 ITP, Review 2.0. http://www.itp.tsoa.nyu.edu/~review/

Weiss, G. M., & Provost, F. (2003). Learning when training data are costly: The effect of class distribution on tree induction. *Journal of Artificial Intelligence Research, 19*, 315–354.

Weiss, G., & Hirsh, H. *(1998), Learning to predict rare events in event sequences. In R. Agrawal & P. Stolorz (Eds.),* Proceedings of the Fourth International Conference on Knowledge Discovery and Data Mining *(pp. 359-363). Menlo Park, CA: AAAI Press.*

Welsh, M., & Mainland, G. (2004). Programming Sensor Networks Using Abstract Regions. In *Proc. USENIX NSDI Conf.*

White Paper. (2006). 802.11n: Next-Generation Wireless LAN Technology. Retrieved from http://www.broadcom.com/docs/WLAN/802_11n-WP100-R.pdf

WHO (World Health Organization). Retrieved from http://www.who.int/mediacentre/factsheets/fs282/en/

Willis, S., & Helal, S. (2005). *A Passive RFID Information Grid for Location and Proximity Sensing for the Blind User.* (Technical Report number TR04-009), University of Florida.

Wireless Short Message Service. (2007). *The International Engineering Consortium*. Web OriForum Tutorials.

Wohlwend, H. (2001). *An E-Factory Vision*. 2nd European Advanced Equipment Control/Advance Process Control Conf., April 18-20.

WSAT. Web Service Architecture Team. (2001). *Web Services Conceptual Architecture, IBM*. Retrieved from http://www.ibm.com/software/solutions/webservices/pdf/wsca.pdf

Xu, Y. *Bien, S. Mori, Y. Heidemann, J., & Estrin, D. (2003).* Topology Control Protocols to Conserve Energy in Wireless ad hoc Networks *(Technical Report 6), University of California, Los Angeles, Center for Embedded Networked Computing*

Xu, Y., Heidemann, J., & Estrin, D. *(2005). Geography-Informed Energy Conservation for ad hoc Routing. In* Proceedings of the 7th annual international conference on Mobile computing and networking. *Rome, Italy. (pp. 70 – 84).*

Xueliang, X., Cheng, T., & Xingyuan, F. (2007). A health care system based on PLC and Zigbee. In *Proceedings of the International Conference on Wireless Communications Networking and Mobile Computing* (WiCom), (pp. 3063-3066).

Yamasaki, R., Ogino, A., Tamaki, T., Uta, T., Matsuzawa, N., & Kato, T. (2005). TDOA location system for IEEE 802.11b WLAN. In *Proc Wireless Communications and Networking Conference, 4*, 2338-2343.

Yau, S. S., Gupta, S. K. S., Karim, F., Ahamed, S. I., Wang, Y., & Wang, B. (2003). Smart Classroom: Enhancing Collaborative Learning Using Pervasive Computing Technology. In *Proceedings of the 6th WFEO World Congress on Engineering Education and the 2nd ASEE International Colloquium on Engineering Education* (ASEE 2003).

Ye, M. Li, C., Chen, G., & Wu, J. (2005). EECS: An Energy Efficient Clustering Scheme in Wireless Sensor Networks". 24th IEEE International Performance, Computing, and Communications Conference, (IPCCC 2005). pp. 535- 540.

Ying, Z., & Debao, X. (2005). Mobile Agent-based Policy Management for Wireless Sensor Networks. *In Proc. IEEE WCNM Conf.*

Yoneki, E., & Bacon, J. (n.d.). *A survey of Wireless Sensor Network technologies: research trends and middleware's role.* (Technical Report, no: 646), UCAM ¡CL¡TR¡646,

Younis, M., et al (2003). Architecture for Efficient Monitoring and Management of Sensor Networks, *(MMNS, LNCS)*

Yu, Y., Govindan, R., & Estrin, D. (2001). *Geographical and Energy Aware Routing: A Recursive Data Dissemination Protocol for Wireless Sensor Networks.* UCLA Computer Science Department UCLA-CSD TR-01-0023

Yun-kyung, L., Hong-il, J., & Hyung-kyu, L. (2006). Secure Biometric Recognition method in Home Network. In *Proceedings of the 32nd Annual Conference of the IEEE Industrial Electronics Society* (pp. 3745-3749). Paris.

Zahariadis, T. B. (2003). *Home Networking Technologies and Standards*. New York: Artech House.

Zander, J. Kim, S.-L. (2001). *Radio Resource Management for Wireless Networks*. Norwood, MA: Artech House.

Zhang, Y., Luo, J., & Hu, H. (2006). *Wireless Mesh Networking: Architectures, Protocols and Standards*. Boca Raton, FL: Auerbach Publications.

Zhang, J., Kulasekere, E. C., Premaratne, K., & Bauer, P. H. (2001). Resource Management of Task Oriented Distributed Sensor Networks. In *Proc. IEEE ICASSP Conf.*

Zhao, Y. J., Govindan, R., & Estrin, D. (2002). Residual Energy Scan for Monitoring Sensor Networks. In Proc. IEEE WCNC Conf.

Ziegler, M., Mueller, W., Schaefer, R., & Loeser, C. (2005). Secure Profile Management in Smart Home Networks. In *Proceedings of the 16th International Workshop on Database and Expert Systems Applications*. Copenhagen, Denmark.

About the Contributors

Athina Lazakidou currently works at the University of Peloponnese, Department of Nursing in Greece as Lecturer in Health Informatics, and at the Hellenic Naval Academy as a Visiting Lecturer in Informatics. She worked as a Visiting Lecturer at the Department of Computer Science at the University of Cyprus (2000-2002) and at the Department of Nursing at the University of Athens (2002-2007). She did her undergraduate studies at the Athens University of Economics and Business (Greece) and received her BSc in Computer Science in 1996. In 2000, she received her Ph.D. in Medical Informatics from the Department of Medical Informatics, University Hospital Benjamin Franklin at the Free University of Berlin, Germany. She is also an internationally known expert in the field of computer applications in health care and biomedicine, with six books and numerous papers to her credit. She was also Editor of the "Handbook of Research on Informatics in Healthcare and Biomedicine" and "Handbook of Research on Distributed Medical Informatics and E-Health", the best authoritative reference sources for information on the newest trends and breakthroughs in computer applications applied to health care and biomedicine. Her research interests include health informatics, e-Learning in medicine, software engineering, graphical user interfaces, (bio)medical databases, clinical decision support systems, hospital and clinical information systems, electronic medical record systems, telematics, and other web-based applications in health care and biomedicine.

Konstantinos Siassiakos holds a diploma (1995) of Electrical and Computer Engineer from the Department of Electrical and Computer Engineering Studies, University of Patras, Greece, and a Ph.D. (2001) diploma from the Department of Electrical and Computer Engineering, National Technical University of Athens, Greece. Dr. K. Siassiakos currently works as visiting lecturer at the Technological Educational Institute of Chalkida, at the University of Piraeus in Greece and Hellenic Naval Academy. Also He currently works as Special Scientific Staff at the Civil Service Staffing Council (ASEP). He has worked as an IT consultant at Ministry of Development (General Secretariat of Industry), Ministry of National Education and Religious Affairs (General Secretariat for Adult Education), Ministry of Health and Social Solidarity and as a researcher at the Department of Technology Education & Digital Systems, University of Piraeus. His research interests include logistics management, electronic customer relationship management systems, applied cryptography, management information systems, web-based learning systems, educational technologies, human computer interaction, quality assurance, business process reengineering, and e-government technologies.

* * *

Georgios Mantas received his Diploma in Electrical and Computer Engineering from the University of Patras, in 2005. In 2008, he obtained the Master of Science in Information Networking offered by Carnegie Mellon University in collaboration with Athens Information Technology (AIT). Since 2008, Mr. Mantas has been pursuing his PhD in the Department of Electrical and Computer Engineering at the University of Patras. His research areas of interest include authentication, integrity, key agreement, routing security in wired and wireless networks, smart cards and biometrics security. Mr. Mantas has knowledge of various programming languages and simulation tools. Mr. Mantas is a member of the Technical Chamber of Greece and IEEE.

Dimitrios K. Lymberopoulos was born in Tripolis, Greece, in 1956. He received the Electrical Engineering diploma and the Ph.D. degree from the University of Patras, Patras, Greece, in 1980 and 1988, respectively. He is currently a Professor in the Department of Electrical and Computer Engineering, University of Patras, where he lectures on communication systems, multimedia communications, and telemedicine services. Since 1982, he has been involved as a Technical Supervisor in various research projects funded by the Greek Government, the European Union, the Greek Telecommunication Organization, and the major Greek Telecommunication industries. He has authored or co-authored over 130 papers in international journals, conferences and technical reports. His research interests include medical communication protocols, telemedicine, context awareness, ontologies in the medical information domain, next generation networks, web multimedia services, data management in medical applications, teleworking (telemedicine) development platforms, and medical communication networks. Prof. Lymberopoulos is a member of the Technical Chamber of Greece and the Greek Society of Electrical and Mechanical Engineers.

Nikos Komninos is currently an Assistant Professor in Applied Cryptography and Network Security, member of the Algorithms and Security Group at Athens Information Technology (affiliate of Carnegie Mellon University) and Instructor of the *Applied Cryptography, ICT Security* and *Computer & Network Security* postgraduate courses. Komninos has over fifteen years of R&D experience in the academia and industry working on the evaluation, analysis and development of practical secure communication systems. His current research areas of interest include authentication, key agreement and intrusion detection in ad hoc networks, design and evaluation of efficient encryption algorithms, attack analysis of cryptographic protocols, transport / network layer security, smart cards and biometrics security. Dr. Komninos has written over 50 journals and conference publications, patents, books and technical reports in the information security research area. He has been invited as technical program committee, guest editor in international conferences and journals and speaker with honours in the field. Dr Kominos is also senior member in various international societies (IEEE, ACM). His full CV can be found in http://www.ait.edu.gr/ait_web_site/faculty/nkom/komninos.html.

Kostas Voudouris, holds a PhD degree on wireless telecommunication systems, from the University of Bradford, U.K. His work experience is extended in the field of telecommunications, initially, as an academic postdoctoral research fellow in the University of Kent at Canterbury, UK (1990-1993), then as a telecoms expert within the incumbent telecom operator in Greece –OTE (1996-2000). In 2000 he joined the Greek telecom regulator (EETT) and the next year he was appointed as advisor to the Deputy-Minister of Transports and Telecommunications. From Oct. 2001 to Sep. 2004 he served as Embassy Counsellor, within the Permanent Representation of Greece to the European Union, responsible (attaché) for Telecommunications, Information Society & Postal Services. Currently, he holds the position of Associate Professor on Wireless Telecommunication Systems within the Department of Electronics of the Technological Institution (TEI) of Athens – Greece. Dr. Voudouris has published over 50 scientific papers in international journals and conferences. From March 2004 until Sept. 2006, Dr. Voudouris served as member of the Management Board of the European Network and Information Security Agency (ENISA). Dr. Voudouris, chaired the Council Working Party on Telecommunications & Information Society Services, during Greek Presidency, 1st semester 2003. From January 1st 2008 he is REWIND's project coordinator an FP7 ICT project funded directly by the EU, involving six (6) high-tech companies from three (3) different countries, with budget of 5,5M for three (3) years. Furthermore he scientifically leads the TEI of Athens research group, in NexGenMiliwave project within the concept of Corallia Cluster.(more info at www.ee.teiath.gr/tea).

Andreas Rigas received his diploma in Applied Physics with major on Telecommunications from the University of Ioannina in 2000. He was also awarded an MSc in Mobile and Satellite Communications from the University of Surrey in 2001 and an MBA with focus on Marketing & Strategy from the Athens University of Economics and Business in 2010. Andreas has worked in the past as a Telecommunications Engineer for Space Hellas S.A. and Siemens Hellas S.A., where he was involved in various mobile telephony and satellite communications projects in Greece, Germany and the United States. He is currently working for OTE S.A. in Wireless & Satellite Communications Laboratory and he is involved in various European and national research projects.

Stamatios Perdikouris received his BEng in Electronics Engineering from the Technological Educational Institute of Crete Department of Electronics, at 2004 and holds an M.Phil in WLAN Embedded Systems from the Brunel University of England (Department of Electronics & Computer Engineering (ECE)) since 2005. Mr. Perdikouris worked as an external partner at Intracom S.A at the time of his M.Phil research and especially he involved in HIPERLAN/2 wireless protocol MAC research and ARM microprocessor architecture. Since 2006 he has been working at the Wireless & Satellite Communications Research Lab of OTE S.A and participates in several European and National research projects.

George Agapiou received the Diploma in Electrical Engineering from the University of Louisville, Kentucky, in 1985, and the M.S. and Ph.D. degrees in Electrical Engineering from the Georgia Institute of Technology, USA in 1987 and 1991, respectively. He worked at the companies Philip Morris, USA at Louisville, in ANCO S.A., Greece and from 1996 as Telecomm Engineer in OTE. He has participated in various FP6, FP7, IST, STREP, Eurescom and e-ten projects and has published more than 30 papers in scientific journals and proceedings.

Emmanouil Patiniotakis holds a diploma of School of Electrical and Computer Engineering from National and Technical University of Athens with a major in Networks and Telecommunications Systems. He is currently study for a Master's degree in Techno-economics systems from the National and Technical University of Athens (NTUA) and University of Piraeus. Since 2007, he has been working as a Telecommunications Engineer at the Wireless and Satellite Communication Labs of OTE S.A. (Hellenic Telecoms). He has participated in several European Community research projects such as REWIND, FUTON, and SELFNET as well as in several national research projects.

Alessia D'Andrea received the degree in Communication Science from the University of Rome 'La Sapienza' in 2006. Currently she is a PhD student in Multimedia Communication with the University of Udine sponsored by the IRPPS of the National Research Council of Italy. She is mainly interested in Communication Science, Social Science, Risk Management, Virtual Communities, Mobile Technologies and Health Studies.

Arianna D'Ulizia received the M.S. degree in computer science engineering from the University of Rome 'La Sapienza', Rome, Italy, in 2005 and the Ph.D. degree in computer science and automation from the University 'Roma Tre', Rome, in 2009. Currently, she is a Researcher with the Institute of Research on Population and Social Policies, National Research Council of Italy, Rome. She is the author of more than 30 papers in international journal, conferences and books. She is mainly interested in human-computer interaction, multimodal languages, visual languages, geographical query languages, risk governance, and knowledge management in virtual communities.

Fernando Ferri received the M.S. degree in electronic engineering in 1990 and the Ph.D. in Medical Informatics in 1993 both from the University of Rome "La Sapienza". He is a senior researcher of the National Research Council of Italy from 2001; where he was researcher from 1996 to 2001. He was a contract professor from 1993 to 2000 of "Sistemi di Elaborazione" with the University of Macerata. He is the author of more than 150 papers on international journal, books and conferences. He was responsible for several projects funded by Italian Ministry of University and Research and European Commission. His main areas of interest are: human-computer interaction, user modelling, visual languages, multimodal languages, sketch based interfaces, social networks, geographic information systems, data and knowledge bases.

Patrizia Grifoni received the M.S. degree in electronics engineering from the University of Rome "La Sapienza" in 1990. From 1994 to 2000 she was a professor of "Elaborazione digitale delle immagini" at the University of Macerata. She is researcher with the National Research Council of Italy from 1990. She is the author of more than 110 papers in international journals, books and conferences. She was responsible for several projects funded by Italian and International Institutions. Her scientific interests have evolved from query languages for statistical and geographic databases, human-computer interaction, multimodal interaction and languages, visual languages, visual interfaces, sketch-based interfaces, Web technologies, social networks.

Costas Chaikalis was born in Athens, Greece, on March 1973. He received the B.Sc. degree in electrical engineering in 1995 from Technological Educational Institute of Lamia, Greece. He also received the M.Sc. and Ph.D. degrees from Department of Electronics and Telecommunications, University of Bradford, Bradford, UK in 1999 and 2003, respectively. During his doctoral studies he worked as a Research Assistant for Mobile Virtual Center of Excellence (Mobile VCE), Terminals Group, UK. Costas Chaikalis is an author or co-author of about 25 technical papers published in international conferences, journals and book chapters. His research interests are in all areas of mobile communications but especially in forward error correction coding, reconfigurable (software radio) architectures, cross layer architectures and DSP applications. Currently, he is a lecturer in the Department of Information Technology & Telecommunications, Technological Educational Institute of Larissa, Larissa, Greece.

Spyros Angelopoulos is currently a Doctoral researcher at Warwick Business School, UK. He holds a Diploma (Dipl-Eng, equivalent to MEng) in Production Engineering and Management as well as an MSc in Management Engineering from the Technical University of Crete, Greece. His current research is on the emergence and evolution of social networks within Public-Private Partnerships and his research interests include Social Networks, e-Government, Information Systems Management and implementation in public services, business transformation and networks as well as complexity and transformation of organizations and socio-economic contexts. His publications include book chapters in Handbooks, papers in Journals as well as presentations in conferences and workshop.

Fotis Kitsios is Lecturer at University of Macedonia, Department of Technology Management. He has graduated from the Technical University of Crete with a diploma in Production and Management Engineering Department, he went on with a master's degree on organization and management and he did a PhD on innovation management with a specialization in services. He has worked as a consultant in several SME's in the field of marketing, management, in adopting innovation techniques and financing. He is also a certified auditor in quality management systems. He has been involved in the implementation and coordination of national and European research projects including: RKMnet, ISTOS, MetaForesight, Innoregio, Leonardo da Vinci, Ecos Ouverture, Adapt, Youthstart, Fair. He has lectured on marketing, management, market research, strategic planning, total quality management, production management, design technologies, data analysis and technological forecasting at Technical University of Crete, University of Macedonia and University of Central Greece, as adjunct professor and he has jointly supervised numerous masters and diploma theses. He also teaches in various public and private vocational training centers and institutions. His scientific research interests mainly focus on new service and product dev, innovation measurement, marketing management and decision-making.

Thanos Papadopoulos is Lecturer in Knowledge and Information Systems Management, Centre for Operational Research, Management Science and Information Systems (CORMSIS), School of Management, University of Southampton, UK. He obtained his PhD from Warwick Business School, University of Warwick, UK. He also obtained his diploma (Dipl-Eng – Equivalent to MEng) in computer engineering and informatics from the School of Engineering of Patras University, Greece, and his MSc in information systems from the Department of Informatics of the Athens University of Economics and Business, Greece. His research interests include innovation and change in public services, business transformation and networks, and information systems' assessment strategies. He has been awarded the Best Paper Award in the 2007 International Conference on the Management of Healthcare and Medical Technology.

Index